The Scholastics and the Jews

*Coexistence, Conversion, and the
Medieval Origins of Tolerance*

THE SCHOLASTICS AND THE JEWS

Coexistence, Conversion, and the Medieval Origins of Tolerance

by

Edmund J. Mazza

Angelico Press

First published in the USA
by Angelico Press 2017
© Edmund J. Mazza 2017

For information, address:
Angelico Press
4709 Briar Knoll Dr.
Kettering, OH 45429
www.angelicopress.com
info@angelicopress.com

pbk: 978-1-62138-273-7
cloth: 978-1-62138-274-4
ebook: 978-1-62138-275-1

Cover design: Michael Schrauzer

CONTENTS

"If the Christian religion were to give careful heed and rightly analyze by use of reason, how inhuman it is and how discordant with piety for it to afflict with many kinds of molestations, and to smite with all sorts of grave injuries, the remnant of the Jews, to whom left as witnesses of His saving passion and of His victorious death, the benignity of the Savior promised the favor of salvation, it would not only draw back its hands from harming them, but as a show of piety and for the sake of the reverence of Christ, it would at least, extend the solace of human kindness to those whom it holds, as it were in tribute."
—Pope Innocent IV (r. 1243–1254)

"We allow the Jews to live with us because they neither know how to cause us harm, nor are they capable of it; rather, they are ever prepared to serve."
—Blessed Humbert of Romans, OP
Master-General of the Dominicans (r. 1254–1263)

"Infidels are men like us and they share our [human] nature."
—Blessed Ramon Lull

"To err is human…"
—Alexander Pope

To *Maria Immaculata*,
the Jewish Mother of *the Christ*,
Who gave Her to me, &
To my beloved wife Tatyana,
who after Her, is my greatest gift from God

Preface

THE 2016 US Presidential Campaign will undoubtedly go down as the most bizarre race in election history. Perhaps it will also be noted that the "Middle Ages" were thrust into the fray thanks to the infamous WikiLeaks emails. In a 2012 email, for example, Voices for Progress President Sandy Newman told Hillary Clinton campaign chair, John Podesta:

> This whole controversy with the bishops opposing contraceptive coverage even though 98% of Catholic women (and their conjugal partners) have used contraception has me thinking. . . . There needs to be a Catholic Spring, in which Catholics themselves demand the end of a *middle ages dictatorship* and the beginning of a little democracy and respect for gender equality in the Catholic church.[1] (emphasis mine)

Quite frankly, pejorative references to the Catholic Church and to the Catholic Middle Ages are common today and certainly not limited to domestic politics. After his September 2006 University of Regensburg address, Pope Emeritus Benedict XVI was roundly criticized for his "medieval" mindset. The deputy leader of Turkish Prime Minister Erdogan's party, Salih Kapusuz, for example, told state media: "He [Pope Benedict] has a dark mentality . . . *the darkness of the Middle Ages*. He . . . has not benefited from the spirit of *reform* in the Christian world."[2] (emphasis mine)

Irate Islamic officials were not the only ones, however, to express outrage over the pope's praise of medieval respect for Truth and his lament over our "modern ages dictatorship" of relativism;[3] rather predictably, so did the editors of *The New York Times*.[4] Stating, "There is more than

---

1. https://wikileaks.org/podesta-emails/emailid/6293.
2. http://www.nbcnews.com/id/14846353/ns/world_news-europe/t/west-bank-churc hes-struck-after-pope-remarks/#.WIUwu32cqUI.
3. http://www.vatican.va/gpII/documents/homily-pro-eligendo-pontifice_20050418 _en.html
4. http://www.washingtontimes.com/news/2016/dec/9/dean-baquet-new-york-times -executive-editor-we-don/.

enough religious anger in the world,"[5] *The Times* in its editorial pages accused the pope of "fomenting discord between Christians and Muslims" because he recounted the "brusque" words of medieval Byzantine Emperor Manuel II Paleologous' dialogue over faith and reason with a Persian Muslim: "God is not pleased by blood—and not acting reasonably (σὺν λόγῳ) is contrary to God's nature. Faith is born of the soul, not the body. Whoever would lead someone to faith needs the ability to speak well and to reason properly, without violence and threats. . . . To convince a reasonable soul, one does not need a strong arm, or weapons of any kind, or any other means of threatening a person with death."[6]

Ultimately, *The Times* branded Pope Benedict a "doctrinal conservative" whose "greatest fear appears to be the loss of a uniform Catholic identity, not exactly the best jumping off point for tolerance or interfaith dialogue." If we understand *The Times* correctly, one is left to conclude that anyone promoting "a uniform Catholic identity" in the world even through the use of rational persuasion is de facto "intolerant."

To express the essence of Benedict's Regensburg thesis we might borrow the prophetic words of Servant of God Archbishop Fulton J. Sheen: "The hardest thing to find in the world today is an argument. . . . Prejudice there is in abundance and *sentiment* too, for these things are born of enthusiasms without the pain of labor. Thinking, on the contrary, is a difficult task; it is the hardest work a man can do—that is perhaps why so few indulge in it. Thought-saving devices have been invented that rival labor-saving devices in their ingenuity."[7] (emphasis mine) Today's soundbites and slogans like "Love Trumps Hate," "Racist, Sexist, Anti-Gay, (*insert name*) Go Away!" or "Keep Your Rosaries Off My Ovaries!" are, to use Sheen's expression, the equivalent of "express trains, carrying the burden of those who are too lazy to think for themselves." As a consequence, young people (and the not so young) believe, for example, that love is just a feeling—no reasoning needed. Indeed, few have ever been reliably informed, even by Catholic professors, that as human

---

5. "The Pope's Words," *The New York Times, The Opinion Pages, Editorial* September 16, 2006; http://www.nytimes.com/2006/09/16/opinion/16sat2.html.

6. T. Khoury, "Manuel II Paléologue, Entretiens avec un Musulman. 7ᵉ Controverse," *Sources Chrétiennes* n. 115, Paris 1966, VII, 3 b–c: 144–45; as cited by His Holiness Pope Emeritus Benedict XVI in "Faith, Reason and the University Memories and Reflections," Address at University of Regensburg, September 12, 2006, http://w2.vatican.va/content/benedict-xvi/en/speeches/2006/september/documents/hf_ben-xvi_spe_20060912_universityregensburg.html#_ftn4.

7. Rev. Fulton J. Sheen, Preface to *Radio Replies*, Revs. Rumble and Carty (St Paul, Minnesota: Radio Replies Press, 1942).

beings they possess more than sense-based sentiments, but also an immaterial soul with an *intellect* that reasons and a *will* which chooses. Fewer still have learned the scholastic definition of love: willing the good for the Other. But if love is willing what is good for someone else, then one's intellect needs rational input to come to understand what exactly is the objective good for the other, the *absolute truth* of the matter, not the contentions of a particular "community." As the Rev. Dr. Martin Luther King, Jr. once put it:

> It is also midnight within the moral order. At midnight colors lose their distinctiveness and become a sullen shade of grey. Moral principles have lost their distinctiveness. For modern man, absolute right and wrong are a matter of what the majority is doing. *Right and wrong are relative to likes and dislikes and the customs of a particular community.* We have unconsciously applied Einstein's theory of relativity, which properly described the physical universe, to the moral and ethical realm.... This mentality has brought a tragic breakdown of [objective] moral *standards*, and the midnight of moral degeneration deepens.[8] (emphasis mine)

Long forgotten in secular circles is Dr. King's definition of a just law: "a manmade code that squares with the moral law or the law of God. An unjust law is a code that is out of harmony with the moral law. To put it in the terms of St Thomas Aquinas: An unjust law is a human law that is not rooted in eternal and natural law."[9]

Regrettably, the decline of the art of rational argument is not only a cancer on our college campuses; it is a malignancy that has infected all modern religious thinking. As long ago as the 1930s, Sheen lamented that among the Christian churches only "one great and fundamental dogma . . . is at the basis of all the other dogmas, and that is, that religion must be freed from dogmas. Creeds and confessions of faith are no longer the fashion; religious leaders have agreed not to disagree and those beliefs for which some of our ancestors would have died they have melted into a spineless Humanism." Cranmer, Latimer, and Ridley come to mind just as easily as Fisher and More. What would they and the countless others who perished on both sides in the sixteenth-century fires of reform have to say today, for example, at the sight of a

8. Rev. Dr. Martin Luther King, Jr., "A Knock at Midnight," August 9, 1964; http://www.thekingcenter.org/archive/document/knock-midnight-o.

9. Dr. King, "Letter from a Birmingham Jail," May 1, 1963; https://www.africa.upenn.edu/Articles_Gen/Letter_Birmingham.html.

statue of Martin Luther on prominent display at a recent papal audience (or a commemorative Vatican postage stamp of Luther in the offing)?[10] "The last thing you must do is 'to say, to convince.' It's not right to convince someone of your faith. . . . Proselytism is the strongest venom against the path of ecumenism."[11] So Pope Francis reportedly addressed thousands of Lutherans in Rome this past October 13th, ahead of the ecumenical commemoration of the 500th anniversary of the Protestant Reformation, while standing beside Luther's statue. Unfortunately, it seems the case, as Sheen argued, that "[t]he man who can make up his mind when proofs are presented [and he who *presents* proofs] is looked upon as a bigot."[12] Meanwhile, the man who "ignores proofs and the search for truth is looked upon as broadminded and tolerant." What depths have we reached, when even a sitting pope speaks this way! And

---

10. Among other disastrous aspects of this idolization of Luther by the current Vatican administration is its complete disregard of Jewish sensitivities. It was Luther, after all, who ranted: "What shall we Christians do with this rejected and condemned people, the Jews? Since they live among us, we dare not tolerate their conduct, now that we are aware of their lying and reviling and blaspheming. If we do, we become sharers in their lies, cursing and blasphemy. Thus we cannot extinguish the unquenchable fire of divine wrath, of which the prophets speak, nor can we convert the Jews. With prayer and the fear of God we must practice a sharp mercy to see whether we might save at least a few from the glowing flames. We dare not avenge ourselves. Vengeance a thousand times worse than we could wish them already has them by the throat. I shall give you my sincere advice:

First, to set fire to their synagogues or schools and to bury and cover with dirt whatever will not burn, so that no man will ever again see a stone or cinder of them. This is to be done in honor of our Lord and of Christendom, so that God might see that we are Christians, and do not condone or knowingly tolerate such public lying, cursing, and blaspheming of his Son and of his Christians. For whatever we tolerated in the past unknowingly—and I myself was unaware of it—will be pardoned by God. But if we, now that we are informed, were to protect and shield such a house for the Jews, existing right before our very nose, in which they lie about, blaspheme, curse, vilify, and defame Christ and us (as was heard above), it would be the same as if we were doing all this and even worse ourselves, as they very well know.

Second, I advise that their houses also be razed and destroyed. For they pursue in them the same aims as in their synagogues. Instead they might be lodged under a roof or in a barn, like the gypsies. This will bring home to them that they are not masters in our country, as they boast, but that they are living in exile and in captivity, as they incessantly wail and lament about us before God.

Third, I advise that all their prayer books and Talmudic writings, in which such idolatry, lies, cursing and blasphemy are taught, be taken from them. . . ."

Luther, *The Jews and Their Lies*, 1543; http://www.ewtn.com/library/ANSWERS/luther.htm

11. https://www.catholicculture.org/news/headlines/index.cfm?storyid=29637.

12. Sheen, *Radio Replies*.

this was no isolated incident, no momentary misspeak. In a Roman address on June 17, 2013, Pope Francis related the following exchange: "'Father, now I understand: it is a question of convincing others, of proselytizing!' 'No: it is nothing of the kind. The Gospel is like seed: you scatter it, you scatter it with your words and with your witness. And then it is not you who calculate the statistics of the results; it is God who does.'"[13] And there was the pontiff's "Top 10 Tips" for bringing greater happiness to one's life (from an interview published in part in the Argentine weekly *Viv*, July 27, 2014). Number Nine was instructive: "Don't proselytize; respect others' beliefs. We can inspire others through witness so that one grows together in communicating. But the worst thing of all is religious proselytism, which paralyzes: 'I am talking with you in order to persuade you,' No. Each person dialogues, starting with his and her own identity. The church grows by attraction, not proselytizing."[14]

Against this backdrop, it came as a surprise to no one when on December 10, 2015, Cardinal Koch and the Vatican's Commission for Religious Relations with Jews issued a document commemorating the 50th anniversary of *Nostra Aetate*, calling for the "principled rejection" of "institutional" proselytization of Jews.[15] Both *Nostra Aetate* and *Dignitatis Humanae* on religious liberty have been viewed as breakthroughs in the Church's relations with non-Catholic religions. Together they have led to much scholarly debate and divergent opinion as to whether the Council's teaching that individuals have a right to immunity from coercion in religious matters represents a rupture with traditional Catholic teaching on truth and tolerance or merely a natural development of doctrine, and the inevitable consequence of the Church's experience of modernity. Furthermore, in the wake of the Council's call for Catholic ecumenical outreach to other faiths, the last half-century has seen the starkest drop in conversions to Catholicism in Western history and, more importantly, in efforts to actively facilitate those conversions. Indeed, tens of millions of Catholics have either left the Faith altogether or no longer actively participate in the Church's liturgical life. And with statements from Pope Francis like those cited above—not the least of

13. http://w2.vatican.va/content/francesco/en/speeches/2013/june/documents/papa-francesco_20130617_convegno-diocesano-roma.html.

14. http://www.catholicregister.org/faith/item/18548-pope-francis-reveals-top-10-secrets-to-happiness.

15. *The Gift and the Calling are Irrevocable* (Rom 11:29), *A Reflection on the Theological Questions Pertaining to Catholic-Jewish Relations on the occasion of the 50th Anniversary of "Nostra Aetate"* (No.4). http://www.vatican.va/roman_curia/pontifical_councils/chrstuni/relations-jews-docs/rc_pc_chrstuni_doc_20151210_ebraismo-nostra-aetate_en.html.

them: "proselytism is solemn nonsense"[16]—many faithful Catholics are wondering whether the Church has left its former teachings—not to mention its senses—behind.

Bishop Sheen averred that "[t]he passing [away] of creeds and dogmas means the passing of controversies." We affirm that the converse is also true: "The passing away of controversies means the passing of creeds and dogmas." It is hoped that this scholarly inquiry into the Church's unsung tradition of evangelical argumentation and peaceful coexistence brings the light of clarity—not to mention the warmth of charity—to the current wholesale social, academic, and ecclesiastical abandonment of reason.

It goes without saying that any faults in this work are, of course, entirely my own. As any author, I owe a great debt of gratitude to a great many, but I wish to especially thank the following persons:

My deepest gratitude goes out to John Riess, Anna Maria Mendell, and the rest of the editorial staff of Angelico Press. My thanks go out to Margaret Coates and Elena Lemeneva for their assistance in translation, as well to all Azusa Pacific University librarians and student assistants, most especially Cheryl Chesler, Irene Molano, Irma Nicola, Dena Simpson, and Larry Handy for their invaluable assistance over the years. During the research and writing of this book I was privileged to access the resources of the Vatican Secret Archives and the Pontifical University of St Thomas Aquinas in Rome, the Dominican House of Studies in Washington DC, Princeton Theological Seminary, Princeton University, and the New York Public Research Library. My gratitude to the kind and helpful staff at each of these and other facilities.

Much thanks are also due to James Kruggel for the years of work he put into helping get this project off the ground a full decade ago, and to all readers of earlier editions of the manuscript, including those who read or heard portions of it in private conversations, published as articles, or presented at conferences. In this regard, I must especially single-out distinguished scholar Dr. Robert Chazan, New York University Professor of Hebrew and Judaic Studies and Co-Director of the Doctoral Program in Education and Jewish Studies at NYU. Robert was kind enough to present at *Christ Among the Medieval Mendicants*, a 2013 conference I organized, hosted by the Medieval Studies Program at the

---

16. http://www.repubblica.it/cultura/2013/10/01/news/pope_s_conversation_with_sc alfari_english-67643118/.

CUNY Graduate Center and the Morgan Library and Museum. The conference commemorated the 750th anniversary of the Barcelona Debate between Dominican Paul Christiani and Rabbi Moses Nachmanides. In addition to presenting, Robert also gave me valuable feedback upon my own research. I should also like to extend my deepest thanks to Dr. Phyllis Roberts, College of Staten Island, CUNY and Graduate Center *emerita* for her sage analysis and advice.

I owe an incredible debt of thanks to the late Dr. Howard L. Adelson, my mentor and director of my doctoral dissertation (from whence this book owes its genesis). Howard was a distinguished professor of Medieval Studies and History at both City College, CUNY and the Graduate Center. He also provided years of service to The Hebrew University in Jerusalem, chairing the Academic Advisory Committee for the Rothberg International School. I would like to acknowledge as well the late Dr. Frederick Purnell, Jr., also of the Graduate Center, under whom I completed my doctorate after Howard's passing.

Lastly, I cannot begin to thank my wife, my father, and all friends, colleagues, and students who gave of themselves to support me along the way.

One final note. The main protagonist of this work is St Raymond of Peñafort, master-general of the Dominican Order and editor of the Code of Canon Law of the Catholic Church. In the vast literature relating to Raymond, his name is spelled in various ways, often depending on the language of the scholarship. I have chosen to keep the anglicized version of his name as it was the form I encountered most frequently. I have also chosen to differentiate Raymond from his saintly contemporary (and my favorite palindrome) Ramon Llull by keeping the native Spanish/Catalan name for the latter.

January 23, 2017
Traditional Feast Day of
St Raymond of Peñafort, OP
San Bernardino County, CA, USA

Introduction:
The Hermeneutics of Intolerance

A doctrinal conservative, his [Pope Benedict XVI] greatest fear appears to be the loss of a uniform Catholic identity, not exactly the best jumping-off point for tolerance or interfaith dialogue.
—Opinion Editors, *The New York Times*, September 16, 2006

Intellectuals are blind where their mental constructs are concerned.
—Pope Emeritus Benedict XVI
(Joseph Cardinal Ratzinger), *Truth and Tolerance*

IT HAS become commonplace in Medieval Studies to speak of the "formation of a persecuting society" or the "development of a dangerous exclusionist tendency" in Catholic Europe of the twelfth and thirteenth centuries.[1] Robert Chazan, for example, author of dozens of works including *Daggers of Faith*, sees a connection between the anti-Jewish violence surrounding the First Crusade and the efforts of Dominicans and Franciscans to make Jewish converts a century-and-a-half later; he claims that although the Church officially repudiated mob violence and

---

1. The following is a representative, but by no means exhaustive, sampling: Robert Chazan, *Daggers of Faith, Thirteenth-Century Christian Missionizing and Jewish Response* (Berkeley, CA: University of California Press, 1989); R. I. Moore, *Formation of a Persecuting Society, Power and Deviance in Western Europe, 950–1250*, Second Edition (Oxford: Basil Blackwell, 2007; 1987); Jeremy Cohen, *The Friars and the Jews: The Evolution of Medieval Anti-Judaism* (Ithaca, NY: Cornell University Press, 1982); Miri Rubin, *Gentile Tales: the Narrative Assault on Late Medieval Jews* (New Haven, CT: Yale University Press, 1999); Christine Caldwell Ames, *Righteous Persecution: Inquisition, Dominicans, and Christianity in the Middle Ages* (Philadelphia, PA: University of Pennsylvania Press, 2009); David Nirenberg, *Communities of Violence: Persecution of Minorities in the Middle Ages* (Princeton, NJ: Princeton University Press, 1996); Dominique Iogna-Prat, *Order and Exclusion: Cluny and Christendom face Heresy, Judaism, and Islam, 1000–1050* (Ithaca, NY: Cornell University Press, 2002).

9

forced conversion, yet the same "desire to provide a more homogenous Christian environment by removing the Jews—manifested itself in more legitimate fashion in an increasingly serious drive to convert the Jews of western Christendom by the force of reasonable argumentation."[2] One is left to conclude that anyone promoting a homogenous Catholic Europe is a threat to Jews, even if his approach involves an appeal to reason rather than the sword. In this, Chazan is supported by another pioneering scholar, Jeremy Cohen. In his classic work, *The Friars and the Jews*, Cohen takes matters even further by posing a new mendicant theology-against-the-Jews: "The prime concern of this book is with the hitherto unappreciated substance of the friars' attack upon the Jews, the basic ideas and theological considerations that underlay their anti-Jewish activities and polemics. I shall argue that the Dominicans and Franciscans developed, refined, and sought to implement a new Christian ideology with regard to the Jews, one that allotted the Jews no legitimate right to exist in European society."[3]

The main force of Cohen's case lies in his analysis of the famous "Barcelona Confrontation" (involving the converted Jew Friar Paul Christiani) and in his critique of the *Pugio fidei*, a missionizing manual for preachers engaging Jews (written by the Dominican Friar Raymond Martini). Based on his analyses, Cohen comes to the conclusion that the mendicants believed that thirteenth-century Jews following rabbinic tradition had broken from the classical Judaism of the Old Testament, thereby making themselves "heretics," and losing their right to be tolerated in contemporary medieval society. Chazan disagrees with this interpretation of the work of Dominicans Christiani and Martini. He argues that in the eyes of medieval Christians (and specifically in the arguments of the aforementioned friars), the true breach of the Jews was not between the Old Covenant of the Law and the Prophets versus that of the Talmud, but in failing to become Christians and confessing the New Covenant, that Jesus Christ had come as Messiah.[4] But as Chazan is quick to state: "While I have disputed Cohen's assertion of a new theological view regarding Judaism and the Jews implicit in the missionizing campaign that we have examined, I agree with his sense of

2. Chazan, *Daggers of Faith*, 1.
3. Cohen, *The Friars and the Jews*, 14.
4. Chazan, 173; "Friar Paul's intention was not to prove that present-day Judaism was a deviation from classical Judaism; his last goal was to prove the age-old Christian contention that Jewish law had been abrogated by the coming of the Messiah but to do so on the basis of rabbinic texts."

deteriorating Jewish circumstances and of an ecclesiastical—or more narrowly mendicant—role in this deterioration."[5]

One could narrow the focus even further and single out the Dominican Friar Raymond of Peñafort and his disciples, as Cohen repeatedly does: "Raymond and his school developed that approach into an organized and aggressive Christian mission to the Jews, very much a novelty in medieval Europe. Raymond de Penaforte was not satisfied with simply ridding Europe of contemporary Judaism; he committed himself to making contemporary Jews believing Christians."[6]

Cohen's charges, however, pale in comparison to the heated rhetoric of the otherwise magnanimous Norman Roth: "That notorious Jew-hater Ramón Peñafort, the DOMINICAN friar then a canon lawyer in Rome and ultimately the author both of the *Decretals* for Pope Gregory IX and the *Siete Partidas* for Alfonso X,"[7] "[h]e went from Castile to his native Catalonia stirring up hatred against Jews. . . . This Jew-hater was later made a saint."[8]

These are serious historical allegations by authors whose books top the reading lists for courses on medieval Christians and Jews at today's leading colleges and universities. Their works have formed the minds of two generations of undergraduate and graduate students. Given this *gravitas*, it is remarkable that in their works none devote more than a thumbnail sketch of the life and work of St Raymond of Peñafort, despite the centrality of the man to the events they purport to investigate. And despite the many viewpoints and actions they allege to be his, it is equally surprising that neither Chazan nor Cohen quote hardly a single sentence from the hand of Raymond of Peñafort himself, relying instead on inferences from the writings and actions of his fellow Dominicans Paul Christiani and Raymond Martini.[9] If their investigations led them to believe that Peñafort was—to steal a phrase from István Bejczy—"the evil genius behind mendicant intolerance,"[10] it is

---

5. Ibid.

6. Cohen, *The Friars and the Jews*, 168–69.

7. Norman Roth, *Medieval Jewish Civilization, an encyclopedia*, "Moneylending," (New York, NY: Routledge, 2003), 455.

8. Ibid., "Canon (Church) Law and Jews," 131; Roth, like Cohen, fails to document a single genuinely "hate-full" expression on Raymond's part; as we shall see, those remarks he does cite hardly qualify as hate-speech.

9. Cf. Chapter 6.

10. István Bejczy, "*Tolerantia*: A Medieval Concept," *Journal of the History of Ideas* 58 (1997): 373; Or, as Chazan writes: "Almost certainly the financial and personnel support reflected in the *Pugio fidei* flows from the missionizing circle at the hub of which sat the active and influential Raymond of Penyafort" (116).

odd that they did not make any serious attempt to plumb the depths of the shadowy figure behind the syndicate.[11] This book shall.

No medieval scholar can deny the contempt, vilification, ridicule, pogroms, murders, expulsions, and other sufferings which millions of medieval Jews endured at the hands of their Christian counterparts, lay and clerical.[12] These matters are not merely academic to this author. My beloved wife suffered years of persecution in the Soviet Union for being a Jew.

However, the axiomatic assumption nowadays is that—at bottom— the historical *beliefs and practices* of the Roman Catholic Church, and in this case, evangelization efforts, are directly to blame for such miseries, not the sins of individuals. And *this* is certainly contestable. Scholars

---

11. To his credit, Roth noted this shortcoming in *The Friars and the Jews*, and in general scholarship decades ago: "Even more serious is the completely inadequate treatment of Ramón de Peñafort. . . . What we are given is a brief summary of his life, part of which is far from correct. . . . It ought to have occurred to authors long before Cohen that since Ramón de Peñafort was the author of the *Decretals*, he deserves further study." *Jewish Quarterly Review* 74, 3 (Jan 1984): 321–25. More than a third of a century later, this *desideratum* has yet to be supplied by anyone in the field, even by Roth himself, whose own work in progress was never completed.

12. To cite an historic admission, on March 26, 2000, Pope Saint John Paul II inserted the following prayer into the "Wailing Wall" of Jerusalem during his state visit to Israel: "God of our fathers, you chose Abraham and his descendants to bring your Name to the Nations; we are deeply saddened by the behavior of those who in the course of history have caused these children of yours to suffer, and asking forgiveness we wish to commit ourselves to genuine brotherhood with the people of the Covenant."

Jewish scholar Kenneth Stow (in other cases a perceptive and balanced historian) argues that "one might accuse the pope of double-talk [since Christians consider themselves 'children of Abraham']. . . . Hence the pope would mean only Christians, perhaps Catholics alone. Yet, I believe the pope was being purposefully ambivalent, allowing all listeners to hear the text as they preferred . . . he certainly meant Jews as Jews too . . . see Chapter 7 for further clarification." Stow, *Jewish Dogs, An Image and its Interpreters, Continuity in the Catholic-Jewish Encounter* (Stanford, CT: Stanford University Press, 2006), 205. There could hardly be any ambivalence, however, given both the totality of the pontiff's words and the fact that exactly two weeks earlier John Paul inaugurated the Church's annual Lenten season with the following prayer:

"*Let us forgive and ask forgiveness!* While we praise God who, in his merciful love, has produced in the Church a wonderful harvest of holiness, missionary zeal, total dedication to Christ and neighbour, we cannot fail to recognize *the infidelities to the Gospel committed by some of our brethren*, especially during the second millennium. Let us ask pardon for the divisions which have occurred among Christians, for the violence some have used in the service of the truth and for the distrustful and hostile attitudes sometimes *taken towards the followers of other religions.*" (last sentence, emphasis mine)

Hurt feelings continue to endure, indeed, when even apologies are misconstrued as multivalent manipulations!

today habitually approach churchmen of the past through the paradigm of the dynamics of power and social control. Though not without merit, if over-used, this modern construct will tend to yield single-minded results, often overlooking the subtler complexities of what was, after all, a medieval situation. No doubt the Middle Ages witnessed the struggle for hegemony among competing social groups no less than today's world, but to view the picture exclusively in these terms is to lose sight of other historical phenomena, no less real for being independent of motivations of power. It is near-universally assumed by today's intelligentsia, however, that any attempt to convert another to one's own religion is automatically a violation and a power-grab. As the Vatican itself not long ago lamented: "It is even stated that the [Catholic] claim to have received the gift of the fullness of God's revelation masks an attitude of intolerance and a danger to peace."[13] In study after study, clerics are called out for being persecutory agents and never once praised for anything "positive." The chapters which follow, however, will challenge the prevailing view of many medieval Catholic figures, institutions, and ideas, and disclose (in some respects for the first time) that it was precisely the religious search for a "uniform Catholic identity" that also contributed to the renunciation of violence, the first European definitions of tolerance, and the beginnings—albeit haltingly—of peaceful interreligious dialogue. However, while the Church's critics have often pointed to the sacrament of the Eucharist as a culprit factor in medieval Christian-Jewish relations, this work will instead have frequent recourse to the not unrelated sacrament of penance or reconciliation, more commonly known as "confession." It is this author's contention that the works of the Scholastics on reason, sin, and sacrament were the true catalysts for the Church's unprecedented involvement in the affairs and works of her Jewish (and Muslim) neighbors and with far nobler intentions and ramifications than many scholars are willing to entertain, nor are many even aware.

Over the last half-century, literally thousands of scholarly books and articles have thoroughly catalogued every aspect of the political, social, and economic machinations of medieval Christian kings, clerics, and communities and their injurious impact on the Jews. The purpose of this present work is not to deny that this well-documented history happened, but to debunk the notion that this was *all* that happened. Serious religious thinking went into the mendicant missions to the Jews, and the fact that this thinking lent itself to distortions—distortions

13. *Doctrinal Note on Some Aspects of Evangelization*, 10, Sacred Congregation for the Doctrine of the Faith, October 6, 2007.

with real-world consequences—should in no way entail interring this thought; all the more so, the deviance demands a deeper explication of the theological reflection. Yet currently, in Medieval Studies, there is not a single work exploring the possible origins of modern tolerance within the realm of medieval meditation on sin, reason, sacrament, and Christian *mission* to Jews, Muslims, and other non-Christians. Indeed, decades of "persecuting-society" scholarship has made it abundantly clear that the dominant intellectual elite of the Academy still view any institution (or representative thereof) with exclusive claims to absolute truth as incapable of tolerance or dialogue, let alone acknowledging its adjunct role as midwife in bringing them to life. Take the following observations of Dominican inquisition:

> One of the most compelling, if unabashedly presentist, arguments in favor of sketching the formation of inquisition's *Christian meanings* is that religious violence and persecution are not relics from a "barbaric" medieval past. Any study of medieval inquisitions arises within a modern religious world that, despite the legacies of *Enlightenment and liberalism*, has still not completely embraced nonviolence, tolerance of difference, and respect for individual creeds, with religion as fundamentally a personal matter. While these are values and practices long advocated in the West, they are not necessarily wholly shared (or identically defined) by persons of diverse religious faiths both there and elsewhere. Long past the Middle Ages, we need not look far to find the marriage of belief and violence in modern religions, the ways in which a perceived obligation to the variously construed divine manifests itself in the restraint of, or harm inflicted upon, the minds and bodies of oneself or others.[14] (emphasis mine)

Though the Christian creed might just as easily be credited with contributing to the origins of contemporary *respect* for persons of difference, such arguments are rarely paid any heed. The answer lies, as John Christian Laursen and Cary J. Nederman observe:

> Over and over in the large Locke[15] literature that great philosopher is featured as the inventor of modern toleration. This literature sometimes seems to feed on itself, and it shows no signs of abating, but if one can escape from the shackles of anglocentrism one discovers that Locke was neither very original in his argumentation nor very broad in his toleration. Catholics and atheists have never thought much of a toleration that excluded them. . . . Yet another distortion is the Inquisition cliché, according to which all of the medieval period and some of

---

14. Ames, *Righteous Persecution*, 232.
15. John Locke (1632–1704), English political philosopher.

the early modern period are seen as an era of relentless persecution. . . .
But the monolithic conception of the Roman Church's reaction to heresy, embodied by the systematic extirpation of heretics through inquis-
itorial procedures, is surely a political construct.[16]

Emblematic of today's "cliché-shackled" scholarship is Mark Cohen's
Under Cross and Crescent: "This book sets out to provide a broad inves-
tigation of medieval Islamic-Jewish and Christian-Jewish relations. . . .
It is *not* a comparative study of tolerance. Neither for Islam, nor for
Christianity prior to modern times, did tolerance, at least as we in the
West have understood it since John Locke, constitute a virtue."[17]

One could also cite Thomas Jefferson. Most Americans know Jefferson as the principal author of the Declaration of Independence and the
nation's third president. But he is also the famed founder of one of
America's oldest institutions of higher education, the University of Vir-
ginia. In this connection he is reported to have quipped that he hoped it
would never retain a faculty of theology,[18] nor ever become a den of
"monkish ignorance and priestly superstition." Jefferson's pontificating
aside, it was precisely these prelates of the Church who invented the
university system in the first place—some six centuries before he did!
Jefferson, however, was a man of his age, the period of the Enlightenment. An ironic appellation, to be sure, for it ushered in unprecedented
shadows of doubt, obscuring centuries of illumination by the scholastic
masters of higher education.

But learning had changed by the time of Locke and Jefferson. Gali-
leo's claim to have proven that the earth was not the center of the universe but that it revolved around the sun seemed to challenge the
accuracy of the teaching authority of both the Catholic Church and the
Bible, as well as the science of the ancient Greek philosophers, notably
Aristotle. Sixteenth-century empirical observations through crude tele-
scopes and microscopes revolutionized man's view of his place in the
universe and made many intellectuals question their common patrimony: the authority of received "tradition," which had been the basis
of medieval education. Or as Jefferson put it: "It is surely time for men
to think for themselves, and to throw off the authority of names so

16. John Christian Laursen and Cary J. Nederman, *Beyond the Persecuting Society:
Religious Toleration Before the Enlightenment* (Philadelphia, PA: University of Pennsylvania Press, 1998), 3–4.

17. Mark Cohen, *Under Crescent and Cross: The Jews in the Middle Ages* (Princeton:
Princeton University Press, 1994), xviii–xix.

18. For the record, UVA has a Department of Religious Studies. Thomas Jefferson, Letter to Thomas Cooper, October 7, 1814, as cited in www. positiveatheism.org/hist/quotes.

artificially magnified."[19] English Chancellor Francis Bacon was another such skeptic of "established authorities" and famously advocated the inductive "Scientific Method" instead:

> But even though Aristotle were the man he is thought to be I should still warn you against receiving as oracles the thoughts and opinions of *one man*. What justification can there be for this *self-imposed* servitude [that] . . . you are content to repeat Aristotle's after two thousand [years]. . . . But if you will be guided by me you will deny, not only to this man but to any mortal now living or who shall live hereafter, the right to dictate your opinions. . . . You will never be sorry for trusting your own strength. . . .[20] (emphasis mine)

Aristotle and the Scholastics are to be rejected because the new science has proven many of their assertions erroneous. Common patrimony gone, the individual must only accept as certain what he can first rationally demonstrate to himself—Descartes' "I think, therefore, I am." This is the beginning of the end of medieval metaphysics, which asserted that a person's existence must certainly *precede* any act of cogitation. With the loss of metaphysics, the entire celestial hierarchy, along with concomitant notions of sin and salvation, death, judgment, heaven, and hell, must needs fall by the wayside. We have only the empirical knowledge of the here and now, concludes Bacon: "Man, being the servant and interpreter of Nature, can do and understand so much only as he has observed in fact or in thought of the course of nature: beyond this he neither knows anything nor can do anything."[21] As John Donne lamented in less prosaic verse:

> New Philosophy calls all in doubt,
> The Element of fire is quite put out;
> The Sun is lost, and th'earth, and no man's wit
> Can well direct him where to look for it.
>
> ....
>
> Tis all in pieces, all coherence gone;
> All just supply, and all *Relation*:
> Prince, Subject, Father, Son, are things forgot,
> For every man alone thinks he hath got
> To be a Phoenix, and that then can be,

---

19. Letter to William Short, August 4, 1820.
20. Francis Bacon, *The Refutation of Philosophies*.
21. Bacon, *The New Organon*.

None of that kinde, of which he is, but he.[22]
(emphasis mine)

Since ancient and medieval authorities had proven incorrect about the natural world, early modern intellectuals threw the baby out with the bathwater, rejecting nearly all of what those commonly accepted authorities had said about the *human* world: God, man, and *public* society. Aristotle's dictum, "man is by nature a social animal" was no longer acceptable. Human nature is not inherently relational. The human race is merely a gaggle of completely separate and unrelated *individuals*. Each of us is not a specimen of a class, but a class unto ourself! Each man is an island . . . a phoenix. As Jefferson wrote, "I am of a sect by myself, as far as I know."[23] This was also Locke's thinking:

> Men being, as has been said, by nature all free, equal, and independent, no one can be put out of this condition and subjected to the political power of another without his own consent. The only way whereby any one divests himself of his natural liberty, and puts on the bonds of civil society, is by agreeing with other men to join and unite into a community for their comfortable, safe, and peaceable living one among another. . . . He [is] absolute lord of his own person and possessions, equal to the greatest, and subject to nobody, why will he part with his freedom, why will he give up his independence and subject himself to the rule and control of any other power?[24]

Rejection of received authority and the enshrinement of the individual were believed to be effective bulwarks against tyranny, and for the promotion of liberty, but they also had the unfortunate effect of forcing all but the most basic religious beliefs to the private sphere. As Elshtain writes,

> There was a worm in the apple from the very beginning of the move for toleration. If one traces that beginning from John Locke's classic *Letter on Toleration* one discovers that in order for religion to be tolerated it must be privatized. There is a realm of private soulcraft and, a realm of public statecraft, and never the twain shall meet. . . . This privatization, even subjectifying, of religion feeds into the bad odor surrounding any hint of proselytization. Proselytizing seemed at best bad manners; at worst a way to try and force something on me that I do not want, am not interested in, but may be gulled or intimidated

22. John Donne, "An Anatomy of the World."
23. Jefferson, Letter to Ezra Stiles Ely, June 25, 1819.
24. Locke, *Second Treatise on Government*, 7; http://www.ucs.louisiana.edu/~ras27 77/judpol/locke.html.

into accepting. The general animus against proselytizing flows from a conviction that those driven in that direction will, almost invariably, be persons of strong religious conviction: those, therefore, who, should they become dominant, would move to end the very toleration that has made their open proselytizing possible. So, in the name of preserving a regime of toleration, we must not tolerate unrestrained proselytism.[25]

Voltaire, a contemporary French *philosophe*, had affirmed as much when he said that one religion was tyranny, two religions civil war, but the toleration of multiple factions a just republic. In other words, Enlightenment toleration is based on the supposition that there can be no certainty with regard to religious claims to truth.[26] "I never will, by any word, or act, bow to the shrine of intolerance, or admit of a right of inquiry into the religious opinions of others," said Jefferson.[27] Men may follow their private beliefs to their own peril, but should not endanger the general welfare on account of their peculiar denominational folly. This is the genesis of the notion of Separation of Church and State and neatly summarizes the prevailing politically correct consensus in Washington, various levels of the judiciary, the "mainstream" media, and academia today. As my colleague Mark Eaton recently observed:

> Some would prefer to exclude believers from public discourse altogether. Stanley Fish never tires of reminding us that religion stands as the litmus test of pluralism. Because there are always "some believers who hold to their faith in a way that is absolute and exclusionary," he argues that religion is ultimately incompatible with pluralism and tolerance, those twin pillars of secular modernity. The philosopher Jurgen Habermas insists that believers must simply come to terms with the "inevitability of religious tolerance," while so-called new atheists like Christopher Hitchens exclaim more shrilly that the "inevitable biases" of believers "should be enough" to exclude them from rational debate. For these and other champions of secularism, religion is safe only when it is confined to the private sphere, since any form of "deprivatized religion," as religious studies scholar Talal Asad puts it, is deemed "intolerable to secularists."[28]

25. Jean Bethke Elshtain, "Proselytizing for Tolerance," *First Things*, November 2002.

26. "The notion that all religions are ultimately equivalent appears as a commandment of tolerance and respect for others. . . . The Christian has to resist this ideology of equality." His Holiness Pope Benedict XVI Emeritus (Joseph Ratzinger), *Truth and Tolerance, Christian Belief and World Religions* (San Francisco, CA: Ignatius Press, 2004), 105.

27. Letter to Edward Dowse, April 19, 1803.

28. Mark Eaton, "Holding Fast to Our Beliefs: Religion and Pluralism Since 9/11," in *APU Life, Azusa Pacific University Magazine*, 23:1 (2010): 17.

Just ask former Amherst College President Anthony Marx about the "bad old days," before religion was privatized:

> In the medieval epochs of Europe, leading right up to the edge of the modern, authority was established by deity or absolutism. Monarchs and priests directed humanity's understanding of nature, of sickness and health, of earth's horizon, of the motion of the stars. It is hard for you now to imagine that way of life, in which such authority was not questioned. But the power of individual insight, yearning and industry were just beginning to coalesce, producing revolutions that replaced despotism with democracy, feudalism with capitalism and fundamentalism with religious choice. . . .
>
> Amherst prizes *individual reason over unearned authority* . . . We believe in "progress": that new knowledge advances us. Just as we believe in science, we also respect and take strength from faith, not as a closed system but as an inspiration [i.e., private not overarching], as another kind of journey, for each to examine and *decide for herself or himself.* Although we know we cannot reach perfection [i.e., certitude], we believe in striving for the improvement for all.[29] (emphasis mine)

Religion may serve as personal "inspiration," but may not condition philosophy, science, or societal structure. According to this view, faith is definitively divorced from reason:

> We could suggest that Descartes, Spinoza, and Kant are points along the way in this process of separation. The attempt at a new comprehensive synthesis by Hegel did not give faith back its proper place in philosophy but tried to transform it completely into reason and to do away with it as faith. To this giving absolute status to the spirit, Marx opposed a system of solely material values; philosophy was now to be based upon exact science. Only scientific knowledge was knowledge at all. . . . A comprehensive theory of evolution, intended to explain the whole of reality, has become a kind of "first philosophy", which represents, as it were, the true foundation for an enlightened understanding of the world. Any attempt to involve basic elements other than those worked out within the terms of such a "positive" theory, any attempt at "metaphysics", necessarily appears as a relapse from the standards of enlightenment, as abandoning the universal claims of science. Thus the Christian idea of God is necessarily regarded as unscientific.[30]

But what if the men of the Scientific Revolution and the Enlighten-

---

29. Anthony W. Marx, Convocation Address, September 3, 2007, Amherst College. https://www.amherst.edu/news/specialevents/convocation/2007.

30. Ratzinger, *Truth and Tolerance,* 177–78.

ment got it wrong? What if God is not merely a fact of religion—*but a fact*? What if sense-knowledge is not the only path to truth? And what if individuals, as a consequence, have an obligation to obey not only material truths, but transcendent truths, if (paradoxically) they truly aspire to freedom? While it is hardly to be doubted they made few miscalculations with regard to planetary motion or representative government, early-modern thinkers were surely not endowed with *infallibility* in their presumption that human knowledge (and therefore pursuit of happiness) was limited to this world? The statement "extraordinary claims require extraordinary evidence," or its synonym, "all propositions are meaningless unless they can be empirically verified," is itself empirically unverifiable![31] And to categorically insist, "There is no such thing as an absolute truth," is actually to proclaim one.

Still the Church is roundly condemned as intolerant for the very reason that it holds to Truth. As Bejczy puts it, "The Middle Ages . . . have no reputation for tolerance, the lack of which is usually attributed to the influence of a powerful Church that was able and willing to suppress all major deviations from the exclusive truth it was convinced it possessed." Whereas, "[t]he enlightened philosophers, who laid the foundations of liberalism and democracy, are . . . hailed as the men who introduced the notion of tolerance as a means of guaranteeing maximum freedom to the individual members of society. . . ."[32]

Speaking of the Church's push for uniformity of thought in the High Middle Ages, Chazan writes: "At this juncture, the drive toward a more homogeneous Christian society emerged in broad segments of society and as indicated convincingly in Benjamin Z. Kedar's excellent study of the alternative tactics of crusade and mission . . . vigorous self-confidence combined with uncertainty and insecurity moved the leadership of western Christendom to press for enhanced homogeneity within and for expansion . . . without."[33] Anna Sapir Abulafia is of similar mindset when she writes: "What twelfth-century theologians had in common was their constructs of Christian *universality* and where they used reason they more often than not used it as that innate human quality that united mankind in knowledge of God. Thus Jews emerged

31. Charles Rice, *Fifty Questions on the Natural Law* (San Francisco, CA: Ignatius Press, 1997), 32.

32. Bejczy, *"Tolerantia,"* 365.

33. Chazan, *Daggers of Faith*, 2.

from their writings as human outsiders . . . the foundations were laid for the institutional marginalization of Jews in the thirteenth century and beyond."[34] (emphasis mine)

Jeremy Cohen, in his own way, looks at the Church's striving for "catholicity" or "homogeneity" as the driving factor in Jewish marginalization:

> The new attitude to the Jews . . . appears to have derived even more from a mounting trend. . . . An overriding concern with the properly ordered wholeness and functional unity of Christendom [which] manifested itself . . . in the spiritual and intellectual climate of the period. Numerous cultural historians have demonstrated how as an interest in a unifying synthesis overcame that in intellectual exploration and individualistic creativity, the humanism of the "renaissance" of the twelfth century gave way to the Scholasticism of the thirteenth. The summa, the complete synthesis and clarification of a field of learning in accordance with accepted philosophical and logical principles, quickly came to constitute the crowning achievement of scholastic writers. . . . Whereas the drive toward realizing the perfect unity of Christendom included the scholastic effort to produce intellectual syntheses which themselves mirrored that unity, the defensiveness of the thirteenth-century Church manifested itself in an attempt to rule and regulate human thought. Ideas or beliefs that did not accord strictly with those of the establishment were seen not only as undermining the Church's authority but as threatening to destroy the Christian unity that the Church struggled to maintain.[35]

It is interesting that Cohen and Chazan both cite the genre of the *summa*,[36] because Dominican Friar Raymond of Peñafort was himself the author of just such a *summa*, the *Summa de poenitentiae*, also known as the *Summa de casibus*, or *Summa confessorum*, the summa for confessors. It might have been just as appropriately named the *Summa*

---

34. Anna Sapir Abulafia, "Twelfth-Century Renaissance Theology and the Jews" in *From Witness to Witchcraft, Jews and Judaism in Medieval Christian Thought*, ed. Cohen (Wiesbaden: Harrassowitz, 1996), 139.

35. Cohen, *The Friars and the Jews*, 249–50; 255.

36. Chazan, *Daggers of Faith*, 26; "The remarkable *summae* of the period convey a sense of confidence in the capacity of the human mind to achieve understanding, in the orderliness of Christian religious tradition, and in the rationality of the Church's teaching. From this perspective, the enhanced ecclesiastical commitment to missionizing can be seen as a reflection of the brimming confidence of the Christian world at this juncture. Sure of itself and its teaching, the Church committed itself in unusual measure to the effort to carry its incontrovertible position to those outside itself, or, in other words, to those in error."

on Sin, for in this lengthy treatise Friar Raymond discusses the various
kinds of sins and the ways a good confessor must discern the offence as
well as the repentance of the sinner. Raymond's work was, in fact,
hugely successful. As William Hinnebusch, OP wrote in his two-volume
History of the Dominican Order, "The timeliness of the *Summa* is indicated by the instant welcome it received both inside and outside the
Order. Few medieval books were so widely distributed. Scholars and
schools wanted it in their libraries; it appeared on the list of book-prices
established by the University of Paris in 1286; manuscript copies stand
on the shelves of most European libraries, great and small."[37]

Could it be more than coincidence that the author of the most popular summa on sin in his day was also the driving force behind the first
systematic campaign to proselytize Jews and Muslims? Is it possible that
the origins of missionary overtures to non-Christians are to be identified not so much with the drive for homogeneity as for holiness?

Neither Cohen nor Chazan treat in their earlier works of the origins
of thirteenth-century missionizing in any direct way, beyond the allu-
sions to universalism and homogeneity quoted above; this investigation
does occur to some degree, however, in later works by both authors.[38]
Several chapters, for example, in Cohen's *Living Letters of the Law* are
devoted to important twelfth-century figures such as St Anselm of Canterbury, Peter Abelard, St Bernard of Clairvaux, Peter the Venerable, and
Blessed Alan of Lille, among others. He summarizes his conclusions
about them thusly:

> Christian theologians of the twelfth century did not yet articulate a
> construction of contemporary, rabbinic Judaism per se as a post-bibli-
> cal Jewish heresy. Nevertheless, some of their pronouncements gravi-
> tated in that direction, and they certainly laid the groundwork for
> subsequent churchmen who did make that formulation explicit. The
> place accorded the Jews on Anselm of Canterbury's map of the world
> had surely been called into question and at times circumscribed, even
> if the poetic imagination of Alan of Lille had not yet eliminated it
> entirely. Perhaps more aptly than she originally imagined, one recent
> student of Alan's opus has observed that had Alan lived just a little
> later, he undoubtedly would have been a mendicant friar.[39]

37. W.A. Hinnebusch, *History of the Dominican Order: Origins and Growth* (Staten
Island, NY: Alba House, 1973), 251.

38. Cf. Cohen, *Living Letters of the Law, Ideas of the Jew in Medieval Christianity*
(Berkeley, CA: University of California Press, 1999), 314; "Indeed, reactions to my thesis
on the significance of the friars, alongside the independent medieval Christian ideas of
the Jew demanded a more conscientious investigation of their antecedents."

39. Ibid., 312.

Cohen approves the suggestion that Alan would have made a good mendicant because Alan includes a polemic targeted at the Jews in his *De Fide Catholica*, which was also directed toward Muslims and heretics. One might also approve the suggestion that Alan would have made a good friar, however, because like Raymond of Peñafort, he also wrote a pioneering treatise on confession, the *Liber poenitentialis*. Unlike the medieval handbooks of penance from former times, which were often little more than lists of sins and their punishments, Alan's work "late in the twelfth century broke clearly with the earlier works of its type. The tariffs had virtually disappeared; the determination of appropriate penances was left entirely to the discretion of confessors."[40]

The revolution in the medieval understanding of the rationality of human repentance inaugurated by Peter Abelard continued its practical development in the new penitential works of individuals such as Bartholomew of Exeter and Alan of Lille. More and more, Catholic priests were encouraged to look beyond the mere application of standard penances based on outward deeds and pursue instead the inward motivations and mitigating circumstances of sin, as well as the heart-felt contrition of the sinner. We do not digress by broaching the issue of the evolution of the Catholic doctrine of penance; rather, I believe it has everything to do with understanding the development of a Christian theology of mission with regard to Jews, Muslims, and heretics. More aptly than she originally imagined did Abulafia observe: "It is true that Abelard concluded in his *Ethics* that the Jews had not sinned by crucifying Jesus Christ. But this had more to do with Abelard's endeavor to find a truly satisfactory definition of sin than an attempt at exonerating those who were held responsible for killing Jesus."[41] I shall argue in this work that it was precisely through the development of a scholastic *sacramen-*

---

40. Lester K. Little, *Religious Poverty and the Profit Economy in Medieval Europe* (Ithaca, NY: Cornell University Press, 1978), 189. Cf. Pierre Michaud-Quantin, *Sommes de casuistique et manuels de confession au moyen age (XII–XVI siecles)*, (Louvain, 1962), 38; "Le *Décret* de Gratien mettait en relief dans la première moitié du XIIème siècle le principe *Poenitentiae sunt arbitrariae*, les pénitences à imposer sont à déterminer dans chaque cas par le confesseur ad arbitrium, selon son appréciation, et exigeait en conséquence qu'il se renseignât sur les circonstances objectives et subjectives qui entouraient la faute avouée. Quelques année plus tard, l'évêque Barthélemy d'Exeter rédigeat un *Poenitentiale*, qui reprenait et accentuait ces dispositions. C'est dans la ligne de cette évolution que se place le *Liber Poenitentialis* d'Alain de Lille, professeur de théologie à Paris, mêlé aux luttes doctrinales contra Cathares du Languedoc par le moine cistercien. Mais cette oeuvre rédigée dans les dernieres années du XII siècle se place résolument sur un plan nouveau et constitue de ce fait le premier des manuels de pastorale pénitentielle cherchant à atteindre les buts définis précédemment."

41. A. S. Abulafia, "Twelfth-Century Renaissance Theology and the Jews," 123.

tality (views concerning sin and the nature of created reality, which we shall explore presently) that the Church came to produce an ideology of mission directed toward Jews and other non-Christians and their inherent dignity. While each of these elements—sin, mission, natural reason, tolerance—are important in the development of the Catholic tradition, they are not necessarily all present in any given theologian.[42] It is, nevertheless, surprising that it has gone unremarked in previous scholarship, that the very men responsible for producing some of the most influential medieval writings on the sacrament of penance (Abelard, Alan, Bartholomew, Raymond of Peñafort, etc.) were also the chief authors of Christian works on Jews. This has largely happened, perhaps, due to the fact that scholars who study Christian-Jewish relations and those who explore mendicant spirituality, or the Church's canon law, rarely sit at the same academic table. There is still a great deal of compartmentalization in today's Academy, and Peñafort is perhaps its principal exhibit.

Nevertheless, I believe an examination of scholastic views on sin and sanctity—not papal monarchy and crusade—is key to understanding unprecedented "rational" approaches to Jews. As we shall explore in more detail in later chapters, Christian intellectuals of the twelfth-century Renaissance may have deplored what they viewed as a lack of exercise of the human faculty of reason on the part of most Jews; however, it does not necessarily follow that "Jews emerged from their writings as human outsiders ... the foundations were laid for the institutional marginalization of Jews in the thirteenth century and beyond."[43] As shall be shown, for the medieval Christian theologian, to *err* was certainly *human*, and formed the basis for a novel medieval construct of *inclusion* that the Dominicans (among others) carried out to its rational conclusion.

What was the "theological justification" underlying the concerted effort on the part of the friars to convert the Jews (and other "infidels")? And was it new? We shall explore the origins and nature of the Dominican concept of "mission." In a very real way, the question compels us to re-examine the very essence of the Order of Preachers itself. What was its *raison d'être*? Did its original mandate include preaching to non-Christians, or was this the singular invention of Raymond of Peñafort? Such an inquiry also necessarily entails an exploration of the "conspicuous" role played by Friar Raymond in the Barcelona Confrontation and the

---

42. This sentence is virtually word for word from my kind anonymous reader, but quotation marks seemed inappropriate.

43. A.S. Abulafia, "Twelfth-Century Renaissance Theology," 139.

subsequent censorship of the Talmud. As one scholar has put it, "In these disputations, and in the broader campaign to expunge parts of the Talmud, the Jewish logos was muted, rendering the conversations between Christians and Jews, at least on these occasions, a monologue."[44]

Modern critics of the medieval Catholic Church—and, more particularly, the Dominican Order—have, admittedly, done much to restore the otherwise muted voices of medieval Jewry. This present study wishes in no way to diminish such praiseworthy achievements of the past half-century of scholarship. What *is* unfortunate, however, is the simplistic kind of role-reversal adopted by most of these same authors in their treatment of mendicancy, one in which the Dominicans are now the "demons" whose "perfidious" press for homogeneity more civilized moderns must now bemoan and beware. Leonard Glick's appraisal is typical:

> by the early thirteenth century all Europe was conceived as Christendom, a single community of the faithful, transcending all regional and national boundaries, presided over by a pope who was beholden to no earthly ruler. Christian society was said to be the earthly equivalent of the mystical body of Christ (Corpus Christi), eternal and indestructible, endowed like its heavenly counterpart with spiritual power surpassing ordinary comprehension. *Nothing was more vital to this vision of Christendom than the idea of order; thus no heresy, no deviation of any sort from designated roles and statuses could be tolerated. But it was becoming evident that Jews were doing just that: deviating from their proper roles far beyond the limits of toleration. . . .* The obvious solution was to step up the effort to eliminate Judaism entirely by converting each and every Jew. . . . [T]he campaign was spearheaded by Dominican and Franciscan friars, who had merged around 1215 as *militant orders dedicated to relentless missionizing and inquisitorial persecution of anyone whose beliefs and practices challenged the supremacy of the Church.*[45] (emphasis mine)

Does this cardboard-cut-out-Christendom-as-fascist-police-state, mendicants-as-storm-troopers construct really help anyone to understand the complexities of a historical situation from which we are now securely seven hundred years removed? As Jonathan Elukin puts it:

> The historiographical fulcrum for much of the recent work on the treatment of the Jews is the claim that twelfth-century Europe became a "persecuting society." The treatment of the Jews in the medieval past thus ominously signals the fundamentally intolerant character of

44. From review by anonymous reader of one of the draft manuscripts of this book.
45. Leonard Glick, *Abraham's Heirs, Jews and Christians in Medieval Europe* (Syracuse, NY: Syracuse University Press, 1999), 189–90.

European states and Christian culture. Although a suggestive characterization, this interpretation reads back into medieval history the
anachronistic power and efficacy of the twentieth-century totalitarian
state.[46]

Subtler than the critiques of Cohen, Roth, and Glick—and potentially far more damaging to the case we hope to construct over the following chapters—are the recent arguments of Christine Caldwell Ames.
Her work, *Righteous Persecution*, has nothing to do with Dominican
involvement with Jews, but it does explore their not entirely unrelated
administration of inquisition against perceived Christian heretics. Furthermore, unlike past scholarship on the friars and the Jews, she astutely
recognizes the critical role of the scholastic theology of sin and repentance in any academic enterprise that purports to grapple with the complexities of mendicant interaction with the "Other." She rightly revises
the scholarship of socio-political homogeneity but unfortunately, she
replaces it with her own model of "spiritual hegemony." As Ames writes:

> Moore needed to distance religion in order to explain the formation of
> the persecuting society . . . yet we have lost something in his "dark,
> persecutory vision" and in its emphasis on social and political
> power . . . clerics' choice not simply to persecute heretics but also to
> evoke and to interpret particular Christian texts and traditions as
> mandating that persecution as sincere piety. . . . The ecclesiastical
> power . . . to define, to interpret, to investigate to punish . . . offered
> itself as an arm of divine power: transcendent, inescapable, terrifying.
> It penetrated clerics themselves; their own power and vision, conse-
> quently was limited, incomplete, and deferred to God, embedded in a
> specific notion of Christian revelation, cosmography, and time. While
> it may resemble Foucault's discursive power, its tone was altered, its
> words interpreted differently, a descant added.[47]

Despite her finer precisions of the persecutory construct, medieval
Church authorities—and more specifically mendicant masters—are
ultimately still *persecutors*. The few scholarly attempts to portray the
institutional Church and its penitentially-minded approaches to others
as something more than intolerance, Ames dismisses out of hand: "For
apologetic Catholic historians, inquisition was 'religious' because heresy
was a genuine, diabolical attempt at religious and social corruption and
inquisitors did Christendom a favor by extinguishing it. This is simply

---

46. Jonathan Elukin, *Living Together, Living Apart, Rethinking Jewish-Christian Relations in the Middle Ages* (Princeton, NJ: Princeton University Press, 2007), 4.

47. Ames, *Righteous Persecution*, 12–13.

unsupportable."[48] Why these contentions are wanting (and how the devil's existence has been definitively disproven[49]) is not specifically mentioned. Ames is equally dismissive when referencing recent medieval-tolerationist scholarship by Laursen and Nederman: "the attempt to revise R.I. Moore's 'persecuting society' quantitatively, marshalling examples of 'tolerance' in medieval literature or legislation that are intended to counter instances of repression, is unhelpful."[50] For Ames, apparently no agglomeration of examples of medieval "tolerance" can explain away the unrelenting religious hegemon that was the "Roman church":

> [It] extended a specific kind of spiritual discipline to individual Christians in the thirteenth century. Heresy inquisitions depended upon that transcendent community governed by God through the pope; reflected the demand for willingly belonging to it; negotiated the inner forum of penance [individual conscience] with the salvific power of an "external" ecclesiastical court.... And as Vauchez observed, the mendicant orders were instrumental in the "monasticization" of the laity.... The Order of Preachers, with its vocation to "save souls," sought "those who go astray," disciplining sinful Christians of all kinds, guiding the will to belong rightly to God's universal monastery... universal *ecclesia*... [and its] discipline of all Christian bodies and souls.[51]

We see again the same "universalist," "homogeneity" construct as alleged evidence of intolerance. Putting the issue of inquisition aside, however, it ought to be asked why so many scholars habitually portray the Catholic hierarchy's attempts at bringing the faithful to drink more fully from the theology of sin and repentance—and more pointedly by direct sacramental experience—almost exclusively in terms of "hegemonic dominance" and "claustration"? Such a sociological hermeneutic is certainly missing much more meaning hidden below the surface.

Despite Ames's protestations to the contrary, the clerical vision of a "transcendent community governed by God through the pope," indispensable elements of a wider conceptualization encompassing all reality—a medieval mindset I dub a "sacra*mentality*"—was a *two*-edged

---

48. Ibid., 13.

49. "*Je pense, donc, je suis*, I know that for a fact, all the rest, all these worlds, God and even Satan—all that is not proved, to my mind. Does all that exist of itself, or is it only an emanation of myself, a logical development of my ego which alone has existed for ever...." The Devil to Ivan Karamazov, Fyodor Dostoevsky, *The Brothers Karamazov*, Part IV, 9; trans. Constance Garnett (New York, NY: Barnes & Noble Classics, 2005), 584.

50. Ames, *Righteous Persecution*, 147, nt. 30.

51. Ibid., 146–47.

sword. Stretched beyond the limits of its own internal boundaries, the distorted construct was, admittedly, the cause of many intolerant consequences, but left to prosper in its proper sphere, the "sacramental" approach to the world could indeed be said to have served as the touchstone of a distinctly *ecclesial toleration* of Jews and other non-Christians.

Before developing this line of thought, a few things seem worth noting first. This study cuts across several major disciplines and, thus, is very likely to leave experts in several fields wanting more. It is, of course, impossible to summarize in one volume what will fully satisfy not only historians of mendicancy, but of moral philosophy, sacramental theology, the western Mediterranean (especially the Crown of Aragon), Jews and Judaism, Muslims and Islam, the papacy, Church councils, canon law, political science, liberty and tolerance, etc. In particular, it should be noted that this book makes no claim to be a comprehensive history of Christian-Jewish relations. Its principal scope is limited to the era that spans the careers of St Anselm of Canterbury, the first of the Scholastics, and Blessed Ramon Llull, who departed from traditional scholastic methods but nevertheless urged an even more intense use of reason in the spread of Christian faith.

This gives us a period of roughly 250 years, which is, nevertheless, the golden age of Scholasticism and the pivot for innovative medieval Christian-Jewish encounter. Thus the central figures in this work are, for the most part, either twelfth-century philosopher-theologians or thirteenth-century early Dominicans. Yet this study does begin in earnest with insights into the Early Christian origins of Scholasticism, tolerance, and of interreligious polemic, and in later chapters inevitably provides appraisals of medieval popes, Church councils, canon law, etc. Regrettably, these parameters leave out many noteworthy individuals such as St Bernard of Clairvaux, Peter the Venerable, Petrus Alfonsi, Nicholas of Cusa and St Vincent Ferrer, to name a few; focusing on the Barcelona Debate of 1263, this book omits other notable Christian-Jewish disputations, such as that of Tortosa in 1413–1414. But as we have said, this book is ultimately about scholastic theology, Dominican mission, and the unsung contributions of pre-modern Christian thinkers toward freedom from coercion in religion.

In the final analysis, this book is, above all, devoted to re-discovering a tradition, the development and implementation of a medieval worldview, or sacra*mentality*, which saw the institutions and inhabitants of this world not primarily as means to the pursuit and maintenance of power, but as sanctified symbols reflecting God's own infinite majesty and simultaneously, flesh-and-blood sinners in need of redemption. How this scholastic "hermeneutic" at one and the same time hindered—and helped—the cause of tolerance is a tale largely yet untold. As one scholar has put it, "placing Dominican words and deeds within the horizon of their own traditions . . . allows us to hear the Dominican voice more fully . . . contributing to the possibility of a fuller dialogos."[52] It is in this sense, that it is hoped this work will be accepted, both as a course correction to current scholarship and—as we mark the 800th anniversary of the birth of the Dominican Order—a new beginning for renewed dialogue—and disputation. This is what we are encouraged to do, not only in innumerable ecclesiastical clarion calls, but by "the most-published person in human history," the recently departed scholar-rabbi, Dr. Jacob Neusner:[53] "to meet one another in a forthright exercise of reason and criticism. The challenges of Sinai bring us together for the renewal of a two thousand year old tradition of religious debate in the service of God's truth."[54]

52. "Review" anonymous.

53. "[He] published more than 900 books devoted to history, source analysis, comparative religion and legal theory. He also edited and translated, with others, nearly the entirety of the Jewish rabbinical texts. His editions of the Jerusalem Talmud and the Babylonian Talmud run to more than 50 volumes. In 'Jacob Neusner: An American Jewish Iconoclast,' the Judaic scholar Aaron W. Hughes called him 'perhaps the most important American-born Jewish thinker this country has produced.'" https://www.nytimes.com/2016/10/11/us/jacob-neusner-judaic-scholar-who-forged-interfaith-bonds-dies-at-84.html?_r=0

54. Jacob Neusner, *Judaism and Christianity, New Directions for Dialogue and Understanding*, eds. Jacob Neusner, Alan J. Aver-Peck (Leiden: Brill, 2009), 8.

1

Setting the Stage

The Jew and the Christian begin to hate one another when both look for *external* causes of their misery, the Jew putting all the blame on the Christian story of the Crucifixion, and the Christian putting all the blame on the Jews.... The Jew and the Christian begin to love one another when both look for the *internal* causes of their misery; that is, their sins and their forgetfulness of the moral law of God.
　　—Venerable Archbishop Fulton J. Sheen, *Love One Another*

IF IT is an understatement to observe that the long history between Christianity and Judaism has, more often than not, involved dispute, not the least of the reasons for this is that the first Christian author, theologian, and missionary was an "apostate" rabbi. Thus, scholars have remarked accordingly upon an ambivalence and an ambiguity toward his former co-religionists in the correspondence of St Paul. Take for example, Galatians 4:21–31:

Tell me, you who desire to be under law, do you not hear the law? For it is written that Abraham had two sons, one by a slave and one by a free woman. But the son of the slave was born according to the flesh, the son of the free woman through promise. Now this is an allegory: these women are two covenants. One is from Mount Sinai, bearing children for slavery; she is Hagar. Now Hagar is Mount Sinai in Arabia; she corresponds to the present Jerusalem, for she is in slavery with her children. But the Jerusalem above is free, and she is our mother. For it is written,

> "Rejoice, O barren one that dost not bear;
> break forth and shout, thou who art not in travail;
> for the desolate hath more children
> than she who hath a husband."

31

Now we, brethren, like Isaac, are children of promise. But as at that time he who was born according to the flesh persecuted him who was born according to the Spirit, so it is now. But what does the scripture say? "Cast out the slave and her son; for the son of the slave shall not inherit with the son of the free woman." So, brethren, we are not children of the slave but of the free woman.

Paul's biblical hermeneutic saw in Abraham's concubine Hagar a figure or "type" of contemporary Judaism and its slavish obedience to the Old Law; while in Sara, it featured a freewoman, a sign or sacrament of Christ's Church, the New Dispensation. The Apostle's penchant for typology (a subject to which we shall return presently) was arguably one impetus for universally disparaging appraisals of Judaism among the (unlike Paul) non-Jewish early Christian apologists, from St Justin Martyr, Melito of Sardis, and Tertullian, down into the late Patristic period with the caustic rhetoric of St John Chrysostom and others (beyond even to Agobard of Lyons in the ninth century). Using typology to justify Jewish debasement, Justin tells Trypho the Jew:

For the circumcision according to the flesh, which is from Abraham, was given for a sign; that you may be separated from other nations, and from us; and that you alone may suffer that which you now justly suffer; and that your land may be desolate, and your cities burned with fire; and that strangers may eat your fruit in your presence, and not one of you may go up to Jerusalem. For you are not recognized among the rest of men by any other mark than your fleshly circumcision. For none of you, I suppose, will venture to say that God neither did nor does foresee the events, which are future, nor fore-ordained his deserts for each one. Accordingly, these things have happened to you in fairness and justice, for you have slain the Just One, and His prophets before Him; and now you reject those who hope in Him, and in Him who sent Him—God the Almighty and Maker of all things.[1]

Melito of Sardis makes similar use of alleged typological "abuse" in an Easter hymn which praises the Paschal mystery and consigns the Jews to history:

O strange and inexpressible mystery!
  The slaughter of the sheep was found to be Israel's salvation,
    And the death of the sheep became the people's life,
    And the blood won the angel's respect.
  Tell me angel, what did you respect?

1. St Justin Martyr, *Dialogue with Trypho*, 16; http://www.theologynetwork.org/Media/PDF/Justin_Martyr-Dialogue_with_Trypho.pdf.

The slaughter of the sheep or the life of the Lord?
The death of the sheep or the model (*typos*) of the Lord?
The blood of the sheep or the Spirit of the Lord?
It is clear that your respect was won
when you saw the mystery of the Lord occurring in the sheep,
the life of the Lord in the slaughter of the lamb,
the model (*typos*) of the Lord in the death of the sheep. . . . (31–33)

This is just what happens in the case of a preliminary structure:
It does not arise as a finished work, but
because of what is going to be visible through its image. . . .
But when that of which it is the model arises,
That which once bore the image of the future thing
    is itself destroyed as growing useless
having yielded that image of the future to what is truly real;
and what once was precious becomes worthless
when what is truly precious has been revealed. (36–37)[2]

Among other uses of invective, St John Chrysostom often interpreted Old Testament figures and passages to paint Jews in a negative light; "I have forsaken my house" (Jer 12:7), is used by him to say: "when God forsakes a place, it becomes a dwelling place for demons." In like manner, the anonymous *Apostolic Constitutions* warns believers to stay clear of Jewish worship: "house of demons or the synagogue of 'Christ Killers,' or the assembly of evil doers."

Perhaps the most objectionable early Christian documents, however, are the Gospels themselves:

"Woe to you, scribes and Pharisees, hypocrites! for you are like white-washed tombs, which outwardly appear beautiful, but within they are full of dead men's bones and all uncleanness. So you also outwardly appear righteous to men, but within you are full of hypocrisy and iniquity.

"Woe to you, scribes and Pharisees, hypocrites! for you build the tombs of the prophets and adorn the monuments of the righteous, saying, 'If we had lived in the days of our fathers, we would not have taken part with them in shedding the blood of the prophets.' Thus you witness against yourselves, that you are sons of those who murdered the prophets. Fill up, then, the measure of your fathers. You serpents, you brood of vipers, how are you to escape being sentenced to hell? Therefore I send you prophets and wise men and scribes, some of

2. Melito of Sardis, *On the Passover*, as quoted in Jeremy Cohen, *Christ Killers, The Jews and the Passion from the Bible to the Big Screen* (Oxford: Oxford University Press, 2007), 63–64.

whom you will kill and crucify, and some you will scourge in your synagogues and persecute from town to town." (Matt 23: 27–32)

They answered him, "Abraham is our father." Jesus said to them, "If
you were Abraham's children, you would do what Abraham did, but
now you seek to kill me, a man who has told you the truth which I
heard from God; this is not what Abraham did. You do what your
father did." They said to him, "We were not born of fornication; we
have one Father, even God." Jesus said to them, "If God were your
Father, you would love me, for I proceeded and came forth from God;
I came not of my own accord, but he sent me. Why do you not understand what I say? It is because you cannot bear to hear my word. You
are of your father the devil, and your will is to do your father's desires.
He was a murderer from the beginning, and has nothing to do with the
truth, because there is no truth in him. When he lies, he speaks according to his own nature, for he is a liar and the father of lies. But, because
I tell the truth, you do not believe me. Which of you convicts me of
sin? If I tell the truth, why do you not believe me? He who is of God
hears the words of God; the reason why you do not hear them is that
you are not of God." (Jn 8:39–47)

In the conclusion to his work, *Christ Killers*, Jeremy Cohen, discussing the historical ramifications of the Gospel of John, quotes fellow
intellectual George Steiner:

> [After leaving the Last Supper] Judas goes into a never-ending night of
> collective guilt. It is the sober truth to say that his exit is the door to the
> Shoah. The "final solution" proposed, enacted by National Socialism
> in this twentieth century is the perfectly logical, axiomatic conclusion
> to the Judas-identification of the Jew.... That utter darkness, that
> night within night, into which Judas is dispatched and commanded
> [by Jesus] to perform "quickly," is already that of the death ovens. Who
> precisely has betrayed whom?[3]

From the Evangelist to Eichmann, it's apparently a very short and
precipitous drop, and it's no less than Jesus Christ who's ultimately to
blame, or at least his first-century publicists.

By no means is this view of the Church's Scriptures confined to contemporary Jewish scholars like Cohen and Steiner; no one perhaps has
propounded it more successfully in recent years than James Carroll, the
ex-Catholic priest, in his *New York Times* bestseller, *Constantine's Sword,
The Church and the Jews: A History*. Carroll longingly awaits the day
when "Vatican III" will be summoned and

---

3. George, Steiner, *No Passion Spent: Essays, 1978–1996* (London: Faber and Faber,
1996), 417, as cited in Cohen, 260.

reorder the Church's relationship to the "troubling texts".... There is no question of simply eliminating them, nor of rewriting them to purge the Epistles and Gospels of what the contemporary ear finds offensive ... but it would be a mistake to do more to let the Gospels off the hook. Indeed, their offensive character is part of what the Church must learn not only to admit but to claim. The anti-Jewish texts of the New Testament show that the Church, even in its first generation, was capable of betraying the message of Jesus, establishing once and for all that "the Church as such" can sin. The Church as such stands in need of forgiveness. The Church must therefore preach the anti-Jewish texts of the Gospel—not against the Jews, but against itself.[4]

Cohen, in his own analysis, gives tacit endorsement to the views of Steiner and Carroll: "In the coming pages, we shall see how Christian religious devotion enshrined the Passion of the human Christ in the minds and hearts of the faithful. As clerics and laypersons alike forged their relationships with God through the experience of the Passion, they internalized a demonic stereotype of the Jew who had caused Jesus his suffering. This image lingered on in Western consciousness long after the medieval preoccupation with the crucified Christ had subsided."[5]

The conclusion is inescapable: ancient and medieval Catholic theology sowed the seeds of modern anti-Semitism and according to some, the Holocaust itself.

But is there an alternative reading?

It is a seemingly indisputable fact of history that Jesus and his Apostles were Jews. It logically follows that the first "Christians" were "Jewish." When the average person makes this statement, however, he has in his mind "Jewishness" as one knows it now in the twenty-first century: an exclusive ethnicity based on birth with the accompanying religious practices associated with Torah and synagogue; and yet this is *not* by any means an exact equivalent to "Jewish" self-identity in the first century, which is the actual subject at hand.[6] There were many groups at that time all claiming to be "Semites," "Children of Abraham," "Doers of the

4. James Carroll, *Constantine's Sword: The Church and the Jews: A History* (Boston, MA: Houghton Mifflin, 2002), 566.

5. Cohen, *Christ Killers*, 126.

6. "So-called Normative Judaism was not normative in the first century," Luke Timothy Johnson, "The New Testament's Anti-Jewish Slander and the Conventions of Ancient Polemic," *Journal of Biblical Literature* (108/3), 1989, 419–41; 427.

Law of Moses." Yet each of them had precious little patience for the others, whom they considered wicked false claimants posing as the true Israel. The disparate sects of the first century are categorized by the contemporary Jewish historian Josephus into: Sadducees, Pharisees, Samaritans, Zealots, and Essenes.

The Sadducees were the nobility in Judea. They were the priests who offered sacrifice in the Temple. They accepted only the Torah as canonical and subsequently differed with the Pharisees (who accepted a wider canon), therefore denying, among other things, the immortality of the soul and the Resurrection of the Body. In fact, we see a dispute between them and Jesus in the Gospel (Mk 12:18–27; Lk 20:27–40). They were particularly resented by their countrymen for being so accommodating to the Roman occupiers. A different high priest each year? Gymnasia in Jerusalem! The Pharisees could hardly restrain their disdain, while the Zealots abandoned restraint altogether, unwittingly sealing Israel's political fate for nearly two millennia. The Essenes (who embraced a wider canon still) had no stomach for the situation and established proto-monastic communities in the Judean wilderness offering a sacrificial meal in place of Temple worship. Then there were the Samaritans, whose ancestors, having been conquered by the Assyrians, had intermarried and intermingled Gentile practices with Hebraic ones. They also refused to worship in the Jerusalem Temple and their fellow Semites refused to have anything to do with them. The fascinating exchange from St John's Gospel between Jesus and the Samaritan Woman may be the earliest recorded Christian dialogue/disputation:

> "Sir, I perceive that you are a prophet. Our fathers worshiped on this mountain; and you say that in Jerusalem is the place where men ought to worship."
>
> Jesus said to her, "Woman, believe me, the hour is coming when neither on this mountain nor in Jerusalem will you worship the Father. You worship what you do not know; we worship what we know, for salvation is from the Jews. But the hour is coming, and now is, when the true worshipers will worship the Father in spirit and truth, for such the Father seeks to worship him. God is spirit, and those who worship him must worship in spirit and truth." (Jn 4:19–24)

Jesus claims that "salvation is from the Jews" not the Samaritans; nevertheless, his saving death and resurrection will usher in the New Covenant wherein the God of Israel is worshipped in spirit and truth, not through a physical location or ritual. The irony was lost on no early believer when later the Pharisees mocked Jesus as a Samaritan: "Are we not right in saying that you are a Samaritan and have a demon?" (Jn 8:48). Similar conventions of contempt of countrymen are especially found among the Essenes, who, for example, cursed all other "Jews" as "sons of darkness" leaving them to languish in hell with the Devil— their father:

> And the Levites shall curse all the men of the lot of Satan, saying: O Be cursed because of all your guilty wickedness!
>
> May He deliver you up for torture at the hands of the vengeful Avengers!
>
> May He visit you with destruction by the hand of all the Wreakers of Revenge! Be cursed without mercy because of the darkness of your deeds! Be damned in the shadowy place of everlasting fire! May God not heed when you call on Him, nor pardon you by blotting out your sin! May He raise His angry face towards you for vengeance! May there be no Peace for you in the mouth of those who hold fast to the Fathers![7]

Simply put then, the first Christians were no more "anti-Jewish" than the Pharisees, Sadducees, Samaritans, Zealots, or Essenes.[8] They, like the others, were simply defending their claim to be the rightful Israel. By the second century, however, the Romans had eliminated the competition so that there were really only two groups left: the Christian Church and Rabbinical Judaism (and really only one ideological arena left in which to fight: the gentile cities of the Empire). As Luke Timothy Johnson writes: "If Jews were so blameless why were Christians so nasty? But our survey shows the use of this language everywhere in the fragmented Judaism of the first century. Readers today hear the NT's polemic as inappropriate only because the other voices are silent. Historical imagination can restore them."[9]

Both groups still had as much right to mutual recrimination as before. Why should it matter that the number of "Gentile" Christians was ever increasing in an inverse ratio to those genetically/ethnically "Jewish"? The Church-as-such still claimed to be the fulfillment of the Covenant, that is to say, authentic "Israel." In this sense then, when the Evangelists or even the Early Fathers defended their claims against the counter-claims of rabbinic Jews, there was nothing *inherently* anti-

7. *The Community Rule*, tran. G. Vermes, 1QS; http://ccat.sas.upenn.edu/gopher/oth er/courses/rels/225/Texts/1QS.

8. Cf. James Dunn, ed. "The Question of Anti-Semitism in the New Testament Writings of the Period," in *Jews and Christians: the parting of the ways, CE 70 to 135: the second Durham-Tübingen Research Symposium on Earliest Christianity and Judaism (Durham, September 1989)* (Grand Rapids, MI: Wm. B. Eerdmans Publishing, 1999).

9. Johnson, "The New Testament's Anti-Jewish Slander," 441.

Judaistic (let alone anti-Semitic) about it. Indeed, as Johnson observes: "By the measure of Hellenistic conventions and certainly by the measure of contemporary Jewish polemic, the NT's slander against fellow Jews is remarkably mild."[10]

The same has been said for the "anti-Jewish" arguments in St Justin Martyr's (AD 100–165) *Dialogue with Trypho*. Since this is the earliest of the historical Jewish-Christian dialogues/disputations and the only extant second century one, it is therefore, worthy of some extended investigation.[11] Scholarly consensus holds that the dialogue is, in fact, based on an actual conversation between Justin and his Jewish counterpart years earlier.[12] As Novikoff explains: "Because of the civility of the exchange and the fact that the two men part as friends, historians have commended the work for its 'courteousness and fairness.'"[13]

Justin extends a definite courtesy to his opponent—many times calling him "friend": "'I excuse and forgive you, my friend,' I said. 'For you know not what you say, but have been persuaded by teachers who do not understand the Scriptures; and you speak, like a diviner whatever comes into your mind. But if you are willing to listen to an account of Him [Christ], how we have not been deceived. . . .'"[14] Justin admits quite openly that his motives—far from sinister—are only for his interlocutor's benefit: "If, then, you have any concern for yourself, and if you are eagerly looking for salvation, and if you believe in God, you may—since you are not indifferent to the matter—become acquainted with the Christ of God, and, after being initiated, live a happy life."[15] The

---

10. Ibid. One should not underestimate the role of Greco-Roman rhetorical practices upon Christian authors in Antiquity and beyond. It was not uncommon to employ hyperbole and to heap abuse upon an opponent and his philosophy. This way of expressing an argument is obviously worlds apart from our commonly accepted standards of discourse. Cf. J.G. Cook, "The Protreptic Power of Early Christian Language from John to Augustine," *Vigiliae Christianae* 48 (1994): 105–34; Robert Louis Wilken, *John Chrysostom and the Jews, Rhetoric and Reality in the Late 4th Century* (Berkeley, CA: University of California Press, 1983); Alex J. Novikoff, *The Medieval Culture of Disputation* (Philadelphia, PA: University of Pennsylvania Press, 2013), among others.

11. Avery Cardinal Dulles, SJ, *A History of Apologetics* (San Francisco, CA: Ignatius Press, 2005), 32.

12. If so, it would be significant, for according to Eusebius of Caesarea, Trypho was "the best known Jew of that time." Eusebius, *Ecclesiastical History*, IV.xviii.6; as quoted in Novikoff, *The Medieval Culture*, 17.

13. Lukyn Williams, *Adversus Judaeos: A Bird's-Eye View of Christian Apologiae until the Renaissance* (Cambridge: Cambridge University Press, 1935), 42; as quoted in Novikoff, *The Medieval Culture*, 17.

14. *Dialogue*, 9; cf. 39.

15. Ibid., 8.

conclusion cannot be overemphasized: zeal for conversion does not preclude peaceful coexistence:

> "For we have found more than we expected, and more than it was possible to have expected. And if we could do this more frequently, we should be much helped in the searching of the Scriptures themselves. But since," he [Trypho] said, "you are on the eve of departure, and expect daily to set sail, do not hesitate to remember us as friends when you are gone."

> "For my part," I replied, "If I had remained, I would have wished to do the same thing daily. But now, since I expect, with God's will and aid, to set sail, I exhort you to give all diligence in this very great struggle for your own salvation, and to be earnest in setting a higher value on the Christ of the Almighty God than on your own teachers."

> After this they left me, wishing me safety in my voyage, and from every misfortune. And I, praying for them, said, "I can wish no better thing for you, sirs, than this, that, recognizing in this way that *intelligence is given to everyman*, you may be of the same opinion as ourselves, and believe that Jesus is the Christ of God."[16] (emphasis mine)

Not only is Justin solicitous for the welfare of his Jewish adversary, he (at times) consciously moderates his rhetoric in keeping with his opponent's sensibilities, as he says at one juncture: "wishing to get him to listen to me, I answered in milder tones . . . "[17]

Nevertheless, Justin is not afraid to testify to Trypho to what he regards as the truth of the matter: "As, therefore, Christ is the Israel and the Jacob, even so we, who have been quarried out from the bowels of Christ, are the true Israelitic race."[18] He also states earlier in the dialogue, "[Prophecies of Christ] are contained in your Scriptures, or rather not yours, but ours."[19] His point is to prove that the Hebrew prophets predicted Christ and to answer Jewish objections to Christianity. In addition, Justin employs typological arguments in support of the Church. As Robert M. Haddad illustrates:

> So, for example, the Passover Lamb (which was slain to achieve Israel's liberation from Egyptian bondage) was for Justin a forerunner of Jesus who, as the Lamb of God, was slain to liberate humanity from the bondage of the devil (*Dial.* 40). Justin saw other types of Jesus in the

16. Ibid., 145.
17. Ibid., 79.
18. Ibid., 135.
19. Ibid., 29.

person of Noah (*Dial.* 138), Jonah (*Dial.* 107,108), Moses (*Dial.* 90, 91, 94, 97, 112), Joshua (*Dial.* 75, 90, 91, 106, 111, 112, 113, 115), the scapegoat (*Dial.* 40), and Rahab's scarlet rope (*Dial.* 111).[20]

Many modern scholars, however, are unpersuaded by Justin's typology:

> However, though allegorical and typological interpretations of Scripture could make a prophecy's fulfillment in Jesus seem obvious to one already Christian, a skeptical or wavering eye would not see it so clearly as having been fulfilled by him. Barnard labels a number of Justin's interpretations as "precarious in the extreme," while Osborne speaks of his "recurring irrationality." Examples include the staffs of Moses and Aaron and all other staffs and trees of the Old Testament— for Justin all these were prefigurations of the cross of Christ (*Dial.* 86).[21]

Many scholars argue that Justin's "Jews," and for that matter, almost all the Jews referenced in the *Adversus Iudaeos* literature of the Patristic era are not "real" Jews at all. They are Scriptural stereotypes constructed by clerics in their polemical writings not to convince real Jews of Christian superiority, but to bolster the faith of the baptized rank-in-file. But whether this approach holds true for a greater or lesser number of instances is not so important for our purposes. What is much more germane is how the use of exegetical "typology," or the construction of the "hermeneutical," or "rhetorical" Jew,[22] impacted the Church's treatment of *actual* Jews in *later* centuries.

What is more, today's Academy generally fails to fathom a terribly vital facet to all this, namely that the Church's use of signification, its typological way of seeing the world—or sacra*mentality*—is not, in fact, chained to rhetoric or exegesis *per se*. Nor, for that matter, does it *always* deleteriously depict Jews. Let us take a moment to delve more deeply.

---

20. Robert M. Haddad, *The Case for Christianity, St Justin Martyr's Arguments for Religious Liberty and Judicial Justice* (Lanham, MD: Taylor Trade, 2009), 146.

21. Haddad, *The Case for Christianity*, 149.

22. "Hermeneutical" Jew is Cohen's expression; "rhetorical" Jew is Paula Fredriksen's, cf. *Augustine and the Jews* (New Haven, CT: Yale University Press, 2010); cf. also David Nirenberg, *Anti-Judaism, The Western Tradition* (New York & London: W.W. Norton, 2013), especially 1–86; Bernhard Blumenkranz, *Die Judenpredigt Augustins* (Basel, 1946).

⊕

"A sacrament," writes St Augustine of Hippo (354–430), "is a sign of a sacred thing."[23] "Thing" is the key word here. As St Thomas Aquinas (1225–1274), famed Scholastic, Dominican preacher, and arguably the most gifted theologian since Augustine, elaborates the Catholic approach to Biblical studies:

> The author of Holy Writ is *God, in whose power it is to signify His meaning, not by words only (as man also can do), but also by things themselves.* So, whereas in every other science things are signified by words, this science has the property, that the *things* signified by the words *have themselves also a signification.* Therefore that first signification whereby words signify things belongs to the first sense, the historical or literal. That signification whereby things signified by words have themselves also a signification is called the spiritual sense, which is based on the literal, and presupposes it. Now this spiritual sense has a threefold division. For as the Apostle says (Hebrews 10:1) the Old Law is a figure of the New Law, and Dionysius says (*Coel. Hier.* i) "the New Law itself is a figure of future glory." Again, in the New Law, whatever our Head has done is a type of what we ought to do. Therefore, so far as the things of the Old Law signify the things of the New Law, there is the allegorical sense.[24] (emphasis mine)

Jean Cardinal Daniélou, SJ observes of Aquinas's remarks:

> The real source and foundation of typology has sometimes been obscured in the course of theoretical discussions about *methods of Scriptural exegisis* [sic]. Aquinas defined it accurately when he showed that it is not a meaning of words but a meaning of things—not a sense of scripture but a sense of history. It begins in the Old Testament, where episodes in the past history of Israel are presented as a figure of what shall come to pass in the end of time. It is thus originally and essentially eschatological. In the New Testament, Christ is shown inaugurating the regime of the last days: it is in this eschatological view that he was pre-figured in the Old Testament. The reality of the last things lives on in the sacraments of the Church during the interim between Christ's ascension into Heaven and his coming again.[25] (emphasis mine)

23. St Augustine, *Letters*, 138, 1.
24. St Thomas Aquinas, OP, *Summa Theologiae*, I, I, 10; www.newadvent.org./Summa; translation from *The Summa of St Thomas Aquinas*, 3 vols. (New York, NY: Benziger Brothers, 1947). Allegory and medieval art/literature is a truly vast corpus.
25. Jean Danielou, SJ, *The Lord of History* (London: Longmans, Chicago, IL: Regnery, 1958), 140–41.

Contrary to popular belief, while Catholicism has always revered sacred Scripture, it has never been "a religion of the book," but of the Word (*Logos*),[26] and that Word has always been viewed by the Church as Someone who not only became incarnate in the Virgin's womb, but in the words and deeds of His Predecessors. As Justin Martyr puts it:

> But these things our Christ did through His own power. For no one trusted in Socrates so as to die for this doctrine, but in Christ, who was partially known even by Socrates (for *He was and is the Word* who is in every man, and *who foretold the things that were to come to pass both through the prophets and in His own person* when He was made of like passions, and taught these things), not only philosophers and scholars believed, but also artisans and people entirely uneducated, despising both glory, and fear, and death.[27]

In the Church's view, Christ's Semitic ancestors, acting as "sacraments," not only foreshadowed in *their deeds* the saving power of *His own*, in some mysterious sense it was Christ Himself who did them. When they spoke, it was Christ speaking through them. (Furthermore, with such a broad Christology, how could the Church do otherwise than "appropriate" the Jewish Scriptures as its own? How could Jewish failure to recognize Christ as Messiah, not also equal blindness to the same Word previously entrusted to them?)

In like manner, it should be noted that the seven sacraments of Christ's Church—"sacraments" in the fullest sense possible—are viewed as post-Resurrection extensions of Christ's historically redemptive acts, which simultaneously deliver and prognosticate the glory of His kingdom to come (a subject to which we shall return in later chapters).

What has all this to do with how the Church perceived and thus treated Jews? To begin with, as Aquinas states, the "spiritual" sense of Scripture "is based on the literal, and presupposes it," therefore, not simply the spiritual, New Testament side of the equation is valid, but—by such typologizing—the literal "Jewish" side, not only really happened, God Almighty willed it (and the figurative, spiritual sense rests upon it).

---

26. *Catechism of the Catholic Church* (Citta del Vaticano: Libreria Editrice Vaticana, 1997), n. 108: "Christianity is the religion of the 'Word' of God, a word which is 'not a written and mute word, but the Word which is incarnate and living.'" (St Bernard of Clairvaux, *S. missus est hom.* 4, 11: PL 183, 86).

27. *2 Apology*, 10.

Thus, there is a transcendent legitimacy—one might say necessity—to the Jewish figures and practices embodied in the Old Law.

Christian doctrine such as this, interpreted by the perceptive and grace-disposed intellect of a *beatus* like Augustine, for example, boded well for the fate of actual Jews. (Especially since no other Church Father comes even close to having as massive an influence upon later scholastic thinking as Augustine.) As Paula Fredriksen argues in her book, *Augustine and the Jews*, though Jewish "literal-mindedness" in observing the precepts of the Law had provided the Church's apologists (and heretics) with convincing demonstration of "Israel's turpitude . . . instead of understanding the Law 'spiritually,' Jews had understood 'carnally' and thus remained enmeshed in the fleshly . . . ," according to Augustine,

> Laws about permissible and forbidden foods, whatever their symbolic aspect, also instructed the people about what they should and should not eat. . . . God, in brief, had charged Israel with more than preserving the divine word of the Law in the text of his book. He had charged them as well with *enacting the commands of that same Law in the flesh, within historical time*. And precisely because these ancient Jews performed the Law *secundum carnem*, "*the lives of these men* as well as their words were prophetic."[28] (emphasis mine) For Augustine, then, the semiotics of prophecy encompasses deeds as well as words, "for material symbolic acts (*corporalis sacramenta*) are nothing other than visible speech (*verba visibilia*)." This likening of physical actions to language in turn provides Augustine with a way to explain why and how the divine truth signified through *sacramenta* can remain the same, even though the sacraments themselves, those ritual acts communicating this truth, clearly changed. (The church celebrates the Eucharist, for example; it does not sacrifice animals.)[29]

In the last analysis, looking at Jews symbolically—even linking them to Christian rituals—could, in fact, lead to an appreciation of Jewish practice.

Beyond the value attributed to the literal applications of the Torah, Augustine's sacramental way of "reading" Jews could also be said to have promoted toleration in other ways. Let us take, for example, his typological comparison of Cain and Abel with "the Jews" and Christ:

> Abel, the younger brother, is killed by the elder brother; Christ, the head of the younger people, is killed by the elder people of the Jews.

28. *Against Faustus*, 4.2.

29. Fredriksen, *Augustine and the Jews*, 244–45; cf. also, idem, "Divine Justice and Human Freedom: Augustine on Jews and Judaism," 392–98, in *From Witness to Witchcraft*, 29–54.

Abel dies in the field; Christ dies on Calvary. God asks Cain where his brother is, not as if He did not know, but as a judge asks a guilty criminal. Cain replies that he knows not, and that he is not his brother's keeper. And what answer can the Jews give at this day, when we ask them with the voice of God, that is, of the sacred Scriptures, about Christ, except that they do not know the Christ that we speak of? Cain's ignorance was pretended, and the Jews are deceived in their refusal of Christ. Moreover, they would have been in a sense keepers of Christ, if they had been willing to receive and keep the Christian faith. For the man who keeps Christ in his heart does not ask, like Cain, Am I my brother's keeper? Then God says to Cain, "What have you done? The voice of your brother's blood cries unto me from the ground." So the voice of God in the Holy Scriptures accuses the Jews. For the blood of Christ has a loud voice on the earth, when the responsive Amen of those who believe in Him comes from all nations. This is the voice of Christ's blood, because the clear voice of the faithful redeemed by His blood is the voice of the blood itself.

Then God says to Cain: "You are cursed from the earth, which has opened its mouth to receive your brother's blood at your hand. For you shall till the earth, and it shall no longer yield unto you its strength. A mourner and an abject shall you be on the earth.". . . That is, the Church admits and avows the Jewish people to be cursed, because after killing Christ they continue to till the ground of an earthly circumcision, an earthly Sabbath, an earthly passover, while the hidden strength or virtue of making known Christ, which this tilling contains, is not yielded to the Jews while they continue in impiety and unbelief, for it is revealed in the New Testament. While they will not turn to God, the veil which is on their minds in reading the Old Testament is not taken away.[30]

On the face of it, Augustine's analogy seems hardly a flattering one, nor one which presages any ecclesiastical benevolence toward the Synagogue; the Jews are "unbelieving" Christ killers, carnally "cursed" in their practice of the Law, and "blind" to New Testament grace. Yet, there is more than meets the eye to this murderous metaphor:

"Groaning and trembling shall you be on the earth." Here no one can fail to see that in every land where the Jews are scattered they mourn for the loss of their kingdom, and are in terrified subjection to the immensely superior number of Christians. So Cain answered, and said: "My case is worse, if You drive me out this day from the face of the earth, and from Your face shall I be hid, and I shall be a mourner and

---

30. St Augustine, *Against Faustus*, 12:9–11.

an outcast on the earth; and it shall be that every one that finds me shall slay me." Here he groans indeed in terror, lest after losing his earthly possession he should suffer the death of the body. This he calls a worse case than that of the ground not yielding to him its strength, or than that of spiritual death. For his mind is carnal; for he thinks little of being hid from the face of God, that is, of being under the anger of God, were it not that he may be found and slain. This is the carnal mind that tills the ground, but does not obtain its strength. To be carnally minded is death; but he, in ignorance of this, mourns for the loss of his earthly possession, and is in terror of bodily death. But what does God reply? "Not so," He says; "but whosoever shall kill Cain, vengeance shall be taken on him sevenfold." That is, it is not as you say, not by bodily death shall the ungodly race of carnal Jews perish. For whoever destroys them in this way shall suffer sevenfold vengeance, that is, shall bring upon himself the sevenfold penalty under which the Jews lie for the crucifixion of Christ. So to the end of the seven days of time, the continued preservation of the Jews will be a proof to believing Christians of the subjection merited by those who, in the pride of their kingdom, put the Lord to death.

"And the Lord God set a mark upon Cain, lest anyone finding him should slay him." It is a most notable fact, that all the nations subjugated by Rome adopted the heathenish ceremonies of the Roman worship; while the Jewish nation, whether under Pagan or Christian monarchs, has never lost the sign of their law, by which they are distinguished from all other nations and peoples. No emperor or monarch who finds under his government the people with this mark kills them, that is, makes them cease to be Jews, and as Jews to be separate in their observances, and unlike the rest of the world. Only when a Jew comes over to Christ, he is no longer Cain, nor goes out from the presence of God, nor dwells in the land of Nod, which is said to mean commotion.[31]

Deicide aside, God will take vengeance upon anyone who "kills" Jews. The preservation of the Jews—not their extermination—is God's priority and Cain is a figure of this providential design. The mark of Cain is "the sign of their Law." The continued practice of Judaism is equivalent to the "life" of the people and simultaneously serves as a "proof to believing Christians." The sacramental quality of the Jewish people is a positive boon to the Christian community. This does not mean, however, that the conversion of individual Jews is not to be hoped for: "Only when a Jew comes over to Christ, he is no longer Cain." Still, no king

31. Ibid., 12.

may coerce Jewish conversion—and so "kill" him; thus, the origins of medieval Catholic toleration.

The wider implications of Augustine's theology for contemporary Jews living in the late Roman Empire are difficult for historians to discern.[32] A causal relation between the Augustinian legacy as it lingered long into the Middle Ages and the treatment of medieval Jews seems easier to appraise: "Augustine's position on the continuing religious importance of the Jewish people, eventually sanctioned by his invocation of Ps. 59:12 ('Slay them not, lest my people forget') ultimately served to safeguard later generations for centuries in medieval Christian Europe. Seldom has a biblical hermeneutic had such an immediate and perduring social effect."[33]

Here too, however, caution is a watchword. Augustine's theological construct of Jews and Judaism was not without its own negative stereotyping, and besides this, his general theological insights, though dominant, had to compete with the views of other apologists and Fathers of the *Adversus Iudaeos* tradition.[34] Even those medievals who accepted Augustine's assumptions modified his treatment of "Jews" to suit their own (changed) circumstances.[35] Nevertheless, it may be argued that an especially Augustinian sacra*mentality* was always present below the surface, and during the High Middle Ages, it would become the special contribution of the Scholastics to plumb the depths of the sacraments both in their symbolic aspects, and in their functions as conduits of God's grace for the remission of sin. Furthermore, for Friederiksen, the sacramental view of the Jew was the by-product of long-suffering meditation on sin and mercy, the mystery of God's righteousness and the unrighteous sinner, of whom Augustine was first:

> But the very clarity of the scriptural prophecies of Jewish unbelief, and their unambiguous confirmation, raised once again the constellation of questions that had dogged Augustine during his earlier reading of Romans and in his examination of his own life. If the sin of unbelief is mandated by heaven (as in the case of Esau, Pharaoh, or anyone languishing *sub lege*), how is God just in punishing the sinner? If sin is mandated, is it nonetheless still voluntary? If it is not voluntary, can it

32. On "actual" Jews and Christians in the age of Augustine: Bernhard Blumenkranz, *Die Judenpredigt Augustins* (Basel, 1946) for decades the magisterial study; cf. Fredriksen, *Augustine and the Jews*, 354–66; "Divine Justice," 52; Cohen, *Living Letters*, 42.

33. Fredriksen, "Divine Justice," 51.

34. Cf. Williams, *Adversus Iudaeos*; S. Krauss and W. Horbury, *The Jewish-Christian Controversy from the Earliest Times to 1789.* Vol. 1. *History* (Mohr Siebeck, 2008).

35. Cf. Cohen, *Living Letters*, esp. 67–145.

still be "sin"? If God is just, how can he condemn those to whom he has chosen not to give grace? If he had offered grace, could the sinner possibly have refused?[36]

The thesis of the chapters which follow is that in the midst of their conscientious excavations of sin and sacrament, and *despite* the prevalence of the existing *Adversus Iudaeos* corpus, scholastic theologians (and canon lawyers) happened upon heretofore untapped channels for tolerance and enlightened Christian views of Jews. But what would make scholastic reflection on sin and sacrament "scholastic" is not simply the systematic application of religious principles, but of *rational* ones. Can we therefore discern Scholasticism's embryonic origins, particularly as they relate to conversion and coexistence in the Patristic era?

For all Justin Martyr's extensive use of the Hebrew Prophets to persuade Trypho into the Christian fold, the catalyst for Justin's conversation with him was Greek philosophy. Indeed, Trypho would never have approached him in the first place had Justin not been clad in philosopher's garb:

> "Whenever I see any one in such costume, I gladly approach him, and now, for the same reason, have I willingly accosted you; and these accompany me, in the expectation of hearing for themselves something profitable from you." . . .
>
> "And in what," said I, "would you be profited by philosophy so much as by your own lawgiver and the prophets?"
>
> "Why not?" he replied. "Do no the philosophers turn every discourse on God? And do not questions continually arise to them about His unity and providence? Is not this truly the duty of philosophy, to investigate the Deity?"
>
> "Assuredly," said I, "so we too have believed."[37]

At Trypho's prompting, Justin narrates in some detail his search for God/Truth among the competing schools of thought of the day and how he finally found the only "safe and useful" one:

> Philosophy is, in fact, the greatest possession, and most honourable before God, to whom it leads us and alone commends us; and these are

---

36. Friedriksen, "Divine Justice," 50.
37. *Dialogue*, 1.

truly holy men who have bestowed attention on philosophy. What philosophy is, however, and the reason why *it has been sent down to men*, have escaped the observation of most; for there would be neither Platonists, nor Stoics, nor Peripatetics, nor Theoretics, nor Pythagoreans, this knowledge being one.[38] (emphasis mine)

As with Augustine some two centuries later, Justin sought "the Divine" in all the wrong places. Going from school to school (which contradicted each other) in his quest for true Wisdom/Philosophy, he was finally led to the Hebrew Prophets in whom he ultimately discovered Christ. Christ is the "*Logos*," which is Greek for "Reason/Truth." This is how Justin put it in both his *1st Apology* and *2nd Apology*[39] and he makes a similar argument here in his *Dialogue*: the argument for the unity of Truth. "Logos" was sent down among men: to the Greeks in the form of philosophy, to the Jews in the form of type and of prophecy.

For whatever either lawgivers or philosophers uttered well, they elaborated by finding and contemplating some part of the Word. But since *they did not know the whole of the Word, which is Christ*, they often contradicted themselves. And those who by human birth were more ancient than Christ, when they attempted to consider and prove things by reason, were brought before the tribunals as impious persons and busybodies. And Socrates, who was more zealous in this direction than all of them, was accused of the very same crimes as ourselves. For they said that he was introducing new divinities, and did not consider those to be gods whom the state recognized. But he cast out from the state both Homer and the rest of the poets, and taught men to reject the wicked demons and those who did the things which the poets related; and he exhorted them to become acquainted with the God who was to them unknown, *by means of the investigation of reason*, saying, "That it is neither easy to find the Father and Maker of all, nor, having found Him, is it safe to declare Him to all." But these things our Christ did through His own power. For no one trusted in Socrates so as to die for this doctrine, but in Christ, who was partially known even by Socrates (for *He was and is the Word* who is in every man, and *who foretold the things that were to come to pass both through the prophets and in His own person* when He was made of like passions, and taught these things), not only philosophers and scholars believed, but also artisans and people entirely uneducated, despising both glory, and fear, and death; since *He is a power of the ineffable Father, not the mere instrument of human reason*.[40] (emphasis mine)

38. Ibid., 2.
39. *1 Apology*, 46; *2 Apology*, 8–10.
40. *2 Apology*, 10.

A second witness to the power of reason and disputation similar to Justin Martyr of Rome may be found hundreds of miles away and more than six hundred fifty years later, in the Turkish village of Haran near the Syrian border:

> It was of immense cultural significance in the early Middle Ages. A home to Jews, Muslims, and Christians, to pagans and to heretics, it was a village alive with religious controversy.... It was a place where ancient philosophical traditions were transformed—translated from Greek and Syriac into Arabic, the tongue of the region's new overlords. There an illustrious series of scholarly families devised an amalgam of ancient Babylonian paganism and Neoplatonism and sought to make it intelligible in a world transformed by monotheism. Living in Haran, in and among the adherents of these many religions, was a small community of Melkites, and caring for the souls of this community in the late-eighth and early-ninth centuries was its bishop, Theodore Abū Qurrah.[41]

In addition to apologetic works addressed to schismatic Christians, Muslims, and pagans, Theodore engages in argument with Jews, with the exception (like Justin) that only with Jews does he repeatedly refer to his ideological opponent as "friend," as, for instance, when he says: "My Jewish friend, I cannot help but be amazed that you accept Moses because of his limited number of wonders but do not accept Christ because of his innumerable and countless wonders."[42] And even more than Justin, he relies not merely on religious arguments, but on rational ones:

> As for you, my Jewish friend, if in the present day you were compelled to bring a rational proof with which to confirm Moses or one of the prophets for even a single person, you would not be able to do so.... This should suffice, my Jewish friend, if you are possessed of intelligence and desire to obtain what is good for your soul. Healing has come to you; and it would have come to you sooner if you had accepted it from the teachers of Christianity who spoke through the Holy Spirit and made clear everything about Christ, using both reason and scripture together. The arguments I have presented above are a compelling confirmation of Christianity. From them, there is no escape for those possessed of reason and good intention, for reason surely leads to Christ, and Christ confirms Moses and the prophets. Both the Old Testament and the New Testament thus belong to us,

---

41. *Theodore Abū Qurrah*, trans. John C. Lamoreaux, *Library of the Christian East*, vol. 1 (Provo, UT: Brigham Young University Press, 2005), xi.

42. Theodore Abū Qurah, b145, Lamoreaux, *Library of the Christian East*, 31.

even as Solomon the son of David said in the Song of Songs, "On our doors are all fruits, both old and new" (Song 7:13).[43]

Once again, it is important to recognize that Theodore has no malevolent intent; he states quite explicitly that he seeks only what is "good for the soul" of a Jew. And he believes Jewish intellects capable of processing his rational arguments. Indeed, for Theodore, reason is the common touchstone for truth. He goes so far as to argue that it is only on the testimony of the Logos of the New Testament that Christians accept the Old, *not* vice versa:

> This is what the gospel teaches us, and we believe in all that it teaches us about Moses, namely that he was sent by God and that these subjects are defective for the aforementioned reasons. It is thus that we believe that Moses and his message are from God. If not for the gospel, however, we would not believe that Moses is from God. Indeed, on the basis of reason we would reject him more earnestly. So also we believe that the prophets are from God on account of the gospel, not on account of reason.[44]

It is important to underscore the appeals to reason in both the works of Justin Martyr and Theodore Abū Qurrah. Though separated by some seven centuries they both display rational disputation and friendly persuasion. Not only do they represent episodes of a phenomenon that will fully manifest itself in medieval Scholasticism, they fly in the face of the charges leveled against the Church by today's secular "schoolmen." Take G.R. Elton's remark:

> Religions spring from faith, and faith, endeavouring to maintain its own convictions, cannot permit the existence of rivals or dissenters. Thus religions organized in powerful churches and in command of their scene persecute as a matter of course and tend to regard toleration as a sign of weakness or even wickedness towards whatever deity they worship. Among the religious, toleration is demanded by the persecuted who need it if they are ever to become triumphant, when, all too often, they start to persecute in their turn.[45]

It would undoubtedly have come as a shock to Elton (as it does to

43. 9th treatise, al-Basha, Qustantin, ed. *Mayamir Thawudurus Abi Qurrah Usquf Harran* (Beirut: Matba at al-fawa id, 1904), B154; Lamoreaux, *Library of the Christian East*, 38–39.
44. Lamoreaux, *Library of the Christian East*, 24.
45. G.R. Elton, *Persecution and Toleration: Papers Read at the Twenty-Second Summer Meeting and the Twenty-Third Winter Meeting of the Ecclesiastical History Society*, ed. W.J. Sheils (Oxford: Basil Blackwell, 1984), xiii; as cited in M. Cohen, *Under Crescent and Cross*, xix.

most) to learn that the phrase "religious liberty" was not invented by French *philosophes* of the eighteenth century, nor by Protestant reformers in the sixteenth century, but by the early Church Father Tertullian in the second century, namely in his *Apology for the Christians* written in AD 197. Tertullian (160–220) was the first Christian theologian to write in Latin instead of Greek and it was he who first coined the name that Christians the world over still use to refer to Almighty God—"the Trinity." The *Apology* was a defense of Christian belief and practice directed at government magistrates in a pagan society that viewed committed Christians as a lunatic fringe worthy of trial and condemnation. Indeed, it was in his *Apology* that Tertullian coined another famous expression, "the blood of the martyrs is the seed of the Church."[46] As for the phrase "religious liberty," here is the context in which it was first used in the Western Tradition:

> Let one man worship God, another Jupiter; let one lift suppliant hands to the heavens, another to the altar of Fides; let one—if you choose to take this view of it—count in prayer the clouds, and another the ceiling panels; let one consecrate his own life to his God, and another that of a goat. For see that you do not give a further ground for the charge of irreligion, by taking away *religious liberty*, and forbidding *free choice* of deity, so that I may no longer worship according to my inclination, but am compelled to worship against it.[47] (emphasis mine)

Or as he writes elsewhere:

> We are worshippers of one God, of whose existence and character Nature teaches all men; at whose lightnings and thunders you tremble, whose benefits minister to your happiness. You think that others, too, are gods, whom we know to be devils. However, *it is a fundamental human right, a privilege of nature that every man should worship according to his own* convictions: one man's religion neither harms nor helps another man. It is assuredly no part of religion to compel religion—to which free-will and not force should lead us—the sacrificial victims even being required of a willing mind. You will render no real service to your gods by compelling us to sacrifice.[48] (emphasis mine)

Though he develops these principles no further, the significance of Tertullian's testimony can hardly be overestimated. One may search the thousand-year history of Greece and Rome and never find a forerunner to Tertullian's plea for individual liberty grounded in reason/natural

---

46. Tertullian, *Apology*, 50.
47. *Apology*, 24.
48. Tertullian, *Letter to Scapula*, 2, 1–2.

law. He recognized that human liberty is rooted in human nature and Nature's God, to be used in accordance with His eternal Law, which Nature obeys blindly, but which man—whose nature is fashioned in the image and likeness of God—may *rationally* choose to obey. That is to say: Liberty is not the right to do whatever you want; it is the freedom to do what you ought. And conversely then, "sin" is defined as "an utterance, a deed, or a desire contrary to the eternal law," to use the words of that infamous-sinner-turned-saint, Augustine of Hippo.[49]

Furthermore, we might state that this definition of liberty is not limited to Christians of Late Antiquity or the Middle Ages. In his 1963 landmark *Letter From a Birmingham Jail*, the Rev. Dr. Martin Luther King Jr. explained in scholastic fashion to fellow Evangelical Christian pastors why he advocated obeying the Supreme Court's *Brown v. Board of Education* decision outlawing segregation in the public schools, while disobeying other so-called "laws" during his civil rights protests in the prejudiced South.

> One has not only a legal but a *moral* responsibility to obey just laws. Conversely, one has a moral responsibility to disobey unjust laws. I would agree with St Augustine that "an unjust law is no law at all". . . . A just law is a manmade code that squares with the moral law or the law of God. An unjust law is a code that is out of harmony with the moral law. To put it in the terms of St Thomas Aquinas: An unjust law is a human law that is not rooted in eternal and natural law.[50]

So according to the greatest civil rights leader our country has ever produced, what makes a law unjust is not that a majority has foisted it on a minority, and not (primarily) because that law conflicts with the US Constitution, but because that law is "not rooted in [the] eternal law" of God.

Unfortunately, neither Tertullian's definition of liberty nor Dr. King's for just law was used as the basis for the landmark decisions of the US Supreme Court in *Roe v. Wade* or in *Casey v. Planned Parenthood* nearly two decades later. Rather, in the opinion of the court:

> The Constitution serves human values, and while the effect of reliance on Roe cannot be exactly measured, neither can the certain cost of overruling Roe for people who have ordered their thinking and living around that case be dismissed. . . . *Some of us as individuals find abortion offensive to our most basic principles of morality, but that cannot*

49. St Augustine, *Against Faustus*, 22.
50. Rev. Dr. Martin Luther King, Jr. "Letter from a Birmingham Jail," https://www.africa.upenn.edu/Articles_ Gen/Letter_Birmingham.html.

control our decision. Our obligation is to define the liberty of all, not to mandate our own moral code. . . . At the heart of liberty is the right to define one's own concept of existence, of meaning, of the universe, and of the mystery of human life.[51] (emphasis mine)

In effect, each majority opinion justice was saying that there is no objective human nature, no objective natural or eternal law to which *all* men must conform, no rational grounds for recognizing Almighty God's sovereignty over the universe. Each individual has his or her own subjective principles of morality, and the state may not impose these on other individuals who hold *their* own subjective opinions. All "truth" is relative; but far from promoting liberty and prosperity, freedom divorced from truth does nothing but install tyranny and poverty. As Pope Francis put it in a 2013 address to the Vatican diplomatic core:

> But there is another form of poverty! It is the spiritual poverty of our time, which afflicts the so-called richer countries particularly seriously. It is what my much-loved predecessor, Benedict XVI, called the "tyranny of relativism", which makes everyone his own criterion and endangers the coexistence of peoples. And that brings me to a second reason for my name. Francis of Assisi tells us we should work to build peace. *But there is no true peace without truth! There cannot be true peace if everyone is his own criterion, if everyone can always claim exclusively his own rights, without at the same time caring for the good of others, of everyone, on the basis of the nature that unites every human being on this earth.*[52] (emphasis mine)

The Christians of Tertullian's day were facing government persecution for refusing to worship the gods of the State, including the "genius" of the emperor. Though sporadic and scattered across two centuries, nevertheless, by Tertullian's time, tens of thousands of Christians had been imprisoned, tortured, and executed especially as spectacle for the crowds.

It was Tertullian, however, who . . . was the first to argue that all human beings possess a natural right to believe and practice a religion of their choice without coercive interference. This was the crucial move that made it possible for a recognizably modern doctrine of religious liberty to emerge, especially when we recognize that Tertullian

---

51. "Beliefs about these matters could not define the attributes of personhood were they formed under compulsion of the State." http://web.utk.edu/~scheb/decisions/Casey.htm.

52. Audience with the Diplomatic corps accredited to the Holy See, Address of Pope Francis, Sala Regia, Friday, 22 March 2013, http://w2.vatican.va/content/francesco/en/speeches/2013/march/documents/papa-francesco_20130322_corpo-diplomatico.html.

was also the first to use the concept and very phrase "religious liberty" .... Furthermore, because religion is in its essence a personal relationship rather than an impersonal transaction, it can yield its proper benefits if and only if it consists of free and authentic choices, in which the worshiper makes a spiritual or "reasonable" sacrifice of her whole self rather than a merely material offering.... A century later, of course, unmistakably building on Tertullian's thought, Lactantius defended religious freedom in similar terms.[53]

Lactantius (AD 240–320), a rhetorician working at the emperor's court in Nicomedia, wrote a groundbreaking Latin work, *Divine Institutes*. He was the first theologian to systematically compare and contrast classical religion and Greek philosophy with Christian teaching. What is more, he is at pains to avoid using Scripture to substantiate his claims, since his target audience is an educated pagan elite. His appeals to reason, however, do not imply that Lactantius is afraid to mince words concerning the many falsehoods in pagan practice, or squeamish to call out the cruelty and ignorance of Roman religious persecution and defend the right of the individual to religious liberty. Born some hundred years after Tertullian, he lived during the most virulent of Roman purges, dubbed the "Great Persecution," which by some estimates claimed as many as a half million victims all by itself. The Great Persecution was promulgated by Emperor Diocletian at the instigation of his imperial colleague Galerius in 303. Bibles were burned, churches demolished. Torture and slaughter followed, especially in the eastern parts of the empire.

As regards Roman persecution and religious liberty, Lactantius writes:

> For they are aware that there is nothing among men more excellent than religion, and that this ought to be defended with the whole of our power; but as they are deceived in the matter of religion itself, so also are they in the manner of its defense. For religion is to be defended, not by putting to death, but by dying; not by cruelty, but by patient endurance; not by guilt, but by good faith: for the former belong to evils, but the latter to goods; and it is necessary for that which is good to have place in religion, and not that which is evil. For if you wish to defend religion by bloodshed, and by tortures, and by guilt, it will no longer be defended, but will be polluted and profaned. For nothing is so much a *matter of free-will as religion*.[54] (emphasis mine)

---

53. Robert Louis Wilken, "The Roots of Religious Freedom in Early Christian Thought," in *Christianity and Freedom*, Vol. 1, *Historical Perspectives*, eds. Timothy Samuel Shah and Allen D. Hertzke (Cambridge: Cambridge University Press, 2016), 55.

54. *Divine Institutes*, 5.

One may not employ an evil means to achieve a good end, especially in the case of religion. Lactantius insists that religious expression must be free, otherwise it is not sincere and becomes impious even, an affront to the Divinity. This would hold true as much for Christians as for their pagan persecutors were their roles reversed.

Lactantius likewise saw no problem with fraternal correction of "the Other." It is rational and charitable to admonish the sinner that he might be converted to the Truth and gain Eternal Life: "Now a wise man never gives himself to the pursuit of gain, because he despises these earthly advantages: nor does he allow anyone to be deceived, because it is the duty of a good man to correct the errors of men, and to bring them back to the right way; since the nature of man is social and benefi-cent, in which respect alone he bears a relation to God."[55]

Ultimately, for Lactantius reason and disputation are the methods proper to religion:

> *Let them call us together to an assembly; let them exhort us to undertake the worship of their gods; let them persuade us* that there are many beings by whose deity and providence all things are governed; let them show how the origins and beginnings of their sacred rites and gods were handed down to mortals; let them explain what is their source and principle; let them set forth what reward there is in their worship, and what punishment awaits neglect; why they wish to be worshipped by men; what the piety of men contributes to them, if they are blessed: and let them confirm all these things not by their own assertion (for the authority of a mortal man is of no weight), but by some divine tes-timonies, as we do. There is no occasion for violence and injury, for religion cannot be imposed by force; the matter must be carried on by words rather than by blows, that the will may be affected. *Let them unsheath the weapon of their intellect; if their system is true, let it be asserted. We are prepared to hear, if they teach;* while they are silent, we certainly pay no credit to them, as we do not yield to them even in their rage.[56] (emphasis mine)

As we shall see, these are the scholastic methods the Dominicans will follow in their missionary efforts directed at heretics and Jews in the thirteenth century.

---

55. Ibid.
56. Ibid.

⊕

As for the fate of the public practice of Christianity, Emperor Diocletian and his henchmen all died over the course of the next few years. In the West, Christians had largely escaped the brunt of his persecution, but they too suffered. Rome was ruled by self-proclaimed Emperor Maxentius, who had Pope St Marcellus arrested for refusing to worship idols. After forced service in the imperial stables, he was martyred. His successor, Pope St Eusebius, was exiled to Sicily by Maxentius and died there.[57]

Further West, Constantine, son of Emperor Constantius, ruled Britain and France, but in 312 marched south to oust the usurper from the imperial capital. On October 27th Constantine and his army encamped alongside the Tiber, a few kilometers to the north at Monte Mario. He was outnumbered, perhaps two to one. According to Church historian Bishop Eusebius of Caesarea, Constantine called on the Christian God in his need: "And while he was thus praying with fervent entreaty, a most marvelous sign appeared to him from heaven . . . about noon . . . he saw with his own eyes the trophy of a cross of light in the heavens, above the sun, and bearing the inscription, CONQUER BY THIS. At this sight he himself was struck with amazement, and his whole army also, which followed him on this expedition, and witnessed the miracle."[58]

If Constantine was praying to *God* and not *a god* right before this solar miracle, it must have been because of his Christian mother, Helena. Constantine was himself a traditional Roman pagan, but with a predilection for one particular deity—the "unconquerable sun." In 310, he claimed to witness a vision of the sun god at the temple of Apollo in Gaul, as recounted in this panegyric: "You saw . . . your Apollo, accompanied by Victory, offering you laurel wreaths, each one of which carries a portent of thirty years . . . you saw and recognized yourself in the likeness of him to whom the divine songs of the bards had prophesied that rule over the whole world was due."[59]

Perhaps this is why, after seeing the Christian sign above the sun two years later, Constantine is said to have "doubted within himself what the import of this apparition could be . . . then in his sleep *the Christ of God*

---

57. Eusebius, *Life of Constantine*, 8; From Philip Schaff, Ed. *The Library of Nicene and Post Nicene Fathers*, 2nd series (New York, NY: Christian Literature Co., 1990), Vol. 1. http://www.ccel.org/ccel/schaff/npnf201.

58. *Life of Constantine*, 28.

59. Nixon and Rogers, *In Praise of Later Roman Emperors*, 248–51; as quoted in Elizabeth Marlowe, "Framing the Sun: The Arch of Constantine and the Roman Cityscape," *Art Bulletin* (June 2006) Vol. LXXXVIII, no. 2: 223–42; 233.

appeared to him with the same sign which he had seen in the heavens, and commanded him to make a likeness of that sign which he had seen in the heavens." (emphasis mine)

None other than Lactantius confirms: "Constantine was directed in a dream to cause the heavenly sign to be delineated on the shields of his soldiers, and so to proceed to battle. He did as he had been commanded, and he marked on their shields the letter 'X', with a perpendicular line drawn through it and turned round thus at the top, being the cipher of Christ."[60] And they obtained victory at the Battle of the Milvian Bridge, October 28, 312.

In February 313, in gratitude to the Christian God, Constantine and his eastern colleague Licinius jointly issued the Edict of Milan:

> Among those things that are profitable to mankind in general, the reverence paid to the Divinity merited our first and chief attention, and that it was proper that the Christians and all others should have liberty to follow that mode of religion which to each of them appeared best; so that that God, who is seated in heaven, might be benign and propitious to us, and to everyone under our government. And therefore *we judged it a salutary measure, and one highly consonant to right reason, that no man should be denied leave of attaching himself to the rites of the Christians, or to whatever other religion his mind directed him*, that thus the supreme Divinity, to whose worship we freely devote ourselves, might continue to vouchsafe His favor and beneficence to us.[61]

By issuing the Edict of Milan Constantine was offering the first formal grant of *individual* religious liberty in more than 4,000 years of ancient history,[62] and anticipating the teaching of the Second Vatican Council more than a millennium and a half in the future:

> men cannot discharge these obligations [to God/Truth] in a manner in keeping with their own nature unless they enjoy immunity from external coercion as well as psychological freedom. Therefore the right to religious freedom has its foundation not in the subjective disposition of the person, but in his very nature. In consequence, the right to this immunity continues to exist even in those who do not live up to their

---

60. Lactantius, *On the Deaths of the Persecutors*, 44; http://www.newadvent.org/fathers/0705.htmc.AD,318–321.

61. https://en.wikiquote.org/wiki/Constantine_the_Great.

62. Galerius, who at first had mercilessly persecuted Christians in the East, ultimately offered them an edict of toleration, but this was done more to save himself from terminal illness—which he feared was the wrath of the Christian god [sic]—and what is more, his edict failed to mention any basis in human nature or inherent right not to be coerced in matters of religion.

obligation of seeking the truth and adhering to it and the exercise of this right is not to be impeded, provided that just public order be observed.[63]

Constantine, very much in keeping with this teaching, rejected religious coercion against his pagan subjects, but in order to safeguard a just moral order, did close a handful of temples that practiced ritual prostitution, for example. But Constantine was a recent convert to the Faith at the time of the edict, and therefore was largely influenced by his immediate Catholic entourage in taking his unprecedented action; among whom, most notably, was the great teacher of reason and rhetoric and tutor to Constantine's heir Crispus, Lactantius.

Constantine's edict applied as much to *any* religious devotee as to a Christian. Perhaps his edict should be just as memorable as his sword.

63. *Dignitatis Humanae, Declaration on Religious Freedom on the Right of the Person and of Communities to Social and Civil Freedom in Matters Religious*, Second Vatican Council, December 7, 1965; http://www.vatican.va/archive/hist_councils/ii_vatican_council/documents/vat-ii_decl_19651207_dignitatis-humanae_en.html. It is not within the parameters of this work to examine the novelty of the wording of this most controversial passage from the documents of Vatican II, nor whether or not it constitutes authentic magisterial teaching; however, it is hoped that this work's millennium-long exploration of tolerance from Lactantius to Llull may offer fruitful resources for these vital and on-going discussions.

2

From Anselm to Abelard

For our faith ought to be rationally defended against the impious, but not against those who admit that they delight in the honor of the name "Christian."
                                    —St Anselm, *Why God Became Man*

Whoever thinks that our persevering zeal, which puts up with so much, is without reward, affirms that God is most cruel.
                                    —The Jew in
              Dialogue of a Philosopher with a Jew and a Christian

AS WE have seen, the missionizing fervor of the thirteenth-century friars has been viewed by most scholars as just another manifestation of that same desire for Christian homogeneity or universality that inspired the massacre of the Rhineland Jews in 1096. Salo Baron was among the first to argue in this vein:

> In the Roman and Byzantine empires, and even in Western Europe before the age of the Crusades, the numerous tracts "Against the Jews" primarily had Christian audiences in mind. Now, on the contrary, the Church viewed apologetic literature as but another weapon in its march toward world domination. The new offensive, seized by the preaching orders, also infused new vigor and introduced novel facets into the polemics which together with the vastly expanding missionary sermons and oral disputations, tried to persuade the Jews of the "foolishness" of their stubborn perseverance.[1]

---

1. Salo Baron, *A Social and Religious History of the Jews* (New York, 1965–83) vol. 9, 101. As cited in David Berger, "Mission to the Jews and Jewish-Christian Contacts in the Polemical Literature of the High Middle Ages," *American Historical Review* 91 (1986): 576–91.

As David Berger notes, this view leads to a historiographic quandary concerning that in-between period, Christian Europe of the 1100s: "Once again, the twelfth century is left in a sort of limbo. Was it a watershed in the use of polemic as a weapon in the church's 'march toward world domination,' or does this questionable distinction belong to the age of the friars?"[2] Berger whole-heartedly agrees with Chazan and Cohen about the universalistic aims of the thirteenth-century mendicants, but he believes "unequivocally" that:

> Despite the proliferation of Christian polemics in the late eleventh and twelfth centuries, the evidence is overwhelming that these works were not rooted in a new or continuing missionary impulse. An examination of the reasons that polemicists gave for writing their tracts reveals a remarkable need to apologize for engaging in an activity considered improper on ideological grounds, and, even when there is no apology, hesitation, or refusal, the reasons given almost invariably do not include the idea that Christians should attempt to proselytize Jews.[3]

Even if Berger's assessment were, on the whole, an accurate one, it would still leave the origins of thirteenth-century Dominican missions unaccounted for. In the time since Berger's article first appeared, scholars like Abulafia and Cohen have come to see an ideological displacement of the Jews in the thought of twelfth-century Christian writers, and have argued vigorously that such an intellectual push of "the Other" to the margins of society preceded and informed later thirteenth-century practices of social exclusion of Jews and Muslims. As we touched upon in the opening chapter, Abulafia blames Christian humanist devotion to reason-as-universalistic-construct of humanity: "But since they also thought that reason was the hallmark of human beings, separating humans from animals, they were led to conclude that those who could not accept their rational conclusions about Christianity were not really human. What developed was a universalistic construct of humanity based on reason which was deemed to coincide with universal Christendom."[4] Or as Cohen characterizes the twelfth century:

> Changing circumstances led to a reclassification of the Jews along with other infidels, especially Muslims, and with heretics; they gave rise to a sense that Judaism constituted but one aspect of the disbelief that threatened the integrity of Christendom. In a word, a process of displacement had begun in Christian thought.... The place accorded the

2. Berger, "Mission to the Jews," 578.
3. Ibid.
4. A. S. Abulafia, "Twelfth-Century Renaissance Theology," 131.

Jews on Anselm of Canterbury's map of the world had surely been called into question and at times circumscribed, even if the poetic imagination of Alan of Lille had not yet eliminated it entirely.[5]

Our investigation of the ideological origins of mission to infidels will thus commence with St Anselm of Canterbury. It shall be our purpose in this chapter to question whether there were any ostensibly missionary motives among twelfth-century Christian humanist writers and/or whether such authors truly characterized Jews as unreasonable and inhuman. It is my contention that a close study of Catholic authors devoted to reason will uncover the true origins of missionary overtures to Jews, Muslims, and other non-Christians. We shall find that it is more than coincidence that the same scholastic authors who produced polemical literature aimed at Jews and other infidels are those who also developed a Catholic theology of sin, repentance, and reconciliation.

Few intellectuals in the history of the West have garnered the praise that St Anselm (1033–1109) has earned. Among other titles, he has been dubbed "the Father of Scholasticism" and "the Second Augustine."[6] He is most famous for the "ontological argument," a purely rational proof for the existence of God as "something-than-which-a-greater-cannot-be thought." If such a thing could be thought not to exist, Anselm argued, then "that-than-which-a greater-cannot-be thought is not the same as that-than-which-a greater-cannot-be thought, which is absurd. Something than-which-a greater-cannot-be thought exists so truly then, that it cannot be even thought not to exist."[7] As Hyman and Walsh observe, "As a straightforward philosophical proof, Anselm's argument has excited discussion in almost every generation since he set it forth; and to judge from recent treatments, its career is far from over."[8]

Anselm's reputation for creativity stems from his vigorous enthusiasm for human reason and its ability to reveal the truth of faith. Our discussion of Anselm centers around his use of rational arguments to convince non-Christians of the truth of the Incarnation, in his work,

5. Cf. Introduction, nt. 39.

6. D. Knowles, *The Evolution of Medieval Thought* (New York, NY: Vintage Books, 1962), 98.

7. M. J. Charlesworth trans. *St Anselm's Proslogion with a Reply on Behalf of the Fool by Gaunilo and the Author's Reply to Gaunilo* (Oxford, 1965), III. As reprinted in Arthur Hyman and James J. Walsh eds. *Philosophy in the Middle Ages, Christian, Islamic, and Jewish Traditions* (Indianapolis, IN: Hackett Publishing, 1973), 150.

8. Hyman and Walsh, *Philosophy in the Middle Ages,* 149.

Cur Deus homo, "Why God Became Man." It is an especially important piece of evidence, for not only was it a work ostensibly directed at answering the objections of non-Christians, it was a treatise that "served for three hundred years as the definitive philosophical and theological explanation of the incarnation of Christ, the central mystery of the Christian faith."[9] As with the ontological argument in his *Proslogion*, however, there has been much debate as to the degree—if any—to which Anselm believed a "straightforward philosophical proof" could turn an infidel into a believer. For in the *Proslogion* itself, Anselm is at some pains to tell God: "For I do not seek to understand so that I may believe; but I believe so that I may understand. For I believe this also, that 'unless I believe, I shall not understand' [Is. 7:9]."[10] If one must believe with faith before reason can enlighten one's mind, then why did Anselm write the *Cur Deus homo*, a philosophical dialogue between himself and his disciple Boso, who asks him questions about Jesus's Incarnation in the name of infidels?

As Boso states at the outset: "Allow me then, to use the words of unbelievers. For since we are fervently seeking the rational basis of our faith, it is fair that I should present the objections of those who are altogether unwilling to approach our faith without rational argumentation. Although they seek a rational basis because they do not believe whereas we seek it because we do believe, nevertheless it is one and the same thing that both we and they are seeking."[11] We find additional support that Anselm thought he could persuade contemporary non-Christians to believe in Jesus Christ as Savior through reason alone at the conclusion of the work: "For you prove the necessity of God's becoming a man, and you do so in such a way that even if the few things you have introduced from our books are removed (e.g., what you mentioned about the three persons of God and about Adam), you would satisfy not only the Jews but also the pagans by reason alone."[12] For these reasons, scholars such as Van der Plaas, Roques, Gauss, and Southern have concluded that Anselm's intended audience was ostensibly Jews and Muslims.

---

9. Thomas F. X. Noble, Barry S. Strauss, et al., eds., *Western Civilization, The Continuing Experiment*, 3rd ed. (Boston, MA: Houghton Mifflin, 2002), 339.

10. Cf. also St Augustine. Thus, Gilson, in his discussion of "The Problem of Christian Philosophy" has the "pure rationalist" put St Anselm and St Bonaventure together as true theologians, but not true philosophers, precisely because of their "stand on faith." Etienne Gilson, *The Spirit of Medieval Philosophy* (Southbend, IN: University of Notre Dame Press, 1936), 5.

11. St Anselm of Canterbury, *Cur Deus Homo*, trans. and eds., Jasper Hopkins and Herbert Richardson (Toronto: Mellen Press, 1976), I.3.

12. Ibid., II.2.

Cohen concurs, calling the *Cur Deus homo* "the treatise that offers the most insight into Anselm's estimation of Jewish unbelief."[13] Cohen emphasizes that "for medieval Christians, the Jews were the most familiar opponents of the doctrine of the incarnation; and, not long before the composition of the *Cur Deus homo*, Anselm spent the winter of 1092–93 together with Gilbert Crispin, abbot of Westminster, who was then at work on his own 'anti-Jewish' treatise, *Disputatio Iudaei et Christiani* (*The Disputation of a Christian and a Jew*)."[14]

Abulafia, however, dissents from this view. She states that: "although Anselm's work on the *Cur Deus Homo* was probably stimulated by his pupil Gilbert Crispin's interest in the Jewish-Christian debate, he himself was not using the term *infideles* to cover Jews. Nor was he referring to Muslims. Anselm's work, including his large number of letters, betrays very little interest in any real non-Christians: Jews, Muslims or pagans. . . . The disbelief he combated was the disbelief of those who were at least nominal Christians."[15] Or as she writes elsewhere: "The fundamental difference between the believers and the unbelievers in his audience is that the first group believes, and whilst believing searches for an understanding of what it believes. The second group has allowed itself to suspend belief until it understands. Both groups are Christians, or at least nominal ones."[16]

I do not think that such an interpretation of Anselm's target audience, however, can be an accurate one, based on what Anselm has to say in another of his writings. Some three to four years earlier, Anselm wrote a letter to Fulk, the bishop of Beauvais, regarding the statements of Roscelin of Compiegne. Roscelin, like Anselm, was a teacher and dialectician who sought to use philosophical concepts to explain Christian doctrine. But as Roscelin and other teachers (notably Abelard) soon found out, such inquiry could often prove as dangerous as navigating a field of land-mines. The difference between orthodoxy and heresy could lie in the use or misuse of a single word or the shade of meaning thereof. In Roscelin's case, Anselm wrote Bishop Fulk to complain that he had heard that Roscelin had been making heterodox statements concerning the nature of the Trinity and that he had ascribed such erroneous opinions to the late Archbishop Lanfranc and to Anselm himself. In his letter, Anselm defends his own adherence to the Apostles' Creed and the

13. Cohen, *Living Letters of the Law*, 172.
14. Ibid., 174.
15. A.S. Abulafia, *Christians and Jews in the Twelfth-Century Renaissance* (London and New York: Routledge, 1995), 44.
16. Ibid., 43.

Nicene Creed and states that any baptized Christian who denies the Trinitarian dogmas contained therein ought to be dispensed with—not reasoned with:

> But if he was baptized and was brought up among Christians, then he ought not at all to be given a hearing. No explanation for his error should be demanded of him, and no explication of our truth should be presented to him. Rather, as soon as the detection of his falsehood is beyond doubt, either let him anathematize the poison which he produces and spews forth or let him be anathematized by all Catholics unless he recants.... For our faith ought to be rationally defended against the impious, but not against those who admit that they delight in the honor of the name "Christian." From these latter it must be rightly demanded that they hold firmly to the pledge made at baptism, but to the former it must be demonstrated rationally how irrationally they despise us.[17]

Clearly then, Anselm did not write the *Cur Deus homo* for Christians "in-name-only," as Abulafia asserts, he wrote it for "the impious," the *infideles* (those who have never been "Christened") for whom he has Boso act as spokesperson, as well as for orthodox Christians who want to better understand the doctrines they already hold on faith. What is also made perfectly clear from Anselm's words is that Jews and Muslims may be "impious," but they are not heretics (as Cohen claims the Dominicans a century-and-a-half later perceived them to be): "For our faith ought to be rationally defended against the impious [*infideles*], but not against those who admit that they delight in the honor of the name 'Christian'" [i.e., heretics]. Yet, Cohen does allege that Anselm "construed Judaism as exemplifying a primitive theological mind-set, representative of an inability to grasp the logic of Christianity, appropriately and necessarily surpassed by faith in Christ."[18]

It is not clear to this author where Cohen gets the idea that Anselm considered Judaism as exemplative of a "primitive mind-set." Nowhere in the *Cur Deus homo* does Anselm make such a claim. In the passage quoted above, when Anselm says that "to the former [*infideles*] it must be demonstrated how irrationally they despise us [Christians]," he is not alleging that the intellect of an infidel is inferior (i.e., irrational) to that of a follower of Christ; Anselm merely means that if only the proper arguments were presented to the said non-Christian, in the proper harmonious arrangement, then that person's intellect would no longer

17. *Cur Deus Homo*, 5.
18. Cohen, *Living Letters of the Law*, 178–79.

reject Christianity, (which is irrational to do, it being so rational) but embrace it. Indeed, one should ask why Anselm would have bothered to go to the trouble of writing the *Cur Deus homo* in the first place, if he felt that Jews and Muslims lacked the proper intellectual hardware for the job of processing it.

By alleging that Anselm construed Jewish minds as "primitive," perhaps Cohen was hearkening to the opening chapter of the *Cur Deus homo* where Anselm states that he will proceed in dialogue form because "issues which are examined by the method of question-and-answer are clearer, and so more acceptable, to many minds—especially to minds that are slower"; also within the same passage, Boso tells Anselm: "what I am asking of you, you will be writing not for the learned but for me and for those who are seeking this solution together with me." Again, these remarks are no slights against Boso, the humble Christian believer, nor against all non-Christians in general; Anselm is merely stating the experiential fact that some minds work faster than others and a good teacher needs to be cognizant of all the students he is trying to reach in choosing his pedagogical methods, not only the prize pupils. It seems quite contrary to the evidence to suggest that Anselm saw non-Christians as any less rational (and therefore less human) than Christians; the very fact that he puts it into the mouth of Boso to state: "Although they seek a rational basis because they do not believe whereas we seek it because we do believe, nevertheless it is one and the same thing that both we and they are seeking," shows a oneness of purpose between Christians and non-Christians, a common humanity united in the desire for truth. And for devout Christians such as St Anselm, was not this the ultimate reason why God became man: "To this end was I born, and for this cause came I into the world, that I should bear witness unto the truth. Everyone that is of the truth hears my voice" (Jn 18:37)? Thus Anselm's treatise is rather an example of the beginning of the development of a Catholic theology of inclusion of non-Christians, rather than exclusion, and for more than one reason. Not only did he believe that infidel intellects were up to the challenge of sifting through his rational arguments for the Incarnation of Christ on an equal footing with believing Christians-seeking-understanding, the arguments themselves demanded a non-Christian, as well as Christian, target audience; deeper meditation on the universal mission of Christ necessarily influenced Christian thinkers like Anselm to compose works targeted at non-Christians. Boso remarks that infidels scoff at Christian claims that God would stoop to be born of a woman, suffer hunger, scourging, and death by crucifixion. Anselm replies that far from insulting God, Christians "proclaim the ineffable depths of His mercy." "He says that if only non-Christians would consider with what beauty the Redemption of man on Calvary paralleled his Fall in Eden, they would no longer take Christians as simpletons, but would instead gain appreciable insight into God's wisdom and love. How remarkable that our ruination began with a woman taking fruit, and our restoration with the fruit of a woman's womb! The devil had seduced man by the pleasure of a tree; tables now turned, Satan would be undone by man suffering on a tree."[19]

Ultimately then, Anselm believes his non-Christian audience just as capable of analyzing his arguments as Christians. This is surely belief in the mental equality of infidel intellects. Furthermore, he demonstrates that his true goal is to see them united with Christians praising God. This is the development of a theology of inclusion based on Christ's redemption: Because God made man in his own image, the human mind is capable of grasping reasonable arguments: Christian and non-Christian minds. Because death had entered into the human race through the disobedience of the first man, all are stained with the same sin: Christians and non-Christians. Because God became man and paid man's penalty for sin on the cross, He is the Redeemer of all and deserving of praise: Christian and non-Christian. With Anselm, we have the beginning of a deeper exploration of the mystery of God's mercy, of the development of a scholastic theology of sin and redemption and its implications for Christians—and non-Christians. Indeed, it is precisely inquiry into human sin and divine mercy that motivates Anselm to write a work answering the objections of unbelievers—for Anselm's investigation leads him to believe that salvation is for them also, and how else shall this redemption reach them if he does not supply rational proofs to convince them?

The main premise of the *Cur Deus homo* is that "as the sin which was the cause of our condemnation had its beginning from a woman, so the Author of our justification and salvation would be born from a woman." Sin and Christ are the two polar opposites; sin was the cause of human alienation from God, Jesus the remedy by which humans are reunited to Him. Anselm argues that to understand who Christ is (why God became man), it is necessary to first comprehend the gravity of sin. To understand the gravity of sin, it is necessary to form a proper appreciation of the One against whom sin is committed—Almighty God:

ANSELM: Since in this inquiry you are assuming the role of those who prefer to believe nothing except what has been established in advance

19. *Cur Deus Homo*, 5.

by reason, I would like for us to agree to accept, in the case of God, nothing that is even in the least degree unfitting.... If angels and men always rendered to God what they ought to, then they would never sin.... The will of every rational creature ought to be subordinate to the will of God.... This is the debt which angels and men owe to God. No one who pays this debt sins; and everyone who does not pay it does sin.... Whoever does not pay to God this honor due Him dishonors Him and removes from Him what belongs to Him ... everyone who sins is obliged to repay to God the honor which he has stolen. This [repayment of stolen honor] constitutes the satisfaction which every sinner is obliged to make God.[20]

The theology of sin, repentance, and redemption centers around the utter transcendence of God and man's complete dependence on Him; hence, the need for all his willful acts to be in accordance with those of His Maker. If we are to understand Anselm's treatise, we must understand his medieval Christian mindset. For Anselm, God and theology are not some quaint pastime, as are stamps and stamp-collecting to a modern philatelist; God is "that-than-which-a-greater-cannot-be thought"! The earth and all its inhabitants, even the totality of the universe itself, is less than a grain of sand in comparison with God. A slight against His honor is not some youthful indiscretion—it's an unconscionable outrage. And herein lay the pitiable plight of man after Adam's sin; his debt was to "make satisfaction in proportion to the extent of sin," that is to the extent of the majesty of Him whom he had sinned against: "you do not make satisfaction unless you pay something greater than is that for whose sake you ought not to have sinned":[21] a metaphysical impossibility for Adam and his race. Boso complains to Anselm about this exceedingly sorry situation in which man was left after Original Sin, and which we as individuals languish in due to the "actual sins" unique to our own doing. Anselm replies that, indeed, the gates to paradise are quite securely shut to man, and man is not in a position to render the satisfaction that can open them again:

ANSELM: But this work can only be accomplished if there is someone who pays to God, for man's sin, something greater than every existing thing besides God. Now, nothing except God surpasses everything that is not God.... Therefore, only God can make this satisfaction.... But only a man ought to make this satisfaction. For in any other case it would not be man who makes it—Therefore, if ... it is necessary that the Heavenly City be completed from among men, and if this comple-

20. Ibid., I. 10.
21. Ibid., I. 13; 21.

tion can occur only if the aforementioned satisfaction is made, and if only God can make this satisfaction and only a man ought to make it: it is necessary that a God-man make it.[22]

Therefore, Jesus Christ was both God and man. God's Justice and Mercy were both satisfied by his Sacrifice. After explaining the theology of the "hypostatic union," or two natures in Christ, Anselm begins to delve more deeply into the mystery of his bodily offering for sin—and its implications for unbelievers:

> Boso: If to put Him to death is as evil as His life is good, how can His death overcome and blot out the sins of those who have put Him to death? Or if it blots out the sin of one of them, how can it blot out any of the sins of other men as well? For we believe that many of the former have been saved and that countless other men are saved.

> Anselm: This question is answered by the apostle who said that: "if they had known it, they would never have crucified the Lord of Glory." For a sin done knowingly and a sin done in ignorance are so different from each other that the evil which these men could never have done knowingly, because of its enormity, is venial because it was done in ignorance. For no man could ever will, at least knowingly, to kill God; and so those who killed Him in ignorance did not rush forth into that infinite sin with which no other sins are comparable. Indeed, in order to ascertain how good His life was, we considered the magnitude of this sin not with respect to the fact that it was committed in ignorance but as if it were done knowingly—something which no one ever did or ever could have done.[23]

Anselm here is pondering the mechanics of the commission of sin through the investigative tool of human reason. In so doing, he is laying the scholastic groundwork for those masters of theology who will come after him, even as he builds on the work of the Fathers and decretists who came before him. Anselm teaches that a sin cannot be considered deadly serious, or "mortal," unless it is done knowingly. If knowledge of the evil of the deed is lacking, then the sin must be deemed slight or "venial." He is espousing a principle (which Abelard shall elaborate further) that sin lies not so much in the objective deed done, but in the subjective mind-set of the doer, or as he says in chapter four of the *De conceptu Virginali et Originali Peccato* (*The Virgin Conception and Original Sin*), "*Nulla essential est iniusta per se.*" As G. R. Evans comments: "Anselm's tag that 'nothing is unjust in itself,' makes this personal choice

---

22. Ibid., II. 6.
23. Ibid., II. 15.

of a good or evil purpose a defining characteristic. He thus gives us a partially 'contextual' theory of injustice."[24] As repeated above, if sin is committed, satisfaction ought to be made to God proportional to the measure of the sin:

ANSELM: Tell me, then: what will you pay to God in proportion to your sin?

BOSO: Penitence, a contrite and humbled heart, fasting and a variety of physical toil, the mercy of giving and forgiving, as well as obedience.

ANSELM: In all these cases what are you giving to God?

BOSO: Do I not honor God when out of fear of Him and love for Him I in contrition of heart cast aside temporal mirth, when in fasting and toil I tread under foot the pleasures and repose of this life, when in giving and forgiving I generously bestow my possessions, and when in obedience I subject myself to Him?

ANSELM: When you render something which you would owe to God even if you had not sinned, you ought not to reckon it as payment of the debt which you owe for your sin.[25]

Anselm is not denying that heart-felt sorrow for sin and some kind of mortifying penance is a necessary condition for its absolution; he is merely reminding Boso that these human expressions would have no value had not the God-man already made satisfaction on his behalf.[26] It is important to note that it is Anselm's inquiry into the theology of sin, repentance, and reconciliation that leads him to a consideration of non-Christians past and present—not some abstract impulse for homogeneity or conformity of thought. The Jews and Romans who put Christ to death in ignorance sinned venially, and through that very death, their sins too may be blotted out. Likewise, contemporary Jews, Muslims, and pagans who reject the Incarnation of Christ through ignorance of the rationality of the doctrine may be persuaded by reasonable argument and so come to salvation. What we have here is the foundation of the theological justification underlying the effort of the friars to convert

24. G. R. Evans, *Law and Theology in the Middle Ages* (London and New York: Routledge, 2002), 15.

25. *Cur Deus Homo*, I. 20

26. As Anciaux says of Anselm: "affirme lui aussi l'efficacité de la penitence en la rattachant aux merites du Christ: '*Sic homo ille redemit omnes alios, cum hoc, quod sponte dedit Deo, computat pro debito quod illi debebant. Quo pretio non semel tantum a culpis homo redimitur, sed etiam quoties cum digna poenitentia redierit, recipitur.*'" P. Anciaux, *La Theologie du Sacrament de Penitence au XII Siecle* (Louvain, 1949), 23 nt. 1; St Anselm, *Meditatio XI* (PL 158: 766).

the Jews, Muslims, and pagans, more than a century later: the beginnings of a theology of inclusion concerning non-Christians, which is
the product of an examination of human sin and repentance.

Anselm's treatise, however, must not be construed itself as indicative
of an Anselmian missionary program to the non-Christians of his day.
Though he lays the ideological groundwork for rational explanation of
the Christian faith to non-believers, the call to an active preaching apostolate has not yet manifested itself. Abulafia documents, at some length,
the lack of any practical contact on Anselm's part with contemporary
Jews or Muslims.[27] Anselm is driven by the desire for holiness, that is to
say, sinlessness and conformity to the will of God. His examination of
the doctrine of sin and repentance leads him to compose a rational
exposition of Christ's redemption so that non-Christians might come to
the faith, but it has not yet dawned on Anselm, or the other Christian
intellectuals of his day, to take these proofs and preach them to tangible
persons in non-Christian precincts. Anselm's attitude, as clearly
expressed at the outset of the *Cur Deus homo*, is to have a ready-made
defensive remedy for turning non-believing adversaries into friendly
co-religionists, when and if they come to assail Christians, not the other
way round:

> For they [Christians] say that these considerations [the rational bases
> for the faith] please them. . . . They make their request not in order to
> approach faith by way of reason but in order to delight in the compre-
> hension and contemplation of the doctrines which they believe, as well
> as in order to be ready, as best they can, always to give a satisfactory
> answer to everyone who asks of them a reason for the hope which is in
> us. Unbelievers habitually raise this particular problem as an objection
> to us, while derisively terming Christian simplicity a foolish simplicity.[28]

Anselm's deep consideration of man's sin and God's mercy drove him
to a consideration for the salvation of non-Christians, but it could not
prompt him to a missionary apostolate; for the same abiding concern
for sinlessness was understood by him largely within an eleventh-cen-

27. Cf. A.S. Abulafia, *Christians and Jews in the Twelfth-Century Renaissance*, 44; "St
Anselm and those Outside the Church," in *Faith and Unity: Christian Political Experience*,
eds., D. Loades and I.C. Walsh, *Studies in Church History, Subsidia* 6 (Oxford: Oxford
University Press, 1990), 11–37; "Theology and the Commercial Revolution: Guibert of
Nogent, St Anselm and the Jews of Northern France," in *Church and City* 1000–1500:
Essays in Honour of Christopher Brooke, eds., D. Abulafia, M. Franklin and M. Rubin
(Cambridge: Cambridge University Press, 1992), 23–40; and "Christians Disputing Dis-
belief: St Anselm, Gilbert Crispin and Pseudo-Anselm" in *Religionsgesprach im Mittle-
alter*, eds., B. Lewis and F. Niewohner (Wiesbaden, 1992), 131–48.

28. *Cur Deus Homo*, I. 1.

tury Christian construct of holiness in which salvation is primarily to be associated with the monastic life. As Abulafia explains generally of the times:

> Remission of sin was a vital quest both for those who sought out the religious life and for those who elected to stay in the world. In the greater part of the eleventh century members of the laity (especially the upper echelons of society) looked towards monasteries to help them find this remission. Gradual changes in perceptions of how and when a penitent was reconciled to the Church had meant that Christian sinners increasingly felt the need to offer some form of satisfaction to counter the temporal punishments they feared in this life and the next—by the end of the eleventh century changes in attitudes towards this idea of the remission of sin become visible. With a growing interest in the make-up of man and society, people began to wonder whether even more might be required of them to achieve forgiveness. They began to look for a more personal experience of penance. That experience was often sought through joining one of the new orders, which stressed the monk's individual seeking for God.[29]

As Abulafia observes of Anselm directly: "He is, as Richard Southern has so brilliantly shown, a man firmly ensconced in his own monastic world. What concerns him most is to show Christians the way to the life of perfect belief and practice, which he thought could be found in the monastery."[30] And we have, in fact, a simile from Anselm which he used to educate the younger monks and which spells out so powerfully his world-view that we must be excused for quoting it at length:

> For God himself displays his enmity towards the devil in the way that a certain king would against a certain prince who was his enemy. For in his kingdom this king has a rather large city [*villam*], in the city a particular castle, and above the castle a vault.... His enemy is so strong that he absconds totally unhindered with whatever he finds outside the city. He frequently enters the city and damages those houses which he finds insecure, and those people who inhabit them he takes captive. Those houses which he finds secure, after he cannot destroy them, he reluctantly leaves them at last. He cannot ascend into the castle nor cause any harm to those who take refuge there, unless they return to the combat of the city. But if they return out of love for their parents, inasmuch as they hear that they are being killed and maltreated, or if they look back through an aperture or window, he can easily kill or

---

29. A.S. Abulafia, *Christians and Jews in the Twelfth-Century Renaissance*, 56.
30. Ibid., 44; Sir Richard Southern, *Saint Anselm: A Portrait in a Landscape* (Cambridge: Cambridge University Press, 1990).

wound them. Wherefore it is necessary that they never heed the cry of their parents nor return to combat nor look back, but always, just as they began, they must flee until they reach the height of the vault. For once they arrive there, they will be entirely secure.

And so that king is God, who wages war with the devil. Within his kingdom he has the community of Christians, within the community of Christians the society of monks [*monachatum*], and above the society of monks the fellowship of angels. Within the community of Christians certain people are ensconced in virtue, though many are insecure. In the monastic world the security is such that if anyone taking refuge there shall be made a monk—unless, recanting, he departs—he cannot be injured by the devil. In the fellowship of the angels there is the joy of such great security that if anyone ascends there he will never wish to return. The king—that is, God—has all this in his domain. Yet his enemy—that is, the devil—is so powerful that he carries off without resistance and submerges into hell all the Jews and the pagans whom he finds outside the community of Christians. He often enters the community of Christians itself and harms through temptation all those whom he finds infirm, and he takes captive the souls inhabiting their bodies. Yet those whom he finds secure, after failing to conquer them, he at last releases, albeit with regret. He cannot break into the monastic world, nor can he cause harm to those who have been made monks, unless they have returned to the secular world in body or in spirit.[31]

Anselm's monastic spirituality is certainly that of "flight from the world." The person truly bent on saving his soul should seek the safety of the cloister, and once he has put his hand to the plough, he must not return to the chaos—temporal and spiritual—that rages beyond its walls. Even should one hear the cries of one's own family members being spiritually "killed and maltreated," not only must that monk not return to defend them against the assaults of the devil, he must not even "look back through an aperture or window," or he will certainly be wounded by the piercing arrows of Satan's wrath. In Anselm's ultimate scheme of things, no one is to attempt to recover family members or non-Christians; they are left to share the same fate: "the devil—is so powerful that he carries off without resistance and submerges into hell all the Jews and the pagans whom he finds outside the community of Christians." The temptations of the world are so many and so evil that the only sure route to salvation is to renounce it completely. Family,

31. Sir Richard Southern and Francis S. Schmitt, eds., *Memorials of St Anselm, Auctores britannici Medii Aevi I* (Oxford: Oxford University Press, 1969), 66–67.

friends, and religious adversaries do not have the Christian understanding or the wherewithal to reach a happy end. In the final analysis, while
Anselm believes non-Christians sinless with regard to Christ's death, he
sees no hope for them without a share in his *Life*. It will be more than a
century before this monastic world-view is turned completely on its
head, when the followers of Dominic Guzman deliberately venture out
into the fray of battle, on what they perceive as a search and rescue mission of Christian *and infidel*. But before they release their arrows in
preaching, "first the bow is bent in study," and for his use of reasoned-
argumentation they are indebted to Anselm.

As cited above, a close friend of Anselm who also engaged in debate
with non-Christians was Gilbert Crispin (1055–1117). Gilbert's most
popular work, the *Disputatio Iudei et Cristiani*, survives in more than
thirty twelfth-century manuscripts.[32] As Abulafia describes it, "The disputation is unique among Jewish-Christian disputations in the amount
of space it allots to the Jewish viewpoint. Reflecting the didactic methods of St Anselm, the tone of the disputation is remarkably mild and the
issues at hand are discussed as civilly as possible."[33] Or as Cardinal
Avery Dulles, SJ once put it:

> One statement that is readily confirmed is "the friendly spirit (*amico
> animo*)" of their debate, for even though the Jew (in some manuscript
> versions) eventually converts at the end . . . a certain level of mutual
> respect is retained throughout. The politeness of their exchanges,
> which is not generally a common feature of anti-Jewish disputational
> writings, may indeed, as has been suggested, be a sign of the original
> conversation on which the work is based. It may equally be a conse-
> quence of the Anselmian approach to arriving at truth through open
> dialogue. In a sense, the same problem of derivation that presents itself
> with Justin Martyr's second century *Dialogue with Trypho*, which was
> purportedly the result of an actual exchange.[34]

Gilbert uses classic Scriptural arguments, but may have viewed them
as insufficient of themselves to convert his Jewish opponent, as Dulles
remarks: "In an effort to supplement his earlier dialogue Crispin later
composed . . . *Disputation between a Christian and a heathen Touching
the Faith of Christ*, in which he ponders more philosophically on certain
difficulties raised by the Jew in the earlier dialogue against the Incarnation. He attempts to show that the taking on of human flesh does not

---

32. Novikoff, *The Medieval Culture*, 52.

33. Anna Sapir Abulafia, "Crispin, Gilbert" in *Medieval Jewish Civilization*, 203–4;
204.

34. Novikoff, 54.

involve mutability in God and is not unworthy of God."[35] Some have considered Gilbert's second dialogue incomplete, perhaps due to his respect for Anselm's *Cur Deus Homo*, which had just appeared; perhaps because he was too fond of exegesis to write a dialogue *sola ratio*.[36]

Gilbert's use of reason to explain Catholic doctrines, particularly those on sin and virtue, would be taken up and carried even further by Peter Abelard; and like Anselm before him, it was precisely Abelard's scrutiny of sin, repentance, and reconciliation that would lead him to a consideration of contemporary non-Christians—in some ways, an even more sympathetic consideration.

Peter Abelard (1079–1142) has been a perennial favorite of medievalists. His independent spirit, his thirst for knowledge, his forbidden love, and, ultimately, his persecution by more conservative peers, have all done much to endear him to subsequent generations of scholars who see much of the "modern man" in this twelfth-century cleric. Abelard's rational treatise on the differences between monotheists, the *Dialogue of a philosopher with a Jew and a Christian*, is often considered in the same favorable light. In Abelard's work, as in Anselm's *Cur Deus homo*, there is none of the venom or vitriol found in other Christian writers who sought to prove the superiority of Christianity over Judaism and Islam. Nonetheless, this was the goal of Abelard's text: to prove to enlightened Jews, and presumably to Muslims steeped in classical philosophy, that Christianity was more perfectly harmonious with reason than the observance of Mosaic, or natural law, before it.[37] The work thus serves as another example of a rational approach to non-Christians, an approach that would later be taken up in earnest by Raymond of Peñafort and the Dominicans. Again we find, as in the former example of the *Cur Deus homo*, that specific inquiry into the question of human sinfulness and virtue has led to a reasoned consideration of those outside the Christian community:

> It is the task of philosophers to investigate the truth by reasoning and in all things to follow the lead of reason, not people's opinion. Therefore, when I had studied for a long time in our philosophical schools and had become learned both in philosophical reasoning and in the

35. Dulles, *A History of Apologetics*, 98.
36. Abulafia, 204.
37. Two centuries before Petrarch, Abelard certainly appears to be dialoguing with the Greco-Roman sages of antiquity.

philosophical authorities, at length I turned my attention to moral philosophy which is the goal of all branches of knowledge; it is so as to study it that all the other disciplines must first be mastered. When I had learned from it as much as I could about the highest good and the greatest evil and about what makes a person truly happy or wretched, I made up my mind to study carefully the various faiths into which the world is now divided. When I had examined them all and compared them, I would follow the one most consonant with reason.[38]

Though the Philosopher is speaking here, it is not hard to hear Abelard explaining the reasons that brought him to writing his own treatise. Abelard, as we shall see, is intensely interested in the nature of sin and holiness. Not only has it driven him to compose a rational appeal to Jews and gentiles, it has colored his own perception of how they must view themselves:

> Jew: Whoever thinks that we shall receive no reward for continuing to bear so much suffering through our loyalty to God must imagine that God is extremely cruel. Indeed, there is no people which has ever been known or even believed to have suffered so much for God—we have borne so much for him without cease, and it should be granted that there can be no rust of sin which is not burnt up in the furnace of this affliction. Dispersed among all the nations, alone, without a king or earthly ruler, are we not alone encumbered with such taxes that almost every day we pay an intolerable ransom for our wretched lives?[39]

Abelard is attempting several things here. In the first place, he is suggesting that a contemporary Jew shares his Christian belief in redemptive suffering—even if he does not share his belief in Christ as Redeemer: "there can be no rust of sin which is not burnt up in the furnace of this affliction." Abelard sees the notion of unmerited-suffering-offered-as-sacrifice-to-atone-for-sin as something that Christians and Jews both share, a common concept in their shared humanity. Secondly, Abelard is attempting to insinuate, albeit in veiled fashion, that a Jew has an innate understanding of the debt of an "intolerable ransom," that is, the debt of Original Sin. This is a second facet uniting Christian and Jew; they are both *poor banished children of Eve*. Stuck in the same mire of sin as a Christian before baptism and forced to carry the same life-long cross of suffering as any post-baptized Christian would, Abelard believes the Jew must have some palpable sense of this shared human

---

38. Peter Abelard, *Collationes*, trans. and ed. by John Marenbon and Giovanni Orlandi (Oxford: Clarendon Press, 2000), 1.

39. *Collationes*, 19.

condition. In fact, he is counting on the truth of these seminal suppositions to ultimately move the Jew to embrace his case for Christianity, once the full arguments are properly presented to him. In his other work on ethics, *Ethica* or *Scito te ipsum* (*Know Thyself*) written shortly after his dialogue,[40] not only does Abelard continue to expound on sin, he continues to propose Jewish belief in this doctrine:

> David says: "For, behold, I was conceived in iniquities" [Psalm 50:7]. In my view ... David's statement that he had been conceived in iniquities or in sins ... represents the general curse of original sin by which everyone is subjected to damnation because of the fault of his parents, in accordance with what is written elsewhere: "No one is free from uncleanness nor is the one-day-old child if he is alive upon the earth" [Job 14:4–5]. ... So when David says he was conceived in iniquities or in sins, he saw that he was subjected to a general sentence of damnation by virtue of the fault of his own parents and he referred these crimes back less to his immediate parents than to earlier ones.[41]

Thus Abelard believes that like David, the Jewish thinker in his dialogue was referring to the shared lot of a common humanity tainted by the sin of its first parents when he said: "Are we not burdened with such great demands that almost every day of our miserable lives we pay the debt of an intolerable ransom?" To those who would argue that this line refers not to shared suffering in Original Sin, but to Jewish guilt for the slaying of Christ, both Abelard's Jew and Abelard himself, are already familiar with this supposition and intend otherwise. As the Jew explains:

> Jew: Indeed, we are thought by everyone to be worthy of such hatred and contempt, that whoever does us any injury believes it to be the height of justice and a supreme sacrifice offered to God. For they say that the disaster of our being made such captives would not have occurred unless God hated us enormously and both pagans and Christians reckon whatever savagery they inflict on us as being done justly in revenge ... the Christians seem to have greater cause for persecuting us since (as they say) we killed their God.[42]

The key word in the above phrase is "seem," for Abelard did not share the commonly held view among Christians that Jews were guilty of the sin of Deicide. In fact, Abelard held quite the opposite view, which he treats at length in the *Ethica*:

40. Peter Abelard, *Ethics*, trans. and ed. D.E. Luscombe (Oxford: Oxford University Press, 1971), xxx.

41. *Ethics*, 20–23.

42. *Collationes*, 19–21.

However, if one asks whether those persecutors of the martyrs or of Christ sinned in what they believed to be pleasing to God, or whether they could without sin have forsaken what they thought should definitely not be forsaken, assuredly, according to our earlier description of sin as contempt of God or consenting to what one believes should not be consented to, we cannot say that they have sinned in this, nor is anyone's ignorance a sin or even the unbelief with which no one can be saved. For those who do not know Christ and therefore reject the Christian faith because they believe it to be contrary to God, what contempt have they in what they do for God's sake and therefore think they do well? . . . [T]he ignorance of such men is not to be imputed to sin at all.[43]

The case of the non-Christians who brought about Christ's death leads Abelard into a deeper investigation of what exactly we mean when we speak of "sin." Properly speaking, "sin is said to be that contempt of God or consent to evil." Human will is key in Abelard's thought, as is the insubstantiality of evil. The sinner does not actually inflict "harm" on God, but rather sins "negatively, that is to say, as not doing or not forsaking what is fitting, we plainly show there is no substance of sin; it subsists as not being rather than being, just as if in defining darkness we say it is the absence of light where light used to be."[44] The greatness of God, sin as contempt of His honor, the need for man to conform all his actions to the will of God: one does not have to strain to hear Anselmian chords reverberating throughout Abelard's moral set piece. The same is also true of Abelard's theory that "sin" is not the will to sin which all men experience—which properly speaking must be called "vice"—but, rather, the *conscious consent* to that drive or will. As was typical of Abelard's turn of mind, he uses an earthy metaphor to get his point across: "There indeed . . . bad will and the sin seem to be the same. For example, someone sees a woman and falls into concupiscence and his mind is affected by the pleasure of the flesh, so that he is incited to the baseness of sexual intercourse. Therefore, you say, what else is this will and base desire than sin?"[45] But as Abelard clarifies, lust for a woman, that is, the desire that tugs at a man and suggests images to his conscious mind, is not itself sinful, but consenting to *willfully* entertain desire, its images and its feelings (and no one knew them better than

43. *Ethics*, 56–57.
44. Ibid.
45. Ibid., 10–15. It seems the direct inspiration for Abelard's statement was the Vulgate verse from Matthew where Christ says: "Whosoever looks upon a woman to lust after her, has already committed adultery with her in his heart" (Matt 5:28). Abelard cites Augustine's commentary; cf. *De sermone Domini in monte*, L 12, n.34 (PL 34. 1246).

Abelard!) is. By making this simple distinction, Abelard was, in fact, actively instigating nothing short of a *revolution* in Western psychology. As Charles Radding remarks: "[Abelard's] thesis [was] ... that neither vice nor the act are themselves sinful but only the sinful intention. The importance of this stress on intention needs no emphasis here. We have already seen that confusion between action and intention was endemic in the early Middle Ages. ... This view had to be refined with great care, and Abelard devotes several pages to this purpose."[46]

What is most important for us, however, is that as Abelard was busy committing his new insights into vice and virtue to writing, he was also engaging Jews and pagans—even discussing Jewish converts. The latter issue specifically comes up as Abelard refines the notion that because something is pleasurable, it must, therefore, be sinful:

> They object that ... pleasure may follow which increases the sin, as in sexual intercourse, or in [gluttonous] ... eating. ... They would not in fact say this absurdly if they were to prove that carnal pleasure of this sort is sin ... if they readily admit this, it is definitely not lawful for anyone to have this fleshly pleasure. Therefore, spouses are not immune from sin when they unite in this carnal pleasure allowed to them, nor is he who enjoys the pleasurable consumption of fruit. ... And lastly the Lord, the creator of foods as well as bodies, would not be beyond fault if he put into them such flavours as would necessarily compel to sin those who eat them with pleasure. For how would he produce such things—if it were impossible for us to eat them without sin? And how can sin be said to be committed in that which is allowed? For what were ... unlawful and prohibited acts, if they are later allowed ... are now committed wholly without sin, for example the eating of swine's flesh and many other things formerly forbidden to Jews but now permitted to us. And so when we see Jews converted to Christ also freely eating foods of this sort which the Law had forbidden, how do we defend them from blame if not by our claim that this is now granted to them by God? So if in such eating once forbidden but now conceded to them the concession itself excuses sin ... [i]f therefore to lie with a wife or even to eat delicious food has been allowed to us since the first day of our creation which was lived in Paradise without sin, who will accuse us of sin in this if we do not exceed the limit of the concession?[47]

46. Charles Radding, *A World Made by Men* (Chapel Hill, NC: University of North Carolina Press, 1985), 210–11.
47. *Ethics*, 16–19.

There is much to be mined from the above passage. The essence of Abelard's moral schema is that whatsoever God created in this material world, He created good. Natural carnal pleasures resulting from eating and reproducing are not sinful, since God invented them and since He explicitly sanctioned them in Eden before the Fall. Making the pleasures of the flesh sinful by their nature would make God the author of evil. The Fall is what is to blame. As a result of Original Sin, Abelard argues, we suffer from more than one disordered passion (bad will), which makes us prone to actual sin, but these inclinations themselves are not sins. Unlawful and prohibited acts like fornication, or the eating of pork by a Jew before the Coming of the Messiah, "formerly prohibited," are now "conceded pleasures" after a man crosses the threshold of the marriage covenant, or the New Covenant of Christ's Church. And Abelard claims that one can "see Jews converted to Christ freely eating foods . . . which the Law had forbidden." His rather casual observation would seem to imply that such conversion was more than just a rare sight—which is intriguing in itself!

Abelard stops well short of suggesting any preaching effort to the Jews. Nonetheless, two things are significant: (1) he chooses to remark that such conversions do take place, and (2) in his *Dialogue*, he advances the same theory of the intrinsic goodness of the flesh, as from his *Ethics*, in the hopes of persuading his Jewish interlocutor to the Christian faith:

> Indeed your law, which repays in this life alone what is due for following or breaking it, and gives reward or punishment here alone, fits everything to this bodily life with the result that there is nothing which it judges clean or unclean according to the soul, nor does it apply any purifications to the stains of souls, which we call sins in the proper sense. Thus it calls foods, in the same way as it calls people, "clean" or "unclean"; often it even calls beds and chairs and all the furniture in a house or even clothes . . . if you count those human uncleannesses for which there exist rituals of purification among those sins which make people wicked, do you not judge that a woman who, by means of a sacrifice, has been cleansed after childbirth, has incurred a sin simply by giving birth, whereas it is rather the woman who leaves no seed in Israel whom you would judge to be cursed?[48]

Abelard's insistence on the inherent goodness of created matter and on sin defined exclusively as consent to a bad will is what motivated him to encourage the Jew of his dialogue to look beyond the Law of Moses. This prompts Abulafia to observe:

48. *Collationes*, 71–73.

In his eyes, Jews looked no further than the letter of the manifold rules and regulations of Mosaic law. To a man interested in man's intention rather than the appearance of his deeds, a purely literal application of the precepts of the Pentateuch to the dos and don'ts of one's daily life could easily have seemed intolerable. Abelard could not acknowledge that Jewish understanding of the Law of Moses had its own spiritual meaning; to him Mosaic precepts and their observance lacked any inner meaning other than being the portent of Christian truth.[49]

Or, as Abulafia says elsewhere: "Jewish refusal to exchange the ceremonial details of the Law of Moses for a christological figurative signification means, in Abelard's eyes, that Jews do not have access to the inner spiritual truth which would direct them to true love of God."[50] I think, however, Abulafia is missing the point. Abelard was a twelfth-century Catholic, not a second-century Gnostic. Nowhere in his writings does he claim that "Jews do not have access to the inner spiritual truth which would direct them to true love of God." For Abelard, reason was something with which all men were endowed, having been created in the image and likeness of God, including Jews. Abulafia, however, argues: "Abelard said that true knowledge was participation in the wisdom of God, he meant participation in Jesus Christ. It was only in and through Jesus Christ that man could build up a loving relationship with God. By definition, Jews could have no part in any of this. Indeed, their denial of Jesus as the son of God could only mean to Abelard that they were not functioning as God meant all men to, not only in the realm of faith but also in the realm of reason."[51] This assessment is partly true, and partly not true. Abelard did believe that to serve God correctly, one needed to be baptized into Jesus Christ through means of his Church, and following well all that She taught; and likewise, he did believe that people served God not only through faith, but by reason as well, since according to the Church, Jesus is the *Logos*, or the wisdom of God Itself. But it is not true that Abelard believed that "Jews by definition could have no part in this." Their denial of Christ was cutting them off from full participation in the life God intended for them, but it did not mean that their intellectual apparatus was incapable of processing logical arguments, which might lead them to the fullness of life in Christ. If, as Abulafia argues, it was their lack of Christianity that made the Jews unreasonable in Abelard's eyes, Abelard (as "the Christian") would have

49. A.S. Abulafia, "Intentio Recta an Erronea?" 28.

50. A.S. Abulafia, "Bodies in the Jewish-Christian Debate," in *Framing Medieval Bodies*, eds., S. Kay and M. Rubin (Manchester: Manchester University Press, 1994), 130.

51. Ibid.

refuted them personally in his dialogue, but it is the Philosopher who engages the Jew in debate, not the Christian—and this is not without its significance. Abelard structured his dialogue in this way, precisely to show that philosophy is a means of reaching Jewish minds, since Jews and Christians are both endowed with reason, united in a common humanity. As a matter of fact, Abelard's Jew is presented as quite a civilized and logical inquirer into truth, and no doubt Abelard hoped for his eventual conversion. A Jew was neither inherently blind nor unreasonable (nor was his obedience to the Law of Moses entirely without praise); Abelard believed he could be persuaded to come to Christianity—indeed, he casually remarks in his *Ethica* that many already have! As Cary Nederman astutely observes of Abelard's construction of inter-religious exchange:

> The conditions of unobstructed rational debate have been met: Each party may express himself openly and without fear, invoking only the standards of reason. . . . His dialogue is a tolerant one, inasmuch as all parties are to be permitted the free expression of their views within the parameters set by a reasoned exchange of ideas. Even the Jew, whose teachings come under the harshest criticism, is presented sympathetically as one whose people has sustained itself despite the "great contempt and hatred" inflicted by both sects, Gentile and Christian alike.[52]

Therefore, the argument that Abelard's appeal to reason somehow diminished Jews as less than reasonable and therefore, less than human is untenable. As for Abulafia's rebuttal that "Abelard, too, resorts to animal imagery when he writes that Jews are 'animals and sensual and are imbued with no philosophy whereby they are able to discuss reasoned arguments,'"[53] we need to place that remark in its proper context.

First off, let us recall that it is Abelard's Philosopher who calls Jews "animals and unable to discuss reasoned arguments," and although Abelard's ideas are often expressed through the mouth of the Philosopher, not all of the Philosopher's sentiments are to be attributed to Abelard, particularly in this case. The Philosopher, being a gentile, is inherently condescending of Jews and Christians, as is clear from the outset, where he says: "I discovered the Jews to be stupid and the Christians insane." Abelard had a fondness for hyperbole, but we must not mistake rhetoric for the substance of his work. As we have seen, his arguments for the sinlessness of carnality were not directed solely at

52. Cary J. Nederman, *Worlds of Difference, European Discourses of Toleration, c. 1100–c. 1550*, (University Park, PA: Pennsylvania State University Press, 2000), 29–30.
53. A. S. Abulafia, "Bodies in the Jewish-Christian Debate," 130.

Jews, but against his more conservative co-religionists as well. Abelard encouraged everyone to use reason to look beyond the parameters of their religious views. He advanced his rational moral theory against his fellow monks as much against non-Christians and received not only scathing criticism for his novelties, but canonical censure.[54] And one of the positions that landed Abelard in trouble was his exoneration of the non-Christians who participated in the Crucifixion. What Anselm had called only a venial sin, Abelard claimed was no sin at all. In fact, he cites more than one instance where non-Christians are seemingly guilty of grave sin and yet innocent, for example, the case of St Stephen, the protomartyr, and his infamous stoning to death by a Jewish mob. Abelard recalls the words spoken by Stephen and how they reecho those of Christ on Calvary, "Lord, lay not this sin to their charge" [Acts 7.601]:

> Furthermore, when Stephen says that what the Jews committed in ignorance against him is sin, he meant sin as that penalty which one bore by virtue of the sin of the first parents, together with other penalties arising from it, or that unjust *action* of theirs in stoning him. [emphasis mine] He asked that this should not be laid to their charge, that is, that they should not be physically punished for this. For God often punishes people here physically although no fault of theirs requires this. . . . Blessed, Stephen, carefully considering this, prayed that sin, that is, the punishment which he took from the Jews or their wrong action, should not be laid to their charge, that is, that they should not be physically punished for this.

> The Lord was also in this mind when he said: "Father, forgive them," that is, do not avenge what they do to me, even with physical punishment. This could in fact have been done reasonably even if there had been no prior fault on their part, in order that others seeing this, or even they themselves, should recognize by punishment that they had not acted rightly in this.[55]

Abelard concludes then, that although the non-Christians who killed Christ and Stephen were ignorant of what they were truly doing, and

---

54. As Radding notes: "Bernard of Clairvaux and William of St Thierry . . . were famous in their time . . . for their eloquent works on inner spirituality, but they had given little thought to propositions that Abelard was ready to put forward in total seriousness: that there was sin neither in desire nor pleasure; that actions themselves are morally indifferent; that anathemas and excommunications, if they are undeserved, do not exclude the believer from God's grace. Abelard's position on these matters must have seemed to them an attack on monastic asceticism and the status of the priesthood in general, and they responded with the persecutions that led to Abelard's condemnation at Sens in 1140." Radding, *A World Made by Men*, 212.

55. *Ethics*, 58–61.

thus did not sin, nonetheless the objectively unjust action they perpetrated may be called a "sin," and they could incur punishment although subjectively sinless. In fact, by the same logic, Abelard reasoned that contemporary Jews and pagans could quite justly suffer eternal damnation, not because of any willful misdeed, or sin, on their part, but simply as a consequence of their ignorance of, and consequent unbelief in, Christ and his Church:

> Moreover, just as what they did through ignorance or even ignorance itself is not said to be properly sin, that is, contempt of God, neither is unbelief, even though this necessarily blocks the entry to eternal life for adults now using reason. It is sufficient for damnation not to believe in the Gospel, to be ignorant of Christ, not to receive the sacraments of the Church, even though this occurs not so much through wickedness as through ignorance. . . .

> However, I think that sin is properly said to be that which can nowhere happen without fault. But ignorance of God or unbelief in him, or those works which are not done rightly, can happen to many people without fault. For if someone does not believe in the Gospel or in Christ for the reason that no preaching has reached him—as the Apostle says: "How shall they believe him of whom they have not heard? And how shall they hear without a preacher?" What fault can be ascribed to him on account of his unbelief? Cornelius did not believe in Christ until Peter, when sent to him, taught him about Christ [Acts 10]. Although previously by the natural law he recognized and loved God, and through this deserved to be heard in his prayer and to have his alms accepted by God, yet if he had happened to depart from this light before he believed in Christ, we should by no means dare to promise him life however good his works seemed, nor should we number him with the faithful but rather with the unfaithful, however eagerly he had worked for his salvation.[56]

Abelard is just as certainly referring to the Philosopher of his dialogue, as he is to the first-century gentile whom the apostle Peter baptized. What Abelard has written in this paragraph from the *Ethica* may be looked upon as a summary of his *Dialogue*, for in both cases he is ultimately declaring that neither the steadfast observance of the Law of Moses, nor the Natural Law of the Philosopher—praiseworthy efforts though they may be—are sufficient for gaining eternal salvation. What is remarkable in hindsight is how Abelard could show so much understanding toward Jews and pagans and then simply leave them to perdi-

---

56. Ibid., 62–65.

tion. For as touched upon earlier, not only does he exonerate them from the sin of crucifying Christ, as did Anselm, Abelard goes so far as to declare that they would have sinned more seriously had they not done so: "And so we say that those who persecuted Christ or his disciples, who they thought should be persecuted, sinned in deed, yet they would have sinned more gravely in fault if they had spared them against their own conscience."[57] Yet for Abelard, though ignorance excuses from sin, it does not admit of faith in the Gospel, and so, consequently, Jews and pagans are as lost in his eyes as in Anselm's dramatic siege simile. Nevertheless, such an attitude is all the more stupefying in Abelard's case, for his study of sin not only led him to consider the lamentable fate of non-Christians, it sparked him to hit upon its salutary remedy, namely, Christian preaching: "For if someone does not believe in the Gospel or in Christ for the reason that no preaching has reached him—as the Apostle says: 'How shall they believe him of whom they have not heard? And how shall they hear without a preacher?'—what fault can be ascribed to him on account of his unbelief? Cornelius did not believe in Christ until Peter [was] . . . sent to him . . . yet if he had happened to depart from this light before he believed in Christ . . . we should by no means dare to promise him life however good his works seemed."[58]

Abelard drops this line of thought about preaching to the unconverted just as quickly as he had picked it up. From this we may note that although Abelard represents the next step in the evolution of medieval thought, i.e., seeing further than Anselm with regard to those outside the Christian community, nonetheless he is one of the middle links in the chain of thinking that ultimately leads to the missionary effort of the mendicants. If Anselm was "a man firmly ensconced in his own monastic world," then Abelard is a next-stage-hybrid: "Peter Abelard was . . . both a monk who spent many years in various cloisters and a schoolman who taught openly in several scholastic centres such as Laon, Paris, Melun, the Mont Sainte Genevieve. . . . Monks and school men—monasticism and Scholasticism—did not wholly share identical interests and outlooks."[59] I would argue that it was Abelard's deeper scholastic exposition of the intricacies of sin and virtue that led him to greater empathy for Jews and other non-Christians, raising the issue of preaching to them, though not acting upon it.

Indeed, Abelard's treatment of human morality was perhaps the most systematic and in-depth endeavor undertaken since Augustine, and

57. Ibid., 66–67.
58. Ibid., 62–65.
59. *Ethics*, xv–xvi.

after discussing non-Christians and the absence of actual sin, Abelard in the *Ethica* next turns to the distinction between mortal and venial sin, a distinction for which he was greatly indebted to the learned Doctor of Hippo.[60] More important to the history of western theology (and psychology), however, is Abelard's contribution regarding the reconciliation of the sinner, of which he sees three stages in the process: "Although therefore we offend God by sinning, there remain ways by which we may be reconciled to him. And so there are three things in the reconciliation of the sinner to God, namely repentance, confession, satisfaction."[61] Repentance is "the sorrow of the mind over what it has done wrong." For Abelard, this repentance can be fruitful or unfruitful. Repentance is fruitful if it is caused by the love of God, and unfruitful if it happens at the thought of some punishment which shall follow. As in Anselm, Abelard is at pains to convince his reader of the greater magnitude of an offense against God, the heavenly King, than against even the most powerful authorities on earth. At the same time, he remarks at the utter desirability of God because of his supreme goodness, and how it ought to inspire our devotion.[62]

60. "Some sins are said to be venial and, as it were, light, others damnable or grave—sins are venial or light when we consent to what we know should not be consented to, but when, however, what we know does not occur to our memory—so sometimes we consent to boasting or to excessive eating or drinking, yet we know this should by no means be done, but we do not remember then that it should not be done. So such consents as we fall into through forgetfulness are said to be venial or light sins, that is, not to be corrected with a penalty of great satisfaction such as being punished on account of them by being put outside the church or being burdened with a heavy abstinence—greater faults . . . perjury, in murder, in adultery, and such like are said to be damnable and weightier sins. We do not incur these like the others through forgetfulness, but commit them with assiduity, as it were, and with deliberation and are made abominable to God." *Ethics*, 68–71. Cf. Augustine, *Enchiridion*, cap. 69–71 (PL 40. 265); *Contra duas epistolas Pelagianorum*, I.14, n.28 (PL 44. 563–4).

61. Ibid., 76–77. "The Apostle invites . . . all who are stubborn and do not take thought for the dreadful judgment of God, saying: 'Or despisest thou the riches of his goodness and patience and longsuffering? Knowest thou not that the benignity of God leadeth thee to penance?' [Rom 2:4]. With these words he plainly declares what is wholesome repentance, proceeding from the love of God rather than from fear, with the result that we are sorry to have offended or to have shown contempt of God because he is good rather than because he is just. For the longer we show contempt of him because we do not believe . . . the more justly therefore he inflicts a heavier punishment for contempt of himself. . . . We are very greatly afraid to presume anything in front of an earthly judge by whom we know we shall be sentenced with only a temporal, not an eternal penalty. Carnal desire makes us do or endure many things, spiritual desire few. Would that we would . . . endure . . . for God to whom we owe all as for our wife or children or . . . mistress!"

62. Ibid., 84–87.

Along with his insistence on human intention in the commission of sin, Abelard was unwavering in his belief that heart-felt repentance was a necessary condition for its absolution. The revolutionary nature of Abelard's theses cannot be overstated. It is indeed an example par excellence of what Colin Morris dubbed the twelfth-century "discovery of the individual": "Germanic society had been generally unaware of the importance of intention. The penal codes usually prescribed punishments for actions and not for the intentions behind them, and the same was true of the Penitentials, where penances were attached to external acts rather than to internal states of mind ... the point had been reached where, after the Battle of Hastings, a penance was imposed without any consideration of the sinner's intention to commit the sin again."[63]

Although the penitents in question were soldiers who would likely kill again, the penitential takes no account of any inward repentance, the concentration is indeed fixed on the outward offence: "Anyone who ... killed a man in the great battle must do penance for one year for each man that he killed. Anyone who wounded a man ... must do penance for forty days for each man he struck. ... Anyone who does not know the number of those he wounded or killed must ... do penance for one day in each week for the remainder of his life; or, if he can, let him redeem his sin by perpetual alms, either by building or by endowing a church."[64] Abelard's approach to sin, therefore, represented quite an advance in moral theology:

It has sometimes been thought that Abelard's emphasis upon the disposition and the intention of the sinner and the penitent was prompted by reaction to the crudities of an existing penitential system under which penances were imposed on sinners according to tariffs which were still set out in current manuals of penance and which were, in the judgment of some, imposed with insufficient regard for the dispositions of the individual penitent or sinner.... Abelard himself in his *Ethics* gave considerable ... importance ... [to] the psychology of the individual sinner or penitent, but it did not at once render obsolete the old penitential collections with their lists of sins, nor were the best of these penitentials, even in the Carolingian age, less concerned with the dispositions of the soul than with tariffs for evil deeds.[65]

63. Colin Morris, *The Discovery of the Individual* (New York, NY: Harper & Row, 1972), 74.
64. Ibid.
65. Ibid., xxxii–iii.

To contrast the view of the penitential of Hastings with the new Abelardian emphasis on repentance, Morris cites a hymn the feisty cleric once composed for the feast of St Mary Magdalene: "Penitents' severe correction, / When they pay long satisfaction, / Tames the flesh, / With their frequent fasts / And with their hair-shirts' cruel rasps. . . . / But the saint did not suffer thus, / Finding God gentler far than us, / For the Judge uses equity / Nor does God who all hearts can see, / Value more a long-lasting sentence / Than a true sorrowful repentance." Abelard believed that God is so good, in fact, that when someone expresses sorrow for sin out of love for One so kind, God actually removes the sin of the sinner before that person has made sacramental confession:

> Moreover, with this sigh and contrition of heart which we call true repentance sin does not remain, that is, the contempt of God or consent to evil, because the charity of God which inspires this sigh does not put up with fault. In this we are instantly reconciled to God and we gain pardon for the preceding sin, according to the Prophet: "In what hour soever the sinner shall sigh, he shall be saved," [Ezek 33:12] that is, he will be made worthy of the salvation of his soul. . . . For although he may be prevented by some necessity from having an opportunity of coming to confession or of performing satisfaction, he by no means meets with hell on leaving this life sighing thus.[66]

Some have characterized Abelard's ideas as a "direct attack on the system of public penance";[67] they suggest that his arguments "implicitly regard penance and confession as essentially human institutions. . . . Strikingly absent is any consideration of penance as a sacrament or as a ritual of the Church at which divine power is invoked."[68] Such views, however, carry Abelard's revolution too far. Though Abelard was the first cleric to propound a theory that sin is remitted by the penitent's inner act of repentance, he does not eliminate the role of the priest, nor does he negate the need for the penances they impose as a satisfaction:

> It is incumbent upon us to deal now with confession of sins. The Apostle James urged us to this saying: "Confess your sins one to another. . . ." . . . There are people who think that confession should be made to God alone. . . . But I do not see what confession avails with God who knows all. . . . For many reasons the faithful confess their sins to one another . . . both, that . . . we may be more helped by the prayers of those to whom we confess, and also because in the humility of confession a large part of satisfaction is performed and we obtain a

66. Ibid., 88–89.
67. Ibid., 71.
68. Radding, *A World Made by Men*, 213.

greater indulgence in the relaxation of our penance.... Lastly, priests, to whom have been committed the souls of those who confess, have to impose satisfactions of penance upon them, so that those who have used their judgment wrongly and proudly by showing contempt of God may be corrected by the judgment of another power, and that they may attend more safely to this the better they follow, by obeying their prelates, the will of these rather than their own.[69]

In Abelard's eyes, though it is God who takes away the sin of the sinner, a priest nonetheless has God-sanctioned power over a sinner's soul, the power of a judge who must apply the correction appropriate to the offence. Whereas before, in the commission of the sin, the sinner had exalted his own will, by submitting himself to the priest the sinner is denying his own will. But the image of priest-confessor as judge of souls is not Abelard's exclusive metaphor; he also sees the priest as divine physician: "But he who seeks medicine for a wound, however foul it is, however smelly, must show it to a doctor so that an effective cure may be applied. The priest in fact occupies the place of a doctor and he, as we have said, must establish the satisfaction."[70] It is incorrect of Radding to state that Abelard does not give "any consideration of penance as a sacrament or as a ritual of the Church at which divine power is invoked." A sacrament, as understood by the Church, is an outward sign, or ritual, expressing an inward act of God's grace obtained by Jesus Christ. The outward minister of the sacrament is most often a priest; Abelard's view of penance/confession does not differ from this. To quote Abelard again: "So cases should be considered, and then the power of binding and loosing should be exercised, it should be seen [by the priest] what fault there is or what repentance has followed after the fault, so that those whom the Almighty visits by the grace of his compunction, those the decision of the pastor may absolve. For then the absolution of him that rules is true when he follows the judgment of the inward judge."[71]

We have not gone off on a tangent by touching upon Abelard's approach to the penitent and the confessor. As shall shortly become evident, it has everything to do with Christian mission to non-Christians and the promotion of toleration.

The first book of Abelard's *Ethica* ends with his study of confession. He started to write a second book, but it was never completed. As Abelard directed much of his first book toward an understanding of vice

69. *Ethics*, 98–99.
70. Ibid., 100–1.
71. Ibid., 120–21.

and sin, so he desired to devote the second to virtue and merit.[72] The task of fleshing out a fuller description lay with "other twelfth-century moralists—for example, the author of the *Ysogoge in theologiam* (*Introduction to Theology*) and after him Alan of Lille."[73] Not surprisingly for us, both these writers are equally distinguished for having written tracts targeted at Jews and other non-Christians.

72. Ibid., 130. The first distinction that Abelard makes is that "prudence, that is, the discernment of good and evil," is not a virtue, but rather, produces all virtues. As for what virtue is, just as he had differentiated between vice and sin, so too he explains the difference between virtue and good deeds. It is possible to get some idea of the scope of Abelard's intended project, both from what he says here and also from what he writes elsewhere, as in his *Sic et non*, and in his commentaries on Scripture. Luscombe points to several passages in Abelard's commentary on Paul's Epistle to the Romans, in which "Abelard reserves three questions for lengthier consideration in the *Ethics*. First, since God's gifts are of grace, in what do merits consist? Secondly, do merits consist in will alone or also in deed? Thirdly, does virtue, which is not manifested in action, suffice for beatitude?"

73. Ibid., xx.

3

Abelard's Heirs:
Odo to Alan of Lille

For, if it is proper for us to exhort those who are fashioned in the faith to live better, surely we should recall the Jews from their erroneous disbelieving sect.

—Odo, *Ysogogue in Theologiam*

We hold discussions with them for their own salvation.

—Bartholomew, *Dialogus contra Judeos*

If anyone shall have killed a Jew or a pagan without premeditated hatred or greed, let him do penance for forty days on bread and water, since the victim was created in the image of God, and the killer has taken away the hope of future conversion.

—Alan of Lille, *De Fide Catolica*

THE "author of the *Ysogoge*," as he is often called, is a hard person to identify historically. Abulafia writes that he is "the author of commentaries on the *Aeneid*, the *Timaeus* and *De Nuptiis*, but as an historical figure he cannot be placed."[1] She notes further that the only extant manuscript of the full text carries a dedication of the work, "written by a certain Odo for Gilbert Foliot, who had been a master in the schools, and prior first at Cluny and then later at Abbeville before returning to England as abbot of St Peter, in Gloucester, in 1139."[2] Although Arthur

1. A.S. Abulafia, *Christians and Jews in the Twelfth-Century Renaissance*, 161, nt.6; cf. M. Evans, "The *Ysogoge in Theologiam* and the commentaries attributed to Bernard Silvestris," *Journal of the Warburg and the Courtauld Institutes* 54 (1991): 1–2.
2. A.S. Abulafia, "Jewish Carnality in Twelfth-Century Renaissance Thought," in *Christianity and Judaism*, ed. Diana Wood, *Studies in Church History* 29 (Oxford: Oxford University Press, 1992), 61.

Landgraf, the modern editor of the *Ysogoge*, argued that this dedication did not properly belong to the work, Abulafia is convinced that Luscombe has more than adequately refuted Landgraf on this point.[3]

While the exact identity of the monk Odo remains a mystery, it is nonetheless evident from his work that he composed his treatise in England sometime between the years 1138 and 1148. What is also clear is that Odo must have studied in Paris, for his *Ysogoge* bears the mark of its two rival schools, that of Peter Abelard, and the other of St Victor, founded by William of Champeaux.[4] Yet, as regards our investigative focus, the treatment of morality, Odo's work is a direct continuation of Abelard's line of thought.[5]

Odo begins his discussion of ethics in the same manner as Abelard, beginning with prudence: "Prudence concerns things good and bad, and the discernment between the two. And therefore between the two it is placed, because nature does not divide good things and bad things from one another, but good from another and bad from another. That is, nature divides good things from the better or the less good, and bad things from the worse or the less bad."[6] Or, as he says elsewhere: "We follow Aristotle, who does not think prudence to be a virtue, because it belongs to neither good things nor bad things, nor is there any merit in it."[7] Likewise, Odo's discussion of the nature of evil, and the relationship between vice and sin, all follow the same Abelardian line: evil lacks being in itself; it is rather, the absence of the good; vices are bad motions

3. Ibid., 61–62; cf. D.E. Luscombe, "The authorship of the *Ysogoge in Theologiam*," *Archives d'histoire doctrinale et littéraire du moyen âge* 35 (1968): 7–16.

4. A.S. Abulafia, *Christians and Jews in the Twelfth-Century Renaissance*, 12; "Jewish Carnality in Twelfth-Century Renaissance Thought," 62; "The text is an interesting mix of ideas coming from the schools of Abelard and the Victorines. Whole chunks of the compendium are based on the *Summa Sentarium*, itself a compilation of many sources, following the tradition of the school of Anselm of Laon [not Canterbury] and William of Champeaux on such issues as original sin and free will . . . taken as a whole, the work can be said to represent the crystallization of anti-Abelardian thought in the school of St Victor."

5. A. Landgraf, "Écrits théologiques de l'école d'Abélard," in *textes inédits-Spicilegium Sacrum Lovaniense* 14 (Louvain, "Spicilegium sacrum lovaniense," bureaux, 1934), L; "Toutefois, la note abélardienne est surtout sensible dans le premier Livre, dans les chapitres consacrés aux vertus, au mérite, au péché. Même explication des vertus théologiques, de leur notion, de leur objet, de leurs rapports. Mêmes opinions au sujet de la division des vertus morales. Plus loin en se recontrent, pour ainsi dire dans les mêmes termes, les fameuses thèses abélardiennes."

6. Landgraf, *Ysogogue in Theologiam*, 65; from Cambridge, Trinity College, MS. B. XIV. 33. ff. 5r–111r.

7. Ibid., 74.

within the soul, not sins in themselves, etc. Odo even goes further by citing the traditional seven from Pope St Gregory the Great's *Moralia*: *superbia, invidia, ira, accidia, avaricia, ingluvies, luxuria.* As for the nature of sin:

> Sin, then, is contempt for God. That is nothing other than to will or not will against knowledge. This happens when we will what we know to displease Him, or do not will what we know to please Him. Indeed we know that what is prohibited by Him displeases Him, and that what is commanded pleases Him.... Sin, moreover, is distinct from vice, because vice is a cause in us, but sin an effect. But in the first man who sinned, sin was the cause and vice the effect. Again, vice is in the corruption of nature, sin in the will.[8]

Odo goes on to discuss the Augustinian delineation between mortal and venial sin, and then undertakes an extended discussion of Original Sin. Much like Anselm before him, Odo explores the great need mankind had to make satisfaction to God for His stolen honor.

> But let us investigate, with reasons brought together from all sides, whether God may forgive some unpunished faults by His mercy alone, or whether justice exacts satisfaction or penalty from every offender.... Beyond that, who may know the creature while he is sinning, how much it lies in him to deprive the Creator of due honor, that is, of the proper subjection of the will? But what is more unjustly done than more justly of the highest justice is preferred than of the highest justice to be taken away and I have not restored just honor? Nothing indeed. But where nothing more unjust is tolerated, by no means is it fitting to bear/uphold the just God. But what is more unjustly done, when the highest justice is more justly preferred, than to take away the just honor of the highest justice and not restore it? Nothing indeed. But where this greatest injustice is tolerated, it is by no means fitting to bear/uphold the just God.[9]

Odo trods the path of Anselm and Abelard in search of a greater understanding of sin, how it impacts the relationship between God and man, and he ends his first book on this note. Yet, just as Abelard surpassed Anselm in discovering the depths of human ethics, so has Odo's treatment of morality brought him beyond the bounds even of Abelardian thought. For Odo opens his second book by declaring a principle as revolutionary as any his irascible mentor ever loosed: "For, if it is proper for us to exhort those who are fashioned in the faith to live bet-

8. Ibid., 106.
9. Ibid., 125.

ter, surely we should recall the Jews from their erroneous disbelieving sect."[10]

Odo makes explicit what was implicit in Abelard's *Collationes* and *Ethica* when he declares that the pursuit of sinlessness is as much for Jews as it is for Christians. Landgraf too, sees much of Abelard in Odo's initiative to Jews:

> The second book of the work is devoted, as we have seen, in great part to the conversion of the Jews. In the *Dialogue between a philosopher, a Jew, and a Christian*, Abelard, without any doubt, wished to make his own contribution to enlightening the conscience of the sons of Israel and to bringing them closer to the truth. One can believe that the zeal employed toward this end by the famous master on the philosophical ground, impelled the author of *Ysagoge* to provide for a like task in the domain of Christology.[11]

To justify an effort at bringing Jews to the Christian understanding of virtue, Odo cites the words of Christ himself: "I am not sent if not unto the lost sheep of the house of Israel" (Matt 15:24). As a second supporting example, Odo cites Jesus's reply to the Pharisees who questioned why he was seen publicly socializing with sinners: "They that be whole need not a physician, but they that be sick" (Matt 9:12). Just as Abelard had described sin-as-wound and penance-as-curative-remedy from the hands of the priest/physician, so too Odo invokes the words of Christianity's Founder in the same context. Odo's thought represents the next stage in the development of a theology of inclusion of non-Christians, based on elaboration of the theology of reconciliation. If it is an obligation to help one's spiritual brother to walk the straight path, it is in some ways even more important to help one's religious adversary, since, presumably, he is in worse spiritual shape. Again we see that the study of sin is an undeniable impetus for persuasive approaches to non-Christians.

---

10. Ibid., 126. As Mews writes: "On many issues, such as his definition of faith or on Christology, Odo steers firmly away from the ideas of Abelard. He is interested in quoting the Hebrew version of the prophets to persuade Jews of the truth of Christian revelation—rather a different goal from that of Abelard in the *Collationes*"; Mews, "Abelard and Heloise on Jews and *Hebraica Veritas*," in *Christian Attitudes Toward the Jews in the Middle Ages*, ed. Michael Frassetto (New York; London: Routledge, 2007), 101.

11. Landgraf, L. "Le second livre de l'ouvrage est consacré, comme nous avons vu, pour une grande part à la conversion des Juifs. Dans le *Dialogue* entre un philosophe, un Juif et un chrétien, Abélard, sans nul doute, a voulu contribuer lui aussi à éclairer la conscience des fils d'Israël et à les rapprocher de la vérité. L'on peut croire que le zèle déployé dans ce but par le fameux maître sur le terrain philosophique, a poussé l'auteur de l'*Ysagoge* à fournir pareille tâche dans le domaine de la christologie."

But not only is Odo to be credited with following the thought of Anselm and Abelard to its logical missionary conclusion, he is responsible for another innovation: the use of the liturgical language of his religious opponent, in this case, Hebrew. Odo writes: "Against those arguments, surely we should more frequently take up the testimonies of Hebrew authors than those points lying in reasoning. For who may not see, in exhortation or discussion, that the Hebrew individual is more moved by Hebrew authority than by anything else brought forth?"[12] Odo believes quite strongly that resort to argumentation in Hebrew is even more effective than the use of arguments from reason in persuading Jews. Notably, he speaks as if from personal experience, or firsthand testimony. Anselm and Abelard had both appealed to the common God-given medium of human intellect in their efforts to answer the objections of Jews and other non-Christians. Odo, now, sees human language as another unifying aspect between Christians and Jews, even as it had once been a punishment that divided men because of sin:

> As it was deserved, divine force restrained the Babylonians with division of languages, when they were provoking heaven with their rash building effort. But now, with wise architects planning to build a more true tower of supernal ascent for all, all kinds of languages have been brought together by divine plan. For what purpose? It evidently appears thus: to strengthen the greatest communion of speech for drawing men together, just as the effective discord separating them is revealed. For how, by determined judgment of mutual will, is the Greek to be successfully drawn to the way of life of the barbarian? Or the Hebrew, to the family ways of the Latin, more than the ass to cohabitation with the ox? For as one kind of nature makes beasts willing to lead life together, so does a common language for men. Wherefore the Church has had word-scatterers teaching an infidel people not at all willing to acquiesce with her, and these teachers are drawing people away from her embrace, when necessarily they should be joined to the same by language.[13]

If among the beasts, how much more among men, a common language leads to a common life together. This is the theology of inclusion. Christians and Jews both confront sin; language is a common means to achieve a common remedy, leading to increased unity. Unlike Anselm secure behind his walled fortress, Odo calls the true Christian to shed not merely external barriers, but even his own identity, in order to achieve reunion of infidels, citing Paul: "I became as a Jew, that I might

12. *Ysogogue*, 127.
13. Ibid.

gain the Jews" (1 Cor 9:20). Paul made his statement within the context of explaining his preaching ministry to the unconverted, a ministry which Abelard raised and which Odo actively promotes. But this ministry to the Jews will first require study and preparation, something Christians are already familiar with for their own good, but must now make an extra effort to embrace on behalf of their religious adversaries: "Beyond this, if scholars among the faithful often enter into conflict over words from the divine page, what is to be done against [when opposing] enemies of the Catholic faith?"[14] Odo is concerned both with the literal level of learning Hebrew—he instructs his reader that it is read from right to left, not left to right as Latin and Greek—and with the allegorical or spiritual sense: this change in reading direction signifies the passing of the message of Christ from the Jews to acceptance by the gentiles. Odo ends the preface to his second book with an explanation of his method of approach: he will incorporate Hebrew itself into his own text; as Abulafia explains, when Odo quotes the Old Testament he will not only render the passage in Latin, but in Hebrew as well, along with a Latin transliteration of it. In addition, for those still mastering the Hebrew alphabet, he explains how he has transferred the Hebrew sounds into Latin script. Unfortunately,

> this projected three-tiered system breaks down almost as soon as it started. Only one Hebrew quotation is transliterated into Latin characters. And only four Hebrew quotations are punctuated. We cannot be absolutely sure whether this was the fault of the scribes involved in the preparation of the Trinity manuscript or whether Odo was loathe to put in all the work his ambitious plan required—the manuscript evidence does speak in Odo's favour. For in each case the Hebrew lines are spaced in such a way that there would have been ample room to accommodate the Latin transliteration.[15]

As we might expect, Odo begins the second book with a continued investigation of morality, notably, an analysis of the Ten Commandments. He explains that the Law was given by God to Moses to assist man after natural law had been vitiated by sin: "The Law was therefore added to the aforesaid things, that it might repair the natural law which had been corrupted by sin, and likewise might prepare the people, by legal figures, for the truth to come."[16] Next, Odo begins both his use of Hebrew and his answers to typical Jewish objections to Christianity. The first argument he makes is with regard to the allegation of Christian

---

14. Ibid.
15. A. S. Abulafia, "Jewish Carnality in Twelfth-Century Renaissance Thought," 65.
16. *Ysogogue*, 132.

idolatry, that is to say, the making of graven images, which would seem to contravene the First Commandment. Odo, however, cites other verses from the Old Testament where God asks that graven images *be made*, both on the Ark of the Covenant and the Temple of Solomon. The underlying assumption is that encountered before in Anselm and Abelard—image-making is not evil "in itself." After examining the Law, Odo moves on to an extended discussion of the Prophets: "By its known effect, the Law was in no way able to provide sufficient remedy for sin; for that reason, there were prophecies to follow the Law. For although the Law showed what was to be done and what to be avoided, the prophets, seeing that the people conformed very little to the Law, administered warnings."[17] Perhaps Odo viewed himself as Christian apologist in something of the same role, *vis-à-vis* the Jews of his own day. At any rate, Odo quotes many passages which he believes point to Christ as Messiah, particularly from Isaiah and Osse. This is the section of his work that contains the most passages in Hebrew.

When Odo finishes his examination of the Prophets, he is ready to take up the use of rational arguments to persuade Jews to come to the Christian faith: "But, Jews, since your infidelity either does not know or pretends not to know the reasons of this mystery of our redemption, let us commence with your concerns in this matter."[18] Abulafia notes that Odo is particularly indebted in this section to Abelard's *Commentary on Romans* and Anselm's *Cur Deus homo*: "In the footsteps of Anselm of Canterbury and Abelard, Odo takes the view that the Devil did not have jurisdiction over man after the Fall. . . .Why, then, was the Incarnation necessary; could God in his omnipotence not simply have pardoned mankind for Adam's sin? Why was it necessary for God to undergo spitting, flagellation, and a most shameful death in order to redeem man? The parallels with Anselm's *Cur Deus homo* are obvious."[19] As she argued before about Anselm, so too Abulafia contends here that Odo's arguments in this section shift from being directed at Jews to being aimed at Christians who have doubts about their faith:

> What is also obvious is that this section, which Odo entitled *Oppositiones Iudeorum*, has merged with internal deliberations about the central doctrine of their faith. Almost immediately we are referred to Christian disagreement about whether or not Jesus saved man from the Devil. Jews are not mentioned at all. At the very end of the section Odo rephrases the relevant phrase in Abelard's commentary to say,

17. Ibid., 139.
18. Ibid., 155.
19. A. S. Abulafia, "Jewish Carnality in Twelfth-Century Renaissance Thought," 70.

"Because this and similar material, which we have introduced from an opponent under the guise of an unbeliever, impels the important question of our redemption, let us repel him who argues in vain by putting forward the reasons transmitted by the Fathers concerning the Incarnation and death of Christ." But the person whom Odo addresses in this section as "you" is hardly an "unbelieving" Jew. For Odo speaks of "your John [the Baptist]" and "your Gospel." At the most, Odo's opponent is a nominal Christian coming up with a number of sticky questions concerning the rationale of the Incarnation.[20]

First off, when Odo says that "this and similar material . . . we have introduced from an opponent under the guise of an unbeliever," he is merely using the same approach as Anselm did in the *Cur Deus homo*, with Boso acting "under the guise of an unbeliever" to advance objections to the Incarnation. Both Anselm and Odo are trying to answer non-Christian opposition, not internal Christian dissent. As for Abulafia's contention that "at the most, Odo's opponent is a nominal Christian" because he speaks of "your John [the Baptist]" and "your Gospel," I hold that Odo was still referring to a Jewish audience and that the context bears this out:

Therefore, if the disobedience of Adam necessarily exacted the death of the Son of God as satisfaction for it, what expiation does the crime committed in His death demand? Might not the first guilt of man be effaced, unless a graver guilt follow it? Therefore, man increases his crimes, because God has not willed to overlook them unless sins are multiplied. But when you say that man is liberated from sin by that death and not otherwise, your statement is plainly false. For before that death, you read, Jeremias and your John were sanctified from the womb.

Therefore they were also liberated from sin. Your gospel also writes that, before His passion, Jesus said to the paralytic: "Have confidence, son, thy sins are forgiven thee" [Matt 9:5]. Likewise concerning the sinful woman, for many sins were forgiven her. If therefore, even before that death, many were liberated from sins, how do you say that apart from it man is by no means redeemed from sin? God extends the highest grace to man whose nature He has assumed if, as you say, He has united man to Himself in one Person. Therefore the lesser grace also, that is to say, the forgiveness of sins, He was able to deliver to man.

Therefore, what necessity do you say there to have been for the highest God to lower Himself to the depths of our nature, and to undergo . . . opprobrium, spitting, scourges, and an ignominious death with

20. Ibid.

evildoers? Or how do you say that man was justified by that death? For he seems to be more guilty, if the wicked slave has committed something for which the innocent Master must die.

Because these and things similar to these, which we have brought in from the opposition under the person of an infidel, do not move the central question of our redemption, we must refute the vain argument by bringing forward reasons handed down from the Fathers for the incarnation and death of Christ.[21]

There is much to unpack from the above passage. To begin with, every time the expression "you say..." (*dicitis*) is used, the "you" in question is not a nominal Christian, it is a devout Christian who already accepts orthodox beliefs on faith, e.g., that God lowered himself and took a human nature, that there is no remission of sin without the sacrifice of Christ, etc. Neither is his accuser a Christian dissenter, but rather, a Jewish believer who cites Old and New Testament texts against the contentions of the Christian. Thus, he refers to "that Jeremiah and your John . . . your Gospel," with "your" meaning that belonging to devout Christians.

Of greater interest to us, however, are the views on sin that Odo imputes to his Jewish interlocutor. The Jew argues against God becoming man because he does not see the death of Christ as the necessary prerequisite for liberating man from sin. He cites the example of the prophets Jeremiah and John the Baptist both being sanctified in the womb, something all true Christians accept—sanctified before Christ's death had occurred. If they could be cleansed from sin before, why the need for His death? Odo's Jew even cites Christ's own words from Matthew's Gospel, when he addresses the paralytic who had been lowered through the roof by his friends: "Be of good heart; thy sins are forgiven thee" (Matt 9:2). Odo makes it clear that sin and the need for its remission constitutes common ground between Jew and Christian—what is at issue is Christ's redemption. There is a unity in the experience of atoning for sin. There is a unity in membership in the human race. Odo's Jew says: "God inclined to our . . . nature," that is to say, the common human nature belonging to Christian and Jew. And since the religious adversaries also share a common human intellect, the Jew is able to raise these logical objections, and the Christian is able to answer with reasoned responses in the hope of successfully persuading his objector.

We know that the objector must be Jewish, because Odo entitles this section "*Oppositiones Iudeorum*," and because he uses Hebrew to explain the Christian's rational answers in the next section: *Rationes Incarnatio-*

---

21. *Ysogogue*, 157–58.

nis. Odo's answer to the aforementioned objections is that no matter
how righteous certain individuals may have been before the coming of
Christ, they could not, of their own merits, make satisfaction to God for
sin and so enter into eternal beatitude: "The prevaricator [one who
walks crookedly], therefore, neither has had anything nor has been able
to do anything, by which he might worthily make satisfaction for faults
committed. Because of this, the most eminent of just men before the
death of Christ went to hell [this term would include the limbo of the
fathers, or 'bosom of Abraham'] because no justice was sufficient for
them."[22] To support his contention, Odo quotes several figures from the
Old Testament: Jacob, Job, David, and Isaiah, who all seem to admit that
they stand outside heaven because of the debt of sin. In this section,
Odo's method is to first give the Hebrew rendering, then the Latin, then
his commentary on the biblical text.[23]

Like Anselm, Odo goes on to describe the mission of the Redeemer
and how He was fitted to the task, having two natures in one Divine
Person. When he completes his discussion of man being saved from sin
by the God-man, Odo next turns to the means through which the saving grace of Christ reaches the sinner, that is to say, the sacraments: "But
up to this point having gone through the reasons of so great a mystery
as that of our redemption, it is now in order to pass from this beginning
to the sacraments. A sacrament, therefore, is the visible form of invisible
grace joined in the very same thing."[24] Of principal interest to our
investigation is Odo's treatment of the Sacrament of Penance. Like
Abelard before him, Odo treats of its three main aspects: "Moreover,
three things are necessary in penitence: compunction, confession, satisfaction. Compunction is contrition of the heart, having arisen from
memory of the crime committed and fear of future judgment. But confession is when, with accusation of himself, he seeks judgment joined to
it; the just man at the beginning of the discourse is his own accuser. Satisfaction is a limited affliction, along with good works, received as a
remedy of the evil done through sins."[25]

In terms of repentance or compunction, Odo explains the need for
inward examination and heart-felt sorrow for sin. Confession is submitting oneself to judgment, and satisfaction a curative remedy for the sinful affliction. As the High Priest Jesus declared that he had come not for
the sake of the sound, but to minister to the sick, so Odo advises the

22. Ibid., 160.
23. He wants to prove that the Hebrew Bible confirms the Christian view.
24. *Ysogogue*, 179.
25. Ibid., 209.

penitent to turn to the priests of the Church for healing: "Although he may make satisfaction, he is still a debtor to the Church, still bound, as long as he is not yet absolved from the future penalty that is still owed. But when he has come to the priest, when the guilty one confesses his fault by accusing himself, and when the suitable satisfaction enjoined by the priest is undertaken, the priest absolves him of the debt of future damnation, that is, God does so through the priest."[26]

As we have seen, Odo's concern for sinlessness inspired him not only to urge the faithful, but Jews as well, to the pursuit of Christian perfection: "For, if it is proper for us to exhort those who are fashioned in the faith to live better, surely we should recall the Jews from their erroneous disbelieving sect."[27] Like Anselm, he had meditated on the mission of Christ to save man from sin, and he borrowed much from the *Cur Deus homo*. Like Abelard, Odo was a moralist who sought to define the grand scheme of human ethics and the importance of "repentance, confession, and satisfaction." The genius of Odo was to blend the work of his predecessors into an unabashedly missionary treatise. Odo did not restrict himself to theoretical argumentation; instead, he took the first practical steps toward effective apologetics by incorporating the use of Hebrew. We ought not to overlook the significance of the fact that he intended his only major theological work, not merely for Christian eyes, but "devoted a disproportionate segment of his *Ysagoge in Theologiam* to argumentation against the Jews."[28] The same view that saw salvation for the Jew as much a priority as for the Christian, may be found in another English cleric who shared Odo's Parisian training and abiding interest in the theology of sin; his name was Bartholomew and he would rise to the Bishopric of Exeter, but not before he had completed a work engaging Jews and an influential penitential on sin.

Bartholomew (1115?–1184) was probably a native of Brittany, though by the time he was a young man he had found his way into the eminent company of the budding scholars surrounding Archbishop Theobald at Canterbury. As his modern biographer, Adrian Morey, describes this circle:

---

26. Ibid., 211–12.
27. Cf. above ft. 10.
28. Chazan, *Daggers of Faith*, 22.

Included among its members [were] the future archbishops of Canterbury and York, as well as John of Salisbury. Probably Bartholomew was one of them, but at what precise period is not known. The older bibliographers assert that he studied at the University of Paris, and it would have been in some such centre of learning that he obtained his great skill as a canonist and the degree of *Magister* which he used later as archdeacon. But his position in the schools at Paris may have been more important than these bare facts would imply.[29]

Morey explains that a contemporary poem called *Metamorphosis Goliae Episcopi* contains a list of the masters teaching at Paris between June 1140 and April 1142.[30] The thirteen masters mentioned include the names of such luminaries as Peter Lombard, Peter Abelard, and Robert Pullen, as well as a certain "Bartholomew."[31] Morey cites scholars such as Poole and Haskins in assigning these lines to Bartholomew of Exeter. If Bartholomew was a member of this distinguished group, Morey argues, it "would account not only for his wide circle of friends ... but for the authority which his Penitential subsequently obtained both in England and on the Continent."[32] Extant manuscripts come from various locations throughout Britain including Bury St Edmund's, St Denis at Southampton, Ramsey, St Mary's Southwark, St Mark's Bristol, and Waltham. Of surviving copies from abroad, two were once owned by St Victor at Paris and a Cistercian abbey in Soissons, and a third is reputed to have come from Clairvaux. As Morey points out: "A total of some eighteen copies of the manuscript exist, and of no English writing on the subject of penance can we say the same."[33]

As we have cited before, the penitential manuals of the early Middle Ages were usually little more than lists of sins and their penances, though these were not without their more extraordinary examples. Bartholomew of Exeter was indebted to such works from the hands of the leading minds of their times, notably, Burchard of Worms, Ivo of Chartres, and Gratian. The *Decretum* of Burchard contains a separate penitential "containing one hundred and fifty nine chapters drawn from all the chief sources including the Celtic penitentials, those of the Carolingian reform, and the *Hadriana*. He establishes a general theory of pen-

---

29. Adrian Morey, *Bartholomew of Exeter, Bishop and Canonist, A Study in the Twelfth Century* (Cambridge, Cambridge University Press, 1937), 4.

30. Cf. *Latin Poems attributed to Walter Mappe*, ed. T. Wright (Camden, 1841), 29.

31. Morey, *Bartholomew of Exeter*, 4.

32. Ibid., 4–5.

33. Ibid., 108.

ance, and gives a list of punishments of the principal sins."[34] Burchard also gives questions for the confessor to use for helping the penitent disclose his sins. The next great canonist, Ivo of Chartres, incorporated about 1600 of the 1784 sections of Burchard's penitential into his own *Decretum*. Ivo's work, in fact, "is probably the main source of the penitential of Bartholomew."[35] It is also not difficult to see the influence of twelfth-century thought in Bartholomew's work, notably the influence of Peter Lombard and Abelard. The Bishop of Exeter "begins his chapter on confession with the usual comment as to its necessity if the penitent has time."[36] Bartholomew writes: "Confession by mouth is necessary, if the penitent will have had time. Whence the Lord says through the prophet, 'Say thou thine iniquities that thou mayest be justified'"[37] [Is. 43:26]. He also cites Ambrose and Augustine on the need to confess,[38] though, as Morey remarks, "he goes on to emphasize, as Abelard had already done in the *Sic et Non*, the classic phrase: 'No one can be justified from sin unless the sin has been done before you confess.'"[39] Citing Bartholomew's Penitential, Anciaux writes, "In the middle of the century the doctrine is general: without contrition of heart, without repentance, there is no remission. To be effective, this interior penitence must meet fixed conditions. On the other hand, modalities of exterior penitence are in accord with the intensity of repentance."[40]

But Bartholomew's chief contribution to the Church's understanding of sin lay not so much in the theoretical understanding of the repentance of the sinner as in its practical expression between penitent and priest.[41] What is most important is that the confessor not merely act in an arbitrary fashion toward the sinner. The priest must exercise the

---

34. Ibid., 170.
35. Ibid.
36. Ibid., 172. From Brit. Mus. Cotton MS. Vitellius A. XII.
37. Ibid.
38. Ibid., 180.
39. Ibid.
40. Paul Anciaux, *La Théologie du Sacrement de Pénitence au XII siècle* (Louvain: Éditions Nauwelaerts, 1949), 463; "Au milieu du siècle la doctrine est générale: sans contrition du coeur, sans repentir it n'ya pas de rémission. Pour être efficace cette pénitence intérieure doit répondre à des conditions déterminées. D'autre part, les modalités de la pénitence extérieure sont en fonction de l'intensité du repentir."
41. Morey, *Bartholomew of Exeter*, 173; "Bartholomew is at some pains to instruct the confessor in the duties of his office, and he echoes contemporary feeling by his insistence on moderation as opposed to rigidity in the application of the penitential canons.... Bartholomew follows the general tendency of the age in favour of mitigating the severity of the penalties for sin."

virtue of prudence, asking questions of the penitent, as Burchard had first advised, in order to assist him in making a good confession:

> I have also said what things there are in which pastoral dispensation is admitted, all which things cannot be imposed upon all penitents, but are to be dispensed in many ways proceeding from consideration of many reasons. In dispensation of which, first of all, the pastor's prudence and his honest life are necessary. Then, the offenders among themselves, and the sins among themselves, and the other things which pertain to increasing or diminishing penances or times of penance, he must prudently consider. He should also know which is true penitence and which false, and he must know that in giving penances the lightness of mercy is more to be followed than the rigor of justice, most of all for those who are believed to be truly penitent, and that if it is possible in assigning penances, vices should be cured with contrary virtues. But most of all, the occasion and cause of sin should be struck down.[42]

Bartholomew's pastoral concern for removing sin from the sinner also motivated him to engage those sheep outside his own flock, namely the Jews. As he writes in his *Dialogus contra Judeos*, "We hold discussions with them for their own salvation." ["*Quotiens enim cum eis pro ipsorum etiam salute conferimus. . . .*"] Most likely written a few decades later than his penitential, Bartholomew's dialogue survives in a single manuscript at the Bodleian Library, Oxford. Though the text remains unedited, sections of it appear in a scholarly essay by R. W. Hunt.[43] For example:

> MASTER: No one of the faithful who have zeal for God along with knowledge of them [that is, of the Jews] endures their calumnies and blasphemies without rejoinder, but neither does he use such rejoinders when he contends about the faith before unbelieving or unlearned persons. For as often as we hold discussions with them for their own salvation, they always hinder the matter in the common way of unquiet creatures, unwilling to understand so that they may act well or believe. Hence as much as it be done with sensible charity, we ought to decline not only meetings with them, but any discussions, knowing that depraved discussions corrupt good morals, and that whoever touches pitch will be defiled by it.
>
> DISCIPLE: How then shall we learn what to respond to them or what we must oppose when the need arises, if not by conferring with them?

---

42. Ibid., 191–92.

43. R.W. Hunt, "The Disputation of Peter of Cornwall against Symon the Jew," in *Studies in Medieval History Presented to Frederick Maurice Powicke*, Hunt, et al. (Oxford: Oxford University Press, 1948), 147–48. The *Dialogue against the Jews* survives in a single manuscript: Oxford, Bodleian Library MS. 482, ff. 1–78.

MASTER: Learn this from the faithful who have a greater part of either testament than the Jews.[44]

We can learn several things from Bartholomew's statements. In the first place, there is a harshness in his approach to Jews, which is lacking in Anselm and Odo. He is reluctant to encourage Christian debate with Jews and seems able only to sanction it in the breach as a necessary evil for the sake of their salvation. The fact that the master discusses the Jews with his disciple, instead of debating a Jew directly, also seems to dull the effectiveness of his approach. In the end, he argues that although Christians and Jews share the Old Testament, Jews do not interpret it in the same allegorical sense that would open their hearts to Christ:

DISCIPLE: I ask first of all, therefore, what may be the principal cause of dissension between us and the Jews?

MASTER: I believe the principal cause to be known to God alone, by whose most just but secret judgment it has happened that there is blindness in the greatest part of Israel, so that the fullness of the Gentiles might enter into the Faith [Rom 11:25]. When this has happened, Israel will be converted to Christ. But of the causes of the dissension between them and us which are known to us, this seems to me to be the first: that every scripture of the Old Testament in which they are able to find a literal sense, they always take according to the letter, unless it exhibits an obvious testimony to Christ. For then either they deny Scripture, claiming that it is not to be found in Hebrew truth, that is, in their books, or spinning fables they change it to something else, or say that they are waiting for something that has not yet happened, or by still other things, with serpentine fraud, when they feel themselves pressed, do they slip away. But they are accustomed never to accept allegory—unless they have another way out [of the difficulty it might create for them]. We, however, mystically interpret not only Sacred Scripture, but also history and things themselves, but in such a way that competent understanding may not be rendered empty through the liberty of allegory, concerning either history or Scripture.[45]

Bartholomew would not be the only Paris-educated cleric to compose a penitential manual for confessors and a polemic on persuading Jews. We shall see that Master Thomas of Chobham, Master Alan of Lille, and their university circle would take an avid interest in sin and repentance and its application toward salvation—especially of unbelievers.

44. Ibid.
45. Ibid.

Alan (1120–1202) was probably born around the year 1120 in the city of Lille in Flanders. As a young man he must have studied at Paris and Chartres under the great masters of the late 1130s and 40s.[46] But it is not until Alan was himself a master at Paris that we can begin to discern some exactness as to the sequence of events of his life and works. At one end of a timeline, his earliest datable work, the *Quoniam homines*, would seem to place him at Paris between 1155 and 1165;[47] on the other, Otto of St Blaise writes in his chronicle that Peter the Chanter and Alan of Lille were both active masters at Paris in 1194.[48] Both Alan and Peter are recognized as the first to acknowledge the distinction between dog-

---

46. G. R. Evans, *Alan of Lille, the Frontiers of Theology in the Later Twelfth Century* (Cambridge, Cambridge University Press, 1983), 2–5; Alan of Lille, *The Art of Preaching*, trans. and ed. G. R. Evans (Kalamazoo, MI: Cistercian Publications, 1981), 3.

47. J. M. Trout, "Alan the Missionary," *Citeaux* 26 (1975): 146–154; 147.

48. John W. Baldwin, "Masters at Paris from 1179 to 1215, A Social Perspective," in *Renaissance and Renewal in the Twelfth Century*, eds., Robert L. Benson and Giles Constable (Cambridge, MA: Harvard University Press, 1982), 147; M. T. D'Alverny, *Alain de Lille, Textes Inédits* (Paris: Librairie philosophique J. Vrin, 1965), 17–18.

Indeed, there seems to have been more than a small rapport between these two academic luminaries of their day. The most vivid evidence for this affinity is a manuscript painting from the Abbey of Ottoburen undertaken under the direction of the Abbot Berthold (1228–1246), which contains a portrait of Alan and Peter together (f. 216 v, 217), and which is reproduced in most every modern work on either author. As D'Alverny describes it: "Le Chantre porte une longue robe, et un tonsure très accentuée, mais Maître Alain est représenté avec une costume de clerc séculier et son bonnet doctoral a un aspect plutôt frivole" (24–26). The fact that Alan is depicted first, donned with his doctoral cap, with his hand and index figure raised would all seem to indicate that the artist wanted to depict Alan as the more important of the two, or at least, that he had something to teach the approving Peter on that particular occasion.

Peter's modern biographer, John Baldwin, acknowledges that when "he turned to theological doctrine, he was prone to adopt the solutions of the *Porretani*, particularly those of Alain of Lille" (I, 48). Baldwin characterizes Peter's interest in practical morality as something more exclusive to the Chanter and his immediate circle; nevertheless, Alan must clearly be considered in the same vein for several reasons. First, as Baldwin himself admits, Peter's distinction between celestial theology concerning articles of the faith, and sub-celestial pertaining to morality in his *Distinctiones Abel* may have been directly inspired by Alan's *De virtutibus et vitiis* (II, 39, nt. 4). Second, there is a similar correlation to be noted between Peter's *Verbum abbreviatum* and Alan's *Ars praedicandi*. The thirteenth-century bibliographer Henry of Brussels considered the *Verbum abbreviatum* Peter's most important writing. Otto of St Blaise identified Alan's *Ars praedicandi* as one of his most noteworthy achievements. Both are less scholarly, more practical theological works dealing with the virtues and vices. D'Alverny cites more than thirty chapters in each work which may be substantively compared with the same chapters in the other (D'Alverny, 148–49).

matic theology and "moral theology"—a phrase that seems to have been coined first by Alan in the 1160s.[49] As Baldwin writes:

> The separation of theology into faith and morality was expressed by the Chanter throughout his works. . . . Elaborating upon this division in the *Distinctiones Abel*, the Chanter divided each part into two additional sections. Theology consisted of a celestial part, which promised divine knowledge by treating the articles of faith and by combating heresy, and of a sub-celestial part which instructed morality by distinguishing between virtues and vices. At the turn of the twelfth and thirteenth centuries most Parisian theologians were discussing the more abstract moral questions, such as the nature of original sin, the influence of sensual appetites, the definition and classification of the virtues, and the role of intention in the moral act.[50]

Alan's *Ars praedicandi*, and *Liber poenitentialis* are entirely devoted to sin, repentance, and the practice of holiness. It was typical of this Parisian circle of theologians to devote themselves to a better understanding of human sin and divine forgiveness in order to better apply the sacra-

---

49. Little, *Religious Poverty*, 175. Little sees Alan as the continuator of Abelard's emphasis on intention in the remission of sin: "But as the new sciences of law and theology evolved, scholars pushed below the surface of mere action to get at the complexities of intention, motivation, peculiar circumstances, rules of evidence, and the psychology of contrition. Abelard was the first great figure in that triumph of the twelfth-century school that Chenu called 'the awakening of the conscience'. The resulting development of moral theology—the term seems to have been used first by Alan of Lille . . . led scholars to the systematic investigation of concrete cases."

Alan is very much an Abelardian when he writes about true contrition for sin in his *Liber poenitentialis*: "That there must be sorrow for sin is proved by manifold authority. For Augustine says, in his book *De poenitentia*, 'Penitence is a certain vengeance of the one sorrowing, punishing in himself what he grieves to have committed.' Augustine also says, 'If you do penance, you are penitent; if you do not repent, you are not penitent.' Behold indeed from this, that if penitence be true, contrition of mind goes along with it, nor does exterior satisfaction or a thick profusion of tears suffice, if these do not proceed from the fountain of the heart. Whence Isidore says, 'I discern which tears to accept as penitence, but sometimes I do not observe the emotion of penitence, because inconstancy of mind does not pour forth tears from the memory of sin, but instead now revives the habit of sin, and those things which they have wept over are committed again.' Sin must also be confessed, for contrition of heart does not suffice, unless confession follow, if you have opportunity to confess" (*Analecta Med. Namurc.* 18, II, 168).

This passage demonstrates the common debt Alan and Abelard owed to the Church Fathers in the elaboration of their twelfth-century Renaissance theology. In Alan's case, he was taking Abelard's bold theory and stating it rather matter-of-factly in practical manuals to be used by priests all over Western Christendom. True contrition is sorrow of the heart, exterior weeping does not suffice; it is the inner workings of the human soul which most concern Alan.

50. Baldwin, 49.

ment in practice.[51] The penitential works of Bartholomew of Exeter and Alan of Lille also aided these early thirteenth-century writers. As D'Alverny says: "In fact, the two manuals which follow most closely upon that of Alan are those of a Victorine, Robert of Flamborough, and of the vice-dean of the chapter of Salisbury, Thomas Chabham."[52] Or as Lester Little writes:

> With the maturing of the sciences of jurisprudence and theology, as well as with the new independence of moral theology, scholars developed the genre of the summa of penance or the summa for confessors. . . . Mention has been made of Alan of Lille's book on penance, with its advice for priests about hearing confessions, and of the canonist Robert of Flamborough's summa, a work that contains a large collection of cases of the Fourth Lateran Council and the formation of the order of friars, Thomas of Chobham wrote a comprehensive summa for confessors.[53]

Thomas Chobham (1160–1230) was also a student of Peter Chanter and later subdean of Salisbury Cathedral (*c.* 1214). His summa was widely influential and was especially noted for its *humanitas*. As Kilian McDonnell writes:

> Thomas Chobham sees the confessor in the mercy business, as indicated in the title of his manual, *Cum miserationes*, completed around 1216. Not by an abrupt command "Tell me your sins" does the confessor begin. Rather he commences with encouraging words: "Perhaps I am a worse sinner than you. I am a man like you, so do not be a respecter of my face." The confessor knows how to move the penitent both with firmness and with gentleness, "A farmhand not only has a stick to prod cows, but also he whistles and sings a song to soothe them."[54]

51. Baldwin, "Masters at Paris," 52–53; "The sacrament of penance . . . attracted the most attention from the Chanter and his followers. . . . The discussion of specific cases for the guidance of the confessor was the Chanter's and [Robert] Courson's important contribution to the medieval development of penance. By concentrating on individual and concrete moral questions Peter and Robert inspired the literature of the 'Guides to Confessors.' Both their general approach and many of their specific solutions were adopted by Robert of Flamborough, [and] Thomas of Chobham."

52. D'Alverny, *Alain de Lille*, 153–54; "De fait, les deux manuels qui suivent de plus près celui d'Alain sont dus à un victorin, Robert de Flamborough, et au vice-doyen du chapitre de Salisbury, Thomas Chabham."

53. Little, *Religious Poverty*, 193.

54. Kilian McDonnell, OSB, "The *Summae Confessorum* on the Integrity of Confession as *Prolegomena* for Luther and Trent," *Theological Studies* 54 (1993): 405–26; 414.

This same condescendence of mercy that the priest offers the penitent extends even further—to Jews (and Saracens)—in an otherwise off-handed remark in Chobham's summa on the *Art of Preaching*:

> But again, it is asked in general whether there should be preaching in all places where there are none but infidels, both in Judaism and in paganism. And it seems that the universal Church may sin in this [by failing to preach].... But again, it is asked why there may not be preaching for the Jews, when they may be compelled by princes and by the Church to hear preaching, and there may be hope that some one of them might be converted to the Faith. To this, certain ones say that pearls should not be cast before swine, because it is clear that they are so incorrigible and obstinate in their hardness that no progress is possible if there be preaching for them. But who can be certain of this, when we often see many Jews converted to the Lord without preaching? Whence there may be great hope that still more might be converted through preaching.[55]

This duty of dispensing charity for confessor *and preacher* alike, this equation of Christian penitent and *non-Christian-prospective-convert* was an unspeakably pioneering advance in the evolution of the medieval penitential sacramentality and presaged St Raymond of Peñafort's impending program.

As for Alan of Lille, like Abelard, Odo, and Chobham, he too considers sin a plague upon the human spirit that needs the merciful ministrations of a physician. As he writes in his own *Ars praedicandi*:

> Remorse is ... the first medicine in the cure of sin. Remorse is a spiritual washing of inner rebirth, without which adult baptism avails nothing.... O happy bath of repentance, which cleanses the human heart as often as necessary.... This is the bubbling lye composed of the ashes of humility and the water of repentance, with which the head of the inner man, that is, the mind, is washed clean of the worms of the vices.... Enter your own conscience; examine it. First consider the state of your own prudence. If it seems to you that it has turned inward through desire; if the throat [has erred) through gluttony, the ear in hearing debilitating melody or by willingly listening to evil-speaking, if the tongue has halted in word, the sense of smell erred in sweet smell-

---

55. Thomas of Chobham, *Summa de arte praedicandi*, trans. and ed. Franco Morenzoni (Turnholt: Brepols, 1988), 85–86.

ing, the sense of touch in theft ... if in any or in all of these you discover sin, wash it away through the act of remorse. According to the
extent of filthiness, measure the amount of the washing; according to
the severity of the sickness, measure out the quantity of medicine.[56]

If true contrition is the first medicine in the cure of sin, the disease
requires further medical attention from a specialist, as Alan says in the
Liber poenitentialis: "Sin must also be confessed, for contrition of heart
does not suffice, unless confession follow, if you have opportunity to
confess. ... For to show that confession belongs to the fullness of penitence, the Lord insinuates so when He commands the healed leper to
show himself to the priest, through which is signified that the spiritual
leper, that is, the sinner, ought to declare the ulcers of sins to the priest
through confession."[57]

Alan is equally concerned that priests should see their role in this
light. He opens the *Liber poenitentialis* thus:

> The wise doctor, therefore, ought to follow the better course, and inves-
> tigate all causes of the malady, without which he cannot determine the
> correct diagnosis. For it is written, "Appear indiscreet in nothing, but
> distinguish what, where, how long, when, and how you should pro-
> ceed." In a different application, the questions might be, "Who, what,
> where, with what helps, why, how, when?" For the same pound of cure
> is not to be weighed out to all. All might thus be restrained from one
> vice, but there should be discretion about the vices to which each is
> subject.[58]

As a good doctor must make careful inquiry in diagnosing an illness,
so, too, a good priest must ask questions of his penitent to get at the
root of the sin. As Michaud-Quantin says of Alan:

> In fact, the author considers the confessor essentially the doctor of the
> spiritual life, and this comparison dominates the directives governing
> his attitude and action. One must cordially greet the sick person (that
> is, the sinner), to give him confidence and persuade him that he can be
> cured, and to give him thus the courage to submit to the treatment
> (that is, to penitence). Then comes the diagnosis, which demands tak-
> ing account of the state and dispositions of the penitent, for these are
> the elements of which his moral responsibility is a function. Also to be
> considered are the circumstances surrounding the fault the penitent

56. G. R. Evans, trans. *The Art of Preaching*, 120–22; PL 210: 109–35; from Bruges MS
193 and Bruges 222.

57. Longère, trans. *Liber poenitentialis*, 168; from Cistercian Abbey of Lilienfield, MS
144 ff. 124r–141v.

58. Ibid., 15.

has committed. A detailed interrogation will put the priest in possession of this information.[59]

The questioning of the penitent was not only meant as an exercise of discovery for the priest, but for the self-discovery of the individual as well. Through dialogue, the confessor helps the sinner to form his conscience.[60]

Alan did not limit his use of the analogy of the physician to his guidebook on administering confession; it is raised with equal force in his handbook on preaching:

> It is proper for the preacher to take up the position of an earthly physician or doctor. Just as an earthly physician varies the forms his remedies take according to the different diseases he treats, so a preacher should apply the remedies of admonition. Thus, if he preaches to the dissipated, let him bring to bear texts which speak against dissipation, and adduce appropriate reasoning.... Now let the preacher cut with the knife by threatening; now let him apply the poultices of consolation. In the same way let him dispute against other vices, according to the way in which he sees his listeners to be entangled by different vices.
>
> If he preaches to the poor, let him discourse on poverty, commending it, and taking his example from our head, Jesus Christ.... If he preaches to the rich, let him invite them to give alms.... If he preaches to soldiers, let him urge them to be content with their own wages, and

59. Michaud-Quantin, 17; "L'auteur en effect considère essentiellement le confesseur comme le médcin de la vie spirituelle, et cette comparaison domine les directives qui gouverneront son attitude et son action. Il faut bien accueillir le malade-le pécheur— pour le mettre en confiance, le persuader qu'il peut guérir et lui donner ainsi le courage de se soumettre au traitement-à la pénitence. Puis vient l'establishment du diagnostic, qui exige de se rendre compte de l'état et des dispositions du pénitent, car ce sont des éléments en fonction desquels vane sa responsabilité morale, et des circonstances qui entourent la faute qu'il a commise; un interrogatoire détaillé, mettra le prêtre en possession de ces renseignements ... "

60. Cf. Roberto Rusconi, L'ordine dei peccati, La confessione tra Medioevo ed eta moderna (Bologna, 2002), 76–77; "Nella nuova letteratura penitenziale delle summae causuum e dei manuali per confessori, malgrado rimanga intato l'interno complesso della metafora sanitaria applicata al sacramento (peccato come malattia, confessore come medico, ecc.), il compito del sacerdote viene presentato in primo luogo come forma d'esercizio di un potere giudizario che spetta all'istituzione ecclesiastica nel *foro interno* della coscienza, come lo definiscono i canonisti.... Un significativo risvolto di questa impostazione appare il fatto che, quando si apre it dibattio sul problema della conscientia erronea-vale a dire sul caso di colui che crede in buona fede di non commettere peccato con un specifico comportamento-l'unica soluzione additata è il deponere conscientiam, cioè accettare le indicazioni di coloro i quali, come predicatori, confessori e curati, sono incaricati di far conoscere la voluntá divina non solo nei lineamenti generali, ma anche nei casi specifici."

not to threaten strangers.... If he speaks to public-speakers let him warn them, lest they support an unjust cause for gain or weaken a just cause out of rancor and hatred.... If he speak to the learned, let him warn them that they should teach as God prompts them, and that they should make God the end of their efforts.... If he directs them to prelates, let him exhort them on the subject of the governance of their people.... If he preaches to the princes of the earth, let [the preacher] warn them, that they should strive after prudence, loath avarice.... If he speaks to cloistered monks and religious, let him bring to bear for their instruction the examples of the Fathers of old.... If he delivers a sermon to married people, let him commend the state of marriage.... If to widows, let him emphasize the burdens of marriage ... if to virgins, let them be recommended to cleanliness of body and purity of mind.[61]

The significance of Alan's *Ars praedicandi* and *Liber poenitentialis* and of the *summae confessorum* in general was that the salvific wisdom of the clerical elite of Paris was now capable of reaching the unlettered, both clerical and lay, throughout all the backwater of medieval Christian Europe. As D'Alverny remarks, "The *Liber poenitentialis* should be considered along with the *Ars praedicandi* and the sermons, because it shows the same moral and apostolic preoccupations. But, even more than the *Ars*, it must have been composed at a time when Alan had the care of souls. Monks practiced the ministry of preaching, but the production of a manual addressed to priests, and to those ready to occupy themselves with the laity, is more the work of a canon secular or canon regular."[62] Indeed, Alan at the very outset of the *Liber poenitentialis* is again at pains to stress the need to reach everyone with the healing message of repentance:

This is the book called Corrector or Doctor. It is very full of medicinal corrections for bodies and souls, and it teaches each and every simple priest just how he may be of help to everyone, ordained or not, rich or poor, child, youth, elder, weak, healthy, sick, at every age, of either sex. It tells when priests must, or profitably may, invite the common people to avail themselves of penitence, and how as a faithful doctor to give them help.... This concerns son and slave, infant, child, youth, ado-

61. *The Art of Preaching*, 146–49.
62. D'Alverny, *Liber poenitentialis*, 153. "Le *Liber poenitentialis* doit être rapproche de l'Ars praedicandi et des sermons, car it témoigne mêmes préoccupations morales et apostoliques. Mais, plus encore que l'Ars, it a dû être composé à un moment où Alain avait charge d'âmes. Les moines ont pratiqué le ministère de la prédication, mais la rédaction d'un manuel qui s'adresse aux prêtres, et a des prêtes qui s'occupent eux-mêmes des laïques est plutôt du ressort d'un chanoine séculier ou régulier."

lescent, the old, the dull, the knowledgeable, layman, cleric, monk, priest, bishop, deacon, subdeacon, in orders or not, married or single, the pilgrim and the poor, virgin and widow, canon, nun, frail, infirm, or healthy, the one who fornicates with animals or with men contrary to nature, continent or incontinent by choice, by necessity, or by chance, whether sinning in public or in secret. It tells by what discretion the priest may reform all these, as he may discern both times and places for penitence.[63]

How far we are from Anselm's analogy of the fortified monastic city! What a difference a century makes in the elaboration of the Catholic theology of sin, repentance, and reconciliation. Where Anselm had depicted practically everyone but monks as destined for damnation, Alan urges the vocation to holiness even upon those who practice bestiality! Where Anselm had urged his brothers to hide behind the safety of the cloister walls, lest they be contaminated by the world; Alan exhorts holy men to seek out all the worldlings they can find and preach repentance to them and confer absolution upon their souls. Anselm's innovation had consisted in ending the monopoly of the exclusive use of the Fathers in the production of works of spirituality; instead, he brought reason to bear on theology and he introduced original sermons. But an even more radical shift occurs with Alan and his circle at Paris—the idea that holiness is not just for the holy:

> The homilies of the Fathers had for centuries provided all that was needed for reading to members of monastic communities. Indeed, it seems to have been so rare for anyone to supplement them with an original sermon in the late eleventh or early twelfth century, that St Anselm's preaching and his "table-talk" aroused much enthusiasm in the monasteries he visited almost as much for their novelty as for their excellence.... Guibert, abbot of Nogent, a younger contemporary of Anselm who remembered with gratitude the spiritual direction he had received from him as a young man, composed a *Book on Making Sermons*.... He envisages the preacher's task in terms of the needs of the monastic community.... In his *Art of Preaching* Alan has not altogether turned his back upon these considerations, but it has a very different air.... Alan wrote within a scholarly milieu very different from that of the monasteries in which Anselm and Guibert lived and worked. He certainly preached to monks, but he addressed himself to fellow-scholars, too, to the heretics, to mixed popular audiences, and ... to groups of widows or soldiers or princes or lawyers. The sheer variety of his experience had taught him a great deal about the

---

63. *Liber poenitentialis,* 15–16.

practical needs of the preacher . . . the change which had taken place between the time Guibert wrote a book on preaching and the period when Alan composed his manual, is obvious enough.[64]

Revolutionary change had occurred in Christian society and in clerical thinking. The example of preaching to heretics is the most illustrative. Anselm's "heretics" were fellow scholars like Berengar and Roscelin who, in their search for theological precision had crossed the line into heterodoxy; as Anselm vociferously stated, they were not to be argued with, they were to be ostracized. Alan's heretics, on the other hand, were whole communities of princes, merchants, and peasants, more populous in some areas—such as certain regions in southern France—than Catholics. Observes Evans: "The pattern began to change as numbers grew and the diffusion of heretical ideas came to depend less on the rise of individual preachers with a talent for demagogy. Heresy which had no obvious leader was harder to deal with and, if anything, more alarming. Bernard of Clairvaux remarked with concern on this new anonymity."[65] Far from ignoring such a threat, Alan crafted theological tracts countering each of their objections, one by one, in his lengthy work, the *De Fide Catholica*, also known as the *Contra haereticos*. Anselm rarely ventured from his monastic confines—certainly never on any missionary endeavors—but by the late twelfth century, even St Bernard's Cistercians were being pressed into service to engage the heretics in Montpellier; Alan himself was there to assist them and with probably more than his scholarly treatise on the faith. As Evans has noted, "there is every reason to suppose that he was involved in [direct] preaching against charges of heretical and unauthorized preaching against the Cathars and Waldensians."[66]

Fomenters of anti-clericalism and lay preaching, Waldes and his followers were ultimately excommunicated by Archbishop John, and two years later, at the Council of Verona, Pope Lucius III formally approved the same. It was during these tumultuous years that Alan devoted the second book of his *De Fide Catholica* to *Contra Waldenses*. J.M. Trout observes a distinction in Alan's treatment of heretics. He considers him close-minded and polemical where Waldensians are concerned, yet deferential toward ostensibly dualist Albigensians.[67] Trout writes further:

64. G.R. Evans, *Frontiers of Theology*, 87–89.
65. Ibid., 103–04.
66. Ibid., 118.
67. Trout, "Alan the Missionary," 151; "Alan is narrow-minded and hostile where the Waldensians are concerned. On the other hand, he treats the Cathari, whose heresy was much more pernicious, as respected opponents."

Of the four books of the *Contra haereticos*, *Contra Waldenses* seems least likely to win a sympathetic response from those against whom it was directed. Alan looses all his power of invective against Peter Waldo and his followers. He accuses them not merely of ignorance, but also of laziness, fraud, and licentiousness. . . . According to Alan, Waldensian gatherings end in orgies: "In their gatherings they give themselves up to gluttony and indulge their lusts, according to those who have left their company. They are lovers of sensual pleasures, preferring carnal pleasures to spiritual." Even hostile observers of the Waldensians, such as Walter Map, granted them an austere virtue.[68]

It is not difficult, however, to determine the source of Alan's animus against Waldo, otherwise known as Waldes, and his followers. Firstly, we are already familiar with Anselm's dictum: "Our faith ought to be rationally defended against the impious, but not against those who admit that they delight in the honor of the name 'Christian.' From these latter it must be rightly demanded that they hold firmly to the pledge made at baptism, but to the former it must be demonstrated rationally how irrationally they despise us."[69] Alan may have held the Waldensians to a higher standard since their heresy was less than a decade old. The Cathars, on the other hand, were already into their second and third generations in certain regions. Most Waldensians were born baptized Catholics; the same may not have held true for Cathars. What really matters is that unlike Anselm, Alan believed heretics needed ministering.

The logical fruit of the practical theology of Alan and his circle at Paris was the recognition that prostitutes and tax collectors can now enter the kingdom of heaven faster than Pharisees. We are, indeed, a long way from Anselm and the analogy of the monastic fortress barred against the world. The evolution of the Catholic theology of sin, repentance, and reconciliation had led to an ever-widening theology of inclusion. Where Anselm had delivered his sermon on the sure path to salvation to young celibate male novices, Alan addressed a new homily, morphing Anselm's metaphor, so as to bring eternal life to individual sinners of the world. His sermon begins with God and the creation of angels and men:

> But when the heavenly king saw that his enemy had established his rampart on earth, he himself wished to situate another [fortress] on earth, from which he could break into the fortress of the devil and subject those taken captive by the devil to his own jurisdiction. . . .
>
> A fortification was thus prepared for the Son of God in the glorious

68. Ibid, 150.
69. Cf. Chapter 2, nt. 17.

Virgin, whom he reinforced with multiple endowments of virtue. . . . Into this stronghold thus fortified went the Son of God, who would wage war on the devil. . . . In this fortress the Holy Spirit made weaponry for him, when he endowed him with a plenitude of virtues. Thus armed he went forth from the castle, when he was born out of this virginal womb. In that very venture he began to attack the fortress of the devil and to release some of his household to his own custody. For from the time that he was born, he was sought for the Gentiles through the faith of the Magi, and he gradually destroyed the weapons of his formidably armed enemy, establishing a new fortress for himself the Church. For through his preaching and the working of his virtue he converted those of the camp of the devil to his own camp—that is, he included them within the unity of the Church. Yet when the devil saw his power weakened and the army of his camp diminished, he devised the death of the eternal king through the agency of his accomplices [complices], the unbelieving Jew [*per infideles Iudaeos*]. . . . Ascending into heaven, he [Christ] left his multiple foundations on earth—that is, the faithful who are the rampart of God, who, endowed with virtues, resist the effronteries of the devil.

Each and every one of us, dearest brethren, *should establish himself as fortress for God so that, finding suitable dwelling therein; he might thereby shut out the affront of diabolic temptation.* Let everyone be aware of the means through which the devil tends to assault the fortifications of the soul: the crossbow of pride which, ascending even up to the heavens, wounded Lucifer. Let one take care lest the arrows of the demons enter through the windows of the senses, lest luxury enters through sight, greed through the ear, gluttony through taste.[70] (emphasis mine)

In Alan's worldview, the rampart against the devil is no longer the cloister; it is the Christian believer himself. To find surety of salvation, one need not belong to a religious community: he can act as a religious individual. For Anselm, spiritual warfare was essentially a passive group-resistance against an exterior foe: "if they look back through an aperture or window, he [Lucifer] can easily kill or wound them. Wherefore it is necessary that they never heed the cry of their parents nor return to combat nor look back, but always, just as they began, they must flee until they reach the height of the vault. For once they arrive there, they will be entirely secure";[71] for Alan, it is active single-combat against the enemy within: "Let everyone be aware of the means through which the devil tends to assault the fortifications of the soul: the crossbow of pride

70. Cohen, *Living Letters of the Law*, 310–11; cf. D'Alverny, *Liber poenitentialis*, 246–49 and Anselm's parable above, Chapter 2.
71. Cf. above, Chapter 2, nt. 31.

which, ascending even up to the heavens, wounded Lucifer. . . . Let one take care lest the arrows of the demons enter through the windows of the senses."[72]

As Alan saw it, a layman—or woman—may aspire to the heights of monastic holiness, as a practicing member of the Mystical Body of Christ, the Church. Alan's deep and abiding interest in moral theology led him to believe that the practice of virtue is something of which each Christian is capable. Each individual acts as a visible foundation, one of many Christ has left on the earth to wage battle against Satan, in much the same way as God established the Virgin Mary, and Christ and his Apostles. Mary, "the glorious Virgin . . . reinforced with multiple endowments of virtue" is now the model, not only for monks, but for each of the faithful, "who are the rampart of God . . . endowed with various virtues."[73] Yet, by declaring that Christians have the self-same vocation to holiness as Christ and the saints, Alan, once again, inadvertently opened wide the doors to lay-preaching. Alan would have the individual layman imitate the example of Christ's virtuousness, but exactly what sort of example did Christ leave? "He [the Holy Spirit] endowed him with a plenitude of virtues. Thus armed he went forth from the castle . . . to re-lease some of his household to his own custody . . . through his preaching and the working of his virtue he converted those of the camp of the devil to his own camp—that is, he included them within the unity of the Church." Christ did not merely practice holiness, he actively preached it in mission to the Jews and Gentiles of his day, "those of the camp of the devil." It is no coincidence that Alan wrote this sermon between 1179 and 1184. It was the time of the Cistercian mission to the Cathars, and more importantly, it was precisely the time of Peter Waldes and his followers: those in the enemy camp who were in most need of God's mercy.

As Alan writes in the *Liber poenitentialis*:

Thus the priest is like a spiritual doctor, when the sinner, spiritually sick, approaches him. First, he ought to attract the sinner with words and soothe him with blandishments, that the sick person may more easily disclose the disease, that is, that he may disclose the sin. Thus, after detection of the sin, the priest, having first set forth words of blandishment, may conclude with blows of satisfaction, warning that the guilty one, led on by shame, must neither disavow his sins nor fear to admit his crimes before a man, for in confessing he speaks not to a man but to God. The priest should further say that one who has con-

---

72. Cohen, *Living Letters of the Law*, 310–11.
73. Ibid.

fessed before the heavenly judge is not held to have been condemned but rather to have been absolved, showing also by multiple authority that guilt is blotted out by the confession of the sin. For authority says: Confess your sins to one another [James 5:16]. And elsewhere: I have said I will confess against myself, and Thou hast remitted the impiety of my sin [Psalm 31:5, or in versions other than Douay, Psalm 32:5], and so on. Even Christ Jesus commanded the cleansed lepers to show themselves to the priest [Luke 17:41]. *Through which is signified that he who labors with spiritual leprosy ought to show himself to the priest through confession of his faults.* Beyond this, the priest should teach that the sin uncovered in the present time will be covered on the Day of Judgment, but that the sin veiled at present will be revealed in the future.[74] (emphasis mine)

Alan would have sinners healed through confession and ultimately attain life everlasting. It is this same pastoral concern for souls that drives him, likewise, to answer the objections of the Waldensians and Cathars in his *De Fide Catholica*. What is significant for our investigation is that Alan thought to include not only the heretics in the scope of his ministry, but also Jews and Muslims, to whom he devotes Books Three and Four of his work: "May there be converted to Catholic unity heretics and pagans renouncing their superstitious opinions, that by doing so they may rise to the unity of eternal beatitude."[75] As Abelard does in his *Sic et non* (and as Aquinas will do later in his *Summa*), Alan presents the views of his opponents in the scholastic fashion, setting out their arguments and then presenting his own solution. Like the other apologists we have examined, Alan uses philosophy in harmony with Scripture in an attempt to persuade Jewish intellects. Let us take, for example, his treatment of the Trinity:

The Jews say the same to be God, and Creator of everything. . . . If God is one, as Sacred Scripture cries out, how does the Christian claim three entities, distinct among themselves, namely, Father, and Son, and Holy Spirit, to be of the one Deity? For if they are several, they seem also to be several gods and not one God. For how may the singular nature of one Person distinct from others, be the nature of another Person? But the Lord says to Israel through Moses: "Hear, O Israel, the Lord our God, the Lord is one" [Deut 9]. Not, therefore, triple, as Christians foolishly say: "The Father is God; the Son is God; the Holy Spirit is God. The Father is one entity; the Son is another; the Holy Spirit yet another." And yet they deny that there are three gods. What is

74. *Liber poenitentialis*, 26.
75. *De Fide Catholica* IV, PL 210:430a.

this monstrosity, that in the Trinity there may be Unity, and in Unity there may be a Trinity?

To the first objection, we respond thus. When God is said to be one, or of one nature, no [concept] of three persons is excluded, for they [the three Divine Persons] are one God, and of one nature, as it is possible to say of these adjectives with varying sounds: albus, alba, album [the Latin adjective "white" in nominative singular masculine, feminine, and neuter forms]. These three say one thing, nor does the one thing exclude varying sounds, for they are one name. It is allowable that the sounds be plural, nevertheless there are not plural names, but one, a name of one root. In a similar way, three Persons are one God and of one essence. For although it may be true in natural things, that as there are substances or natures, just so many are the subsisting persons, still He Who created nature is not subject to nature. It is allowable that there be three Persons still of one nature. If [in God] there were plurality of natures, the principles of things might be said to be plural, [a concept] which the Catholic Faith abhors.[76]

Understanding, as Anselm did, that Jews do not accept the authority of the Christian Scriptures, Alan sought to employ philosophy to persuade them to accept the Church's understanding of God as Trinity. But note how, unlike Anselm, Alan evinces a strong sympathy for the Jewish point of departure, that is to say, how strange the Christian doctrine must first appear as seen through their eyes. The ability to place oneself in the shoes of those with whom one debates represents an advance in the development of Christian psychology as well as theology. Note further how purposefully Alan couches his words so as to show commonality between his Jewish opponents and himself, notions that are abhorrent to their intellects are just as abhorrent to Catholic minds: "What is this monstrosity, that in the Trinity there may be Unity, and in Unity there may be a Trinity?"[77] Far from seeing Jews as less than reasonable, and therefore, less than human, Alan is capable of displaying a certain empathy and equality of intellectual capacity. But not only in these ways does Alan's thought represent a progression in Christian conceptualization of "the Other." He is also ahead of the curve in demonstrating familiarity with Jewish anti-Christian polemical arguments,[78] and in going so far as to invoke an argument in his work—seemingly in his favor—from the Talmud itself.

76. Ibid., 401–2.
77. Ibid.
78. Cf. David Berger, "Gilbert Crispin, Alan of Lille, and Jacob ben Reuben, A Study in the Transmission of Medieval Polemic," *Speculum* 49 (1974): 34–37.

In its greatest part the law has been abolished; it seems therefore that the law has no validity. Indeed in *Sehale* Elias says that the world will endure six thousand years—two thousand shall have been of vanity, which refers to the time before Mosaic Law, two thousand under Mosaic Law, and the following two thousand of the messianic age. But it is obvious that more than four thousand have passed; thus it is apparent that the law has passed and the messiah has come.[79]

Amos Funkenstein, among others, sees Alan's use of the Talmud as a critical step in the history of Christian polemic. As Cohen admits, "Alan's *De fide* marks a new stage in the role played by postbiblical, talmudic literature in Christian anti-Jewish polemic; for whereas Peter Alfonsi and Peter the Venerable condemned [contemporary] Judaism for its allegedly absurd rabbinic lore, the *De fide* cites a well-known talmudic homily in support of its claim that the messiah has already come."[80] On the other hand, Cohen does not view one Jewish quotation as representative of any major transformation:

Alan's writings contain no evidence of any personal familiarity with rabbinic literature. Making his sole reference to a passage in talmudic lore that he claimed bespoke the truth of Christianity, Alan hardly betrayed an awareness of the groundbreaking significance that Amos Funkenstein and others have attributed to his citation. . . . The objections to Christianity refuted in the *De fide* may well reflect some knowledge of contemporary Jewish polemics, but the *De fide* adduces—and refutes—them in a highly theoretical non-confrontational mode of discourse. And although the *De fide* makes no reference whatsoever to the Augustinian doctrine of Jewish witness, it makes no suggestion that the Jews have outlived their distinctive function in Christendom. Whether or not Alan believed that the Jews served a purpose in a properly integrated Christian society, he certainly deemed them worthy of inclusion in his virtual summa on disbelief within that society.[81]

It would be more appropriate to define Alan's work not so much as a summa on disbelief in society, as a summa on the sin of disbelief in society. It is approaching Alan in entirely the wrong way to speak of whether he believed Jews had "outlived their distinctive function," or "served a

---

79. Alan of Lille, *De Fide Catholica* RIO, PL 210: 410; as quoted in Cohen, *Living Letters of the Law*, 309; David Berger first identified "Sehale" as the Babylonian Talmudic book, *Sanhedrin*, 97a. in his review of Cohen's *The Friars and the Jews*. However, the idea of a six thousand year world history may, in fact, be a rabbinic borrowing from early medieval Christian sources.

80. Cohen, *Living Letters of the Law*, 308–9.

81. Ibid., 312.

purpose in a properly integrated Christian society."[82] Alan was a twelfth-century missionary, not a nineteenth-century utilitarian. He saw Jews as sinners, not as a social group, and it was their inclusion in the society of the saints in heaven that most concerned him. Alan had vertical horizons, a Catholic sacramentality.

Alan saw his work as a Church prelate as the continuation of the priestly mission of Christ himself: "He began to attack the fortress of the devil and to release some of his household to his own custody ... through his preaching and the working of his virtue he converted those of the camp of the devil to his own camp—that is, he included them within the unity of the Church."[83] Thus Alan preached to the Jews and the Muslims because he saw them as "weapons of his formidably armed enemy [Satan]" and simultaneously as "those taken captive by the devil to his own jurisdiction," though originally "of his [God's] household."[84] This is the trailblazing significance of Alan's work: he sees preaching to Jews and Muslims as much a priority as preaching to lay Christians and heretics, because all sinners are the legitimate creation of God and should not be in the devil's possession. Alan was helping God take back His own. As for those who would argue that we have no direct evidence that Alan ever preached to heretics, let alone Jews and Muslims, it must be answered in reply that Alan's medieval definition of "preaching" was less restrictive than our modern construct: "There are three kinds of preaching that which is by the spoken word, of which it is said: 'Go, preach the Gospel to every creature.' Another is by means of the written word as when the Apostle says that he has 'preached' to the Corinthians because he has written them a letter. The third is by deed, as it is said: 'Every work of Christ is our instruction.'"[85] By Alan's definition, his *De Fide Catholica* against the errors of Cathars, Waldensians, Jews, and Muslims is a work of preaching, as would be subsequent works by Dominican friars.

In his *DFC*, Alan was clearly more concerned with the threat to the integrity of Jewish souls than with any danger they themselves posed to Christian Europe. Alan and his circle at Paris were intensely interested in the revitalization of human souls. Penance and preaching were the inseparable hallmarks of all their social directives. Alan did not seek to displace or eliminate heretics, Jews, or Muslims on a spiritual, or secular

82. Ibid.
83. Ibid., 309.
84. Ibid.
85. *Art of Preaching*, 120.

level; his interest was in their eternal welfare—a welfare he now equaled with the same urgency as that of right-believing Christians. This is Alan's contribution. Far from contributing to any theoretical or practical marginalization of Jews, his *DFC* actually promoted tolerance, both in the medieval and in the modern senses of the word. As Joseph Pearson explains: "[Alan's] *Contra Iudaeos* is mild in tone, with few direct references to Jews at all.... Even by today's standards, this text is not very passionate in its polemic against the Jews; and by the standards of the late twelfth century, Alan's *Contra Iudeos* is exceptionally restrained and impersonal. The familiar anti-Jewish tropes, alleging blindness, irrationality, and malice of the Jews never appear."[86]

Pearson points out, however, that besides his *De Fide Catholica*, Alan also authored a *Summa "Quot Modis,"* or *Distinctiones dictionum theologicarum*, which "frequently mentions Jews and Judaism ... in the most abusive terms."[87] Alan's *DDT* is a conspicuous example of that genre of literature scholars term "distinctions-collections," which medieval authors composed for the benefit of preachers. His "Bible Dictionary" lists in concordance fashion selections from Scripture containing certain words or phrases and provides the definitions of these terms as understood according to their various interpretive "senses."[88] Within this format Jews are repeatedly referenced in vituperative vocabulary as:

> obstinate (225D), supercilious (962D) ... blood-drinking (934A) ... poisonous vipers (1005A), lions (835C) and fire-breathing dragons (776A) ... cursing (763A), plotting (938B), dangerous (782B)—they despise and maltreat Christ, killing him out of envy (748A, 1011D) and a desire to hold on to their power (942D) ... the Jews are to be scattered (959D) throughout the world, condemned to a lowly status. In the life to come, they will be consigned to damnation. When Alan comes to define "burning" (*torrens*) in his dictionary, he immediately thinks of the Jews in Hell (977A–B).[89]

Although the material in his dictionary was culled from centuries of Patristic and Carolingian commentaries and did not necessarily represent his personal views, Alan's exacting compilation acted as an incredi-

---

86. Joseph H. Pearson, "The Anti-Jewish Polemic of Alan of Lille," in *Alain de Lille, Le Docteur Universel: Philosophie, théologie et literature au XII siècle*, eds. Jean-Luc Solère, Anca Vasiliu, and Alain Galonnier (Turnhout: Brepols, 2005), 83–106; 93, 98.

87. Ibid., 93.

88. Ibid; for the genre, cf. M.A. and R.H. Rouse, "*Statim invenire*: Schools, Preachers, and New Attitudes to the Page," in *Authentic Witnesses: Approaches to Medieval Texts and Manuscripts* (Southbend, IN: Notre Dame University Press, 1991), 191–219.

89. Ibid., 102–3.

ble catalyst for the spread of anti-Jewish caricatures: "Because preaching was the mass communication of the Middle Ages, the anti-Jewish tropes of the *DDT* found their way into hundreds of sermons and eventually into many thousands of church-going ears. By collecting together so many anti-Jewish references and putting them at the disposal of the preacher, Alan transmitted them to a public well-beyond the scholarly circles to which they had previously been confined."[90]

What are we to make of the night-and-day treatment of the Jews that exists between the two contemporaneous treatises of Alan of Lille? The answer is simple: like Abelard before him (and the Dominicans after him) Alan is caught between two traditions. On the one hand, there are the demeaning stereotypes of the Jews that are as old as the era of the first apologists; on the other, there is the more reasoned approach (in their finer moments) of Augustine, Anselm, and Abelard and his succes-sors. The result? The *Distinctiones dictionum theologicarum* AND the *De Fide Catholica Contra Iudeos*. As Pearson observes, "a preliminary analy-sis of the anti-Jewish references of the *DDT* indicates that many cita-tions are of earlier authors; seldom indeed is Alan speaking in his own voice. Most of the anti-Jewish material is drawn from standard patristic sources, from Jerome and Cassiodorus or the *Moralia* of Gregory the Great."[91] His *De Fide Catholica*, on the contrary, contains a preponder-ance of original material[92]—even recourse to the Talmud.

Alan, like other twelfth-century Renaissance theologians, was trying to take the best of his Catholic patrimony and attenuate it to his own times. He *did* blaze a trail toward tolerance, but like all trailblazers, he could also revert to form. To expect more than this is to hold him to an unreasonably high standard. Within his own limited milieu, however, it can be safely said that he took the first steps down a path of progress. This is perhaps best shown in his repeated claims that neither Christian heretics, nor Jews are to be killed or in anywise molested, as he states in the *DFC, Contra Waldenses*:

> And as an earthly judge must not usurp a Church office, neither should a Church judge usurp an earthly office. The Church therefore ought to defend those guilty of blood. This does not mean only that she ought not to punish with corporal penalties, but even more that

90. Ibid., 104.

91. Ibid., 103–4; St Jerome from *DDT*, 210:716C = PL 26, 698B, Cassiodorus, 707A = PL 70, 1101D, 1102A, and Gregory, 809D = PL 76, 505D, 506A; 819C, 833D = PL 76, 68C; 826D, 863A = PL 76, 64D.

92. Ibid., 95; "Since it is generally conceded that about 40% of Book III [of the *De Fide Catholica*] is taken from [near-contemporary Gilbert] Crispin, it follows that approximately 60% of the *Contra Iudeos* is apparently original."

she should intercede with earthly judges on behalf of the guilty. When the Lord says, "I do not will the death of the sinner" [Ezekiel 18], this is not to be understood of bodily death, but of the death of the soul. For He does not will the death of the soul, but rather that [the sinner] be converted and live spiritually. We say therefore concerning Jews, that they ought not to be killed. If however they commit those crimes, for which the law dictates that a man is to be killed, the judge is able to kill them, that he may serve this law well. In a similar way, heretics are not to be killed for heresy, but because of the Christian character they bear [that is, because of the sacramental character of baptism], they are to be led back to the fold of the Church.[93]

Trout remarks of this statement, "Alan maintains that neither Jews nor heretics should be killed for their beliefs. Although *Contra haereticos* is directed to Moslems as well as Jews and heretics, he neglects to include Moslems in his plea for mercy. Perhaps Alan is absent minded. On the other hand, the omission might suggest that the work was written in the period of the Third Crusade, after the fall of Jerusalem."[94] The former is more likely the case, for in his *Liber poenitentialis*, Alan reiterates his protection of Jews and this time includes the "pagans," his alternate expression for Muslims: "If anyone shall have killed a Jew or a pagan without premeditated hatred or greed, let him do penance for forty days on bread and water, since the victim was created in the image of God, and the killer has taken away the hope of future conversion."[95] Alan, of course, could only speak of the penance that the Church is able to administer, having already explained above the separation of the temporal and spiritual powers in punishing offenders. What is more important is that, based on Alan's statements above, it is hardly the case that Alan "eliminated almost entirely the place accorded Jews in Christendom," or that he did so because they "threatened its integrity."[96] It is insinuated that Alan would have made a good Dominican because of such beliefs. In Cohen's assessment, Alan and the friars are ultimately responsible for the theological underpinning of a persecuting society:

Thus, as Moore has shown, leper, heretic, and Jew became virtually interchangeable designations in twelfth-century Christian taxonomies of society, exemplifying marginality and an impurity that threatened the fabric of Christian existence. At the end of the century, one encountered in Alan of Lille's *De fide catholica contra haereticos* a new

93. *De Fide Catholica*, PL 210, 396C, D.
94. Trout, "Alan the Missionary," 149.
95. Longère, 77; *Liber Poenitentialis*, II, 58.
96. Cohen, *Living Letters of the Law*, 312.

genre of polemical treatise, which debated systematically and in turn heretics, Saracens, and Jews. Not long thereafter, the Dominican canonist Raymond of Penyafort followed the lead of Gratian and other twelfth-century masters by grouping together all "those who dishonor God by worshiping him vilely, namely Jews, Saracens, and heretics."[97]

To view Alan, or Raymond and the Order of Preachers, through the lens of the dynamics of power and exclusion is to run the risk of importing modern societal suppositions into twelfth-century treatises, and of overlooking the presence of a distinct medieval construct of inclusion based on human sinfulness and divine redemption. As we have seen above, Alan believed that heretics, Jews, and Muslims were objectively guilty of the sin of offering improper worship to God, but in his handbook for confessors he makes it equally clear that although Jews and pagans are sinners, they are, nonetheless, human beings "created in the image and likeness of God," and must not be violated, under pain of sin.

Neither Alan nor Raymond viewed Jews as heretics, but as sinners. The scholastic syllogism runs thusly: all heretics are sinners, but not all sinners are heretics. As Evans writes: "Alan describes the Cathars as *haeretici temporis nostri*; the Waldensians are *haeretici* and their leader is a *haeresiarcha*, but the Jews and the Moslems are not strictly heretics. They do not call themselves Christians and Alan refers to the Jews as *Judaei* as though no further comment was required. The Moslems, he tells us, are called, vulgarly, *saraceni vel pagani*. Alan would not, then, want to call all the unbelievers to whom he addresses himself in the *Contra haereticos* 'heretics.'"[98] Still, it must not go unrepeated that Alan was more responsible than most for helping to spread prejudiced views of Jews. His *Distinctiones dictionum theologicarum* certainly scattered the seeds of *traditional* anti-Judaism farther and wider than they might otherwise have been.

Anselm and Abelard had offered rational defenses of Christian theology for the benefit of non-Christian audiences, with Abelard in particular attempting to persuade Jews to look beyond the Law of Moses in the attainment of moral perfection. Odo and Bartholomew went into even more detail: "If it is proper for us to exhort those who are fashioned in the faith to live better, surely we should recall the Jews,"[99] even holding "discussions with them for their own salvation."[100] Alan's advance was

97. Ibid., 157–58.

98. G. R. Evans, *Alan of Lille, The Frontiers*, 128.

99. Landgraf, *Ysogogue in Theologiam*, 126.

100. R. W. Hunt, "The Disputation of Peter of Cornwall against Symon the Jew," 147–48.

to agitate for an active preaching apostolate, not only for the faithful, but for heretics, Jews, and other infidels. He considered them as deserving of pastoral attention as Christians, imbued with dignity by having been created in the image and likeness of God. On the practical level, Alan developed a more sophisticated Christian polemic, one that incorporated the objections of actual Jewish polemic, as well as verses from the Talmud itself. The stage was set for the *coming of the friars*.[101]

101. Thomas of Eccleston, thirteenth-century English chronicler.

4

Dumb Dogs,
Domini Canes, and Canon Law

Before his mother conceived him, she saw in a vision that she would bear in her womb a dog who, with a burning torch in his mouth and leaping from her womb, seemed to set the whole earth on fire. This was to signify that her child would be an eminent preacher who, by "barking" sacred knowledge, would rouse to vigilance souls drowsy with sin, as well as scatter throughout the world the fire which the Lord Jesus Christ came to cast upon the earth.
—Blessed Jordan of Saxony, OP, *The Libellus*

By barking is understood preaching, which arouses fear through speech; and by the staff the punishment which is given by the good works which they themselves do and exhort others to perform. However, the punishment by deed, should be imposed with moderation and great prudence, and with love and not ill will; in order that men may understand that it is done more through the love of God.
—St Raymond of Peñafort, OP, *Siete Partidas, Book One,* XLII

OF THE MYRIADS of tourists who frequent Florence each year, many visit the venerable Church of Santa Maria Novella to admire Giotto's Crucifix or Masaccio's *Holy Trinity.* Others, however, come to visit the Dominican chapterhouse attached to the church to see the great fresco in the Spanish Chapel by Andrea di Buonaiuto, *The Allegory of the Dominican Order.* The painting shows St Dominic holding the cane of a master, about to release a pack of black and white dogs against wolves that are ravaging sheep. The symbolism is lost on no one familiar with medieval preaching. The black and white dogs symbolize the Dominican preachers in their black and white habits. The wolves are heretics and the sheep are the faithful of Christ's fold. Perhaps chiefly from this painting, the legend has spread that the earliest Dominicans were also known as "*Domini canes*," "Hounds of the Lord." This pun, however, is a popular fiction, as the followers of Dominic were never called "Dominicans" at that time, let alone "*Domini canes*."[1] Nevertheless, this chapter contains "Dumb Dogs and *Domini Canes*" in its title because in the Middle Ages, the dog was, in fact, a very potent symbol for authentic Catholic preaching and for St Dominic and his Friars Preachers in particular.

"Preachers need knowledge ... [but] there is a certain cultivated ignorance, when someone is able to learn and chooses not to; this is stupid and lazy and easily put right; therefore it is inexcusable."[2] So Alan of Lille, the twelfth-century master of Paris, lamented the spiritual state of the bishops of his day for their neglect of education and their lack of enthusiasm for preaching to poor sinners. The crisis in clerical education and episcopal zeal was leading to a corresponding crisis in evangelization and the pastoral formation of the people of God. It was not enough that over the past century the clerical elite had developed penitential theology; freedom from sin and the extension of God's mercy must now reach the masses.

As we have seen quoted above and from the analysis of the preceding chapter, Alan of Lille was a great university educator and preacher himself, and so could not stomach the spiritual sloth of contemporary prelates. He viewed their failure to learn and to preach as a betrayal of the bishops' calling to be watchful guides for the flock of Christ. To underscore his point, he compares the mediocrity of the bishops to the muzzling of canines:

> They are priests and prophets without reason, teachers of impossibilities, guessing at secrets. O vile ignorance, abominable folly, which imposes silence upon the prelate, and makes our watchdog, that is the shepherd, mute; This is the frog which, when it is thrust into a dog's mouth, silences his barking. The prelates of our time seat themselves upon a throne before they are instructed beneath the birch: they don the robes of a Master before they undertake the hard work of the student. They choose to be eminent, not to be useful; the reward of honor,

1. P. Mandonnet, *St Dominic and His Work*, OP, trans. Benedicta Larkin (St Louis and London: B. Herder, 1948), 448–49.

2. Alan of Lille, *The Art of Preaching*, trans. and ed. G. R. Evans (Kalamazoo: Cistercian Publications, 1981), 144.

not the burden of hard work. To such a prelate it can be said: "Physician, heal yourself."[3]

Alan cites several sources for the pastoral malaise. The first is episcopal pride, a lack of personal holiness and a desire for worldly gain. Second, he notes the bishops' refusal to submit to the rigors of intellectual formation. Lastly, there is the sin of the Pharisee, when bishops "teach, but do not do," laying instead heavy burdens on other men's backs that they themselves refuse to shoulder. It is important for us to take note of these three vices which Alan alleges behind the pastoral vacuum, as they shall be remedied by St Dominic a generation later by three corresponding "virtues."

Alan was not alone in his fulmination against the failure of bishops to preach, nor was he the only one to employ dog-imagery in doing so. It seems even hell itself could find no better epithet for the prelate who neglected his preaching than "dumb dog":

> But to the confusion and ignominy of the *prelati* and of those who ought to have instructed the people, the Lord preached the truth of the Gospel, or permitted it to be preached, through an evil spirit in a certain demoniac, who was then in Germany. When the latter was asked what his name was, or (*vel*) by whose authority he presumed to preach and to teach people, he would reply: "My name is Pen-in-ink. For I am compelled by the Lord to preach the truth to shame (*in contemptum*) the dumb dogs who are unable to bark, and because I am unable to say anything except what is true and deserves to be written down, *Pen-in-ink* is my name."[4]

The above account of the demoniac is related by another university-trained master—later turned bishop—James of Vitry, in his *Historia occidentalis*. In the first four chapters of his work, James describes the sins of Christendom, where everyone from usurers to princes is weighed in the scales and found wanting; he titles his fifth chapter "The Negligence and Sins of Prelates," because he considers their failure as pastors the root of all the evils outlined in chapters one through four: "The

---

3. Ibid; "Orator, plead for yourself, you who are a vicar of Christ, imitate his work, who 'Began to do and to teach.' He who teaches but does not do, defiles Christ. He lays on those subject to him an unbearable burden, yet he is not willing to put out a finger to move it. . . . Some hide in a handkerchief the talent of divine wisdom which has been committed to them—that is, those who, out of idleness, do not wish to preach. Some hide it in the dung-heap—that is, those who in their deeds contradict their own words; others hide it in the mud—those who hide the word out of envy."

4. James of Vitry, *Historia occidentalis*, Chap. 5, in D. L. D'Avray, *The Preaching of the Friars, Sermons diffused from Paris before* 1300 (Oxford: Oxford University Press, 1985), 14–15.

cause of all these evils is to be found in the bad morals, deficiencies, and ignorance of prelates."[5] James too, used dog analogies, as for instance "when he related the old fable of the shepherds and the wolves, in which the latter agree to leave the sheep to the shepherds, provided the shepherds gave up their dogs. The moralist reflected: 'The infernal wolves know very well that if they could triumph over these dogs, namely the preachers, they would easily strangle the sheep.'"[6]

By the dawn of the thirteenth century, even the curia of Rome were aware of a pastoral vacuum sustained by the negligence of bishops and priests, and filled by only-too-eager groups of "heretics." Pope Innocent III assesses the scene, invoking again the dog metaphor: "Since the dogs of the flock do not bark, the (heretics) themselves bark, not that they may ward off the attacks of the wolf, but rather that they may cause the flock to stray away."[7] Oddly enough, even heterodox groups viewed their ministry in somewhat the same light, i.e., bearing a preaching burden the clergy refuse to shoulder: "The Apostle [Paul] rejoices whatever way Christ is preached, whether through the wicked or the good, with a right intention or a wrong one. Why then should not the bishops also rejoice when Christ is preached by us? But they contradict us."[8] Such was the Waldensian lament.

The Waldensian belief in strict apostolic poverty and preaching tied their movement in common cause with the other major alternative Christianity of the day, the Albigensian or "Cathar" churches. Throughout the course of his reign, Pope Innocent III made no secret of his contempt of the Cathars, nor his disappointment with the rank-and-file bishops over the neglect of their primary pastoral duties, which had precipitated the Cathar crisis. Innocent had frequent recourse to the now familiar canine-theme in his castigations of the clergy: "His watchmen all blind, dumb dogs, unable to bark, hide the talent committed to them in the napkin like the unprofitable servant, since the word of the Lord has been bound in their mouth."[9] Only a few short months after he had ascended the throne of Peter in 1198, Innocent had recruited a handful of devoted Cistercian monks to bear the episcopal burden of preaching to the Cathars and Waldensians. But the Cistercians achieved little, if any, success in southern France. They were ridiculed for the lux-

---

5. Ibid.

6. Mandonnet, 453, citing T. Crane, *The Exempla of Jacques de Vitry* (1890), 17.

7. Innocent III, *PL*, 215:819.

8. Foncaude, *Adversus Waldensium sectam*; *PL*, 204:817.

9. *PL*, 214:904; Reginald Ladner, OP, "The Plight of Preaching in the Twelfth Century," in *St Dominic and His Work*.

urious manner in which they traveled and only seemed to confirm the heterodox in their belief that the Church of Rome was the "whore of Babylon" foretold in Revelation. Missionizing was not according to the rule of the cloistered and the Cistercians repeatedly petitioned Innocent to accept the resignation of their commission.

It was at this desperate hour that two unlikely prelates appeared in Rome and provided an unwitting solution to what had seemed to popes and theologians for decades now a "doggedly" insoluble problem. Meeting with Innocent III en route to a diplomatic mission in Denmark was one Diego, bishop of Osma, Spain and his trusted cathedral canon, Dominic Guzman. They had come to ask Innocent not to absolve them of a mission program, but to approve one. Diego and Dominic sought papal permission to preach to the pagan Cuman peoples of Hungary. Doubtless, Diego sought to impress Innocent when he recounted a singular example of the resourcefulness of his young priest Dominic as they had passed through France. It seems that during their stopover in Toulouse, they had chanced to make the acquaintance of their innkeeper, a zealous Cathar, and that he and Dominic spent the whole night in debate over Scripture rather than slumber. By daybreak, Dominic's Catholic commitment and apologetics had secured the man's safe return to the fold. Understandably, Innocent denied their request to preach to the Cumans and sent them back to the Cathars. This zealous bishop and priest were just the shot in the arm his Cistercians needed. When Diego met with the Cistercians in Languedoc he and Dominic urged reforms in their mission: "putting everything else aside, they [threw] themselves even more fervently into their preaching. Moreover ... they should follow and teach the example of the Pious Master, proceeding in all humility, going on foot, with neither gold, nor silver, imitating in everything they did the apostolic way." In the end, the more conservative Cistercians finally acquiesced: "If some duly authorized person wished to go ahead of them and show the way, they would follow him most willingly."[10]

Heterodox lay movements had urged a return to apostolic poverty and public preaching as means of combating the pastoral crisis of the High Middle Ages. The bishop of Osma, for his part, could find no fault in the lofty ideal of Christ's poverty as preparation for ministering the Word. It seemed, in fact, the perfect remedy for episcopal arrogance. As a bishop himself, he knew the temptation to pride and the covetousness of worldly prizes and praises. Thus, Diego was confident that if ortho-

---

10. Peter of Vaux-de-Cernay, *Hystoria Albigensis,* II, 20–21, in Little, *Religious Poverty,* 155.

dox representatives like himself met the Cathars on their own terms, it would have the desired effect of turning them back to the ranks of the faithful. He had already witnessed how the personal sincerity, scriptural sagacity, and unflinching oratory of his priest Dominic had managed to convert one obstinate Albigensian innkeeper in just a single night's stay. In this incident we see the added importance not only of being scholastically equipped for successful episcopal evangelization, but of the power of teaching by good example: "those who teach—and do." Dominic's deed inspired Diego, whose deeds would goad on the Cistercians—and, hopefully, the heretics they had come to reclaim. It was this combination of first, personal sanctity reflected in poverty, second, love of learning, and third, preaching—in word and deed—which would repair the three root vices behind the current episcopal vacuum, which Alan of Lille earlier outlined above. It was these three virtues, in fact, which would come to characterize St Dominic's fledgling "Order of Friars Preachers," the embryonic origins of which may first be discerned in that first season of preaching in 1206/1207. Ultimately, the fledging Order would take the speculations of the cloister—of Anselm, Abelard, and Alan—and embody them in penitential proclamations. Soon, not only fallen Christians but the rest of fallen humanity would prove their oyster.

Much virtuousness would be demanded of Dominic. First, his trusted Cistercian companion Ralph of Frontfroide died in September 1207, then "later in the autumn Diego returned to Osma to tend to his duties there, though with the firm intention of returning to the anti-Cathar mission and of bolstering it with some of the resources of his diocese. Diego died at home on December 30th, 1207. Two weeks later Peter of Castelnau was assassinated and Rome reacted by putting in motion the machinery of a crusade."[11] So we see that, after some initial success, Dominic was thrust into heading the mission in Diego's absence and, in the earliest weeks of his new leadership, was facing a crisis with the potential to undo all the collective labor of their previous months of work. Despite the violence of war, Dominic's preaching to the heterodox would continue. The source of his perseverance, according to Jordan, was his Christ-like humility and self-sacrificing charity:

> On one occasion a public debate was organized against the heretics. The local bishop proposed to go to it with an imposing entourage, but St Dominic said to him, "No, my lord and father, that is not the way to go to meet such people. The heretics are to be convinced by an exam-

---

11. Little, *Religious Poverty*, 155.

ple of humility and other virtues far more readily than by any external display or verbal battles. So let us arm ourselves with devout prayers and set off showing signs of genuine humility and barefooted to combat Goliath." The bishop accepted ... and he sent his equipage away and they set off barefooted. The place they were going to was many miles away. On the way there they began to be uncertain of their route, so they asked the way of someone they thought was a Catholic, but in fact he was a heretic. "Certainly," he said, "Not only will I show you the way, I shall be delighted to escort you there myself." While he was taking them through a wood somewhere, he led them away so viciously, through thorns and thistles, that their feet and legs became quite covered in blood. The man of God endured all this with the utmost patience; breaking out into a hymn of praise to God, he encouraged the others to praise God too and to be patient. "My friends," he said, "hope in the Lord, Victory will be ours, because even now our sins are being washed away in blood." The heretic saw their extraordinary and blissful patience, and he was pricked with compunction at the good words spoken by the man of God, so he admitted the poisonous way he had deceived them, and renounced his heresy. When they reached the place of the debate, everything came to a satisfactory conclusion.[12]

Here we see again, not only the first virtue of humility, but also the last, perseverance-in-teaching-by-doing. As St Dominic's contemporary, St Francis of Assisi, was to instruct his friars: "Preach always ... when necessary use words."

Venerable Jordan of Saxony, the man who had succeeded St Dominic as master-general of his Order, had much to say about the Christ-like motivations of his mentor. In 1233, Jordan wrote: "Frequently and particularly he [Dominic] prayed that God would deign to give him true charity, efficacious to help and assure the salvation of men; for he thought he would only be a true member of Christ when he spent himself wholly, to the limits of his strength, for the welfare of men's souls, as the Savior of all, the Lord Jesus, offered himself for our salvation."[13] St Dominic's charity for souls, particularly non-Catholic ones, must have been an especially strong penchant, since multiple witnesses to his cause of canonization swear to it under oath. Brother William of Monferrato testifies:

---

12. Gerald de Frachet, *Lives of the Brethren*, in *Early Dominicans, Selected Writings*, ed. Simon Tugwell, OP (New York, NY: Paulist Press, 1982), 87–88; from B.M. Reichert OP in *Monumenta Ordinis Fratrum Praedicatorum Historica*, vol. I (Louvain, 1896).

13. Blessed Jordan of Saxony, *On the Origins of the Order of Preachers*, Chapter 13, in Brooke, 164.

Going to Rome once, when I was still in the world, I went to stay in the house of the bishop of Ostia, . . . and there I consorted with brother Dominic who used to come and see the cardinal frequently, and I recognized him as a holy man and I liked his way of life. I began to love him and I often spoke with him about the salvation of others. . . . I went to Paris to study theology for two years, and there I received the habit of the Preachers from the blessed Dominic, although we had previously agreed to go and convert unbelievers.[14]

Let us note how frequently the word "love" is intertwined with notions of "converting others."

Brother Rudolph of Faenza's sworn testimony amplifies this point: "I never saw a man whose service of God pleased me more than did that of the blessed Dominic. He longed for the salvation of all men, including Christians and Saracens, and especially the Cumans, to whom he wanted to go."[15] Brother Paul of Venice adds: "He longed jealously for the salvation of believers and unbelievers alike. He sometimes said to me, 'When we have established our Order, we shall go to the Cumans and preach the faith of Christ and win them for the Lord.'"[16] Let us note well, Dominic said: win them for the Lord Jesus—not the Lord Pope! Lastly, Brother Frugerio of Pennabilli reiterates these points: "He was zealous for souls, not only those of Christians, but also Saracens and other unbelievers. As evidence of this, he proposed to go to the pagans and die there for the faith, once he had organized his brethren."[17]

It was at the first General Chapter which St Dominic and his friars had held in 1220 that the founder and his brethren first proposed to "clarify the institutional identity of their order, and to expand their early customary into a set of formal Constitutions."[18] As such, their "mission statement" may be found in the prologue which they drafted: "Our Order, is recognized as having been especially instituted from the beginning for preaching and the salvation of souls, and our study should be principally and ardently directed to this end with the greatest industry, so that we can be useful to the souls of our neighbors."[19] Thus, it was Dominic's "zeal for souls" that was formally recognized as the purpose of their Order, with study and preaching serving as the first means to

14. *Acta Canonizationis s. Dominici* 12, in *Early Dominicans,* 69–70; from Bologna, Bibl. Univ. MS. 1999, ff. 21–26.

15. Ibid., 77.

16. Ibid., 83.

17. Ibid., 84.

18. M. Michele Mulchahey, *First the Bow is Bent in Study . . . Dominican Education before 1350* (Toronto: Pontifical Institute of Medieval Studies, 1998), 3.

19. Ibid.

this end. It is no accident that Dominic asked one of his brothers, Paul of Bologna, to complete the first Dominican handbook on confession that same year, nor was it coincidence that it was Paul whom he then promptly sent to the pagan Cumans, the infidels to whom Dominic, himself, had always desired to preach. The connection between concern for sinners in the confessional and concern for sinners who have never been baptized is palpable in the first decades of the Dominican Order. The case of Paul of Hungary (the epithet by which he came to be definitively known) is informative.

After Dominic had received papal approval for a universal apostolate in 1217, he had dispersed the majority of his membership to Paris, a few to Bologna, and a few elsewhere. These two university towns provided him with students and masters of intelligence and fervor, the kind he needed to serve an ever-widening circle of souls; Friar Paul was such a man. Paul had been a professor of canon law at Bologna when he was enticed into the Order by the preaching of Friar Reginald of Orleans in 1219.[20] By January 1221, he had been promoted to prior of the Dominicans in Bologna, who were attached to the Church of St Nicholas. Thus, he begins his manual on confession by saying: "This manual exists because they [confessors] work among the perils of souls, and sometimes difficulties emerge. May it contribute to the honor of God and of blessed Nicholas, and to the usefulness of the brothers as well as the salvation of their penitents."[21] Of his *Summa de poenitentia*, we may observe three general features: first, it is succinct and practical; second, it shows the influence of his study of canon law; and third, it shows its indebtedness to the pastoral approach of St Dominic himself.[22]

Some of the authorities that directly influenced Paul, by his own admission, were the new regulations concerning confession set down in Canon Twenty-One of the Lateran Council, which he refers to as the "*nova constitutio.*" And of course, there was the authority of his master, Dominic: "*ubi dicit prior noster, Magister dominicus.*" Dominic's concern that priests imitate the "longing for others" and the total self-sacrifice of Christ comes through in Paul's directions:

> It follows from the speech of the priest and from his meek leading toward what should be confessed. The priest ought to set forth the love of God the Father when He sent His Son for sinners, and the charity of

20. Ibid., 530.

21. "*Rationes poenitentiae, Fratrum Praedicatorum,*" in *Bibliotheca Casinensis, seu codicum manuscriptorum qui in tabulario casinensis asservantur,* t.4 (Monte Cassino, 1880), *Florilegium Casinensis,* 193.

22. Mulchahey, *First the Bow is Bent,* 531.

Christ for sinners needing redemption. Christ died crowned with thorns, pierced with a lance, fixed to the cross by nails in His hands and feet. This may lead one to confess that the death of Christ profits him. Other motives include the following. First, Christ did not come for the just, but for sinners. Next, the Lord does not will the death of sinners but their conversion (the priest may quote, "I do not will the death of a sinner," or other words of the Lord). Also, one or more of these examples may be encouraging: the denial of Peter, the persecution by Paul, the sin of the Magdalene, the confession and faith of the good thief, the adultery of David, and what was done by the tax collector. These persons, although they sinned gravely, obtained forgiveness through penitence, and certain ones of them were afterwards apostles and saints. Finally, the spiritual doctor, following the example of the corporal doctor, may soothe the sick person with sweet words, may show compassion, and thus may strengthen the feeling of spiritual health in the infirm one.[23]

As Christ had answered in defense of his ministry, "It is not the well that need a physician, but the sick," (Matt 9:12) so too did Paul, as Abelard, Odo, Bartholomew and Alan before him, encourage confessors to view their role as an extension of Christ the divine physician. Paul himself was soon asked to teach not only by word, but by his own example. In one of his last official acts before he left this world, Dominic commissioned Paul and four companions to go preach and convert the Cumans. A Turkish-related people, the Cumans had ruled for several decades the territory stretching from the Volga to the Danube.[24] During the 1220s the Hungarians both checked their advance and sought their conversion. Paul and his companions began their mission in Hungary and then moved eastward. As Friar Gerald of Frachet relates it, the Dominican mission to the Cumans was to be a labor of many years that involved much Christ-like suffering and self-sacrifice:

Remembering the desire of Blessed Dominic to go and convert the pagans, especially the Cumans, who had absolutely no instruction about God, they invoked the guidance of the Holy Spirit and decided to send some virtuous brothers to that nation. There, after experiencing suffering and incredible hardships, they were rejected and forced to come back [to Hungary]. But the fire of the Holy Spirit and zeal for souls inspired them to try again. After a very difficult journey they

23. *Florilegium Casinensis*, 193.
24. Gerald de Frachet, *Vitae fratrum*, trans. and ed. Joseph Kenny, OP, www.op.org/ nigeriaop/kenny/VF.htm. (Now:www.josephkenny.joyeurs.com/VitaeFratrum.htm#INT RODUCTION); from Reichert, *MOPH* I.

reached those people near the Diepner [sic] river. There they often suffered hunger, thirst, lack of covering and persecutions, some of them were held captive and two were killed, but the others persevered in the preaching mission they had begun.[25]

After much hardship, their tireless missionizing eventually bore fruit, most notably in the case of the conversion of a Cuman leader named Boris, along with some of the members of his family. This success was followed up by the conversion of an even more important chieftain named Membrok and about a thousand people of his clan. Unfortunately for the friars, their preaching apostolate among the Cumans coincided with the coming of the Mongols, who brought death and destruction on an unprecedented scale to Dominican and Cuman alike:

> After much hard work, by God's help, a convent was established, and the brothers began to preach confidently among the people. Only God can count the number of people who were converted to the faith of our Lord Jesus Christ day after day. While the brothers' fervour and zeal for the conversion of these pagans was increasing more and more, God's hidden judgment permitted a persecution from the Tartars. This not only impeded the preaching of our brothers, but forced many of them to go sooner to the heavenly kingdom. Up to ninety brothers flew to the kingdom of heaven, some by the sword, others by arrows, spears, or fire.[26]

Gerald of Frachet also reproduces a letter from the Dominican missionaries, dispatched to the master-general of the Order, which testifies to their spiritual progress as well as to the continuing Mongol menace: "Many thousands of nobles and ordinary people of both sexes of that people received the grace of baptism, and they try as best they can to practice the Catholic faith. . . . But the cruelty of the Tartars is threatening them no less than other peoples in the east; it is even threatening them more, because they are nearer to the invaders."[27] Clearly, the Dominicans among the Cumans saw their role as missionary preachers

---

25. *Vitae fratrum*, 6.
26. Ibid., 6.1., "The mission to these pagans [Cumans] was interrupted while, as a result of the Tartar persecution, the Cumans were scattered to different parts of Greece, Bulgaria, Serbia, and other nearby regions. Finally most of them came to Hungary, where the king welcomed them. There, by common counsel and with the indispensable help of the king and queen, who were zealous for the faith, ten brothers were sent to preach to them. Up to today they are day and night at work in their office of preaching and have baptized many thousands of Cumans. Day by day, with God's help and the brothers' zealous work, more and more are being baptized and united in the faith."
27. Ibid., 6.2.

as an extension of the work of Christ and His Apostles. They are concerned with the liturgical and sacramental life of their new Cuman converts, as well as with the threat posed to their physical lives by the Tartars ("the men from Tartarus," i.e., hell). As was stated at the outset, I believe there is much to the fact that Dominic chose Friar Paul, the author of the Order's (then) only manual on penance, to head the team that was sent to convert the pagan Cumans, the pagans Dominic loved most. The "zeal for souls" of the Dominican missionaries in Hungary is in fact very reminiscent of that possessed by their founder.

That the friars were more interested in saving the Cumans from devils (temporal and eternal) than in ensuring that another "outside group" walk in lock-step with homogenous Catholic Europe is evident not only from the above accounts, but even more clearly still from others. Confession and worthy reception of Communion, the intercession of saints, and the ever-present threat of tempting devils constitute the most important elements in the Dominican tales of Cuman converts. Boris, the King of the Cumans, after receiving Baptism and practicing Catholicism for some years, confesses and receives Holy Communion before his death in the chapel of the Holy Virgin, where he is also eventually buried.[28] A similar story concerns Membrok. We are told that King Andrew of Hungary (the father of Saint Elizabeth) had the great joy of being this powerful chieftain's godfather. Membrok too, in his last end, was assisted by the brothers; in his throes he said, "Let all Cuman pagans leave me now, because I see horrible demons around them; let only the brothers and the baptized Cumans stay, because the two brothers who were martyred are waiting for me to take me to the joys that they preached." He then died "with wonderful joy" and was buried in the same chapel of the Blessed Virgin Mary.[29] Acting in concert with the sinless Blessed Virgin as co-redeemers in the salvation of others was the guiding spirit of the Dominican mission to the pagans:

> In the early days of the Order a brother was commanded to go to the Cumans to help in their conversion. He was gravely disturbed at this assignment and asked a hermit friend of his, who was a true friend of God, to pray to the Lord for him, since he could hardly believe that such an assignment was useful for him. The following night that pious and holy man prayed to the Lord with the greatest affection for him. The Lord showed him this consoling vision: He seemed to see a large river with a bridge over it, and men of different religious orders going over it happily, but one by one. The Preaching Brothers did not go over

28. Ibid., 6.1.
29. Ibid.

the bridge, but swam across the river, each of them dragging a vessel full of men. When some of them began to fail because of the excessive labour, he saw the Blessed Mary helping and lifting them up with her kind hand, so that they crossed by her help. After they crossed the river, he saw them with those they had carried in a most pleasant place, rejoicing with unspeakable joy. The hermit told this vision to the brother, strengthened very much by it, he fulfilled his assignment, clearly recognizing that brothers who work for the salvation of men have heavier but more fruitful work to do than other religious who work for their own salvation. This work is full of unspeakable joy and in it they have the Blessed Virgin as their special helper.[30]

An Order of monks who work *directly* for "the salvation of men," rather than "for their own salvation," was unprecedented in Christian history. Yet it was precisely this charism which defined the Order of Preachers.

In November of 1215, more than 400 bishops and more than 800 priors and abbots answered Pope Innocent III's summons for the opening of the Fourth Lateran Council. Canon ten treats of the role of the bishop and of preaching:

Among other things that pertain to the salvation of the Christian people, the food of the word of God is above all necessary, because as the body is nourished by material food, so is the soul nourished by spiritual food, since "not in bread alone doth man live but in every word that proceedeth from the mouth of God" (Matt 4:4). It often happens that bishops, on account of their manifold duties or bodily infirmities or because of hostile invasions or other reasons, to say nothing of *lack of learning, which must be absolutely condemned in them and is not to be tolerated in the future,* are themselves unable to minister the word of God to the people, especially in large and widespread dioceses. Wherefore we decree that bishops provide suitable men, powerful in work and word, to exercise with fruitful result the office of preaching, who in place of the bishops, since these cannot do it, diligently visiting the people committed to them, may instruct them by word and example. And when they are in need, let them be supplied with the necessities, lest for want of these they may be compelled to abandon their work at the very beginning. Wherefore we command that in cathedral churches as well as in conventual churches suitable men be appointed

30. Ibid., 1.6.

whom the bishops may use as coadjutors and assistants, not only in the office of preaching but also in hearing confessions, imposing penances, and in other matters that pertain to the salvation of souls. If anyone neglect to comply with this, he shall be subject to severe punishment.[31]

Here, again, we see the concern of Diego and Dominic even at the level of the Church universal. Lateran IV was especially concerned with the second of our episcopal virtues: education. The council fathers condemn the bishops' "lack of learning," and threaten that it will "no longer be tolerated."

Dominic and his followers were trained in Scripture and theology; they were therefore the perfect vicars for their bishop in fulfilling his office of preaching:

Unlike earlier lay preachers, Dominic and his priests aspired to be known as orthodox and theologically informed evangelists. Armed with an education considered sufficient and appropriate by their diocesan, the preachers of Toulouse aimed to do what only bishops and legatine preachers had been allowed to do before: they would preach doctrine. Foulques' official sanction for them to do just that more than anything else set Dominic's friars apart from most other contemporary preachers. Those lay groups which had earlier been given papal approval for their preaching had been limited to moral exhortation and had been excluded quite explicitly from teaching doctrine . . . even Francis and his followers initially could do no more than preach penance. What the Church needed, and needed badly, were preachers who would not suffer from such restraint, nor feel the pull of the cloister, preachers who were educated and who could be trusted to represent the Church's teaching and to defend it from all attacks. This is the gap Dominic and his confreres attempted to fill with the help of Bishop Foulques, right from the start.[32]

"He who moves the hearts of the people by preaching causes fruit to grow. But he who hears confessions bears fruit, because with his conscience as witness he knows what he has accomplished in the person who goes to confession. For to preach is to sow, but to hear confessions is to reap."[33] So averred Peter of Reims, prior of the Dominican convent of St Jacques and prior provincial of France. Peter was underscoring the profound connection between preaching and hearing confession within

31. Lateran IV, *Internet Medieval Sourcebook*; www.fordham.edu/halsall/sbook.html (From H. J. Schroeder, *Disciplinary Decrees of the General Councils: Text, Translation and Commentary* (St Louis, MO: B. Herder, 1937), 236–96.

32. Mulchahey, *First the Bow is Bent*, 8–9.

33. Pierre de Reims, in D'Avray, *The Preaching of the Friars*, 50.

the context of the theology of sin, repentance, and reconciliation. This Dominican prior's statement is in harmony with the pronouncements of the Fourth Lateran Council, which also drew attention to the pastoral connection between preaching and confession.[34] Peter's profession is also proof that there was a like connection between the mission of Dominic's order and the mandate of the council. As good coadjutors, they could sow the seeds of repentance for sin in the field of preaching and reap the harvest in the absolution of the confessional

> faithfully and to the best of their ability the penance imposed, receiving reverently at least at Easter the sacrament of the Eucharist, unless perchance at the advice of their own priest they may for a good reason abstain for a time from its reception; otherwise they shall be cut off from the Church (excommunicated) during life and deprived of Christian burial in death. . . . Let the priest be discreet and cautious that he may pour wine and oil into the wounds of the one injured after the manner of a skillful physician, carefully inquiring into the circumstances of the sinner and the sin, from the nature of which he may understand what kind of advice to give and what remedy to apply, making use of different experiments to heal the sick one.[35]

The council fathers have here employed the same theological language of sin-as-wound and confessor-as-divine-physician that we have encountered previously in Parisian-authored manuals for confession and preaching. Lateran IV took the analogy quite literally, as evidenced in canon twenty-two:

> Since bodily infirmity is sometimes caused by sin, the Lord saying to the sick man whom he had healed: "Go and sin no more, lest some worse thing happen to thee" (John 5:14) we declare in the present decree and strictly command that when physicians of the body are called to the bedside of the sick, before all else they admonish them to call for the physician of souls, so that after spiritual health has been restored to them, the application of bodily medicine may be of greater benefit, for the cause being removed the effect will pass away. We publish this decree for the reason that some, when they are sick and are advised by the physician in the course of the sickness to attend to the salvation of their soul, give up all hope and yield more easily to the danger of death. If any physician shall transgress this decree after it has

---

34. "We command that in cathedral churches as well as in conventual churches suitable men be appointed whom the bishops may use as coadjutors and assistants, not only in the office of preaching but also in hearing confessions, imposing penances, and in other matters that pertain to the salvation of souls."
35. Lateran IV.

been published by bishops, let him be cut off (*arceatur*) from the Church till he has made suitable satisfaction for his transgression. And since the soul is far more precious than the body, we forbid under penalty of anathema that a physician advise a patient to have recourse to sinful means for the recovery of bodily health.[36]

The Council clearly sought to inspire a thorough reform of pastorship throughout Christendom, a renewal of the *cura animarum*, a renewal that Dominic's order was uniquely qualified to implement. Thus Katherine Jansen speaks of "the concomitant emergence of mendicant preaching, and the Fourth Lateran Council's reformulation of the sacrament of penance ... the friars worked out the practical implications of the Council's penitential theology."[37] It would appear that an active and innovative collaboration between Dominic and the newly-elected pontiff, Honorius III, made the merger a reality. In the face of canon thirteen, which forbade any new religious orders, the late Pope Innocent had sent Fulk and Dominic back to Toulouse, encouraging them to meet with their confreres and to decide upon an already established monastic rule which should govern their order. As a cathedral canon regular, Dominic was quite comfortable with selecting the Rule of St Augustine. This ancient rule was also the centerpiece of the more recently conceived Premonstratensian Order. Dominic and his group made the necessary verbal alterations that would enable this rule to work for them.[38]

On December 22, 1216, Pope Honorius approved Dominic's order in the bull "*Religiosam vitam*," placing the new community at Toulouse under his patronage. It would seem, however, that the young prior's "longing for the salvation of all," which Friar Jordan purports back to Dominic's days in Osma, emboldened him to propose to the pope a more universal endeavor. No more than four weeks had passed before Honorius signed another bull, "*Olim in partibus Tolosanis*," in which he implored the masters and students of Paris to come to Toulouse to assist "the Catholic preachers," who were actively missionizing there. We are thus led to believe that Dominic himself, or his associates together with him, were about to leave the precincts of Toulouse, if for no other reason than to recruit new foot-soldiers. The choice of Paris and its traditional "concern for practical moral problems" was deliberate, and tells us much about Dominic's intentions for his rising order. Dominic and

36. Ibid.
37. Katherine L. Jansen, *The Making of the Magdalen: preaching and popular devotion in the later Middle Ages* (Princeton, NJ: Princeton University Press, 2000), 201.
38. Mulchahey, *First the Bow is Bent*, 19.

Honorius, however, were not finished yet. Two days after the release of "*Olim in partibus Tolsanis*," the pope issued "*Gratiarum omnium*," in which, for the first time, the word "*praedicatores*" is used to denote Dominic's followers. The other significance of "*Gratiarum omnium*" was that it clearly established that the order no longer answered to a local bishop, but to the bishop of Rome. A third bull, "*Justis petentium*," was released on February 7, 1217. "*Justis petentium*" was a crucial amendment to his first bull of approbation, "*Religiosam vitam*." This latest document changed the profession of Dominic's members from a profession to a "church" (*ecclesia*) to that of a "monastery" (*monsterium*). Fulk had gifted the Church of St Romain to Dominic for his use in Toulouse, and St Romain is directly referred to in "*Religiosam vitam*." By substituting the word "monastery," Honorius was freeing Dominic and his friars from an exclusive attachment to the Church of St Romain, or the diocese of Toulouse. Significantly, he also changed the wording of Dominic's formal title from "Prior of St Romain" to simply "you as prior, my son." There could be no question now: Dominic and Honorius had created wide enough legal loopholes to fit a universal Order of Preachers outside the gates of the city of Toulouse.

During the first years of its official existence, the Dominican Order found a welcome home in many quarters and a grudging acceptance in others. Almost four years to the day he issued "*Justis petentium*," Honorius felt confident enough to issue a final salvo, this one addressed to all archbishops, bishops, and priests of Christendom. On February 4, 1221, the pontiff released the aptly entitled encyclical letter "*Cum qui recipit prophetam*," in which he declared for the first time that Dominicans who were priests be allowed to hear confessions. It was a priority the pontiff surely had in mind since the close of the Lateran Council; canon ten's prescriptions for "suitable men" who could serve as episcopal coadjutors resounds loudly enough in *Cum qui recipit prophetam*.[39]

The timing of the release of *Cum qui recipit prophetam* may have been another "Dominican event" coordinated by Dominic in concert with Honorius. Besides the fact that it was issued at the start of Lent, the traditional penitential time of the Church year, it may also have been promulgated in advance of the General Chapter meeting which the Order was to hold on Pentecost of that year (May 30). It was Dominic's plan at this meeting to authorize preachers to be sent to Britain, Ireland, Scandinavia, Poland, the Near East, and to his beloved Cumans in Hungary. If the encyclical and the chapter were coordinated, it would further dem-

39. Vladimir Koudelka, ed. *Monumenta diplomatica*, no 143, 145–46, in Mulchahey, *First the Bow is Bent*, 53.

onstrate that "Dominican mission," properly understood, was driven by meditation on the theology of sin, repentance, and reconciliation.

While the tradition of sin, pardon, and preaching to the faithful (even the infidel) that we have been elucidating thus far hit its stride in the opening decades of the thirteenth century and received confirmation in the canons of the Lateran Council, it had to share the stage with another tradition—the same anti-Judaism we first witnessed among the Fathers. It remains to be examined how the two coexisted in the Church's canons and vied for expression in its practices.

Four brief canons (67–70) comprise the sum total of the Fourth Lateran Council's pronouncements regarding Jews. However, although they comprise but a small portion of its legislation, these Lateran laws are important, not only for their ultimate impact on the Jewish community, but for the fact that they represent the first time that Jews are addressed at any length in the documents of a general council of the Church. Canon 67 is ostensibly concerned with Jews and the economic well-being of Christendom. It states that as the Church has been increasingly successful in curbing the faithful from charging usurious interest rates on loans, it has done so only to find that "Jewish perfidy" has come to occupy their place in extorting "heavy and immoderate" interest from Christians.

Without denying an underlying pastoral concern for sin (in this case usury), it is probably closer to the truth to see in this canon more temporal and mercenary motives. But for our purposes, the chief significance of this statute would seem to lie in its overt hostility toward the Jews exemplified by the word "perfidy." Legion are the references to the "perfidy" of the Jews (and others "infidels") in centuries of letters from popes, as well as in legislation of local councils. Although the primary Latin definition of *perfidia* would seem to be "faith-less-ness," or "disbelief," Edward Synan seems to observe rightly that its secondary meaning, "treachery," "cannot have been far from the mind of Latin speakers":[40] treachery, as in guilty of the *sin* of "treason" against the King of the uni-

---

40. Edward A Synan, *The Popes and the Jews in the Middle Ages* (New York, NY: Macmillan, 1966), 175, nt. 15. "Furthermore, since both Judaism and Christianity are religions of covenant, any deficiency of faith is in some way a violation of trust as well as a failure to assent to dogmatic propositions." Synan provides the following bibliography: Erik Peterson, *Le mystère des Juifs et des Gentils dans l'église, suivi d'un essai sur l'Apocalypse* (Paris: Desclée, de Brouwer, 1935).

verse, the Lord God, for not accepting His Son as Messiah and Savior. This indictment by Catholic prelates was routinely laid at the door of the Jewish community as if Jesus's messianic appearance, salvific Death, and Resurrection were self-evident biblical truths.[41] Catholic prelates of the Middle Ages seem to have forgotten the incredulity of Christ's closest companions![42]

This hostility toward the Jewish people because they were perceived as flagrantly disregarding the obvious is also evinced in canon 69: "Since it is absurd that a *blasphemer of Christ* exercise authority over Christians, we on account of the boldness of transgressors renew in this general council what the Synod of Toledo [589] wisely enacted in this matter, prohibiting Jews from being given preference in the matter of public offices, since in such capacity they are most troublesome to the Christians."[43] (emphasis mine) Few Christian rulers actually took this prohibition to heart, so what seems most important about this measure is, again, the mentality it reveals of the people who enacted it.

To paraphrase Louis Bouyer, while many, if not most, educated Christians today "tend to assume that our non-Christian antagonists are in complete good faith and to be respected *a priori*, indeed that their ignorance [of the truth of Christianity] must be invincible [sincere], it seems undeniable" that the prevailing assumption of medieval Church authorities was quite otherwise. It seems right to say "authorities," because it is hard to generalize about the overwhelming majority of Catholic lay persons for whom we have no written evidence regarding their actual Chris-

---

41. Cf. Guido Kisch, *The Jews in Medieval Germany* (New York, NY: Ktav Pub. House, 1970), 323; Roth, *Medieval Jewish Civilization*, "Church and Jews," 168; as Nancy Turner writes: "Many popes, theologians, and secular rulers . . . reacted with anger and frustration at what they saw as the stubborn unreasonableness of the Jews for refusing to accept what Christians believed to be logically demonstrable Christian doctrines," 198, "Jewish Witness, Forced Conversion, and Island Living: John Duns Scotus on Jews and Judaism," in *Christian Attitudes Toward the Jews in the Middle Ages.*

42. Lk 24:13–35: "While they were conversing and arguing together, Jesus himself also drew near and went along with them; but their eyes were held, that they should not recognize him. . . .But one of them, named Cleophas answered and said to him, 'Art thou the only stranger in Jerusalem who does not know the things that have happened there in these days?' And he said to them, 'What things?'

"And they said to him, 'Concerning Jesus of Nazareth, who was a prophet, mighty in work and word before God and all the people'. . . .

"And he said to them, 'O foolish men, and slow of heart to believe all that the prophets have spoken! Was it not necessary that the Christ should suffer these things and enter into his glory?' And beginning with Moses and all the prophets, he interpreted to them in all the scriptures the things concerning himself."

43. Lateran IV, 69.

tian beliefs, let alone their views of Jews.[44] Roth, for example, maintains that

> Probably few ordinary Christians could have known precisely what being a Jew meant, since ignorance of the Bible and indeed of their own religion was so widespread. Most Christians, including even the nobility, were illiterate. Few went to church at all ... the local clergy were usually as illiterate as the laypeople, and sermons were rarely preached. .... Sources indicate that even in the High Middle Ages supposedly educated nobles often had little or no knowledge of the basic Gospel stories, and much less did the peasant or working class.[45]

If this worst-case historical scenario is an accurate one, then Roth has just penned one of the best *apologiae* for an Order of Preachers ever written!

As for the Catholic hierarchy's view of the Jews as guilty of the sin of deliberate disobedience to God, this is a mentality deserving of deeper examination, but we are more concerned with refuting charges that mendicancy developed a *novel* anti-Judaism than that it failed to reject an inherited, centuries-old institutionalized one. That later Dominican and Franciscan literature contains variations and permutations of the Church-sanctioned stereotypes of Jewish blindness and treacherousness is a fact not to be glossed over. We shall, however, limit our comments at present. Let it be noted for now that mendicancy inherited these prejudiced views; it did not invent them. Furthermore, we shall continue to find, even as we already have found, that certain theologians and preachers practiced and encouraged a medieval "toleration" simultaneously as they absorbed, even *reinforced*, prejudiced notions of "the Other." This is the novelty—one might say the paradox—we are examining.

To the casual student of history, canon 68 seems perhaps the most intrusive and intolerant of the whole Lateran Council:

> In some provinces a difference in dress distinguishes the Jews or Saracens from the Christians, but in certain others such a confusion has grown up that they cannot be distinguished by any difference. Thus it happens at times that through error Christians have relations with the women of Jews or Saracens, and Jews and Saracens with Christian women. Therefore, that they may not under pretext of error of this sort, excuse themselves in the future for the excesses of such prohibited intercourse, we decree that such Jews and Saracens of both

---

44. John Arnold, *Belief and Unbelief in Medieval Europe* (London: Hodder Arnold, 2005), 4.

45. Roth, *Medieval Jewish Civilization*, "Christian-Jewish Relations," 151.

sexes in every Christian province and at all times shall be marked off in the eyes of the public from other peoples through the character of their dress. Particularly, since it may be read in the writings of Moses [Num 15:37–41], that this very law has been enjoined upon them.[46]

The West today knows little of sumptuary legislation. In the East, however, hundreds of millions of women, for example, can testify to its deep and abiding persistence. In antiquity, laws distinguishing clothing were most often designed for distinguishing between social classes. Purple, for instance, as a color reserved solely for the emperor, springs to mind from Justinian's Code. When the Muslim Arabs conquered the Christian, Greco-Roman cities of the Middle East, sumptuary laws again distinguished the followers of Muhammad from the "People of the Book." As far as Medieval Christendom is concerned, the question that needs to be addressed is why the Church should have chosen in the opening decades of the thirteenth century to reassert an ancient, even biblical principle.

The "scholarship of intolerance" sees this canon (and Lateran IV in general) as the resurrection of full-blown persecution, the most strident attempt at polarization to date by the over-centralizing, over-reaching Roman Church. As Moore famously writes:

What is essential to the present argument is that Lateran IV laid down a machinery of persecution for Western Christendom, and especially a range of sanctions against those convicted, which was to prove adaptable to a much wider variety of victims than the heretics for whom it was designed. Jews had been the objects of increasing brutality during the previous two or three decades. . . . Jews had not enjoyed the legal rights to hold land or transmit property by inheritance, or the use or protection of the public courts in many parts of Western Europe, and to that extent their position was already similar to that which Lateran IV laid down for heretics. But the prescription of identifying clothing (a device which the inquisition later applied to the punishment of heresy, and found to be greatly feared) and the prohibition of Jews from public office served to underline their disabilities, and to confirm their place with heretics in the category of those who were subject to repression . . . the apparatus for the persecution of Jews in Europe was fully worked out during the thirteenth century . . . it was not until this time that drawings which depict Jews as physically distinctive—particularly with long, hooked noses—began to appear: like the badge of shame they were necessary. . . .[47]

46. Lateran IV, 68.
47. Moore, 10.

While we have no doubt that the *homogeneity factor* is present at some level in ecclesiastical legislation of this sort—as it is in most human laws—we find it far from a conclusive factor. Furthermore, it ought to be said that Moore's uses of words like "machinery," "victims," "repression," "badge of shame," etc. are nearly as pejorative and injurious to the reputation of the Catholic Church as the medieval Christian stereotypes he so deplores were for Jews.

The facts of the matter are these: in the first place, Lateran IV's legislation never actually called for a "badge," and neither do they necessarily impute "shame." What is more, in certain kingdoms, like those of Spain, the Lateran statutes (and repeated papal letters) went widely unheeded by temporal authorities. Although in "the same year [1215] the pope wrote to the archbishops and bishops of France, and *no doubt similar letters were sent to other countries,* clarifying that Jews should be ordered to wear 'clothing by which they might be distinguished from Christians,'" yet Innocent III specifically stipulated "that they *should not be forced to do so if this would incur danger to their lives.*"[48] (emphasis mine) Hardly a persecutory consideration!

To what primary motivation then ought we to attribute the Council's regulation of clothing for non-Christians? Few scholars seem willing to accept canon 68 at face value: "through error Christians have relations with the women of Jews or Saracens. . . . Therefore, that they may not under pretext of error of this sort, excuse themselves in the future for the excesses of such prohibited intercourse . . ." Is sex really to blame? Could interreligious intercourse be happening at such an alarming rate that it sent scads of celibate old prelates scurrying to put pen to parchment to squelch it? Well, if Roth is right that "few ordinary Christians could have known precisely what being a Jew meant, since ignorance of the Bible and indeed of their own religion was so widespread. Most Christians, including even the nobility, were illiterate. Few went to church at all," then what is so improbable about couplings so instinctual?

However, even if we lack statistical data on "sex and the single serf" as it were, David Nirenberg has proposed that the Church's anxiety over

---

48. Neither is it entirely fair, as some do, to compare the Church's statute distinguishing between Jewish and Christian garb with the totalitarian, anti-Semitic imposition of the yellow star on German Jews by the Nazis. In the first place, the Church's clothing requirement was targeted at Muslims as well as Jews, so there was nothing inherently anti-Semitic about it. (For that matter, anti-Semitism, strictly understood, is a racist theory from the nineteenth century).

such interfaith intimacies depended "not so much on the quantitative reality of sexual interaction (anxieties need not correspond to the real) but on far more complicated cultural logics."[49] "Modern commentators" have assumed, he writes, "that the language of crisis and of sex was a pretext for discriminatory pressure intended to further evangelization"; but the driving motivations of Church authorities might have been far more "psychologically and theologically complex." Or as Stow remarks, "The concept of special Jewish dress was not itself a new one. Quite likely, it was borrowed from the . . . centuries-old Islamic practice of making Jews wear honey-colored turbans or sashes. It is also becoming increasingly clear that Innocent III was not rationalizing. . . . Sexual contact between Christians and non-Christians—whether Jews or Muslims—was a reality, and one that had long been a thorn in the ecclesiastical side."[50]

Further canonical appraisals of Jews are found twenty years later in the *Decretals*, a systematic codification of all the Church's law ordered by Gregory IX and undertaken by none other than Raymond of Peñafort himself. Title Six of the *Decretals* is dedicated to "Jews, Saracens, and their slaves." Thirteen of its chapters cover Christian-Jewish relations. The first two chapters, as well as the last chapter, prohibit Jews from owning Christian slaves; while chapters five, eight, and thirteen forbid other Christians from close service to Jews. Chapter one is an extract from the Council of Macon and chapter two is an extract of a letter from Pope Gregory the Great to the bishop of Lucca. Chapter eight is taken from a letter of Pope Alexander III and chapter thirteen is from Innocent III. These excerpts were culled from the *Decretum*, so, again, we see that canon law is essentially case law and that Raymond of Peñafort added no novelty or personal opinion.[51]

What is most pertinent for us about these chapters, however, is their strong prejudiced thrust. The Council of Macon, for instance, declares that: "It is abominable that a blasphemer of Christ hold in the chains of servitude one whom the Lord Christ redeemed."[52] Once more we see the contumelious categorization of *Jews-qua-Jews* as sinners, collectively guilty of blasphemy for not recognizing Christ as Messiah. Even more

---

49. David Nirenberg, "Conversion, Sex, and Segregation: Jews and Christians in Medieval Spain," *American Historical Review* (Oct. 2002): 1065–1093. Thanks to Krista Sue-Lo Twu for reminding me.

50. Kenneth Stow, *Alienated Minority, The Jews of Medieval Europe* (Cambridge, MA: Harvard University Press, 1992), 247–48.

51. These issues reappear in his *Summa de poenitentia*, but here they are treated almost last (4.6–7), though in greater detail.

striking is the caustic rhetoric of Pope Alexander, who not only classifies them as obstinate sinners, but portrays them as maniacally plotting the destruction of the innocent: "The Jews, moved by their enmity for the human race, through continual conversation and excessive familiarity, bend the souls of the simple to their superstition and perfidy."[53]

But perhaps the most derisive remarks of the *Decretals* are those of Innocent III: "Rather as slaves rejected by God, in whose death they wickedly conspired, they shall . . . recognize themselves as the slaves of those whom Christ's death set free at the same time that it enslaved them. For as soon as they begin to gnaw in the manner of a mouse and to bite in the manner of a serpent, one may fear lest the fire that one keeps in his bosom burn up the gnawed parts."[54]

Vitriolic indeed, but one must remember that in its original context this quote from Innocent was an indignant response to purported Jewish outrages against Jesus in the Eucharist (and the bodily integrity of Christian women).[55] Furthermore, as Stow observes, "Although various researchers have seen it as either an outpouring of gratuitous wrath and hatred . . . or . . . as an expression of a desire to eliminate the Jew from society and an attack on the foundations of Jewish existence, *Etsi iudeos* must, rather, be seen as an outburst of papal anger at Jews who have broken the terms" of their social "contract" with Christians, in which one group is clearly the superior and the other the inferior.[56]

52. Chap. 1, Chazan, *Church, State, and Jew in the Middle Ages*, 28; from Emil Friedberg, *Corpus Iuris Canonis*, vol. II (Leipzig: Bernhard Tauchnitz, 1881), 771–78; English translation adapted from Grayzel, *The Church and the Jews in the XIIIth Century*, 2 ed. (New York, NY: Hermon Press, 1966).

53. Ibid., Chap. 8, 31.

54. Ibid., Chap. 13, 33.

55. "Furious that the Jews at Eastertime were forcing Christian wet-nurses to express their milk following reception of the Eucharist, Innocent declared that the Jews must realize [sic] that their 'guilt has consigned them to Perpetual Servitude' and that their actions must exemplify this state. The Jews' 'servitude', as canonists like Hostiensis stressed, was neither a real one, nor was it a foil with which to parry imperial claims to power. It was rather a concept, a mnemonic device, combining the principle of 'subservience' enunciated in 1063 by Alexander II with the exegetical consensus based on Paul in Galatians (4:23) that the Jews were the offspring of Hagar the serving woman. Its purpose was to emblemise [sic] correct Jewish behavior and to remind Christians as well as Jews, of the rightful parameters limiting Jewish behavior and of the need to maintain their integrity." K. Stow, *The New Cambridge Medieval History*, 1198–1300, ed. D. Abulafia (Cambridge: Cambridge University Press, vol. 5, 1999), 206–7.

56. Stow, "Hatred of the Jews or Love of the Church?" *Popes, church, and Jews in the Middle Ages: confrontation and response* (Aldershot, Great Britain; Burlington, VT: Ashgate, 2007), 81.

Nevertheless, we see that the rhetoric of the-Jews-as-Christ-killers has formally made its way into the canon law of the Catholic Church. The Jews are said to be serving a collective sentence of servitude because the leaders of their forefathers conspired to kill Jesus. "Keeping them in their place" will keep them from fresh blasphemies. It must be said, therefore, that by including such opprobrious papal phrases in the Church's definitive canonical code Raymond should be held reasonably responsible for reinforcing and disseminating demeaning stereotypes of the Jew. And this all the more so, since as Muldoon writes, "non-Christians had only a small place in the *Decretum* and because of the manner in which that book had been constructed, material dealing with non-Christians could be uncovered only with some difficulty. The *Decretals,* however, was compiled in such a way as to facilitate the identification of material concerning such persons."[57] However, it is equally to be remarked that, in stark contrast to the *Decretals,* Raymond, in his own *Summa de poenitentia,* apart from repeating the technical charge of "vile blasphemy," does not record a single slanderous sentence or demonic depiction of the Jews (though he had a perfect opportunity to do so); and we have already made mention of his *Summa's* wide and lasting influence in its own right.

Several things seem discernible in the attitude of the Church hierarchy disclosed through the *Decretals*: first, an inability on the part of churchmen to see that their teachings were not self-evident and second, a failure to perceive what might be deemed cultural snobbery. The successors of St Peter seem as guilty as their first-century co-religionists whom Paul reprimanded:

> If the root is holy, so are the branches. But if some of the branches were broken off, and you a wild shoot, were grafted in their place to share the richness of the olive tree, do not boast over the branches. If you do boast, remember it is not you that support the root, but the root that supports you. You will say, "Branches were broken off so that I might be grafted in." That is true. They were broken off because of their unbelief, but you stand fast only through faith. So do not become proud, but stand in awe. For if God did not spare the natural branches, neither will he spare you. (Rom. 11:16)

This leads us to believe that the vulgar expressions used in the Church's canons toward Jews have as much to do with fallen human nature's propensity to dislike the "Other" as with the actual content of

57. James Muldoon, *Popes, Lawyers, Infidels: The Church and the Non-Christian World, 1250–1550* (Philadelphia, PA: University of Pennsylvania Press, 1979), 4.

Christian doctrine.[58] However, this is not to say that Christian theology played no detrimental role toward Jews; this is witnessed in chapters fifteen, sixteen, and eighteen of the *Decretals*, which reiterate the teachings of Lateran IV, of Innocent III, and Gregory IX that Jews may not hold temporal office over Christians nor give "invitation" for intimacies with them by lack of distinguishing dress. (These matters are likewise treated by Raymond in his *Summa*.) As we have witnessed already, they demand a more satisfactory explanation than mere "prejudice" or "power." The anti-Judaistic tradition originally found in the Fathers and reappearing in the medieval canons seems first and foremost to be the fruit of a *misapplication* of the Catholic sacramental principle.

The striking feature, even of a cursory examination of these ordinances from the *Decretals*, is the Church's preoccupation with symbolism, or sacramentality. If, for example, one accepts the principle that Jesus *has* liberated Christians from the slavery of sin (unseen reality), it is incomprehensible that they can now be in servitude (seen reality) to those not in Christ (Jews and Saracens) and not so liberated. Likewise, if the point of princes and princely government is to so regulate society (seen reality) as to prepare men and advance them on their pilgrimage to the Heavenly Jerusalem (unseen reality), then how could those tied to the earthly Jerusalem—notably Jews—possibly be permitted to rule over (i.e., assist, encourage) those baptized subjects and heirs to the Kingdom? As Stow explains, "Reality was thus to mirror the belief that Christianity had superceded [sic] Judaism, liberating the Christian through grace while the Jew remained enslaved under the 'Law.' Only through their Perpetual Servitude and inferiority to Christians could the Jews serve as a true witness to Christian liberation."[59]

To put it perhaps clumsily, but maybe all the more accurately: Church leaders saw the society of men as a tangible reality which must needs mirror certain theological realities. If the Jews were adversely impacted by its canons, this had more to do with the Church's scrupulousness to make the temporal "pegs" of medieval civilization fit preternatural

58. As Pope Emeritus Benedict XVI writes: "Not only a communal dynamic exists [uniting disparate peoples], but equally communal divisions, barriers against others, contradictions that exclude.... We have been talking just now about the unity of the human being and about his being secretly touched by the truth spoken by God. We are now brought to recognize that there must be in opposition to this a negative factor in human existence: an alienation that hinders our perceiving things and that, at least partially, cuts men off from the truth and thus also from one another." Pope Benedict XVI (Joseph Cardinal Ratzinger), *Truth and Tolerance,* 65.

59. Stow, "Hatred of the Jews," 81.

"holes" than with actual lived experience of the Jewish community and consequent contempt for it. One could say a "sacra*mentality*" taken to its extremes is the root cause of ecclesiastical anti-Judaism. As Romano Guardini writes:

> The immediacy with which the Middle Ages saw the absolute reality of God and the promised eternal life as the essential thing, threatened . . . to depreciate the finite and temporal. The finite appeared merely as the shadowy reflection of the absolute, and time as the antechamber of eternity, without any reality of its own. The symbolic character of creation was so strongly felt that creation itself was not looked upon as having sufficient reality. . . . Truth [however] remains truth, no matter what the price. And it was indeed truth which the modern conscientiousness recognized in opposition to the Middle Ages: the genuine, meaningful reality of finite being, which demands our action. In all our admiration for the greatness, the unity and the fervor of the medieval concept of the world we must not forget that it contained, at all points, the religious short-circuit. The absolute was so strongly felt that the finite and its own meaning were not given proper and proportionate consideration.[60]

"The symbolic character of creation" leads us to consider more deeply the Church's understanding of the term "sacrament." "A sacrament," writes St Augustine "is a sign of a sacred thing."[61] In its broadest definition, then, we may say that, beginning with the Book of Genesis, Jews and Christians have always viewed reality in sacramental terms, and thus it is appropriate to dub this mental outlook a sacra*mentality*: "In the image of God he created him, male and female he created them" (Gen 1:27). Not simply man, however, but all reality in the Judeo-Christian experience is said in some way to show forth the countenance of its Creator:

> For all men were by nature foolish who were in ignorance of God, and who from the good things seen did not succeed in knowing Him Who IS [YHWH], and from studying the works did not discern the artisan; but either fire, or wind, or the swift air, or the circuit of the stars, or the mighty water, or the luminaries of heaven, the governors of the world, they considered gods. Now if out of joy in their beauty they thought them gods, let them know how far more excellent is the Lord than these; for the original source of beauty fashioned them. Or if they were

---

60. Romano Guardini, *The World and the Person*, trans. Stella Lange (Chicago, IL: Henry Regnery Co., 1965), 14–15.
61. Augustine, *Letters*, 138, 1.

struck by their might and energy, let them from these things realize how much more powerful is he who made them. For from the greatness and beauty of created things their original author by analogy is seen. (Wis. 13:1–5)

From the seen we come to "know" the unseen. This was the testimony of St Paul, the converted Jew, Saul of Tarsus: "Ever since the creation of the world his invisible nature, namely his eternal power and Deity, has been clearly perceived in the things that have been made" (Rom. 1:20). This is one level of sacramental approach to the universe, the level according to created nature.

But, as in the Book of Wisdom, so too Paul warns that to reject God's created order is to carve idols of one's own making and constitutes the essence of human sin:

So they are without excuse; for although *they knew God they did not honour him as God or give thanks to him, but they became futile in their thinking and their senseless minds were darkened.* Claiming to be wise, they became fools, and exchanged the glory of the immortal God for images resembling mortal man or birds or animals or reptiles. Therefore God gave them up in the lusts of their hearts to impurity, to the dishonouring of their bodies among themselves, because *they exchanged the truth about God for a lie* and worshipped and served the creature rather than the Creator, who is blessed for ever! Amen. (Rom. 1:20–25) (emphasis mine)

To Church authorities like Paul, all sin begins with the rejection of God and his natural order. Sin is a violation of objective truth—which all men ought to know by the use of their reason. No mention is made of any "leap" of "Christian faith."

The notion of human reason's unaided ability to know God's existence and the objective truth about man is, of course, the centerpiece of the scholastic philosophy of St Thomas Aquinas. It is expressed throughout his *Summa contra gentiles and Summa theologiae*:

Since all things subject to Divine providence are ruled and measured by the eternal law ... among all others, the rational creature is subject to Divine providence in the most excellent way, in so far as it partakes of a share of providence, by being provident both for itself and for others. Wherefore it has a share of the Eternal Reason, whereby it has a natural inclination to its proper act and end: and this participation of the eternal law in the rational creature is called the natural law ... thus implying that the light of natural reason, whereby we discern what is good and what is evil, which is the function of the natural law, is nothing else than an imprint on us of the Divine light. It is therefore evident that the natural law is nothing else than the rational creature's participation of the eternal law.[62]

For medieval theologians like Thomas, any human law must agree with the natural law (God's Truth) or it is automatically an "unjust" law. How then can human law "sanction" Jewish (or Muslim) worship, since, from a Christian standpoint, these activities no longer reflect the "right form" of religion? This brings us to the heart of the medieval Catholic idea of toleration.

In antiquity, *tolerantia* was especially found in the writings of the Stoics, and it meant the bearing of anything troublesome to the mind or body. The term is also plentiful in the writings of the Church Fathers, where the term takes on a religious significance.[63] The individual Christian believer patiently endures the wrongs of this life, not so much to become the stoic master of himself as to become the humble servant of an all-provident God, who allows the rain to fall equally on the just and the unjust. But with the dawn of medieval Christendom, *tolerantia* began to take on societal, rather than individual, connotations. The word found its way into legal usage within the context of sin and its wider place in society. "Toleration" came to denote "not taking punitive action" against what were considered objectively disordered acts, either by individuals or groups of individuals. The development of *tolerantia* was especially aided by the growth of canon law. Both the *Decretum* of Gratian (1140) and the *Decretales* of Gregory IX (1234) repeatedly give instances in which evil practices should be borne with, and both use the word *tolerare.* As we shall see, examples of Jewish worship are maintained in both collections as conspicuous examples of practices to be "tolerated."[64]

One further item of Christian-Jewish contention must first be addressed, however, one which also involves anti-Jewish allegations against the Dominican Order and Raymond of Peñafort, charges involving denigration of the Talmud.[65] This episode clearly shows the tension

62. *Summa* I. I. 91.2; www.newadvent.org/Summa.

63. Bejczy, "*Tolerantia,*" 368.

64. Ibid., 368–69.

65. "Raymond de Peñaforte—who served as papal confessor when Gregory IX received Donin at the curia, who stood at the helm of the Order of Friars Preachers when the Dominicans played a leading role in the *auto de fe* of 1242 against the Talmud ... clearly shared the view of contemporary postbiblical Judaism as a heretical departure from the biblical norm." As shall become evident, Cohen, in an attempt to make the pieces of his thesis fit, is mistaken on virtually all three of these counts.

between the twin traditions of anti-Judaism and that of formal forbearance we have been following thus far.

The story of the "Paris Talmud Trial" begins with Nicholas Donin, a Christian convert from Judaism about whom little is known except for the fact he had a serious axe to grind. In 1236, he approached Pope Gregory IX "with a list of charges against rabbinic Judaism—the postbiblical, 'oral' tradition to which the Jews of his day adhered. Donin leveled most of his accusations against the Talmud, but he also used Jewish liturgy, rabbinic commentaries on the Bible and Talmud, and various collections of *midrashim* to substantiate his charges."[66] When Gregory IX finally got around to investigating Donin's charges against the Talmud, he issued a letter addressed to the Christian kings of Europe, in which he repeated Donin's allegations and asked that on the first Sabbath of Lent of the following year (March 3, 1240), while Jews would be gathered at synagogue, all their books be taken for proper examination and given into the custody of trusted Dominicans and Franciscans.[67] It would seem, however, that only Louis IX of France actually carried out the pope's orders, and that, furthermore, he was disposed to allow the rabbis an opportunity to defend the Talmud before consigning it to flames.[68]

The existence of the Talmud was apparently something of a "revelation" to thirteenth-century prelates. As Hyam Maccoby remarks upon the Talmudic defense of Rabbi Yehiel ben Joseph:

66. Cohen, *The Friars and the Jews*, 60; Cohen emphasizes that the first nine of Donin's theses "concern the Jews' allegiance to rabbinic doctrine and their neglect of biblical precepts" (Cohen, *Living Letters of the Law*, 321). He argues that Donin was trying to paint the Talmud as a deviation from the Old Testament and that Raymond of Peñafort (as papal chaplain) and Gregory IX—individuals already obsessed with doctrinal regularity—came to view the Talmud and contemporary Jewish use of it, as heresy (ibid., 322). In the first place, by April of 1236, Raymond was on a boat bound for Barcelona, and thus was probably nowhere near the pope when he received Donin's thirty-five theses. Moreover, because of severe ill-health, it is highly unlikely that he was still conducting much official business for Gregory IX while he was at the curia during the first three months of that year. The evidence suggests that Raymond was not a party to the Donin matter in any direct way. As for the pope, he did not even respond in any official capacity for another three years. Cohen himself, in his more recent *Living Letters of the Law*, has toned down his language regarding a supposed role for Raymond in the Donin affair: "He served as Gregory's personal confessor, perhaps even until Nicholas Donin brought his indictment of the Talmud to the curia" (334).

67. Solomon Grayzel, *The Church and Jews in the XIIIth Century* (Philadelphia, PA: Dropsie College for Hebrew and Cognate Learning, 1933), 239–43.

68. John Hood, *Aquinas and the Jews* (Philadelphia: University of Pennsylvania Press, 1995), 35.

Yehiel's impassioned reply that the Talmud *was* Judaism must have come as something of a surprise to his Christian interlocutors. They had thought of the Talmud as something new-fangled and extraneous to Judaism. As Inquisitors, therefore . . . they were in something of a quandary. For it was not their business to interfere with Judaism itself, which had to remain in a state of suspended animation, so to speak, until the time of the conversion of the Jews as a body to Christianity. The very existence of the Talmud (which has been the central feature of Judaism for the previous thousand years or more) was a surprise to them, since they were used to identifying the Jews with the people of that name in the Old Testament and the Gospels. . . . Their first impulse was to sweep the Talmud out of existence altogether as an annoying irrelevance and a "heretical" innovation, in that it complicated needlessly their picture of what it meant to be a Jew. The Paris Disputation represents this reaction.[69]

Even more so the 1242 Paris bonfire that followed![70]

Gregory was succeeded by Innocent IV in 1244, a pope who initially followed the same harsh policy toward the Talmud. In a letter to the king, the newly-minted pontiff writes that the "wicked perfidy of the Jews," which has blinded them to Christ and Christian kindness has also led them to "despise the law of Moses and the prophets and follow certain traditions of their elders . . . called 'Talmud' in Hebrew. It is a large book, exceeding in size the text of the Bible. In it are often found blasphemies against God and His Christ, obviously entangled fables about the Blessed Virgin, abusive errors, and unheard of follies."[71] Innocent goes on to charge that Jews keep their children ignorant of the Law and the Prophets for fear they will read in them obvious proofs of Jesus's Messiahship and forsake Judaism for the true faith. He mentions the trial and burning of the Talmud and directs the king "in the name of the Lord Jesus Christ to strike down with merited severity all the detestable and heinous excesses of this sort" by ordering the confiscation of any remaining manuscripts of the Talmud—and commentaries on it— throughout all the kingdom of France, having them suitably consumed by flame.

69. Hyam Maccoby, Ed. And Trans., *Judaism on Trial* (London; Washington: Littman Library of Jewish Civilization; Washington, DC: Distributed in the U.S. by B'nai B'rith Book Service, 1993), 4.

70. As much as twenty-four wagonloads of Talmuds may have perished. But it must be said that Raymond was no party to this incident, as Cohen claims he was. His two-year tenure as master-general of the Dominicans ended in 1240—not 1242.

71. Chazan, *Church, State, and Jew,* 232; taken from Grayzel, *Church and Jews,* 1966, 251–53.

However, in 1247, in an almost complete about-face, Innocent told Louis that as pope, beholden to both the

> wise and the foolish, he must harm no one unjustly, but is bound to exact what is just and to render to each his due. When, therefore, the Jewish masters of your kingdom recently asserted before us and our brothers that, without that book which in Hebrew is called "Talmud," they cannot understand the Bible and their other statutes and laws in accordance with their faith, we then, bound as we are by the divine command to tolerate them in their law . . . do not want to deprive them of their law.[72]

Now the matter of papal-mendicant intolerance and complicity in a matter concerning heresy-by-Jews is a complex one. To begin with, Pope Gregory certainly disregarded any modern notion of tolerance, as did King Louis, by his intrusion into Jewish worship services and by his confiscation and destruction of religious texts. Whether such unprecedented affronts were done to eradicate "heresy" is the question that is open to debate. Maccoby, for one, believes that what might have started out as a heresy inquisition was dropped *specifically when the papacy recognized that contemporary Judaism was not the same as biblical Judaism*: "One of the results of the Paris Disputation . . . was that the Church did tacitly acknowledge the paramount place of the Talmud in the definition of Judaism and no longer regarded it as heresy, within the jurisdiction of the Inquisition, for a Jew to study the Talmud. Instead, the second charge that the Talmud contained blasphemies against the Christian faith continued to be pressed, as a matter on which the Inquisition was entitled to regulate Jewish conduct."[73]

Seen in this light, far from branding Jews as heretics for deviating from the Law and the Prophets, the Church "confirmed," or "tolerated," their current practice (shriven any Christian insult); thus, far from proving the intolerant nature of Catholic leadership, the Paris Disputation ultimately shows the Church in rather a tolerant light. As Roth writes of Innocent's letter: "This important letter . . . uses the term 'tolerate,' and so also in his earlier letter to the archbishop of Vienne . . . for the first time in connection with Jews. We also learn from this letter that by no means were all of the copies of the Talmud burned in the fire at Paris."[74]

72. Ibid., 234.
73. Maccoby, *Judaism on Trial*, 25.
74. Roth, *Medieval Jewish Civilization*, "Talmud, Condemnation of," 635.

Perhaps the most inherently conservative institution in history, the governing authority of the Roman Catholic Church—despite its ingrained commitment to orthodoxy—proved itself capable of listening to "the Other" and adjusting its policies accordingly. One would not want to stretch this point out of proportion, however; ten years later, Pope Alexander IV again ordered the seizure of Talmudic literature in France (though nowhere else).[75] But as Hood writes, though "the Talmud was subjected to sporadic ecclesiastical censorship over the next three centuries," still "no perpetually binding canon against it was ever promulgated."[76]

It is interesting that, in 1247, Odo (Eudes) de Chateauroux, chancellor of Paris and bishop of Tusculum, one of the leading participants of the "Talmud trial," presented the new pope with a summary of the inquiry's findings in an attempt to dissuade him, arguing that "tolerance would seem to mean approval. Saint Jerome . . . says that there is no perverse doctrine that does not contain some truth, and so likewise no heretics are to be found who do not think well of some one article of the Faith. These are books that contained errors, and hence no matter how much good they contain, they were, nevertheless, condemned by the authority of the councils, in the same way that heretics are condemned although they do not err in everything."

The first item worth observing is that Odo was *not* a Dominican. It should also be noted that even a churchman as anti-Judaistic as Odo grudgingly admitted that Jewish books contained "some good things." More importantly, as we attempt to put Odo's judgment into its historical context, the question becomes: must a document that is considered "error-full" necessarily be categorized as "heretical"? When Odo compares the books of the Talmud to the heretical writings condemned at historical Church councils, is he saying that they are similar in that they both contain a mixture of error and truth, or is he saying that they are similar because they are both heretical?

As he sees the case against the Talmud:

---

75. One wonders if Odo is again to blame. As Roth points out, not only did he try to convince the pope to reverse his decision regarding the toleration of the Talmud, but "without, apparently, waiting for the pope's answer, Odo assembled an 'apostolic court' in Paris, consisting of no fewer than forty-four clerics, including the renowned Albertus Magnus, and again condemned the Talmud as blasphemous and 'unworthy of tolerance.' He stated that he was aware of other books not shown him by the rabbis, and that he would do whatever was necessary to get these books." Cf. Grayzel, *Church and Jews*, 1933, 276–79.

76. Hood, 35.

[O]ne set of claims involved internal Jewish discomfort with the Talmud, a sense that it represented deviation from the norms of biblical teaching. Although given an initial hearing by the officials of the papal court, this line of attack was quickly dropped. More important from the point of view of the Church were the allegations that the Talmud sanctioned, and even recommended, behaviors that were anti-Christian (contravening the prohibition of actions harmful to the Christian host society), that it contained material that blasphemed Christianity (yet another kind of harm), and that it taught doctrines that were fundamentally absurd and hence intolerable. All these allegations were based on firsthand reading of the talmudic sources and roused considerable concern in ecclesiastical circles.[77]

We would agree with Chazan's interpretation, which is in line with Ben Kedar's earlier work arguing that the papacy was not acting against Jews for heretical violations of Christianity, but for their perceived errors in following the Law of Moses.[78] As far as the Dominican involvement in the Talmud trial, it is not necessary to postulate a new mendicant ideology against Jews to explain their role in the affair. As we have seen from the outset of this chapter, the principal role for a Dominican friar was to be an episcopal coadjutor. Whatever commission fell under the scope of a bishop, it could be carried out by a member of the Order of Preachers. When it fell to the lot of the bishops of France to seize and examine the Talmud, the Dominicans were naturally there to assist them. As Chazan writes: "the Dominicans and Franciscans of Paris ... [their] involvement in the anti-Talmud campaign was a reasonable extension of their general responsibility for the propriety of doctrine in Christian society."[79] As a matter of fact, it may have been none other than "Raymond and his circle" who ultimately helped *save* the Talmud from extinction.

As we have seen above, following the lead of his predecessor Gregory IX, Innocent IV in 1244 seemed bent on obliterating the Talmud, not sparing even its existing commentaries. Only three years later, after meeting with a delegation of rabbis, did he suddenly discover the milk of human kindness? No sufficiently adequate explanation has as yet been

77. Chazan, *Daggers of Faith*, 33.

78. Benjamin Z. Kedar, "Canon Law and the Burning of the Talmud," *Bulletin of Medieval Canon Law* 9 (1979): 79–82.

79. Chazan, *Daggers of Faith*, 34; and Vose adds: "Actual scope for independent disciplinary actions against non-Christians by mendicant friars or other clergy remained questionable and limited indeed"; Robin Vose, *Dominicans, Muslims and Jews in the Medieval Crown of Aragon* (Leiden: Cambridge University Press, 2009), 170.

adduced to account for this papal reversal. Stow has argued that the pope's about-face may have had more to do with meeting threats to papal primacy than with dealing even-handedly with Jews: "For Paris, Innocent knew, had long been the home of those protagonists who preferred scriptural to papal interpretative authority. . . . Just as the Talmud was said by its Parisian opponents perversely to have supplanted the Bible . . . so might the same be said of the papal canons [the *Decretals*]."[80] As Stow points out, twenty-seven of the forty-two signatories of Odo's condemnation were secular masters at the University of Paris, a "second seat of discontent" for Rome. Innocent's reversal, therefore, may merely have been a way of checking early "conciliarist" pretensions. Stow further poses a link between papal "protection" of the Talmud and its use by Dominicans in their polemics preaching Christ as Messiah (cf. Chap. six below): "And these developments were not necessarily unrelated. Innocent IV's original order of 1247 to return certain Hebrew books may have provided the stimulus prompting the Dominicans first to weigh the Talmud's possible Christological verities. The conduit linking the pope to the friars would, of course, have been Raymond of Penaforte, the Dominican General, who both edited Gregory's *Decretals* and dominated events in Spain."[81] Once again, the hidden but influential Raymond is postulated as the vital link.

To us, however, it seems far more likely that Master Raymond and his friars influenced Innocent IV than the other way round. As Stow admits, no pope of the era demonstrated any first-hand knowledge of the Talmud itself; whereas, Raymond may already have been familiar with Alan of Lille's use of *Sanhedrin* in his *De Fide Catholica*, since as the author of the *Summa poenitentiae*, Raymond is also likely to have read Alan's own moral treatise. Furthermore, we know that Raymond began his unique mission to the Jews of Spain as early as 1240, after he retired from his post as head of the Order. It is entirely probable that it was during the early years of that decade (if not sooner) that Raymond and his confreres succeeded in converting people like the learned Jew, Paul Christiani (whom we shall examine in Chapter six), who had extensive knowledge of the Talmud. As Stow writes: "The Dominicans purposefully incorporated rabbinic texts into sermons, which they forced the Jews to hear, and for which they obtained royal enabling licenses in 1245, the 1260s, and in 1296."[82] And Baer adds: "In the early

80. Stow, "Hatred of the Jews," 257.
81. Ibid., 258.
82. Kenneth Stow, *Popes, Church, and Jews in the Middle Ages, Confrontation and Response* (Burlington, VT: Ashgate Variorum, 2007), I, 27–28.

1240s the mendicant friars in Aragon embarked on an intensive missionary campaign.... In a short polemic which appeared about this time, the author, R. Jacob of Venice, rebukes a certain convert [Paul] who spread calumnies concerning the Jewish prayers [and] sought to foment hatred against the Talmud."[83] To us, therefore, it seems more plausible that Innocent would have reversed himself on the Talmud's existence by 1247 because the septuagenarian Raymond (perhaps with Paul Christiani) persuaded him that—if purged of perceived blasphemies—it could furnish the Dominican arsenal with Christological proofs than that the pontiff was swayed by rabbinic appeals alone.[84] Stow himself seems to suggest as much when he writes in another work: "The discussion had shifted from the burning of books to censorship alone. Did the shift occur in Spain at the behest of Dominican Hebraists, or was censorship already under consideration by Innocent IV?"[85] If it could ever be proven more than conjecture, what irony of ironies that the Dominican friar condemned for arch anti-Judaism was perhaps the only Christian who prevented the Talmud's complete consignment to oblivion in western Christendom. It is to that man we must now turn.

Little is known of Raymond's early life aside from the fact that he was probably born in Peñafort, near the village of Vilafranca del Penedes outside Barcelona, between the years 1175 and 1180.[86] In 1210, he and another canon of the cathedral of Barcelona departed to study law at

83. Yitzhak Baer, *A History of the Jews in Spain*, vol. 1 (Philadelphia, PA: Jewish Publication Society, 1961), 151–52.

84. Vose, like Stow, although not speaking directly to our contention, nevertheless supports it in a general fashion when he writes: "Whereas at Paris Nicholas Donin had denounced the Talmud alone as a heretical book ... Paul Christiani ... chose to use Talmudic passages as part of his argument that even rabbinic writings supported Christian theological doctrines when properly interpreted. The Talmud had its uses, and was therefore to be carefully expurgated rather than eliminated outright," 172; additionally, it would be interesting to see what relation, if any, the First Council of Lyons (1245–1247) might have had on Innocent in this matter, since, at the least, it may have distracted him from his immediate prosecutorial intentions.

85. Grayzel, *Church and the Jews*, ed. Stow (New York, NY: Jewish Theological Seminary of America, Detroit, MI: Wayne State University Press), revised ed. 1989, v. II, Stow nt. 9, 102.

86. Ribas, *Estudios historicos y bibliograficos sobre San Ramon y Penyafort* (Barcelona, 1890), 11–15.

Bologna.[87] Raymond had a successful university career leading to a pro-
fessorship and to authorship of his own book on canon law, the *Summa
iuris*. Most likely completed between 1218 and 1221,[88] the *Summa iuris*
demonstrates both Raymond's skill at jurisprudence and his fervor for
an educated clergy in association with the reforms of the Lateran Council.[89] Raymond's work addressed the need for ordinary priests to
become more familiar with Church law. A properly informed clergy was
the prerequisite for their pastoral vocation.[90]

T. M. Schwertner suggests that Raymond was himself brought back
from Bologna to Barcelona by Bishop Berengar de Palaciolo to assist in
just such a capacity.[91] With him, Berengar also brought the first group
of Dominicans to his diocese. Raymond may have worked with them as
Berengar's coadjutors and, by 1222, was sufficiently convinced of their
merits to enter their ranks himself. It may have been at this time that
Raymond authored the *Summa pastorales*, or *Libellus pastorales de cura
archdiaconi*.[92] Although its date is uncertain, its inspiration is not: "At
the insistence, moreover, of certain bishops, he supplied to all bishops
and prelates a most useful and honest pattern according to which they
might visit churches committed to their care and usefully provide for
the salvation and honesty of both clergy and laity."[93] In his work, Raymond is concerned first and foremost with instilling in prelates a zeal
for souls. He states that it is the chief duty of an auditing prelate "to
teach by exhorting, arguing, reproving and insisting opportunely and

87. Franciscus Balme and Ceslaus Paban, *Raymundiana: Seu documenta quae pertinent ad S. Raymundi de Pennaforti vitam et scripta*, II, *Monumenta ordinis fratrum
praedicatorum historica*, IV (1898–1901), 3; from Reichert, *MOPH* I.

88. Mandonnet, "La Carrière Scolaire de S. Raymond de Pennafort," *Analecta sacris
ordinis fratrum praedicatorum* 14 (1920): 277–80; Denifle first called attention to this
summa in *Die Universitäten*, I, 15, no. 76. Cf. Stephan Kuttner, "The Barcelona Edition of
St Raymond's First Treatise on Canon Law," *Seminar* 8 (1950): 52–67.

89. *Raymundiana*, II, 5.

90. Lateran IV, 11; "Not only in every cathedral church but also in other churches
where means are sufficient, a competent master be appointed by the prelate with his
chapter, or elected by the greater and more discerning part of the chapter, who shall
instruct gratis and to the best of his ability the clerics of those and other churches in the
art of grammar and in other branches of knowledge. In addition to a master, let the met-
ropolitan church have also a theologian, who shall instruct the priests and others in the
Sacred Scriptures and in those things especially that pertain to the *cura animarum*."

91. T. M. Schwertner, OP, *Saint Raymond of Pennafort of the Order of friars preachers*;
Revised and edited by C. M. Antony (Milwaukee, WI: Bruce Pub. Co., 1935), 36; cf.
Raymundiana I, 20.

92. Echard, *Scriptores*, I, 106–110; Leopold Delisle, *Catalogue des Manuscripts*, I (1849),
592–649.

93. *Raymundiana*, I, 28.

persistently and especially by preaching." Preaching by example is also of the utmost importance. The visitator is to find out how the pastor of the church is conducting not only the sacraments, but himself.[94]

But Raymond's greatest pastoral work was his *Summa de poenitentia*, also known as the *Summa confessorum* or the *Summa de casibus conscientiae*. It was during these first years as a Dominican friar that Raymond likely completed his manual, incorporating much material from his previous *Sunma iuris*.[95] In his university days, Raymond had written glosses on Gratian's *Decretum*, and this experience with the Church's canons would prove invaluable to his new manual for confessors; his experience was essentially that of case law, and his task was to take papal precedents and apply their general principles to particular situations.[96] As Mulchahey puts it, "The *Summa de casibus* aimed to help the confessor see the relationship between the cases presented to him, on the one hand and the principles embodied in the legislative dispositions of the Church, on the other. It is case law."[97]

Raymond of Peñafort, even before he edited the *Decretals*, was thoroughly conversant with Gratian's canons and in his twin *summae* he gave his own recension of *tolerantia*:

> Now then since Jerome says that, following the advent of Christ, the cult of the law does not differ from idolatry and Origen also says that now one cannot serve God through the law, why is it that the Church gives them [Jews and non-Christians] the right to sin mortally, since it commands that they not be obstructed from observing their rights? Likewise if they sin mortally in such observance, why should they not be punished as for other crimes? Say to this that the Church does not give them the right to sin, but it grants *permission*, as Pope Gregory says, lest those whom reason might easily win over be forced back by adversity.

94. Schwertner, 102–03.

95. Kuttner, "Zur Entstehungsgeschichte der Summa de casibus des hl. Raymund von Pennafort," *Zeitschrift der Savigny-Stiftung für Rechtsgeschichte* Kan. Abt. 85 (1953): 419–48.

96. Mulchahey, *First the Bow is Bent*, 534; 536. "The sort of law with which Raymond of Peñafort dealt as a teacher . . . was case-law, law composed principally of the decisions of popes in response to questions which had been put to them. The job of the teacher or compiler of such law was to explain the particular decision in terms of patristic authority or other precedent, and to extend the principle it implied to form a general rule, which, in its turn, could be applied in new situations. Raymond's experience with this approach led him to apply a very similar one in treating the topic of penance in his *Summa de casibus conscientiae*. . . . According to the canon lawyer's point of view, sin or moral fault occurs when the divine will is violated. And because the divine will is expressed in the Church's law, sin can be judged understanding if or how a particular case, given its particular circumstances, transgresses the law."

97. Ibid.

Moreover, if Jews were prohibited from this or punished temporally for this, then they would be forced into the faith, which should not be done, as noted above.[98] (*Summa de poenitentiae*) (emphasis mine)

And again:

Permission is taken in three different ways. First, when something is allowed that is not forbidden by any law.... Second, when something is indulged that runs counter to human rules.... This is properly called the true and absolute permission, and it excuses from sin. The third type of permission occurs when lesser evils are permitted so as to prevent greater ones. This is called the *permissio comparativa*, and it does not excuse from sin. It should, however, be called *tolerantia* rather than permission.[99] (*Summa iuris*) (emphasis mine)

Raymond's definition of tolerance would thus seem to contain two pertinent aspects. In the first place, tolerance does not mean, as it does in modern discourse, that two contrary affirmations of truth are to be considered equally valid; only one can be accurate, the other a falsehood, hence sinful, or "evil." Therefore the "toleration" of something necessarily implies that the something in question is, to a greater or lesser degree, not in harmony with the fullness of God's Truth, upon which Justice itself is based and so human law. Thus Raymond writes: "*quod ea quae permittimus, non approbamus.*" The second component to his definition is the idea that although certain tolerated acts are inherently sinful, it does not follow that corrective action must be taken to eradicate them. As a matter of fact, if doing so would lead to a greater sin, then the original sin must be left untampered with, that is to say, tolerated. Bejczy notes that later canonists took the definition of tolerance even further: "Joannes Andreae ... distinguished three types of tolerance: *permissio simplex*, the mere abstention from punishing evil acts; *permissio tollens impedimentum*, which, moreover, obliged the Church to restrain other people from proceeding against the evil acts in question; and *permissio praestans iuvamen*, the case in which the Church was required to foster actively the occurrence of some evil act (e.g., the punishment of criminal clerics)."[100]

It would seem, from our initial examination of Friar Raymond's ideology, that, far from advocating "ridding Europe" of Jews and Muslims, he was, rather (by his own definition), tolerant. As Bejczy writes:

98. *Summa de poenitentiae*, 5; Chazan, *Daggers of Faith*, 40.
99. *Summa de iure canonico*, trans. and eds. Xaverius Ochoa and Aloisius Diez, *Universa Bibliotheca iuris* I. A. (Rome, 1975); Bejczy, "*Tolerantia*," 369–70.
100. Johanes Teutonicus, Glossa D. 3 C. 4 ad v. permittit., Ibid., 370.

The concept of *tolerantia* was chiefly developed as an answer to the question of how ecclesiastical authorities should deal with the practices of Jewish religion. Jewish rites were considered an evil that had to be tolerated; the major evil that was thus prevented was the forced conversion of the Jews, for conversion to Christianity had to be a matter of free-will. Moreover, the Jews would be more willing to embrace the Christian faith, the canonists argued, when they were treated with benevolence.[101]

The most celebrated ecclesiastical edict embodying *permissio tollens impedimentum* was *Sicut Iudaeis*. Substantially the work of that tremendously influential Latin Doctor of the West, Pope St Gregory the Great, *Sicut Iudaeis* was first re-issued by Pope Calixtus II (1119–1124); it would subsequently be reissued six times over the next hundred years. It not only mandated non-interference with Jews, but threatened sanction against those who molest them:

> Just as the Jews ought not to be allowed to do more in their synagogues than the law permits, so too they should suffer no reduction in the privileges that have been previously granted them. That is why, though they prefer to remain obstinate rather than acknowledge the words of the prophets and the secrets of their own scriptures and come to a knowledge of Christianity and salvation, because they have sought our protection and aid and in accordance with the mercy of Christian piety...we grant them their petition and offer them our shield of protection. We also decree (*statuimus*) that no Christian shall use violence to force them to be baptized if they are reluctant or unwilling; but if any of them seeks refuge among the Christians because of his faith, after his willingness has been made clear, he shall become a Christian without suffering any calumny. For it is impossible to believe that one who comes to baptism unwillingly truly possesses the Christian faith. Also, absent due authority, no Christian shall presume to harm them, kill them, take their money, or alter the privileges they have become accustomed to in that region. In addition, during the cel-

---

101. Bejczy, "*Tolerantia*," 371; "Accordingly, Joannes Andreae mentioned the Jewish rites as an example of acts that should meet with *permissio tollens impedimentum*: the Church should not only leave the rites unpunished but should also prevent others from disturbing them. The same arguments for tolerance applied to other unbelievers, notably to Muslims. Canon law mostly treated Jews and Muslims under the same headings, although canonists often took a harsher stance against the latter because, as a result of the crusades, Christianity was at war with them. The canonists agreed, however, that Muslims who lived in peace with Christians ought not to be attacked or expelled and other infidels living on the borders of Christendom (Prussians, Lithuanians) had to be treated analogously."

ebration of their festivals, no one should assault them with sticks or stones, nor should any services be required of them except those which have long been customary. And, in opposition to the depravity and avarice of evil men, we decree that no one shall desecrate or diminish Jewish cemeteries or, with the object of extorting money, exhume those buried there. If however—God forbid—someone knowingly acts in defiance of this decree, he shall suffer loss of honor and office, or be restrained by excommunication, until he makes satisfaction. We wish, however, to place under the protection of this decree only those who have not presumed to plot in the subversion of the Christian faith.[102]

Raymond of Peñafort, as we have seen from the start, is roundly criticized for categorizing Jews as "heretics" and mounting his Dominican missionary effort in an attempt to have done with them. But it was Raymond-the-chief-canonist who actually saw to it that the principles of *Sicut Iudaeis* would be given a wide and lasting hearing by specifically including it as Chapter Nine of the *Decretals*. He also includes the following phrase from Alexander III (Lateran III) as Chapter Eight: "Indeed, if old synagogues fall or threaten to fall, it can be tolerated that the Jews rebuild them. . . . In any case, they should clearly have the right to be tolerated in their old synagogues and observances."[103]

Instances like these prompt Bejczy to disagree strenuously with the prevailing characterization of Raymond: "Moreover, the influence of canon law on Scholasticism in matters of tolerance invalidates Cohen's distinction between tolerant popes and canonists on the one hand and intolerant mendicants on the other—a distinction which is little convincing anyway, since the canonist Raymond of Peñafort (who gave an authoritative definition of tolerance, as we have seen above) is depicted by Cohen as the evil genius behind mendicant intolerance."[104]

The fact of the matter is that while Jews did suffer legal restrictions as outlined above, the same Church canons granted them a degree of religious freedom and protection unthinkable for Christian heretics.[105] Friar Raymond, it must be remembered, in collating the canons was

---

102. *Sicut Judeis*, in John Hood, *Aquinas and the Jews* (Philadelphia: University of Pennsylvania Press, 1995), 29–30.

103. Chazan, *Daggers of Faith*, 30.

104. Bejczy, 373, nt. 38.

105. Ibid., 375; "Heretics and homosexuals were not even in theory allowed to dwell in the margins of society, like Jews and prostitutes. Heresy and homosexuality were not seen as minor evils that society could afford; heresy endangered the very core of Christian civilization, whereas homosexuality was felt to threaten the distinction between the sexes. . . . *Tolerantia* was a way of walking honestly towards outsiders; towards insiders, strictness prevailed."

culling through centuries of anti-Judaistic sentiment dating back, as we have seen, to the earliest Fathers. That he did not allow this tradition complete sway, that he saw fit to incorporate Augustine's and Pope Gregory's more enlightened approaches as anchor of Christian-Jewish relations, seems an otherwise praiseworthy achievement. If Raymond was operating under an alleged new Dominican ideology that viewed Jews as heretics, he passed up a splendid opportunity to brand them as such for all to see, in the definitive codification of the Catholic Church's law.

Furthermore, one year later, in the final edition of his *Summa de poenitentiae*, Raymond again regarded the two groups separately: "We have spoken above of Jews and pagans who by their infidelity dishonor God, now we treat of heretics, who by deviating from the faith sin in many ways against God." ("*Dictum est supra de Iudaeis, & Paganis, qui per infidelitatem Deum inhonorant nunc agendum de Haeretics, qui a fide deviantes in Deum multipliciter peccant.*")[106] This authoritative distinction between infidels (Jews, Muslims, and pagans) and heretics became widespread among priests of the Dominican Order, as well as among secular prelates throughout Christendom owing to the enormous popularity and circulation of Raymond's *summa*. As Mulchahey writes:

> The *Summa de casibus* was welcomed with open arms by Raymond's fellow Dominicans, for whom, as we have seen, it became one of the fundamental textbooks for their discussions "*de moralibus*," just as the sentences of Peter Lombard stood as the set text for the *schola*. The *Summa de casibus* is one of the few works ever mentioned by name in Dominican educational documents: even the famous *ratio studiorum* of 1259 recommended it. The Roman Province early encouraged the brothers of Tuscany, and especially all young priests, to study the *Summa de casibus* diligently, right alongside the Bible, the Lombard's *Sentences*, the *Historia scholastica*, and the writings of the Fathers.[107]

106. St Raymond of Peñafort, *Summa de Poenitentia* (Rome, 1603), I, 6.

107. Mulchahey, *First the Bow is Bent*, 538–39. "Humbert of Romans, in his book of Instructiones, listed the *Summa de casibus*, as one of the books all conventual libraries were to obtain, and even mentions Raymond of Penafort by name when he tells confessors that they should refer to the Summa "*magistri Raymundi*" before absolving excommunicates or simoniacs. It was also from Humbert we first learned that the *collationes scientificae* designed to train the friars in moral science were meant to focus on the *Summa de casibus* and similar texts. The work was one familiar to all the friars—Dominican convents from Florence to Barcelona had their own copies—and it was distributed by the Paris stationers to the wider world. Raymond of Peñafort's modern reputation may rest on the *Liber extra* and perhaps on his later services as master-general of the Dominican order, which included the revising of the order's Constitutions in 1239, but his contemporary fame was largely owing to his confessor's manual, the *Summa de casibus*."

If there was a distinct Dominican ideology toward Jews, it was the one set down by Raymond in his *Summa* for confessors: Jews, along with other "infidels," were sinners because they did not worship God in the manner that was now ordained, i.e., through Christ and his Church; by the same token, however, they did not sin as "greatly" as "heretics," who "deviated" from their Christian faith. Not only did Raymond make a clear distinction between Jews and heretics, but unlike in the *Decretals,* in the *Summa* he repeats the expression of Gregory the Great (and included in the *Decretum*) concerning the appropriate manner of approaching Jewish conversion: "Both Jews and Saracens should be induced by authoritative texts, by reason, and by blandishments rather than by harshness, to accept anew the Christian faith. They should not, however, be compelled to do so, for forced servitude does not please God." Authoritative texts, reason, and kindness were the very measures Dominic himself had employed and, as we shall see in the next chapter, these methods served as ideals for Raymond's own mendicant mission to the Jews and Muslims of Spain (if not always observed in the breach).

In this section, Raymond also elaborates a specific legal policy of medieval toleration, including some material also found above in the *Decretals*:

> It appears from what precedes that the Church judges those who are outside her, and inflicts many penalties upon them. Against this, the Apostle says in I Corinthians 5, "For what is it to me, to judge them that are without?" Solution. The Church cannot judge concerning them, such that she inflicts spiritual penalties or imposes rules of religion on them, but she can inflict temporal penalties, and also spiritual ones indirectly, by removing Christians from communion with them. For example, in a case already mentioned, the Pope judges concerning an inheritance to be restored to converts to the Faith—against the legitimate case of outsiders who claim to be sons. Reply that the Pope does this by reason of the Faith which they have received. Another instance is the following. Since Jerome says that the cult of the Law, since the advent of Christ, does not differ from idolatry, and Origen also says that now it is not possible to serve God by following the Law (16 q.7), an objection can arise. What is this? The Church gives them authority to sin mortally, as long as she teaches that they are not to be impeded from observing their own rites. And, if they sin mortally in this, why are they not punished as for other offenses? To this objection, say that the Church does not give them authority to sin, but permits the sin, lest (as Gregory says) those whom reason can fairly call back, adversity might drive farther away. Besides, if Jews were prohibited from observing their rites, or were punished temporally for doing so,

they would be compelled toward the Faith, which ought not to be done, as is said above.[108]

As we have cited previously, Raymond's *Summa* had one of the widest diffusions of any book of the High Middle Ages. His *tolerantia* toward Jewish existence, and in particular his citation of canon law to support his point, had an incalculable effect upon forming tolerant Christian attitudes toward the infidel. No doubt he spread the already-established notion that Jews and Muslims were sinners, yet precisely because they *were* he argued that they ought to be "tolerated." Yet Raymond's reputation has suffered from even another law code and another modern critic.

Norman Roth denounces Raymond in the harshest rhetoric for his "indirect" impact upon Jews through Spanish civil law: "Ramon de Peñafort . . . was the major anti-Jewish figure of thirteenth-century Spain. After he had completed his malicious work in writing the Castilian legislation (*Siete partidas*) which for the first time in Spanish codes expressed hostility to Jews, although fortunately it remained only a reference work with mere advisory status at best, he returned to his native Catalonia to wreak similar havoc."[109] Or as he writes elsewhere:

> Although the decidedly anti-Jewish legislation of the Visigothic councils was utilized in the *Decretum*, it was largely ignored in the *Decretals* . . . [they] were never binding in civil courts, nor did they have any particular influence on European civil law. . . . In Spain, the influence was indirect, chiefly through Ramon de Peñafort. While the *Siete partidas* never were accepted fully as an operative "national code" of law in Castile, even in the fourteenth century, there is no doubt about the influence of the attitudes contained in it as reflected in some later local ecclesiastical councils. In Aragon the situation was quite different. The *Fueros*, also the work of a canonist (Vidal de Canellas), became the law of the kingdom, and the same canonist wrote the *Furs* of Valencia and other local ordinances. He was a disciple of Ramon de Peñafort.[110]

It is a puzzling approach to history that uses one hand to blame Raymond for foisting anti-Jewish legislation on the otherwise tolerant kingdoms of Christian Spain, while the other hand fails to praise him for the fact that his compilation of the *Decretals* "largely ignored" much of the "decidedly anti-Jewish legislation of the Visigothic councils . . . utilized in the *Decretum*." Secondly, Roth never ceases to speak about Raymond as if the good Dominican (like John on Patmos) "dreamt up" this entire

108. Ibid., 1, 4, 5.
109. Roth, *Conversos*, 205–206.
110. Roth, *Medieval Jewish Civilization*, "Canon (Church) Law and Jews," 134.

legal prospectus on his own—"he confined *his* anti-Jewish sentiments to *his* prolific and dangerous legal codes"[111] (emphasis mine) when virtually every paragraph related to the Jews in the *Partidas* is either directly or indirectly taken from the *Decretum,* Lateran IV, or the canons of earlier councils and correspondence of popes. As Larry J. Simon plainly states: "An item by item survey of the enactments reveals that most of the eleven laws in this title correspond to legislation contained in the nineteen chapters of book V, title vi, 'Concerning Jews, Saracens, and their slaves,' in the *Decretales* of Pope Gregory IX."[112]

To tar-and-feather Raymond as a "Jew-hater" is to similarly stigmatize all earlier councils and popes as "Jew-haters" (including Pope Gregory the Great!). But even where we might possibly venture to discern the personal touch of Peñafort in the *Partidas,* there is no justification for declaring him even "extremely anti-Judaistic," let alone malevolent; in fact we may infer just the opposite in some cases. For example, in *S.P.* 1.23.8 Raymond offers a solution to the following dilemma: To whom should one give alms, if the choice is between a fellow Christian and one's own father who has become a heretic or "a believer in some other religion"? Raymond declares: "Alms should be given to the father, on account of the relationship existing between the parties, although he may not be Christian."[113] The good friar was not so "extreme" as to deny the principle that "charity begins at home," merely because one's parent was a Jew. Similarly, in Title 10 of his *Summa on Marriage,* Raymond pronounces another counter-intuitive verdict in the case of a non-Christian couple where one spouse converts to Catholicism and the other does not. He outlines the Church's position on "mixed marriage," including the "Pauline privilege":

> When the spouses are [both] unbelievers such as Jews or Saracens, there is a true marriage. But if one is converted to the faith and the other remains in Judaism or in the error of paganism, if the unbeliever does not wish to cohabit with the believer, or if he wishes to cohabit but not without injury and blasphemy to the name of Christ, or to draw him to infidelity or to another mortal sin, in these three cases the affront to the Creator dissolves the right of marriage for the believer and so the believer can licitly marry [another].
>
> If, however, the unbeliever wishes to cohabit with the believer with-

---

111. Ibid., 210.

112. Larry J. Simon, "Jews in the Legal Corpus of Alfonso el Sabio," *Comitatus* 18 (1987), 86.

113. Burns SJ, ed., *Las Siete Partidas,* vol. 1 Title 23, Law 8 (Philadelphia, PA: University of Pennsylvania Press, 2001), 260.

out any of the aforesaid, the believer, if he wishes to cohabit with the unbeliever, does well because the Apostle admonishes the Corinthians saying, "If a brother has an unbelieving wife [and she consents to dwell with him, let him not put her away]" etc. (1 Cor 7.12). If he does not want to cohabit with the unbeliever, he must not be forced, *but as long as the unbeliever is living the believer cannot marry because the marriage endures.*

Although some have made a distinction, saying it is one thing for Jews another for pagan converts because a Jew converted to the faith ought not cohabit with an unbelieving wife who wishes to cohabit, but a converted Saracen or pagan can, it seems that today the same judgment applies to both cases.[114] (emphasis mine)

Again, a tie that binds is not so easily dismissed, even when the case involves a Jew. Raymond even goes against the grain of some church-men by granting Jews the same privileges as other non-Christians. His overriding interest is in *intangible* "affront to the Creator," that is to say, sin; not in proscribing a dissenting sub-group in order to preserve the dominance of the elite group in some back-handed sociological fashion. One further case is revelatory of a certain tolerance on the part of Peñafort. *S.P.* 1.4.63 addresses proper behavior for a Jew or Muslim toward Jesus in the Eucharistic "Bread" when it is being carried through the street to the home of some sick person. Raymond does not demand, but asks for some sign of humility on the part of the said non-Christian, but if he or she is unwilling, "we direct that he leave the street" so as to avoid any disrespect toward God. Anyone found offending is to be incarcerated for three days by the local judge of that district, but only "after he has been proved guilty." This "presumption of innocence" was arguably rare even for Christians in the secular courts of Raymond's day, let alone for non-Christians. If the person is obstinate enough to offend a second time, the punishment is doubled to six days. And if the offender "does not repent," but commits instead a third violation,

we order that he be arrested and brought before the King, that he may inflict what punishment he may deem right for such an act, if, how-ever, the King should be at such a distance from the place that this can-not be done, the guilty party must be securely guarded until the King is informed. . . . First that the Jews and Moors may not be able to say that they are wrongfully subjected to injury in our dominions; second that the judges, or those whose duty it is to try them, may not advise them to do wrong, through a wish to obtain their property, or on account of

114. Pierre Payer, trans. and ed., *Summa on Marriage* (Toronto: Pontifical Institute of Medieval Studies, 2005), 51.

the pleasure they may derive in inflicting corporeal injury upon them by reason of the hatred they bear them.[115]

It is a strange "Jew-hater" who frames laws to protect Jews from those who bear them "hatred."

It is hard to escape the conclusion that Roth's treatment of Raymond and the *Partidas* is one-sided. Furthermore, he is mistaken when he writes: "It is of interest to consider the laws dealing with Jews in the *F.R.* [*Fuero Real*]. In theory, a Jew is like a heretic (indeed, in CANON LAW, the *Decretals* of Gregory IX, written also by the same Ramon de Peñafort who wrote the *Partidas*, *most of the laws dealing with Jews are in the title on heretics*)."[116] (emphasis mine) Title VI of the *Decretals*, as we have seen above, is entitled by Raymond: "Concerning Jews, Saracens, and their slaves"; a separate title (VII) is devoted to "Heretics."

Current scholarship on intolerance makes frequent reference to the Dominican role in the torture and execution of heretics. Raymond is, as always, ubiquitous and iniquitous: "In 1242, together with 'other wise men,' he succeeded in persuading the Council of Tarragona to issue a decree that heretics should be turned over to the 'secular arm,' i.e., the government, to be burned at the stake, while those who recanted were, mercifully, to be imprisoned for life!" But Raymond was simply encouraging the episcopacy to implement Canon 3 of Lateran IV. As we have seen, the council had called for coadjutors to assist the bishops and this was *the* mendicant mandate.

Or again, Roth observes: "Also according to the *F.R.*, no Christian is allowed to convert to Judaism or Islam, on pain of death. Similarly, the *Partidas* condemn to death any Christian 'so unfortunate as to become a Jew' or so 'insane' as to become a Muslim."[117] To a Christian, these apostate actions would constitute grave sin and *sin* was considered the ultimate form of insanity. Besides, it is facile to assume that Raymond personally embraced every action of the Church unequivocally, simply because he was under obedience to promulgate its decisions.[118] As the late John Kemp, SJ wrote: "Raymund of Peñafort, advisor to the pope, insisted that there be no death penalty for heresy. But his advice was not heeded by the determined pontiff."[119]

115. Burns, *Las Siete Partidas*, 43.
116. Roth, *Medieval Jewish Civilization*, "Jews in Spanish Law," 616.
117. Ibid.
118. "A hazardous enterprise," is how Simon qualifies it, speaking of scholarly attempts to "discern Alfonso's personal attitude toward Jews in his law codes," 89.
119. John A. Kemp, SJ, "Gregory IX," in *The Catholic Encyclopedia for School and Home*, vol. 5 (New York, NY: McGraw Hill, 1965), 15.

In the end, the *Siete Partidas* need not be viewed as an intolerant code. As Dwayne Carpenter concludes:

> As a medieval king and devout Christian, Alfonso was unquestionably influenced by centuries of ecclesiastical formulations and canonical prescripts. Therefore, on an essentially theoretical level, neither juridical novelties nor expressions of tolerance should be sought in "De los judios." Rather, an examination of the question of tolerance must rely on the evidence of the individual laws of *SP* 7.24. While at times the Alfonsine legislation regarding Jews hardly appears to reflect a spirit of disinterested benevolence, it nevertheless adheres to the essential meaning of the Latin *tolerare*, "to endure, to allow." Thus, in its strictest sense, tolerance does not require a preference for or understanding of that which is tolerated. Justice, then, not love, is the essence of tolerance, and, in this respect at least, Alfonso was not only Learned, but also Tolerant.[120]

Which for us, is as much as saying, "Raymond of Peñafort was not only Learned, but also Tolerant."

While it is understandable that Raymond should have treated Jews and Muslims in his collection of canon law and in the civil code of Castile, why, might we ask, did he include them in his manual for confessors? It is not as if a priest was likely to encounter them in his confessional![121] (Nor indeed did he have jurisdiction to absolve them if they were.) It could be said, again, that Raymond wished local pastors to be apprised of the canons of the Church, or that he was just being particularly thorough in a *summa* on sin, or that he was trying to educate woefully inept parsons on exactly what the distinctions were between members of Church and synagogue. To this list might we also add that they were included because Christians and Jews shared a common humanity as "sinners"? In an interesting passage from the *Siete Partidas*, Raymond not only discusses the Original Sin of Adam, he speaks of a *common belief shared with Jews and Muslims:* "Adam was the first man whom our Lord God created . . . and on this both Jews and Moors are agreed. Hence he is, and will be called the Father of all, because he was the beginning of the race of men."[122]

In light of the above, can we not read the deliberate inclusion of Jews and Saracens in his *Summa* as—on some level—a way of "including" otherwise dubious "outsiders"? In April of 1233, at the very time that

---

120. Dwayne E. Carpenter, *Alfonso X and the Jews: An Edition of and Commentary on Siete Partidas 7.24 "De los judos"* (Berkeley, CA: University of California Press, 1986), 105.
121. I speak, of course, rhetorically, the confessional "box" being a later invention.
122. Burns, *Las Siete Partidas*, 133.

Raymond was in his employ, Pope Gregory wrote about the Jews to the bishops of France, referencing not merely their common sinfulness with Christians in the manhood of Adam, but common "Christ-hood" in the scheme of salvation of the New Adam:

> Although the perfidy of the Jews is to be condemned, nevertheless their relations with Christians is useful and in a way, *necessary*; for they *bear the image of our Savior,* and were created by the Creator of all mankind. They are therefore not to be destroyed, God forbid, by His own creatures, especially by believers in Christ, for *no matter how perverse their midway position may be, their fathers were made friends of God, and also their remnant shall be saved.* . . . Such kindliness must be shown to Jews by Christians, as we hope might be shown to Christians who live in pagan lands.[123] (emphasis mine)

These are extraordinary verses. Let us begin our examination with Gregory's last phrase: "No matter how perverse their midway position may be, their fathers were made friends of God, and also their remnant shall be saved." Gregory's tri-partite scheme for understanding the Jew of his day by observing (simultaneously) his past and his future is an example of a medieval sacra*mentality* of the highest order. For while we have already observed that each item in creation, most notably man, is a kind of "sacrament," a tangible sign of an intangible reality yet, according to the Church's teaching authority, more wondrous still are the seven sacraments signifying and instituted by Christ himself. In the following quote from the *Summa theologiae,* let us note how strikingly Thomas's phraseology on the sacraments parallels that of Gregory IX on the Jews:

> A sacrament properly speaking is that which is ordained to signify our sanctification. In which *three things* may be considered; viz. the very cause of our sanctification, which is Christ's passion; the form of our sanctification, which is grace and the virtues; and the ultimate end of our sanctification, which is eternal life. And all these are signified by the sacraments. Consequently a sacrament is a sign that is both *a reminder of the past,* i.e., the passion of Christ; and an indication of that which *is* [*now*] effected in us by Christ's passion, i.e., grace; and a prognostic, that is, a *foretelling of future* glory.[124] (emphasis mine)

This is the sacra*mentality* of the Church and the medieval Catholic origins of modern tolerance.

---

123. Grayzel, *Church and Jews,* 201.
124. *Summa* III.60.3.

The Jewish people, like a sacrament, are a benefit to Christians, "in a way, necessary." The Jewish people, like a sacrament, "bear the image" of Christ. The Jewish people, like a sacrament, are a sign "that is both a reminder of the past . . . and a prognostic, that is, a foretelling of future glory." And just as the sacraments are not to be treated unworthily, so too the Jews ought to be protected from desecration. Indeed, they deserve the same kindness that the pope hopes "be shown to Christians who live in pagan lands." This is the "Golden Rule" of love, laid down by Christ himself: "Do unto others as you would have them do unto you" (Luke 6:31). It is the definition of "tolerance" par excellence. Indeed, it was precisely this transcendental view of human dignity and *caritas* which the papacy again raised centuries later as its clarion call on the ominous eve of Hitler's rise to power: "The Catholic Church habitually prays for the Jewish people who were the bearers of the divine revelations up to the time of Christ. . . . Actuated by this love, the Apostolic See has protected this people against unjust oppression and, just as every kind of envy and jealousy among the nations must be disapproved of, so in an especial manner must be that hatred which is generally termed anti-Semitism."[125]

And this statement was further interpreted by a committee of European Catholic scholars in 1937 to mean:

> By disapproving of the hatred against the Jews and condemning it as irreconcilable with the Gospel, the Church professes her own charity toward the people of Israel. She expects and demands, therefore, that every Christian individual and every Christian nation treat the people of Israel according to the words of Our Lord: "All things, therefore, whatsoever you would that men should do to you, do also to them" (Matt 7:12).[126]

Although many academics have treated the Catholic view of the beneficial "witness" of the Jews as found in Paul, Augustine, and other saints and doctors, to my knowledge current scholarship has yet to

---

125. Decree of the Holy Office March 25, 1928; https://removewittenbergjuden-sau.com/2016/03/25/25-march-1928-pope-pius-xi-closes-friends-of-israel-otdimjh/.

126. *The Church and the Jews, A Memorial Issued by Catholic European Scholars,* trans. Gregory Feige, 26 (Washington, DC: The Committee on National Attitudes of the Catholic Association for International Peace/New York: Paulist Press, 1937), 16. Cf. also *Documents of the Second Vatican Council, Nostra Aetate,* 4, October 28, 1965: "Furthermore, in her rejection of every persecution against any man, the Church, mindful of the patrimony she shares with the Jews and moved not by political reasons but by the Gospel's spiritual love, decries hatred, persecutions, displays of anti-Semitism, directed against Jews at any time and by anyone."

make the connection between Catholic views of the Jews and the subtler notion of sacramental witness.[127]

Gregory's sacramental view of the Jews, however, was no fleeting literary topos. We see it repeated in response to a horrific slaughter of French Jews, in separate letters to both the bishops and the king of France. It needs to be quoted at length:

> Yet these Crusaders, along with others, plot impious designs against those Jews and pay no heed to the fact that *proofs for the Christian faith come, as it were, from their archives and that, as the prophets testify, although they should be as the sands of the sea, yet in the end of days a remnant of them shall be saved, because the Lord will not forever spurn His people.* These Crusaders try to wipe the Jews almost completely off the face of the earth. In an unheard of and unprecedented outburst of cruelty, they have slaughtered in this mad hostility two thousand five hundred of them—old and young, as well as pregnant women. Some were mortally wounded and others trampled like mud under the feet of horses. They burned their books, and for greater shame and disgrace, they exposed the bodies of those thus killed as food for the birds of heaven and their flesh to the beasts of the earth. After foully and shamefully treating those who remained alive after this massacre, they carried off their goods and consumed them. And in order that they may be able to hide such an inhuman crime under the cover of virtue and in some way justify their unholy cause, they claim to have done the above and threaten to do worse, on the ground that the Jews refuse to be baptized. They do not sufficiently consider that, when a storm arose in this great and spacious sea and humankind was endangered by this tempest, then the true Jonah, Jesus Christ, the Son of God, came into these depths and permitted himself to be submerged in this storm, so that by His blood he might win us back to God and renew us through the font of regeneration which is consecrated by it. *He did not make distinctions of condition of life, or of sex, as a result of which anyone of any people can be raised to adoption among the children of God. But to those to whom God wants to be merciful are not to be compelled to the grace of baptism, rather they must want it voluntarily. Just as man fell of his own free will when he succumbed to the serpent's guile, even so, when called by the grace of God, he ought to bring about his own rise in complete freedom of will.*[128]

Once again, we see that meditation on the theology of sin, salvation, and sacrament has led to a consideration of the Jews and their dignity as

---

127. Cf. Cohen, *Living Letters*; Fredriksen, *From Witness to Witchcraft*; idem, *Augustine and the Jews*; Robert E. Lerner, *The Feast of Saint Abraham: Medieval Millenarians and the Jews* (Philadelphia, PA: University of Pennsylvania Press, 2001), 23–24.

128. Chazan, *Daggers of Faith*, 109–10.

men. Christian actions toward the Jews must mirror the merciful grace of Almighty God. Once again, Jews are viewed in the sacramental time sequence of Jesus Christ: "yesterday, today, and forever" (Heb 13:8). Gregory credits them with providing Christians their Old Testament, according to which it should come as no surprise that in the present day they are as numerous as the sands of the seashore (Gen 22:15). Importantly, the pope (seven hundred years in anticipation of the Second Vatican Council) points out the Jews are *still* "His people," and both vengeance and mercy toward them are of times and seasons which are God's alone. And not merely of God the Father: in his previous letter, Gregory says that Jews, even though they be unbaptized, still "*bear the image of our Savior.*"

None of the Church's modern detractors have (so far as I am aware) drawn any attention to the phrase: "Jews . . . bear the image of our Savior." This is precisely the Catholic sacra*mentality* we have been elaborating. The Jew is a human being (seen reality), the sign, the image of Jesus Christ (unseen and *Ultimate Reality*). In the annals of papal history no greater praise, it appears, was ever paid to the Jewish community than this one. Gregory's sacramental sentiment was an echo of an earlier remark by St Bernard of Clairvaux: "Whoever touches a Jew so as to lay hands on his life, does something as sinful as if he laid hands on Jesus himself."[129]

Although a handful of future popes would yet regard Jews and Judaism with utter disdain, Gregory had established a tolerant precedent by his sacramental elaboration of the doctrine of Jewish witness. Neither were his remarks isolated ones in the history of the papacy or the period. In a letter of May 1247, we find similar expressions of *reason* and *love* from the pen of his successor Innocent IV:

> If the Christian religion were to give careful heed and rightly analyze by use of reason, how inhuman it is and how discordant with piety for it to afflict with many kinds of molestations, and to smite with all sorts of grave injuries, the remnant of the Jews, to whom *left as witnesses of His saving passion and of His victorious death, the benignity of the Savior promised the favor of salvation*, it would not only draw back its hands from harming them, but as a show of piety and *for the sake of the reverence of Christ*, it would at least, extend the solace of human kindness to those whom it holds, as it were in tribute.[130] (emphasis mine)

Once again, "contemporary" Jewry reflects "once and future" glory.

---

129. Synan, *The Popes and the Jews*, 75.
130. Grayzel, *Church and Jews*, 265.

They give witness to Christ's salvific death on Calvary and shall be the recipients of its benefits before the end of time. The Jew is a living symbol of the Savior. Seeing Jesus reflected in Jews and reverencing Him vicariously through them was a sacramental principle guaranteeing Jews fundamental human dignity whenever and wherever it should be invoked; it was the institutional Church alone, not the vulgar masses, nor the emerging nation-state, which viewed Jews in such sacral terms. Nederman, though he does not explore the sacramental aspect, summarizes matters well when he writes:

> From the patristic era onward, it was argued that forbearance toward Jewish communities by Christianity was justified by their function as witnesses to the law of the Old Testament as well as by the scriptural promise of Jewish conversion at the end of the world. While this was hardly sufficient to halt popular expressions of anti-Semitism, it did afford to the Jewish faith a sort of formal (albeit limited) toleration, the significance of which should not be disparaged. If the incidence of intolerance toward the Jews was on the rise during the later Middle Ages, as has been documented, this may well have been due to the erosion of ecclesiastical influence over secular government rather than the result of pressure brought to bear on temporal authorities by the Church.[131]

Furthermore, when the avowedly secularist anti-Semitism of National Socialism reared its ugly head in Germany and the rest of central Europe in the 1930s, it was precisely the medieval Catholic view of the Jew and his sacramental dignity that was raised in alarm by concerned Christian scholars:

> It is quite certain that the people of Israel, as well as every individual Israelite, should be an object of pious awe to the Christian for the simple reason that the Logos became Man in Israel. Even as the Christian loves the land which bears the footprints of the Lord, so also should he love the people among whom the Lord was born. Just as it grieves him if the holy places are devastated by the heathen, so also his love of Christ will sadden and trouble him when he sees the devastation ... brought on the people of Israel.[132]

In the medieval context, it is worth underscoring the fact that these exceptional pronouncements of respect for Jews based upon their sacramentality are chiefly found where Raymond of Peñafort is found: the years Peñafort acted as Gregory IX's confessor and chief advisor, and the years that Peñafort first spearheaded Christian mission to Jews (and

---

131. Nederman, *Worlds of Difference*, 21.
132. *The Church and the Jews*, 11.

may even have persuaded Innocent to spare the Talmud). Let us turn, therefore, to a further investigation of Pope Gregory's dictum: "Jews . . . *bear the image of our Savior.*"

As we have noted above, the Apostles, like St John, the Beloved Disciple, had taught from earliest times that the only Son of the Father was the *Logos* through whom all things were made: "In the beginning was the *Logos*, and the *Logos* was with God; and the *Logos* was God. He was in the beginning with God. All things were made through him, and without him was made nothing that has been made" (Jn 1:1–3). Thus, even before there was a Fall from grace requiring a "redemption," Jesus Christ, the later "*Logos*-in-the-flesh" (Jn 1:14), had a claim on each creature in his creation. Indeed, Paul in his missionary labors speaks of "*re-establishing all things in Christ*" (Eph 1:10). All human life is holy because it is the living reflection of the only One Who IS Holy.

Like Alan of Lille before him, Gregory IX states that Jews are "created by the Creator of all mankind. They are therefore not to be destroyed, God forbid." These are the medieval Catholic strands in the umbilical cord of the modern rights discourse of four and five centuries later: "We hold these truths to be self-evident that all men are created equal, that they are endowed by their Creator with certain inalienable rights and among these are life." A medieval and ecclesial sacra*mentality* is, therefore, a significant factor in the formation of the Western notion of tolerance.

It cannot be overstated that Raymond's *Summa* was representative, not merely of his own views on spirituality and society, but of the fledgling Dominican Order at large. Indeed, after Dominic himself, he seems to have been the greatest single personal influence that molded the mentalities of the first Dominicans, an influence that extended from one end of Europe to the other.[133] As the late Leonard Boyle writes:

> These four manuals, the most celebrated of which is the *Summa de casibus* of Raymond of Pennafort, first drafted at Barcelona about 1224, represent the very first literary activity of the Dominican Order, something which is all too readily forgotten, if ever mentioned, by histori-

133. Leonard Boyle, OP, *The Setting of the Summa Theologiae* (Toronto: Pontifical Institute of Medieval Studies, 1982), 2; "At least four useful manuals of the administration of the sacrament of penance had been put together by members of the Order at Bologna, Paris, Cologne, and Barcelona and soon were circulating . . . beyond France, Italy, Spain, and the Rhineland . . . to Britain, Ireland, Scandinavia, Poland, Hungary, and the Near East."

ans of the Order. . . . By and large these manuals and aids were meant for the generality of the members of the Dominican Order, for the *"Fratres communes"* generally engaged in the twin function of the Order, preaching and hearing confessions.[134]

Perhaps due in part to his fame as a former master from Bologna, and partly because of the popularity of his *Summa pastoralis* and *Summa* on sin, Raymond attracted the attention of the papal legate to Spain, Cardinal John of Abbeville. From 1227 to 1229, Raymond acted as John's coadjutor, assisting him in everything from the pastoral reform of the clergy to the sensitive matter of the validity of the king's marriage to the preaching of a new crusade against the Moors.[135] It was, however, particularly in the realm of sin and repentance that Friar Raymond achieved his reputation.[136]

Raymond's reputation preceded him all the way to Rome itself, where he was summoned to the court of Pope Gregory IX. According to Raymond's biographer, the Pope was ready to pay the highest honors to Raymond's penitential facility.[137] Besides, therefore, the privilege of being the pope's own confessor, Raymond was also given the office of papal penitentiary, in which case he administered confession in place of the pope himself. The office of Apostolic Penitentiary was a new and developing position within the curia, as a recent treatment states: "According to documents of 1200, a certain Cardinal Giovanni 'de S. Paolo' heard confessions for the pope. Quite probably he was assisted by other confessors placed under his authority. In the time of Pope Honorius III (1216–1227), the cardinal who exercised that office was known as 'Penitentiary,' 'General Penitentiary,' then 'the Highest Penitentiary'. . . . He had collaborators among whom were some 'friars' later called 'Minor Penitentiaries.'"[138]

Again we see an example of the developing importance of confession in the eyes of the papacy and of the friars as coadjutors or "expeditors of God's mercy." Being a friar, a canon lawyer, and the author of a lengthy summa on the subject, Raymond was naturally chosen to hear the pope's confessions, as well as those who would wish to confess to the pope (certain sins being reserved to the absolution of the bishop of

134. Boyle, *The Setting of the Summa,* 2.

135. *Raymundiana,* II, 10–13; from *Vita S. Raymundi de Penaforti ordinis Praedicatorum per fratrem Petrum Marsilii ejusdem ordinis olim conscripta et nunc primum per Francisco Diago, etc. in lucem edita* (Barciononae, Sebast. Cormellas, 1601).

136. Ibid., I, 23.

137. Ibid.

138. "Penitentiary, Apostolic," in *New Catholic Encyclopedia* (Washington, DC: Catholic University of America Press, 2001), 75.

Rome). Interestingly, Raymond's biographer explains that the office also involved ministering to those who had petitioned the Holy See and those who suffered from poverty.[139] These facts underscore Raymond's role—the role of chief confessor—as both judge of souls and physician of souls, an extension of the "charitable" mission of Christ and his vicar on earth. Lastly, it was around this time (1230) that the pope entrusted another prodigious task to Raymond, that of collecting and codifying all existing canon law into one harmonious whole.[140] His subsequent multi-volume collection came simply to be known as the *Decretals* of Gregory IX, or the *Liber extra*.

In pursuit of Peñafort we have come to a pinnacle and a point of confluence. The Dominican canonist and author of his own *summae* on law and sin was now perhaps the highest-placed prelate in Christendom, save the supreme pontiff himself. Doubtless, Raymond's task was no mean feat: he poured over endless glosses on Gratian, pronouncements of the popes, and the Church Fathers and councils, in particular the recent reforming rubrics of Lateran IV. It was now up to his discretion to make order out of chaos, to lay a matrix that would endure in substance into the twentieth century. But we should like to know with greater certainty just how much of a free hand Gregory gave Raymond (what to keep from Gratian's tome, what not?). We can only speculate. One thing seems probable; it is hard to imagine that Raymond in codifying the canon law of the Catholic Church was allowed anything akin to his own "bully-pulpit." Unlike many modern western jurists, he saw his role not as an activist "creator" of law, but as a preserver, keeping what was best and deleting what was outmoded. Thus, it should go without saying that reading the *Decretals* of Gregory IX, the *Siete Partidas* of Alfonso X, the Wise—even Raymond's *Summa de poenitentia*—is *not* the same as reading his own "blog"!

Like Paul of Hungary, though, Raymond of Peñafort could not content himself with works on canon law and confession. Ultimately, as a disciple of Dominic, he was moved to immerse himself in the culture of the "un-churched" in hopes of bringing them into the one fold, into the loving arms of an eternally Good Shepherd. From the Dominican standpoint, it was the duty of a good sheepdog to chase, to bark, to plead, to threaten; *practically any* cost was permissible—to save the sheep [the sinner: Christian, Jew, or pagan] from being devoured by the infernal wolf. This is not to excuse Dominican excesses, but to see them more in the light of a medieval morality play than a modern power-play.

139. Ibid.
140. *Raymundiana*, I, 23.

5

Coexistence & Conversion

> But if your brother shall offend against you, go, and rebuke him
> between you and him alone. If he shall hear you, you shall gain your
> brother. And if he will not hear you, take with you one or two more:
> that in the mouth of two or three witnesses every word may stand. And
> if he will not hear them: tell the Church. And if he will not hear the
> Church, let him be to you as the heathen and publican.
>
> (Matt 18:15–17)

> Let us preach to the Jews, wherever we can, in a spirit of love, whether
> they welcome our words or spurn them. It is not for us to boast over
> them as *branches broken off* (Rom. 11:17). Rather let us consider by
> Whose grace, and with what loving kindness, and into what kind of
> Root it was that we were grafted. For then, as not minding high things,
> but agreeing with the humble (Rom. 12:16), we shall be able to say to
> them without exulting over them—though we exult in God—*Come let
> us walk in the light of the Lord* (Isa 2:5).
>
> —St Augustine, *Adversus Judeos*

IF THERE EVER was a chief spokesman for Dominican theology—or
for the catechesis of the Catholic Church *in toto*—Thomas Aquinas
(1225–1274) was surely it. The famous author of the *Summa theologiae*
and master of the universities of Paris and Naples was uniquely posi-
tioned to elucidate centuries of Christian doctrine, not only in the light
of contemporary Scholasticism's distillation of the fathers and doctors
of the Church, but also through the arc of Aristotelian and Islamic traditions. If there was a distinct "Dominican ideology towards the Jews,"
undoubtedly we should find it at his doorstep. Furthermore, inasmuch
as St Raymond of Peñafort instructed Aquinas to compose a missionary

manual, we might do well to observe his notion of *tolerantia*, and glimpse perhaps more clearly the imprint of his master Peñafort and his formative influence upon him. As Boyle writes:

> Scholars allow that Thomas, who may have embarked upon his *Summa contra Gentiles* (1259–1264) at Raymund's request, probably owes many of his civil and canon law references in the *Summa [theologiae]* and in the *Scriptum super Sententiis* to the *Summa de casibus* [of Peñafort]. But the dependence runs much deeper than this. Thomas had a healthy respect for Raymund as the fine legist and able moralist that he was. There is a manifest reliance on Raymund in St Thomas' treatment of matrimony in the *Scriptum super Sententiis* (1252–1256). There are large and unsuspected borrowings from the *Summa de casibus* ... on simony in the *Secunda secundae*, which corresponds to the opening chapter of Raymund's *Summa*. The whole of the *Ad quintum* in 2-2, 100, 1 is word for word from Raymund, as are the *Ad sextum* in 2-2, 100, 2 and the long Ad *quintum* in 2-2, 100, 6.
>
> A professional familiarity as Lector at Orvieto with the *Summa de casibus* and with the system of cases and *"collectiones morales"* certainly stood Thomas in good stead later when he came to compose his *Summa theologiae*, and particularly the *Secunda secundae*, and it enabled him to field with ease the many questions concerning the pastoral care.[1]

St Thomas, in fact, was one of a commission of five which in 1259 recommended a *Ratio studiorum* for the Order to the General Chapter of Valenciennes. Among other things, his report urged "that priories without Lectors should set up private classes for the brethren on the *Historia scholastica* (of Peter Comestor), the *Summa de casibus* (of Raymund) ... to offset any danger of idleness."[2] When Thomas was himself a Lector at Orvieto, he would have treated the moral problems of practical theology found in Raymond's *Summa*. Indeed, in 1262–1263, he received a series of such questions from his Florentine counterpart at Santa Maria Novella, James of Viterbo. The future archbishop of Taranto was having difficulty interpreting Raymond's *Summa* on the buying and selling of credit and sought the Angelic Doctor's view.[3] Thomas, after consulting with an archbishop, a cardinal, and "a passing glance at what Raymund of Pennafort had to say in the *Summa de casibus* ... penned the brief, lucid reply which is now among his *Opera omnia* as *De emptione et venditione ad tempus* and upon which he later

1. Boyle, *The Setting of the Summa*, 7.
2. Ibid., 5.
3. Ibid., 6.

based part of an article in the *Secunda secundae* of his *Summa theologiae*."[4]

Having discerned something of Raymond's pedagogical stamp upon Aquinas, let us turn to his *Secunda secundae* and his teaching on tolerance. He writes: "Among unbelievers there are some who have never received the faith, such as the heathens and the Jews: and these are by no means to be compelled to the faith, in order that they may believe, because to believe depends on the will: nevertheless they should be compelled by the faithful, if it be possible to do so, so that they do not hinder the faith, by their blasphemies, or by their evil persuasions, or even by their open persecutions."[5] We see then that Thomistic tolerance is the same as that which we have already encountered in *Sicut Judaeis* and Raymond's *Summa*. Jews are not to be forced against their will to convert, because true faith requires the free acceptance of the will. Freedom of conscience, therefore, in the contemporary sense, owes no small debt to centuries of Catholic insistence on this point. What is more, though there are some today who argue for "animal rights," anyone familiar with medieval theology—and Thomas in particular—knows the teaching that only humans have rights, because only humans have free will. So in effect, every time the Church taught that Jews were not to be forcibly baptized, it was tacitly re-affirming the *humanity* of the Jews, a contribution to modern rights discourse she is seldom credited for.

As for Thomas's phrase, "they should be compelled by the faithful, if it be possible to do so, so that they do not hinder the faith, by their blasphemies, or by their evil persuasions, or even by their open persecutions," it is clear that he is not so much thinking of Jews as he is of Muslim potentates in Spain, Africa, and the Holy Land. For he adds: "It is for this reason that Christ's faithful often wage war with unbelievers, not indeed for the purpose of forcing them to believe, because even if they were to conquer them, and take them prisoners, they should still leave them free to believe, if they will, but in order to prevent them from hindering the faith of Christ."[6] His words apply to Jews, however, in the traditional sense that they were not allowed to proselytize Christians, nor openly ridicule their faith, ruin them by usury, etc.

Furthermore, the charge that the Dominicans no longer saw a place in Christendom for the Jews is utterly refuted by Thomas's own words:

---

4. Ibid.
5. *Summa theologiae*, II. II. 10. 8; www.newadvent.org/Summa.
6. *Summa*, II. II. 10. 8.

The Church does not forbid the faithful to communicate with unbelievers, who have not in any way received the Christian faith, viz. with
pagans and Jews, because she has not the right to exercise spiritual
judgment over them, but only temporal judgment, in the case when,
while dwelling among Christians they are guilty of some misde-
meanor, and are condemned by the faithful to some temporal punishment. On the other hand, in this way, i.e., as a punishment, the Church
forbids the faithful to communicate with those unbelievers who have
forsaken the faith they once received, either by corrupting the faith, as
heretics, or by entirely renouncing the faith, as apostates, because the
Church pronounces sentence of excommunication on both.[7]

This section seems a direct borrowing from Raymond's *Summa*.[8] He
teaches that the Church does not exercise spiritual judgment over Jews,
only temporal. Thomas also reiterates that heretics sin more grievously
than Jews in their unbelief, wherefore the Church prohibits the faithful
from intercourse with them, but not necessarily from Jews. Indeed,
Thomas taught that, while Jews may not keep Christians as slaves, they
may employ them as laborers.

Human government is derived from the Divine government, and
should imitate it. Now although God is all-powerful and supremely
good, nevertheless He allows certain evils to take place in the universe,
which He might prevent, lest, without them, greater goods might be
forfeited, or greater evils ensue. Accordingly in human government
also, those who are in authority, rightly tolerate certain evils, lest certain goods be lost, or certain greater evils be incurred: thus Augustine
says (*De Ordine* ii, 4): "If you do away with harlots, the world will be
convulsed with lust." Hence, though unbelievers sin in their rites, they
may be tolerated, either on account of some good that ensues therefrom, or because of some evil avoided. Thus from the fact that the Jews
observe their rites, which, of old, foreshadowed the truth of the faith
which we hold, there follows this good–that our very enemies bear witness to our faith, and that our faith is represented in a figure, so to
speak. For this reason they are tolerated in the observance of their rites.

On the other hand, the rites of other unbelievers, which are neither
truthful nor profitable are by no means to be tolerated, except per-
chance in order to avoid an evil, e.g., the scandal or disturbance that
might ensue, or some hindrance to the salvation of those who if they
were unmolested might gradually be converted to the faith. For this
reason the Church, at times, has tolerated the rites even of heretics and
pagans, when unbelievers were very numerous.[9]

7. Ibid., 10. 9.
8. *Summa de poenitentiae*, 313; cf. Ames, 268, nt. 47.
9. *Summa theologiae*, II. II. 10. 11.

Bejczy comments:

> Those who are in power, Thomas explained, rightly permit certain evils
> lest some good be brought to nothing or greater evils take their
> place.... Thus, the rites of the Jews should be tolerated, because they
> foreshadow the Christian faith, which is a good; for in this way we
> obtain testimony to our faith from our enemies. The rites of the other
> infidels, from which no good proceeds, can be tolerated so as to avoid
> scandal or hatred towards Christianity.... Tolerance for the sake of the
> good that may result from the permitted evil seems to have been Tho-
> mas' own idea. This idea did not alter the fact that the tolerated evil
> remained as evil as it ever was. Thomas alleged that the Jews sin in their
> rites and he called them "our enemies." His argument shows that one
> did not have to like the Jews to be tolerant; to the contrary, one had to
> dislike them to be tolerant, for tolerance only applied to evil. Tolerance
> was not an imperative of love but a restraint on one's hatred. It is thanks
> to this restraint however, that Jews, in the Thomistic concept, were per-
> mitted to live their own lives within the bonds of a Christian society.[10]

Actually, toleration of Jewish rites because of the good (witness) that
results from them was not "Thomas' own idea," as Bejczy suggests. As
we have seen, the idea of the "sacramental" quality of the Jews is at least
as old as St Paul, was perpetuated by centuries of popes and doctors,
and was enshrined into canon law by Raymond of Peñafort. Secondly,
Thomas never says that the Jews themselves are evil, but that their manner of worship falls into this category—and by "evil," he really means
sinful or "incorrect," not that they are evil by their very nature. Lastly,
the phrase "tolerance was not an imperative of love but a restraint on
one's hatred" is a major imprecision on Bejczy's part, as demonstrated
in the following argument.

Although Thomas says that "unbelievers sin in their rites," and these
rites may consequently be called "evil," they may be tolerated, not only
on account of "some good [witness] that ensues therefrom," but also
"because of some evil avoided." Thomas says that the evil avoided is
"some hindrance to the salvation of those who if they were unmolested
might gradually be converted to the faith. For this reason the Church, at
times, has tolerated the rites even of heretics and pagans, when unbelievers were very numerous." This seems, again, a direct borrowing from
Raymond's *Summa*.[11] Tolerance is practiced toward Jews, Muslims—

---

10. Bejczy, 372.
11. *Summa de poenitentiae*, 313; cf. Caldwell Ames, 268, nt. 47: "But the church's toleration in 'permitting' the 'sin' of their continued 'idolatry' was only for the purpose of
encouraging future conversion, indeed suggesting transcendent universality."

conceivably even to heretics (if there are enough of them)—in order to avoid any "hindrance to their salvation." Mendicant tolerance properly understood, then, meant seeking the supernatural good of those who did not practice the Catholic religion. This is not the passive "restraint of hatred," it is the *active practice of love*, the vocation of every Dominican, and, for that matter, every believing Christian. Oftentimes, love demands reminding a brother of his "error," and so Aquinas quotes Augustine [*De Verb. Dom.* xvi, 4]: "'You become worse than the sinner if you fail to correct him.' But this would not be so unless, by this neglect, one omitted to observe some [moral] precept. Therefore fraternal correction is a matter of precept [binding all]."[12] As Takashi Shogimen has pointed out, this view was not peculiar to Aquinas: "The basic pattern of the discourse on fraternal correction was formulated by Alexander of Hales in the early thirteenth century. The set of questions that he posed remained unchanged in theological scholarship from the late thirteenth to the early fourteenth century.... Hales wrote that the universal duty of fraternal correction was shown in Matt xviii. 15–17."[13] The English translation of the Vulgate reproduced at the head of this chapter runs thusly: "But if your brother shall offend against you, go, and rebuke him between you and him alone. If he shall hear you, you shall gain your brother. And if he will not hear you, take with you one or two more: that in the mouth of two or three witnesses every word may stand. And if he will not hear them: tell the church. And if he will not hear the church, let him be to you as the heathen and publican."

For Aquinas, then, depending on one's circumstances, it was either a duty of charity *not* to correct a sinner (if it was felt that doing so would make him worse), or a duty *to* correct the sinner:

> The correction of the wrongdoer is a remedy which should be employed against a man's sin. Now a man's sin may be considered in two ways, first as being harmful to the sinner, secondly as conducing to the harm of others, by hurting or scandalizing them, or by being detrimental to the common good, the justice of which is disturbed by that man's sin. Consequently the correction of a wrongdoer is twofold, one which applies a remedy to the sin considered as an evil of the sinner himself. This is fraternal correction properly so called, which is directed to the amendment of the sinner. Now to do away with anyone's evil is the same as to procure his good: and to procure a person's good

12. *Summa theologiae*, II. II. 32 a.8.

13. Takashi Shogimen, "From Disobedience to Toleration," *Journal of Ecclesiastical History*, 52, no. 4 (October 2001): 601–2.

is an act of charity, whereby we wish and do our friend well. Consequently fraternal correction also is an act of charity, because thereby we drive out our brother's evil, viz. sin, the removal of which pertains to charity rather than the removal of an external loss, or of a bodily injury, in so much as the contrary good of virtue is more akin to charity than the good of the body or of external things. Therefore fraternal correction is an act of charity rather than the healing of a bodily infirmity, or the relieving of an external bodily need. There is another correction which applies a remedy to the sin of the wrongdoer, considered as hurtful to others, and especially to the common good. This correction is an act of justice, whose concern it is to safeguard the rectitude of justice between one man and another.[14]

Indeed, as far as Aquinas, Raymond, and their Dominican confreres were concerned, tolerating Jews and preaching to Jews were *not* mutually exclusive: "Fraternal correction is not opposed to forbearance . . . on the contrary it results from it. For a man bears with a sinner, in so far as he is not disturbed against him, and retains his goodwill towards him: the result being that he strives to make him do better."[15] *Fraternal* correction, applied to infidels, logically demands that said unbelievers are to be considered "brothers." Yes, they must be corrected, for the good of their souls (charity)—and of Christian society at large (justice)—but they must also be borne with (tolerated), as must all sinners.

Aquinas's quintessential Dominican approach to Jews and Muslims must be seen as an extension of the admonishment of the sinner, the penitential subject of the preacher and confessor, a subject we have treated at length in preceding chapters. Teaching and reproving Jews, then, far from constituting hostility, was more an act of charity than of justice:

It is fitting for a religious order to be established for the works of the active life, in so far as they are directed to the good of our neighbor, the service of God, and the upkeep of divine worship. Now the good of our neighbor is advanced by things pertaining to the spiritual welfare of the soul rather than by things pertaining to the supplying of bodily needs, in proportion to the excellence of spiritual over corporal things. Hence it was stated above (Question 32, Article 3) that spiritual works of mercy surpass corporal works of mercy. Moreover this is more pertinent to the service of God, to Whom no sacrifice is more acceptable than zeal for souls, as Gregory says (*Hom. xii in Ezech*).[16]

14. *Summa*, II. II. 33. 1.
15. Ibid.
16. Ibid., II. II. 188. 2.

Aquinas argues that his Order of Preachers has been established chiefly for the spiritual good of others. Willing "the good" for Jews means loving them and considering them "friends." As he writes:

> Love is not divided into friendship and concupiscence [selfish desire], but into love of friendship, and love of concupiscence. For *a friend is, properly speaking, one to whom we wish good: while we are said to desire, what we wish for ourselves....* When friendship is based on usefulness or pleasure, a man does indeed wish his friend some good: and in this respect the character of friendship is preserved. But since he refers this good further to his own pleasure or use, the result is that friendship of the useful or pleasant, in so far as it is connected with love of concupiscence, loses the character to true friendship.[17] (emphasis mine)

This preaching-as-love-of-neighbor was the same approach taken by Aquinas's master Raymond of Peñafort:

> And preaching must be in one of the following ways, namely: either to explain to them how they may know and understand the belief in the Faith and how to avoid committing sin after they have understood it: or how they can perform Penance for their sins after they have committed them. In order to do this properly, he who preaches must possess three qualifications: first, charity, which means the love of God, more than anything else, as well as love of himself and of his neighbor.[18]

It would have startled medieval university faculty like Raymond and Thomas to hear their modern successors describe their program of preaching and proselytism as a will-to-power to "bring the world to order":

> Nothing was more vital to this vision of Christendom than the idea of order; thus no heresy, no deviation of any sort from designated roles and statuses could be tolerated. But it was becoming evident that Jews were doing just that: deviating from their proper roles far beyond the limits of toleration.... The obvious solution was to step up the effort to eliminate Judaism entirely by converting each and every Jew ... the campaign was spearheaded by Dominican and Franciscan friars, who had emerged around 1215 as militant orders dedicated to relentless missionizing and inquisitorial persecution of anyone whose beliefs and practices challenged the supremacy of the Church.[19]

---

17. Ibid., II. II. 26. 4.
18. Burns, *Las Siete Partidas*, I. V. XLII.
19. Glick, 189–90.

In Dominican eyes, persuading "Others" into the One Fold was more the act of a lover seeking union with his beloved:

In like manner when a man loves another with the love of friendship, *he wills good to him, just as he wills good to himself*: wherefore he apprehends him as his other self, in so far, to wit, as he wills good to him as to himself. Hence a friend is called a man's "other self" (*Ethic.* ix, 4). . . . The first of these unions is caused "effectively" by love; because love moves man to desire and seek the presence of the beloved, as of something suitable and belonging to him. The second union is caused "formally" by love; because love itself is this union or bond. In this sense Augustine says (*De Trin.* viii, 10) that "love is a vital principle uniting, or seeking to unite two together, the lover, to wit, and the beloved." For in describing it as "uniting" he refers to the union of affection, without which there is no love: and in saying that "it seeks to unite," he refers to real union.[20] (emphasis mine)

As the late Thomistic scholar and Muslim missionary Fr. Joseph Kenny, OP put it:

Love of God and neighbour is further manifested in mercy, another state of mind whereby, because of our love for our neighbour, we regard the evil that he is suffering as our own, we have sympathy for him and are motivated to do whatever we can to relieve him of his suffering.

When it comes to words, love is again the opposite of hate. Love rejoices in the truth, even the hard and bitter truth which it bravely upholds. It also accords praise where praise is due, gives credit where credit is deserved, and expresses gratitude where benefits have been received.

And as for actions, love builds up where hate tears down. It is beneficent and gives liberally. Above all, it translates mercy into zakāk. To relieve bodily needs, it leads one to feed the hungry, give drink to the thirsty, clothe the naked, house the homeless, visit the sick, redeem captives and bury the dead. To relieve spiritual needs, it leads one to pray for others, teach them, counsel them, console them, correct them, forgive them, and put up with their defects.

Where we saw hatred at its worst, in converting its victim into a devil by bad example, we see love at its best in the exercise of fraternal correction. While public authority can do this on a coercive level, through police and prisons, on a non-coercive level it is the equivalent of:

كُر ن م ال عن نﻪي وال عروف م ال ب ر الأم .

It is an attempt on the part of any private citizen to persuade someone who is leading a bad life to make a turn-about, a conversion to a good

---

20. Ibid., II. II. 28. 1.

or a better life. *Love is at its best and most effective level of operation when, with God's grace, it can change a human devil into a saint.*[21]

Saintly proselytizers, far from viewing Jews as "demon-dogs," saw them as their "other selves," and wished to share with them the greatest good which they themselves possessed: Jesus Christ and the fullness of his faith. If Raymond and his friars were prompted by such motivations, then their interest in the Talmud is all the more explicable; besides fear of potential blasphemies, it was a case of the lover seeking to "know" the beloved:

> The beloved is said to be in the lover, inasmuch as the beloved abides in the apprehension of the lover, according to Philippians 1:7, "For that I have you in my heart": while the lover is said to be in the beloved, according to apprehension, inasmuch as the lover is not satisfied with a superficial apprehension of the beloved, but strives to gain an intimate knowledge of everything pertaining to the beloved, so as to penetrate into his very soul. Thus it is written concerning the Holy Ghost, Who is God's Love, that He "searcheth all things, yea the deep things of God" (1 Cor 2:10).[22]

Even someone as patently hostile (as we shall see) as Raymond Martini was—on some level, it seems—attempting to "love his enemies." Martini would not accept students at his language school who were merely academically curious about non-Christians, only those who wished to learn the liturgical languages of Jews and Saracens in order to save souls. As one of his pupils put it: "I have often hoped, dearest father, that the seed of the Hebrew language, which the zeal of the religious brother R. Martini sowed in the garden of my heart, should be useful not only for myself, but also for the eternal salvation of others of the faithful."[23] This was the original mandate for Dominican language schools for training preachers in Hebrew and Arabic: "We enjoin the prior provincial of Spain that he ordain some place of study for learning

21. Fr. Joseph Kenny, OP, "The Anatomy of Violence," Dominican Institute, Ibadan Conference on Islam, terrorism and African development organized by the Department of Arabic and Islamic Studies, University of Ibadan 8–10 February 2006: http://www.dhspriory.org/kenny/AnatomyViolence.htm.

22. Ibid., II. II. 28. 2.

23. Arnold of Villanova, *Allocutio super significatione nominis Thetragrammaton*, ed. Joaquín Carreras I Artau, "La 'Allocutio super Tetragrammaton' de Arnaldo de Vilanova," *Sefarad*, 9 (1949), 80–105; As cited in Mark D. Johnston, *The evangelical rhetoric of Ramon Llull: lay learning and piety in the Christian West around* 1300 (New York, NY: Oxford University Press, 1996), 56. Arnold was not a friar, but an active layperson and translator.

the Arabic language, in the religious house of Barcelona or elsewhere, and assign there some friars, of whom it may be hoped, that from this mode of study they may become proficient in the saving of souls. Moreover, whoever and from whatever province may have wished to learn the Arabic language, let him write to this teacher/master."[24]

Indeed, what present-day professors call "hatred" or "aggressiveness" on the part of mendicant missionizers and Talmudic censors might just as easily be categorized in medieval terms as the "zealousness" associated with one who loves deeply:

> love of friendship seeks the friend's good: wherefore, when it is intense, it causes a man to be *moved against everything that opposes the friend's good.* In this respect, a man is said to be zealous on behalf of his friend, when he makes a point of repelling whatever may be said or done against the friend's good. In this way, too, a man is said to be zealous on God's behalf, when he endeavors, to the best of his means, to repel whatever is contrary to the honor or will of God; according to 1 Kings 19:14: "With zeal I have been zealous for the Lord of hosts." Again on the words of John 2:17: "The zeal of Thy house hath eaten me up," a gloss says that "a man is eaten up with a good zeal, who strives to remedy whatever evil he perceives; and if he cannot, *bears with it* and laments it."[25] (emphasis mine)

Ultimately, all things which the Christian faith categorized as sinful or lacking in the fullness of the truth were considered obstacles to Jewish-Christian "re-union" and Raymond and the Dominicans acted earnestly to "repel" them wherever they saw them; even if it meant (as we shall see) censoring passages of the Talmud or forced sermons in synagogues, such "zeal" was considered acceptable. Unable to bring Jews to embrace the fullness of Gospel truth, devout Christians practiced "forbearance" toward Talmudic literature and Jewish ritual, while simultaneously "lamenting it."

It may sound absurd to some to call religious proselytism "love," but what hermeneutic gives us better historical insight: using the "mental constructions" of the participants themselves, or importing twentieth-century academic discourse concerning "elites and minorities"?

> He who announces the Gospel participates in the charity of Christ, who loved us and gave himself up for us (cf. Eph 5:2); he is his ambassador and he pleads in the name of Christ: let yourselves to be reconciled with God! (cf. 2 Cor 5:20). It is a charity which is an expression of

---

24. *Acta I* (Valenciennes, 1259), 101; in Mulchahey, *First the Bow is Bent*, 348.
25. Ibid., II. II. 28. 4.

the gratitude that flows from the heart when it opens to the love given in Jesus Christ, that Love which, as Dante wrote, is displayed throughout the universe [39]. This explains the ardour, the confidence, and the freedom of speech (parrhesia) evident in the preaching of the Apostles (cf. Acts 4:31; 9:27–28; 26:26, etc.) and which Agrippa experienced when he heard Paul speaking: "You will soon persuade me to become a Christian!" (Acts 26:28).[26]

Even some present-day scholars have, at times, seen the wisdom in the medieval approach:

> If I want to engage in dialogue with you, I must recognize your otherness, your fundamental difference from me. . . . But I must not remain mute because you are Other: I must speak to you, provoke you, understand you—speak my love to you (you who are so close to me, you who are so far away from me) and at the same time let myself be won over by you. In this dangerous game, and it is much more than a game, you can lose your soul, I can lose my soul. . . . I believe that certain authors of the twelfth and thirteenth century reached this fine point of tenuous grace, achieving a dialogue which can serve as a model for us today.[27]

At the very least, modern scholars ought to accept as evidence of "dialogue" or "tolerance" what they cannot themselves admit as "love." The late Richard Popkin, for instance, does exactly this when, after surveying several early modern millenarian Christian movements (including mendicant missionaries in Mexico) and their relations with Jews and unbelievers, he concludes by saying:

> The millennial tolerationists covered above almost all expected the end result of their toleration policies would be to make everybody pure and true Christians if God so willed. In the interim (which they did not think would be too long), a legally tolerant world had to be created in order to prepare for this. Their advocacy and action to create such a world probably did at least as much to create modern tolerant societies as the deist and nonreligious groups in Europe and America in the seventeenth and eighteenth centuries.[28]

26. *Doctrinal Note on Some Aspects of Evangelization*, 11.
27. Gilbert Dahan, *The Christian Polemic against the Jews in the Middle Ages*, trans. Jody Gladding (South Bend, IN: University of Notre Dame Press, 1998), 118.
28. Richard Popkin, "Skepticism About Religion and Millenarian Dogmatism: Two Sources of Toleration in the Seventeenth Century," in *Beyond the Persecuting Society, Religious Toleration Before the Enlightenment*, eds. John Christian Laursen and Cary J. Nederman (Philadelphia, PA: University of Pennsylvania Press, 1998), 244.

The fact is, even a cursory reading of the medieval sources makes it clear that *supernatural* categories of love and sin were at the heart of mendicant relations with non-Christians, not some sociological agenda to make infidel minds walk in lock-step in one universal *temporal* entity: "Christian Europe." Dominican mission to Jews was more akin to the mentality of Mother Teresa than of Machiavelli. In her private correspondence the modern day "saint of Calcutta" reveals that it was a supernatural vision of Jesus and his desire to save "sinful" souls that launched her heroic service to the poorest of the poor: "*Little one give me souls—give Me the souls of the poor street children.—How it hurts—if you only knew—to see these poor children soiled with sin. I long for the purity of their love.—If you would only answer My call—and bring Me these souls—draw them from the hands of the evil one—If you only knew how many little ones fall into sin every day.*"[29]

What was at stake in the thirteenth-century approach of the friars to the Jews was, in the words of Raymond of Peñafort, "sin," the violation of "the honor of God," the identical expressions found in Anselm's rational dialogue with infidels of a century-and-a-half earlier. For the Dominicans to simply "leave the Jews alone" would have been a betrayal of both God and man. As one modern Catholic theologian put it:

> Apart from the contradiction with the words of Christ and the Apostles, indeed with the whole teaching of the Church, this notion of leaving the Jews alone shows a very great lack of love for the Jews. For the deepest core of true love of neighbor is the concern for the eternal salvation of the neighbor. Therefore, one should encounter no man without seeing in him a living member of the Mystical Body of Christ or a catechumen *in spe* (a prospective catechumen).
>
> Let it not be objected that he can also attain his eternal salvation outside the Church, as a Protestant or as a non-Christian. This is, of course, a dogma which was defined at the First Vatican Council, but it changes nothing of the mission which Christ gave us: "Go forth into all the world and teach all peoples and baptize them," nor of the enormous importance of the adoration of God in truth, in Christ, *per ipsum, cum ipso, et in ipso*. There is after all an infinite value in the glorification of God which is present in the true Faith, in union with God through sanctifying grace and all the sacraments. And this desire to glorify God is an apostolate which flows from the true love of Christ,

29. Blessed Mother Teresa of Calcutta, Letter to Archbishop Périer, January 13, 1947, as cited in *Mother Teresa: Come Be My Light, The Private Writings of the "Saint of Calcutta,"* ed. Brian Kolodiejchuk, MC (New York and London: Doubleday, 2007), 49.

cannot be separated from true love of neighbor, which is grounded in the love of Christ alone.[30]

Caritas was uppermost in Dominican minds, the eternal salvation of Christian—and non-Christian—souls and the glory this gives Almighty God; they did not have to brand Jews "heretics" to justify a missionary approach to them. *This* is the innovative ideology behind the school of Raymond of Peñafort: that Jews, Muslims, and other infidels are capable of salvation and need as much pastoring as Christians.

The world-at-large in the mid-thirteenth century, however, was as hostile to the "otherworldly" peace of Christ as it had ever been. Consider the wave of devastation, stretching thousands of miles, littered with millions of corpses: the arrival of the Mongols. Southern, in his book, *Western Views of Islam in the Middle Ages*, characterizes "the appearance of the Mongols on the scene of history" as the

> event which did more than anything else to change the whole aspect of the Islamic problem ... the Mongols greatly enlarged the geographic horizon.... Peter the Venerable [had estimated] ... that Islam contained a third, or possibly even half of the people of the world.... By the middle of the thirteenth century, it was seen that this picture was far too optimistic. There were ten, or possibly a hundred unbelievers for every Christian.... We see that [Roger] Bacon ... now ... had a true measure of the place of Christendom in the world: "There are few Christians; the whole breadth of the world is occupied by unbelievers, and there is no one to show them the truth."[31]

Peter the Venerable of Cluny was one of the first medieval Christians to grasp the enormity of the non-Christian population of the world. Peter's groundbreaking response was to work toward a Latin translation of the Qur'an. Like his neighbors the Cistercians, who took the first grudging steps to proselytize heretics, the Venerable Cluniac was pioneering the Christian use of non-Christian religious texts. Alan of Lille,

30. Dietrich Von Hildebrand, *The Devastated Vineyard*, trans. John Crosby and Fred Teichert (Chicago, IL: Franciscan Herald Press, 1973), 93–94. Von Hildebrand, incidentally, was forced to flee Austria when Hitler and the Gestapo placed him especially high on their elimination list. His outspoken defense of truth (and of Jews) very nearly cost him his life.

31. Sir Richard Southern, *Western Views of Islam in the Middle Ages* (Cambridge, MA: Harvard University Press, 1962), 42–43.

and later Raymond of Peñafort and the mendicants, would refine such practices in evangelizing the infidel both at home and abroad. In addition, language study was to become a priority that would especially occupy the energies of Peñafort and his Franciscan contemporary Roger Bacon, as would the enduring twelfth-century tradition of wielding rational philosophical arguments in the service of Christian outreach.

More than two hundred years of wielding swords of steel had accomplished little in the spread of the reign of Christ. "Pop-history" notwithstanding, though the Crusades were not particularly about *converting* infidels, nevertheless, repeated thirteenth-century military failures such as the Fourth Crusade (which sacked Christian Constantinople instead) and the Crusade of St Louis of France (which exacted a king's ransom for his safe return), not to mention the utter devastation wrought upon civilized men by the wrath of the Mongols, added a sense of urgency to the mission of those Christians who thirsted for the redemption of unbelievers (and the preservation of Christendom). In a frighteningly short span of years, the Mongols had brutally subjected the civilizations of China, Russia, Central Asia and eventually even the Eastern Islamic Empire. The news reached anxious European ears: "It is evident that the Tartars have destroyed nearly the whole dominion of the Saracen on the north, east, and south as far as Egypt and Africa. Thus it happens that their Caliph, who holds the position of a pope among them, was destroyed thirteen years ago, and Baldach [Bagdad], a city belonging to that Caliph, was captured with a great number of Saracens."[32] This apocalyptic backdrop should not be forgotten—as it so often is—in works treating thirteenth-century mendicant approaches toward Jews. If we do not understand the wider context, we shall certainly fail to adequately appraise the novel mission programs of Raymond of Peñafort and others.

It was in 1235, while Raymond was actively ministering to Gregory IX as confessor and penitentiary, that the pontiff issued the bull *Cum hora undecima*, which was a universal appeal for the evangelization of the unbaptized: "Since the eleventh hour has come in the day given to mankind . . . it is necessary that spiritual men [possessing] purity of life and the gift of intelligence should go forth with John [the Baptist] again to all men and all peoples of every tongue and in every kingdom to prophesy because, according to the prophet Isaias, the salvation of the

---

32. Roger Bacon, *Opus Maius*, trans. ed. Robert Belle Burke, 2 vols. (New York, NY: Russell & Russell, 1928; reprinted 1962).

remnant of Israel will not occur until, as St Paul says, 'the *plenitudo gen-tilium* enters first' into ... heaven."[33] The Roman Church—at least in its finer moments—did not limit this supernatural love to its camp-followers, but encouraged its practice toward all men. Witness St Augustine's echo of St Paul cited above: "Let us preach to the Jews, wherever we can, *in a spirit of love*, whether they welcome our words or spurn them. It is not for us to boast over them as branches broken off (Rom. 11:17)." (emphasis mine) The point of our present study is precisely this: that the motive of Christian love of God and neighbor is visible not only in papal decretals aimed at protecting Jews, but in Dominican *mission* to them and to other "infidels." Caritas was, at the very least, no less a factor than fear or self-preservation for the Church's leadership in its dealings with an un-Christian world. Pope Gregory IX, for example, writing to the Dominicans in 1238, offered them the same indulgence for proselytizing Muslims in the Holy Land as Lateran IV had granted to Christian knights for its military recapture: "It is no less commendable in the eyes of the Redeemer to convert the infidels to the faith by preaching the divine word than it is to subdue by arms the perfidy of the Saracens."[34] This was the essence of the Catholic Church and of the Order of Preachers, a subject we now take up in earnest.

Muldoon explains the biblical significance of Gregory's "eleventh-hour appeal":

> The bull ... contained the basic statement of the church's missionary function.... The opening lines ... reflected the apocalyptic tradition that was strong among the members of the Franciscan order in its early years.... The task of the missionaries was to fulfill Christ's injunction to preach the gospel to all men so that the process of salvation might be completed. They were to strengthen those Christians whose faith was weak, to correct the false doctrines of heretics, and to bring the non believers into the fold. In order to facilitate the missionaries' work, Gregory IX granted them a number of special privileges, including the right to hear confessions anywhere, to absolve excommunicates, to dispense converts from various kinds of irregularities, probably referring to minor impediments involving marriage and generally to ease the way into the fold of those outside of it.[35]

---

33. Pope Gregory IX, *Cum hora undecima*, in James Muldoon, *Popes, Lawyers, and Infidels* (Philadelphia, PA: University of Pennsylvania Press, 1979), 36–37; Vose, *Dominicans, Muslims and Jews*, 40–43. Original text in Latin in A. Tautu, ed., *Acta Honorii III et Gregorii IX* (Rome, 1950), 286–87 (#210).

34. Kedar, "Canon Law," 142.

35. Ibid.

These special privileges were exactly the kinds of works with which Raymond of Peñafort especially busied himself as penitentiary; thus over the course of the years 1234–1235, we must surely recognize Raymond's hand, not only in the codification of the Church's law, but in the charting of a "new evangelization." Once again, the theology of sin, repentance, and reconciliation is exposed as the undergirding beneath the Church's missionary efforts. As early as 1225, Pope Honorius III had granted the mendicant orders in North Africa permission to preach to infidels and apostate Christians.[36] Ten years later, Raymond authored a set of canonical responses in reply to questions of sin posed to the Holy See by Dominicans and Franciscans already at work in Tunisia. As Muldoon explains:

> During the pontificates of Honorius III (1216–1227) and Gregory IX (1227–1243), the missionary zeal of the Franciscans and Dominicans led to further papal contact with the ruler of Morocco. In order to ease their way, Honorius authorized some modifications in the garb they wore so that they would not attract unnecessary attention. Some years later, Gregory IX wrote to the ruler of Morocco inviting him to receive baptism at the hands of the friars working in his land, an invitation that was refused. . . . On the other hand, the ruler of Morocco was not uninterested in relations with the papacy. In 1235 he sent an embassy consisting of two Genoese merchants to the pope seeking to arrange a treaty with the papacy. The embassy, which is known from Gregory's response, led to the dispatching of a Franciscan friar to Morocco for discussions with the Moroccan ruler. The use of a Franciscan as the papal envoy suggests that the main purpose of an agreement with the Moroccan ruler was the protection of the Christians living there and the friars who were being sent to minister to them. In addition, the friars were expected to preach to the Moslems.[37]

In his reply to the Dominicans and Franciscans, Raymond makes it clear that he is interested in the eternal salvation of both the Christians and Muslims in Tunis, and he is not unmindful even of the temporal welfare of the infidels at Christian hands. Though his answers are mostly about sins and sacraments, he also says: "Certain ones steal Jews or Saracens and most of all women, and leading them into the land of the Saracens, they make them, by coercion, profess to the Saracens that they are Christian men and women, and under the Christian name they sell them. We ask whether such are excommunicated because of the

---

36. Ben Kedar, *Crusade and Mission, European Approaches toward the Muslims* (Princeton, NJ: Princeton University Press, 1984), 143.
37. Ibid., 39–40.

injury they do to the Christian name? We answer: They are not excommunicated, but they sin mortally."[38]

In the same year which saw the release of *Cum hora undecima* and Raymond's replies to the friars of Morocco, the saint obtained approval from Pope Gregory for an Order specifically devoted to the redemption of Christian slaves from Muslim captivity. The Order of Our Lady of Ransom (also known as the Order of Our Lady of Mercy) had first sprung in the 1220s from a collaborative effort between Raymond, St Peter Nolasco, and King James I of Aragon, involving a shared vision of the holy Virgin, who had requested its inauguration. Peter, fleeing war-torn Languedoc with young James, had first approached Raymond, not surprisingly, in the confessional at Barcelona. He held a passionate concern for Christian prisoners of war, as did Raymond, according to his biographer.[39] Thus it was that Raymond applied his juridical talent in establishing yet another set of laws governing a religious society. The Order of Our Lady of Mercy borrowed from the rule of St Augustine and the Dominicans, but it was essentially a military-monastic Order; Peter Nolasco and other nobles of a spiritual bent had first started out as a confraternity in Barcelona to care for the sick in hospitals, as well as for ransoming Christian prisoners. The establishment of the Mercedarians was, therefore, a solidification and continuation of this initial venture. The Order sought to ransom the captive by money; they wept with those who wept, and sold themselves into captivity for the liberation of Christian slaves, as their fourth vow has it: "And if necessary, I shall remain captive in the hands of the Saracens, for the redemption of the faithful of Christ."[40]

The Christ-like self-sacrifice of the Mercedarians had both individual and corporate precedents. Jordan of Saxony writes that St Dominic once offered himself in ransom to the heretics, while his namesake, St Dominic of Silos, a member of the Order of the Most Holy Trinity for the Redemption of Captives, had done likewise many times himself. In 1198, Innocent III had written a letter of introduction for the Order of the Trinity to the ruler of Morocco on behalf of their efforts. His letter also suggested that "the prince might be interested in exchanging Moslems held by Europeans for Christians held captive in Morocco."[41] Thus it was that popes and holy men had for some time been interested in

---

38. One could assume that the mortal sin here also concerns inhumane treatment of infidels, besides the primary affront to the word "Christian"; *Raymundiana*, I, 31–32.

39. *Raymundiana*, I, 36.

40. Schwertner, 49.

41. Muldoon, *Popes, Lawyers, Infidels*, 39.

establishing various missions to Muslims in North Africa, and not always of a hostile nature.

If Gregory IX's Moroccan policy had its forerunners, it also had its successors. Innocent IV (1243–1254) reissued *Cum hora undecima* in 1145 and in that same year sent a delegation of Dominicans to the sultan while on mission to the Mongols:

> After an unsuccessful attempt to obtain the assistance of the sultan in crossing over from the Moslem-held lands of the Near East into the Tartar lands, the two Dominicans reached the Tartars by different routes. One byproduct of the Dominican contact with the sultan was a letter from him to Innocent IV concerning the possibility of a disputation between representatives of both faiths. The sultan pointed out that the Dominicans did not know Arabic and that there was no one among his subjects sufficiently learned in Christian teachings to debate the Dominicans effectively.[42]

Whether as a direct result of the sultan's criticism or not, it was in the years that followed (1245–1255) his observations that the first Dominican school of language was established in Tunis. As with the creation of the Mercedarians, it was a feat involving a miraculous vision and the cooperation of Raymond of Peñafort and James of Aragon.[43] The master-general who gave Raymond license to begin his *studium lingue* was his successor, John Wildeshausen. Master John was a Dominican who was himself devoted to the study of languages, to preaching to infidels, and, notably, to confession and absolving penitents on behalf of the papacy. In his entry for the year 1241, Gerald of Frachet writes:

> Brother John was elected Master at Paris. He was a German from the town of Wildeshausen in Saxony. . . . He was received in the early days of the Order [1220–1221], and was an outstanding preacher in many languages: German, Italian, French and Latin, and his preaching produced good results everywhere he went. Therefore he was taken as assistant to many cardinals and acted as penitentiary in various Papal missions. While he was prior provincial of Hungary, he was made bishop of Bosnia.[44]

Hungary, as we have seen, was mission territory for the Dominicans. It was here that Friar John established a reputation for sanctity in the *cura animarum*, as King Bela of Hungary testified to the Order after John's death in 1253:

42. Ibid., 43.
43. *Raymundiana*, I, 32.
44. *Vitae fratrum*, 7.

How wonderful was the virtue and good life of Bishop John of Bosnia, of holy memory, who first lived among us and then became the Master of your Order. As we and the people of our kingdom take delight in recalling his memory, we are stirred to devotion and contrition. He was a kind father to the afflicted, using his little episcopal revenue only to help the poor. In a word, he took pity on the pitiable and suffered for the suffering. His preaching was inspired by the Holy Spirit, enlightening and moving his listeners as he attracted them like honey. He was a true witness of Christ, filled with the grace of God and was loved by all. His merits could not stay hidden, but were brought to light by miracles as people with unruffled faith asked for his prayers. We and others can testify that he raised a dead man, made the crippled to walk and the blind to see. We also, impressed by his holy life, often confidently asked for his prayers to help people who were seriously ill.[45]

It speaks to the spiritual motivations behind the Dominican schools of language that two men proposed as saints were responsible for their creation. We may also observe the hand of Master John in the promotion of Raymond's *studia* from another historical source, specifically, the Spanish provincial chapter of 1250, held in Toledo. As Mulchahey writes: "In 1250, the Spanish provincial chapter announced its plans to establish a new convent in North Africa, and fluency in Arabic was wisely noted as key to the friars' success there. By way of explanation for a mission outside its own borders, the chapter declared its concern for infidel souls, but also cited an order the Spanish friars had received from master-general John of Wildeshausen that they choose from amongst themselves who would devote their energies to the study of Arabic."[46]

Mulchahey's translation of the minutes from the chapter reads as follows:

Wishing to fulfill the command of the master and conscious of the usefulness of the plan to present lives, but especially to those who will come after us, we assign brother Amoldo Guardia, brother Pedro de Cadireta, brother Ramon Martin, brother Pedro Ariam, brother Pedro de Puteo, brother Pedro de San Feliz, brother Dominic Estevan, and Pedro de Canoles, to study Arabic [*ad studium Arabicum*], enjoining this in remission of their sins by our authority and that of the master, in the name of the Father and of the Son and of the Holy Spirit. We designate the above-named Arnoldo Guardia the others' superior, and

45. Ibid., 6.
46. Mulchahey, *First the Bow is Bent*, 345.

we shall bring their number up to twelve at the first opportunity God provides.[47]

In addition to a foundation at Tunis, we are told of a second school in Murcia. As Peter Marsilio, the distinguished Dominican and counselor to James II, writes: "He established schools of languages for the brothers of his Order of Tunis and Murcia, to which he caused chosen Catalan brothers to be assigned, who became a beautiful mirror of their nation, and brought forth much fruit in the way of souls."[48] As for the *fructum animarum*, Raymond's biographer writes: "From which the greatest fruit followed, for more than ten thousand Saracens were converted by the brothers preaching to them, and the truth of the Christian faith was made known among Saracens in both Spain and Africa, and soon so approved that many of them were quickly disposed to receive the truth of the Catholic faith and, as a matter of fact, nearly all of the brothers' teachers in the Arabic language were converted by their industry."[49]

"Ten thousand Muslim converts" may be a greatly exaggerated figure, but the bottom line is that Raymond's school-to-mission effort undoubtedly achieved much initial success in both Tunis and Murcia. A report from Raymond to the Order from *c.* 1258 reads as follows:

The progress made by the ministry of the brothers in Africa and Spain can be summarized in the following areas:

First, among Christian soldiers staying there, many of whom are hungry for the word of God.

Secondly, among the Aramaeans, who are Christians but slaves of the Muslims. They understand only Arabic and greatly desire brothers to teach and strengthen them.

Thirdly, among apostates who are being brought back to the faith through the efforts of the brothers. Many Christians tempted to apostatize because of extreme poverty or because of allurements by the Muslims have held onto their faith and have been strengthened in it through the efforts of the brothers.

Fourthly, both Muslims and many Christians misled by them thought that Christians are idolaters because of the images that they venerate in church. Many of these have, by the grace of God and the teaching of the brothers, been brought back to the truth.

---

47. Ibid.
48. *Raymundiana*, I, 12.
49. Ibid., I, 32.

FIFTHLY, among Christian captives, whom the brothers instruct and strengthen in their faith; sometimes even get them released.

SIXTHLY, there is progress among the Muslims themselves, especially among their princes, notably with the *amîr al-mu'minîn*, or king of Tunisia. God has given them more grace and favour than it is advisable to write about at present. The door seems to be open for inestimable fruit, as long as the harvesters are not lacking. Many Muslims, especially at Murcia have been converted to the faith both secretly and openly.[50]

We can learn several things from Raymond's report. In the first place, the brothers' knowledge of Arabic is not only a tool for the conversion of Saracens, it is part of a broader effort to save Christian, as well as infidel, souls. Raymond speaks of Dominican approaches to Christian slaves, who understand only Arabic, and of Christian soldiers and prisoners who also need the ministrations of Catholic priests. Among the Muslims, Raymond especially indicates a degree of success among Tunisian nobles, including the king himself. It seems that much progress had indeed been made in the decade since the sultan exchanged embassies with Pope Innocent IV. Paraphrasing Christ's words, Raymond notes that the potential harvest is great and thus, more laborers are required.

It is within this context that we must understand the address of the new master-general of the Dominican Order, Humbert of Romans, to the General Chapter of 1255. Humbert not only called for a renewed missionary effort, he admonished those friars who were reluctant to minister to non-Christians because of their lack of training in foreign tongues. He attributed their fault not to their intellects, but their wills: "Scarcely any of the Brethren wish to study" foreign languages, because of an inordinate affection for their native lands and families.

Humbert concludes his letter by appealing to the friars to exhibit some of that same Christ-like self-sacrifice as Dominic himself first displayed on behalf of souls:

> If therefore, under the inspiration of the Grace of God, any one of you is willing to apply himself according to our wish to the study of Arabic, Hebrew, or Greek languages, or any other barbarian tongue; or if there be anyone disposed to go out from his own country to pass into Palestine, Greece, or any other provinces which lie adjacent to infidel countries, where there is great need of Religious who are capable of suffering much for the Order, for the Faith, for the salvation of souls

---

50. *Vitae fratrum*, 6.

and the Name of our Lord Jesus Christ, I beg him to make it known to me.[51]

Christ had preached: "Greater love hath no man than to lay down his life for his friends" (Jn 15:13). He followed up this preaching the next day with its excruciatingly difficult practice on the cross. For the mendicants, the Mount of Calvary was their chief example and the "school of love" of neighbor. The fact that masters Dominic, Raymond, John, and Humbert all spearheaded missions to Jews, Muslims, and pagans, far from demonstrating the rise of a thirteenth-century persecuting society which saw such segments as subhuman, proves precisely the opposite; for as Humbert succinctly states in his *Treatise on the Formation of Preachers*: "Preaching is directed at *man*."[52] (emphasis mine) Furthermore, he then, in good scholastic fashion, explains why preaching has *nothing* to do with earthbound motives (would that today's academics understood him on this point):

[Preaching] is concerned with the soul, not the body . . . it is souls that are sought by preaching. And what it seeks with regard to them is only what is relevant to salvation. . . . A job done for a king is more noble than a job done for his horses, and a job done in a temple is more noble than one performed in the stables. So what a noble job it must be [preaching], which is concerned with the most worthy of all creatures [man], and with the more worthy part of that creature [the soul], and with the more worthy aspect [salvation] of that part of the most worthy creature![53]

This is surely proof of the vertical-sacramental mindset of the Dominicans. Humbert goes on at length about the necessity of preaching, continually referencing spiritual, not temporal, ends: "Preaching hastens the end of time when all creation shall finally show its full measure of glory, it spreads supernatural knowledge and so reduces the number of souls falling into hell, it sows the word of God and makes lives fruitful, it liberates souls from the subjugation of demons, and it stirs the hearts of men to hope for heavenly rewards." This especially includes non-Christians, according to Humbert: "Again, [preaching] is supremely necessary for the barbarian peoples of the world to come to faith in Christ, because without it they cannot be saved . . . people cannot have such faith unless someone preaches to them."[54] Later, Hum-

51. Burns, *Las Siete Partidas*, 102.
52. Humbert, *Treatise on the Formation of Preachers*, 186.
53. Ibid.
54. Ibid, 186–88.

bert invokes the same language Lateran IV laid down concerning the sacrament of penance with regard to preaching:

> Again, the word of God is the medicine which heals everything (*Wisd* 16:12), and *preachers are doctors*, as Matthew 9:12 shows, "It is not the healthy who need a doctor, but the sick"; and so, when there is a lack of preaching, epidemics of disease rage unchecked. This is why, by contrast, Wisdom 6:26 says, "An abundance of wise men is the health of the world," which the Gloss paraphrases, "The company of preachers is the health of the world."[55] (emphasis mine)

At the following year's meeting in Paris, we find him evidently satisfied: "From Spain we learn that the Brethren, who for some years have given themselves up to the study of the Arabic language, have made great progress, and what is still more praiseworthy is that they have converted Saracens, many of whom have already received Baptism."[56]

Incidentally, years later, in preparation for the Second Council of Lyons (1274), we again encounter Humbert's witness concerning conversion of the infidel. Though Christian losses in the Crusades have dimmed immediate prospects for peaceful coexistence with Muslim states, Europe's Jews are explicitly segregated from persecution: "Jews are tolerated because 'the remnant of Israel will be saved' (Rom 9:27; Is. 10:22). Also, because it would be cruel to kill their subjects. Also, because of the prohibition of the Prophet, saying: 'Do not kill them, lest at any time my people forget' (Psalm 59:11)."[57] Thus, Stow observes: "Those who would argue a Dominican conspiracy against the Jews, based on the premise of an aggressive, anti-Christian Judaism, should contend with explicitly contradictory statements like Humbert's here."[58] In fact, Humbert goes out of his way to point out that the Jews do not constitute a threat to Christian society: "We allow the Jews to live with us because they neither know how to cause us harm, nor are they capable of it; rather, they are ever prepared to serve."[59] This statement is all the more remarkable as it was made (as we shall see) at the precise moment when Dominican efforts aimed at Iberian Jews began to intensify.

---

55. Ibid, 189.

56. Humbert, as cited in Schwertner, 114–15; cf. Mulchahey, *First the Bow is Bent*, 347.

57. Humbert, *Opusculum tripartium*, chap. 15, in Grayzel, *Church and the Jews*, v. II, 130.

58. Grayzel, *Church and the Jews*, v. II, 130, nt. 2.

59. Humbert, in J.D. Mansi, *Sacrorum Conciliorum Collectio*, 59 vols. (Venice, 1779–1782), 24, 115, as cited in Stow, "Hatred of the Jews or Love of the Church?" *Popes, church, and Jews in the Middle Ages: confrontation and response* (Aldershot, Great Britain; Burlington, VT: Ashgate, 2007), 82.

Papal support for Raymond's *studia linguarum* was not lacking in the face of early achievement.[60] The pertinent section of Pope Alexander IV's letter to Raymond runs thusly:

> You have informed us, and we have heard gladly, that Friars Preachers sent by our mandate to Tunisia and other foreign nations, both for converting infidels and also for strengthening the faithful, are producing significant fruit through the grace of Jesus Christ. And because to you, with your son the prior provincial of Friars Preachers of Spain, it is committed that you be able to send friars of the same kind to the lands of the Saracens and to other nations of infidels, We, favorably inclined to his supplications, concede by the authority of these present words, that you and whatever friar of your order, to whom the aforesaid prior shall have committed his functions in this matter, may validly by our authority send friars suitable for this to these same places and works, and you may validly enjoin upon them jurisdiction for the remission of sins.[61]

It is possible to trace the development of two other language schools for this period in Barcelona and Valencia City. As for the former, the chapter of 1259 had this to say: "We enjoin the prior provincial of Spain that he ordain some place of study for learning the Arabic language, in the religious house of Barcelona or elsewhere, and assign there some friars, of whom it may be hoped, that from this mode of study they may become proficient in the saving of souls. Moreover, whoever and from whatever province may have wished to learn the Arabic language, let him write to this teacher/master."[62] Once again, we are reminded of the "other-worldly" purposes of these language schools and the conversant missionaries they produced.

---

60. A. Berthier, "Les écoles de langues orientales fondées aux xiii siècle par les dominicaines en Espagne et en Afrique," *Revue africaine* 73 (1932): 92–93. "Une série de bulles dans lesquelles le pape s'intéresse au sort des Prêcheurs de Tunis, confirme cette opinion. En 1256, Alexandre VI ordonne au provincial d'Espagne d'envoyer des religieux à Tunis. Il renouvelle ce commandement en 1258. Le 15 juillet 1260, il ecrit à Raymond de Péñafort, qui lui a rendu compte du succès de la mission de Tunis, et lui confirme la délégation donée par le provincial d'Espagne de pouvoir envoyer des religieux à Tunis. Il semble aussi que ce soit au groupe des frères de Tunis que se rapporte, dans le Chapitre provincial de Saragosse de 1257, l'avertissement donné aux frères de penser au *negocium arabicum* et la recommandation faite aux prieurs de les engager à prier frequemment dans les chapitres, pour les religieux assignés *huic negocio*."

61. "Diplomatari de San Ramon de Penyafort," ed. and trans. Fernando Valls y Taberner, *Analecta sacra tarraconensia* 5 (1929): 35.

62. Mulchahey, *First the Bow is Bent*, 347 nt. 376.

The issue of salvation in the Christian-Muslim encounter was a priority for Raymond and had been for some time. Coming, as he did, from Catalonia, he could not have remained uninfluenced by the *Reconquista*. Indeed, to some degree, as papal legate, he had actively instigated it. Enhanced concern for the temporal and eternal welfare of souls was a natural outcome of a revolution in Iberian hegemony. Because of its acquisition of Muslim towns and villages, in just one generation the kingdom of Aragon witnessed a population increase of almost fifty percent.[63] It is also against this backdrop that we must contextualize Raymond's overtures to infidels: the reality of Iberian *convivencia*.

The rediscovery of Aristotle through Jewish and Islamic transmitters in the opening decades of the thirteenth century put Western Christians in possession of an extensive body of learning which had been lost to them for centuries. But as Lutz-Bachmann points out:

> The Latin West did not just recover important texts of the antique philosophy and the epistemology of sciences, but also benefitted from the exchange with the tradition and culture of Arabic-speaking Islam, Judaism, and Greek-speaking Byzantium, *and with the religious concepts embedded in these respective cultures.* The centers of translation of the Greek, Arab, and Jewish philosophy and theology were at the time located in Spain, in particular the translation school connected to the Toledo cathedral.[64] (emphasis mine)

Indeed, Toledo during the reign of Alfonso VI (r. 1072–1109) has long been seen as "the epitome of the tolerant co-existence in the Middle Ages of the three major 'religions of the Book': the *cuidad de la tolerancia y la convivencia*."[65] In fact, there are some scholars who interpret the practical cooperation between Christians and Jews in their translation projects as a genuine form of "dialogue." One could point, for example, to the Jewish writer Abraham Ibn Daūd, author of *Sefer ha-Kabbalah* (*The Book of Tradition*) and *Emunah ramah* (*The Exalted Faith*). He has been characterized by some as intolerant because in the *Book of Tradition* he rests his case for the truth of Judaism on the basis of coherence

63. Anthony Bonner, trans. and ed., *Selected Works of Ramon Lull*, 2 vols. (Princeton, NJ: Princeton University Press, 1985), I, 94–95, in Chazan, *Daggers of Faith*, 5.

64. Mathais Lutz-Bachmann, "Rationalität und Religion. Der Beitrag des Thomas von Aquin zu einer rationalen Grundlegung des Religionsdialogs in der *Summa contra gentiles*," in *Juden, Christen, und Muslime: Religionsdialoge im Mittelalter*, eds. Mathais Lutz-Bachmann and Alexander Fidora (Darmstadt: Wissenschaftliche Buchgesellschaft, 2004), 96–118; 96.

65. Alexander Fidora, "Abraham Ibn Daūd und Dominicus Gundissalinus: Philosophie und religiöse Toleranz im Toledo des 12. Jahrhunderts, 10–26," in *Juden, Christen, und Muslime: Religionsdialoge im Mittelalter*, 10–27; 10.

between the Scriptures and rabbinic commentary upon them; clearly his views are authority-based, not rationally demonstrated.[66] Abraham has also been seen as anti-Christian because he repeats the charge that the Gospels are historically inaccurate because they depict Jesus as born in the time of King Herod, whereas he claims Jesus was known to have lived a hundred years earlier.

But in his book, *The Exalted Faith*, it is not faith alone that is exalted, but man's rational faculties as well: "The *Mutakallimun* [The masters of the science of discourse] affirm [that there are] rational religious rules.... [Examples of] this [judgment are rules] such as righteousness is good, injustice is evil, it is good to praise him who is good."[67] As Fidora interprets Ibn Daūd: "Every religion is founded on two pillars: some propositions which may be proven through a philosophical discourse with rational arguments, as well as some which are only accessible through revelation and a tradition to validate them."[68]

While Ibn Daūd admits that Jewish observance of the Sabbath, dietary laws, etc. are religious rules based on revelation and so peculiar to Jews, "[the religious rules] that are called 'rational' do not vary from nation to nation."[69] Further, he specifically broaches the issue of disparate religions occupying the same territory and their (generally negative) religious interchange: "[Also], different nations agree about [generally acknowledged religious rules], so that there may be in a single [political] state communities of human beings [who have] many [different] religious rules, [who] believe in opposite traditions and [who] degrade, deny, and mock each other's traditions." Yet "the generally acknowledged rules bring them together."[70] One hundred years later, in an apologetic manual commissioned by none other than Raymond of Peñafort, Thomas Aquinas will argue the same: "Natural reason ... all are constrained to respect [it]."[71] Ibn Daūd, therefore, in arguing for moral absolutes discoverable to all men, has laid the groundwork for interreligious dialogue.[72] What is perhaps most fascinating about Abraham's statements is that he is expressing them at the very same moment in history when Master Odo, Bishop Bartholomew, and Alan of Lille are

66. Ibid., cf. Manuel Alonso, *Temas filosóficos medievales: Ibn Dāwūd y Gundisalvo* (Santander: Universidad Pontificia Comillas, 1959).

67. Abraham Ibn Daūd, *The Exalted Faith*, trans. and ed. Norbert M. Samuelson (Cranbury, NJ: Associate University Press, 1986), 204.

68. Fidora, "Abraham Ibn Daūd," 15.

69. *The Exalted Faith*, 204.

70. Ibid.

71. St Thomas Aquinas, *Summa contra gentiles* II, 2.

72. Fidora, "Abraham Ibn Daūd," 15.

incorporating reasoned elements into their own religious outlook and outreach to the "Other." And just like them, so, too, among Ibn Daūd's chief subjects in the *Exalted Faith* are the greatness of God and the subsequent necessity for humans to practice virtue and avoid vice: "The basic principle and pillar of the Torah is faith. Next is virtue and conduct. If it were not for them the ordering of the world would cease and civilization would be destroyed. Thus, you will find that all the nations agree or almost agree about state laws."[73] As did the Christian humanists of the Latin twelfth century, Ibn Daūd sees his work in a medicinal capacity. He titles the last chapter of his work, "On the Healing of the Soul," and he states that of its two chapters, "The first chapter is general discourse about virtues, [instances of] conduct, laws, statutes, pleas, and prayers. The second chapter is about additional examples of those who are spiritually ill and the ways of healing them."[74]

The case of Abraham Ibn Daūd clearly demonstrates that Anselm, Abelard, and their heirs were completely justified in their reasoned approaches to Jews: "Different minds are brought together by generally acknowledged religious rules."[75] Furthermore, we may ask, is it any surprise that it was Spain—not France, England, or Italy—which produced in succession Dominic Guzman, Raymond of Peñafort, and Ramon Llull?

For Raymond and other polemical pioneers, herein lay the answer to Christendom's weighty problem: If that hour of history had been reached when Christian Europe found itself demographically outnumbered and militarily outmaneuvered, still it had not yet come before Christendom came into possession of a singular weapon, the likes of which it had heretofore never been equipped: a more complete depository of the philosophical wisdom of the ancients. Raymond thus imposed upon Thomas Aquinas to create a *Summa contra gentiles,* as Peter Marsilio, one of Raymond's earliest biographers, explains regarding his master's missionary fervor and the philosophical insights of Aquinas:

> As well, ardently desiring conversion of the infidels, he asked the eminent doctor of the sacred page, brother master of theology of his same Order, Thomas Aquinas, who was held to be greatest among all clerics of this world after brother Albert the philosopher, to write a work against the errors of the infidels, through which the darkness of shadows might be lifted, and the doctrine of the true sun expounded to those unwilling to believe. That master wrote what the humble prayer

73. *The Exalted Faith,* 263.
74. Ibid., 259.
75. Ibid., 204.

of such a father asked, and created the work entitled *Summa contra gentiles*, which I believe to have had no equal in its subject.[76]

Vose, however, attacks the veracity of Peter Marsilio's witness. Vose must; the central thesis of his work is that scholars have made far too much of an alleged Dominican preoccupation with missionizing Jews and Muslims. The belief that Aquinas wrote an ostensibly missionary treatise is part and parcel of this "myth":

> In fact Thomas Aquinas wrote no treatise devoted to mission in any form. A persistent myth, originating in the writings of the fourteenth-century Catalan Dominican Peter Marsili, claims that the *Summa contra gentiles* was written expressly for use as a missionary manual by Spanish preachers facing Muslim audiences.... The myth has been convincingly refuted by R.-A. Gauthier.... It is only one of the pious tales recorded in three chapters devoted to recalling Raymond's sanctity. These chapters were among Marsili's additions to the original Catalan version of the *Libre dels fets*, which originally had nothing to do with Raymond.[77]

But as the late Robert Burns, SJ explains (considered by many the preeminent scholar of medieval Iberia of our time), neither Vose nor Gauthier, are the first to doubt the missionary motives of Aquinas's *Summa*:

> Unaware of this future revolution in dating and innocent of the complexity of Mudejar Spain, seeing only the "gentiles" of the Paris academic scene as his target, thus M.M. Gorce rejected the witness of Peter Marsili, Penyafort's fellow Dominican and biographer, on the grounds that "except for some teachers or rabbis in the realms of Aragon, one cannot see very well what profit could be drawn from this work of extreme erudition and real philosophical difficulty." The puzzlement betrays ignorance of the high civilization flourishing in Valencian and Murcian Islam during the centuries leading up to the crusade; it also rests on a misunderstanding as to the nature of the Dominican schools for which the work was desired.[78]

And as for Peter's credibility:

> Besides, Marsili was a man eminent in the Islamic mission, distinguished in letters and learning, a counselor to James II, and well placed to know the facts. When he put his account together at the Barcelona center, thirty-five years after the death of its director Penyafort, many

76. *Raymundiana*, I, 12.
77. Vose, *Dominicans, Muslims and Jews*, 53; nt. 117.
78. Burns, *Las Siete Partidas*, 100–1.

who had known that great man were still alive to dispute irresponsible claims. His witness is definitive.... Aquinas surpassed Penyafort's request for a handbook, of course, creating a master work useful against not only the Greco-Arab views in their Parisian and varied Islamic forms but against the full range of *errores infidelium* facing Christendom."[79]

It bothered more than a few churchmen to see pagan truths intertwined with biblical teaching, for which point, among others, the new mendicant orders were coming under increasing fire from the secular clergy. Aquinas defended his novel approach by asserting that the Bible could never be in conflict with natural reason. Speaking of the Scriptures, Aquinas wrote:

> No opinion or belief ... sent to man from God is contrary to natural knowledge. And therefore the Apostle says: "The word is near in thy heart and in thy mouth, that is, the word of faith which we preach" (Rom. 10:8). But because it surpasses reason it is counted by some as contrary to reason, which cannot be. To the same effect is the authority of Augustine (*Gen. Adlitt.* 2, 18): "What truth reveals can nowise be contrary to the holy books either of the Old or New Testament."[80]

Another Parisian master who whole-heartedly agreed with Aquinas on this point was Roger Bacon. Bacon, an Englishman by birth, after completing his studies at Oxford, went on to the University of Paris, where he became regent master of the arts. Sometime around 1247 he joined the Franciscan Order, and from 1257 to 1266 he was teacher of mathematics, perspective, and philosophy at the *studium* of the Franciscans in Paris. Between 1266 and 1268 Bacon wrote his most famous work, the *Opus Maius*, at the request of Pope Clement IV. In it, Bacon strongly contends that the proselytization of Muslims and pagans must be accomplished by appeals based upon reason, as opposed to arguments based on Scripture, nor did he see any conflict between the two:

> [W]e are not able to argue in this matter by quoting our law, nor the authorities of the Sacred Writers, because unbelievers deny Christ the Lord, and his Law, and the sacred Writers. Wherefore we must seek for reasons in another way which is common to us and to unbelievers, namely philosophy ... the power of philosophy is in perfect accord with the divine wisdom, nay, is a vestige of the divine wisdom given by God to man, that by this vestige man might be stimulated to comprehend divine truth.[81]

79. Ibid.
80. *Summa contra gentiles*, I, 9.
81. *Opus Maius*, 793.

Philosophy was, as it were, a propaedeutic to theology, and this was only rightly so, since reason and revelation were common to one another, having both one and the same divine Author: "Nor do these things belong exclusively to philosophy, but are common to theology and philosophy, to believers and unbelievers, given by God and revealed to philosophers, to the end that the human race might be alien to the Faith or outside its principles, but are drawn from its roots, as will appear from what is to be said."[82] Since philosophy was "common to believers and unbelievers alike," Bacon believed it better suited for persuasion than the Bible. His idea was to use the philosophical knowledge gained from the Muslims to gain in turn their own conversion.

Likewise, within his *Summa contra gentiles* (c. 1259–1269), Aquinas sought to return philosophy back to the Muslims "enriched by revelation," but without changing its rational content. This is the "Christian Philosophy" of which Etienne Gilson was so fond of speaking. Gilson's expression was controversial, for if philosophy (considered in itself) is truly philosophy (truth which can be apprehended by the mind of man without the aid of Scriptural or Apostolic revelation), then "the idea of Christian philosophy has no more meaning than 'Christian physics' or 'Christian mathematics.'"[83] What Gilson meant, however, is that the Christian philosopher chooses to focus on certain philosophical problems that the non-Christian philosopher does not. Because Aquinas accepted certain biblical truths on faith, he specialized his philosophical enquiry in particular areas: "Since the Christian revelation teaches us only truths which are necessary to salvation, its influence could extend only to those parts of philosophy that concern the existence and nature of God, and the origin, nature, and destiny of the soul,"[84] which is how his *Summa contra gentiles* is ordered. Speaking of the "order and mode of procedure" in his work, Aquinas again makes a distinction, but not an opposition, between natural reason and biblical faith:

> There is then a two-fold sort of truth in things divine for the wise man to study: one that can be attained by rational enquiry [philosophy], another that transcends all the industry of reason [that is, revelation]. . . . To the declaration therefore of the first sort of truth we must proceed by demonstrative reasons that may serve to convince the adversary. But because such reasons are not forthcoming for truth of the second sort, our aim ought not to be to convince the adversary by

82. Ibid., 793.
83. Etienne Gilson, *The Spirit of Medieval Philosophy*, trans. A. H. C. Downes (Southbend, IN: University of Notre Dame, 1991, reprint of Charles Scribner's Sons, 1936).
84. Ibid., 38.

[biblical] reasons, but to refute his reasonings against the [Bible's] truth, which we may hope to do since natural reason cannot be contrary to the truth of faith.[85]

Rather than attempt to use philosophy to explain all the truths contained in Scripture, Aquinas advises, instead, to use philosophy to discredit non-Christian teachings which are in opposition to those found in the Bible. To those who stubbornly cling to the use of Scripture alone in persuading the infidel, Aquinas warns that this method may very likely have the opposite effect:

> The special mode of refutation to be employed against an opponent of this second sort of truth is by alleging the authority of Scripture confirmed from heaven by miracles. There are, however, some probable reasons available for the declaration of this truth to the exercise and consolation of the faithful, but not to the convincing of opponents, because the mere insufficiency of such reasoning would rather confirm them in their error, they thinking that we assented to the truths of faith for reasons so weak.[86]

An example of this theory is found in contemporary practice in the account of the Franciscan Friar William of Rubruck during his stay at the court of the great Mongol Khan Mangu in 1254. The khan had allowed a free and open debate between Christianity and the other religions, and the weapon William made use of when engaging his opponents was not the sword of Scripture, but the sword of philosophy. When his Nestorian Christian counterparts wanted to take on the Buddhists, William asked them, "Suppose I am a follower of their religion; they say there is no God, prove that God exists."[87] According to his account: "The Nestorians did not know how to prove anything, they could only repeat what the scriptures tell. I said: 'These people do not believe in the Scriptures; if you tell them one story, they will tell you another.'" So William spoke for the Christian side, and because he was able to articulate *rational* proofs for the existence of God, as Bacon writes, "the Idolaters were confounded and convinced."[88]

Actually, William had all he could do to convince his Nestorian counterparts not to battle the Muslims first: "They said they would like first to have a debate with the Saracens. I pointed out that this was not a good idea, for the Saracens agree with us in that they say there is one

85. *Summa contra gentiles*, I, 9.
86. Ibid.
87. Christopher Dawson, trans. and ed. *Mission to Asia* (Toronto: University of Toronto Press, 1955; reprint 1992), 191.
88. *Opus Maius*, 796.

God; they would therefore be on our side against the tuins [Buddhists]."
Bacon agreed with William's approach:

> The advocate of a religion in the first place must know how to answer
> the questions that are asked about God in general. He must not, how-
> ever, enter into a discussion of all the particular truths at once, but
> should proceed gradually and begin with the easier topics in this
> way.... God, then, is the first cause antecedent to which there is no
> other, a cause that did not emerge into being nor will it be possible for
> it to cease to be, of infinite power, wisdom, and goodness.... And in
> this definition Tartars, Saracens, Jews, and Christians agree.[89]

William's strategy again proved decisive; when William got his Bud-
dhist opponent to declare "no god is omnipotent," the Muslim section
burst into hysterical laughter. Not only that, but just as William was
ready to let the Nestorians have their go at them, the Muslims reportedly declined to argue: "We concede," they said, "that your law is true
and that the Gospel is true: we have no wish to dispute with you." And
they confessed that in their prayers they prayed for a Christian death. So
the dispute came to an end, as Southern puts it, "Christians and Moslems joining together in common triumph over the Buddhists, and all
drinking copiously."[90]

One can only imagine the impression this story left upon Roger
Bacon as he heard it from William's own lips sometime in 1257. More
than anything else, it must have grounded him securely in his belief that
"blood and sword must give way to dialectical argument and preaching,
the darkness of war to the light of knowledge." Clearly, Bacon the mendicant was more concerned about the eternal salvation of non-Christians than he was about the creation of a homogenous Catholic political
order in this world. As Southern summarizes Bacon's view:

> The aims of Christendom have been wrong ... because they have been
> perverted by the desire for domination which frustrated the work of
> conversion. The wars have been unsuccessful; but even if they had
> been successful ... [it would be] impossible to occupy so much terri-
> tory, and second ... the survivors would have been inflamed against
> their conquerors, dangerous to live with, and impossible to convert—
> as, he alleges, we can see in many parts of the Islamic world today.
> Preaching is therefore the only way in which Christendom can be
> enlarged.[91]

89. Ibid.
90. Southern, *Western Views of Islam*, 50.
91. Ibid., 57.

But even preaching will come to naught unless friars are willing to learn foreign languages in the cause of the conversion of unbelievers. This lesson, perhaps more than any other, was impressed upon Bacon by William's experiences. As Bacon writes:

> The knowledge of languages is necessary to the Latins for the conversion of unbelievers. For in the hands of the Latins rests the power to convert. And for this reason Jews without number perish among us because no one knows how to preach to them nor to interpret the Scriptures in their tongue, nor to confer with them, nor to dispute as to the literal sense.... Then the Greeks and the Rutheni and many other schismatics likewise grow hardened in error because the truth is not preached to them in their tongue; and the Saracens likewise and the pagans and the Tartars, and the other unbelievers throughout the whole world.... Oh, how we should consider this matter and fear lest God may hold the Latins responsible because they are neglecting the languages so that in this way they neglect the preaching of the faith. For Christians are few, and the whole broad world is occupied by unbelievers; and there is no one to show them the truth.[92]

It is not hard to hear Raymond of Peñafort pleading for his language schools in the above words of his contemporary Roger Bacon.

Thomas Aquinas had said that the two obstacles to Christian preaching to the unconverted were Christian ignorance of non-Christian sacred texts and the lack of weight which Christian Scripture carried among infidels; while Aquinas focused on the latter of these two difficulties, his fellow Dominican and patron, Raymond of Peñafort, tended to focus on the former. It has been suggested that as counselor and sometime confessor to James I, Raymond was responsible for the king's initiative to hold the famed Christian-Jewish Barcelona Disputation and to compel the Jews of Catalonia to listen to the sermons that he and other Dominicans, notably Friar Paul Christiani, delivered with missionary intent. Furthermore, we may speculate that it was just such preaching on Raymond's part that was responsible for bringing Friar Paul, a former Jew named Saul, into the Christian fold in the first place.[93] This brings us for the first time in this essay directly to the issue of Raymond's novel

92. *Opus Maius*, 608.
93. Williams, *Adversus Judaeos*, 244; cf. Cohen, *Friars and the Jews*, 108 and nt.14.

mission program to the Jews of Spain. By way of introduction to that community, the following observation speaks volumes:

> First of all, it is necessary to realize that Jews lived in medieval Spain longer than they had in any other country in the world, including Israel ... approximately twelve centuries of continuous Jewish presence.... Second, more Jews lived in medieval Spain than in *all* the other countries of Europe combined. Finally, and this is generally not realized, unlike other countries the Jews in Spain lived scattered throughout the length and breadth of the land, in the tiniest villages and in the major cities. Most indeed, were rural rather than urban dwellers. This could be possible only in a situation where Christians generally were not only tolerant but friendly towards Jews, and where Jews felt entirely safe in living, sometimes only two or three families, in a remote Christian village.[94]

The above description ought to give any historian worth his salt a pause bordering on awe. This is all the more so for anyone aspiring to articulate a better understanding of Christian-Jewish relations. Medieval Iberia was extraordinary in its Jewish presence, and, we might add, extraordinary precisely *because* of it, as we have seen in the case of Ibn Daūd.[95]

But soon after the arrival of the Black Death in 1349, the Jewish communities of Spain found themselves scapegoats for the plague, which killed as much as a third of the population in some cities. In the decades that followed, thousands of Jews found themselves and their loved ones repeatedly threatened and victimized by civil war and religious bigotry, including the unprecedented pogroms of the summer of 1391. This was followed in its wake by intense Dominican preaching, forced attendance at sermons, and compulsory presence at "debates" that lasted for months. By the 1430s, one third to one half of the Jewish population of the peninsula had converted to Catholicism. By 1492, the remnant that had refused was expelled from the country—a fact equally worthy of a moment of observed silence.

In some ways, then, it is no wonder that Raymond of Peñafort, the friar who first inaugurated Dominican mission to Jews, should be so vilified, especially by leading Jewish scholars. But it is just that, a vilifi-

94. Roth, *Conversos, Inquisition, and the Expulsion of the Jews from Spain* (Madison, WI: University of Wisconsin Press, 1995), 9.

95. "Here biblical commentary and the scientific study of the text were born; here, too, was the miraculous 'renaissance' of the Hebrew language made possible by the creation of Hebrew grammar, which in turn gave birth to Hebrew secular poetry and literature on the Arabic model" (Roth, *Conversos*, xi).

cation, a "black legend"; one that serves no useful purpose in the pursuit of truth. Not even Peñafort was prescient enough to foresee, in 1242, the waves and watersheds that would wash across Iberia over the next 250 years. As we shall see, apart from forced sermons in synagogues and compulsory attendance at Christian-Jewish debates, there is little from that later era for which we may blame/credit Raymond. We must insist that, rather than reading back the deteriorating Jewish circumstances of later centuries, the origins and essence of Raymond's unprecedented mission to Jews must be sought squarely in the penitential literature of the twelfth century and increased concern for the eternal fate of the laity exemplified by the preaching of St Dominic and his earliest associates.

If *first the bow is bent in study*, it is loosed in preaching and disputation. The missives of thirteenth-century mendicant mission swiftly constituted a penumbra stretching from farthest Mongolia to Raymond's own Catalonia. As we have noted in passing, Dominic and his first friars not only preached to heretics, they often debated them, a form of "preaching" later mendicants would employ in earnest with Jews and Muslims—even, as we have seen, with Buddhists! Though some view Christian-Jewish debate itself as a form of Christian anti-Judaism, they would do well to note the frequent use of this form of engaging the "Other," starting with the very founder of militant mendicancy. As Blessed Jordan of Saxony relates in a passage that needs to be quoted at length to be fully appreciated:

> There were frequent disputations under chosen judges at Pamiers, Lavaur, Montreal and Fanjeaux and on the days appointed noblemen, knights, women and common folk came wanting to be present at the discussion of the faith. It happened that one particular celebrated disputation was arranged at Fanjeaux; for which a large throng of faithful and heretics gathered. *Several of the faithful prepared pamphlets first, laying out arguments and authorities to confirm their faith; when they had all been examined the blessed Dominic's leaflet was reckoned the best and received general approval,* and was laid before the three judges chosen to determine the disputation by the consent of the parties, beside the heretics' leaflet, which they had written on their own account. *The aim was that whichever party's leaflet was reckoned by the judges the more reasonable, their faith should be accepted as superior.* After much dispute the judges could not agree to support either party, and they fell on the plan of throwing both leaflets into a fire, so that if either was not burned it would doubtless contain the true faith. And so a large fire was kindled, and they threw in both leaflets. The heretics' book was immediately consumed, but the other, written by Dominic, that man

of God, not only remained unharmed, but leapt a great distance out of the flames in the presence of all. It was thrown in a second, and a third time, and each time was thrown out of the fire; and so it demonstrated openly the truth of the faith and the holiness of the man who had written the leaflet.[96] (emphasis mine)

The element of the supernatural aside, there is much that is tangible that we can take away from Jordan's hagiography. If there was ever a prime example of the medieval Catholic origins of modern free-and-open-debate, it is this one. We see that the embryonic Dominican Order believed that its religious opposition ought to be given the chance to lay out its best arguments in an impartial fight, and that above all, "reasonableness" should be the deciding criterion that proves the truth of the faith of the winner. Thus the mendicants were pioneers in the practice of reconciling differences through recourse to rational disputation and adjudication rather than violence and punitive retribution. We are, however, still grounded in the Middle Ages; when the judges deadlock, we see an immediate return to pagan Germanic "trial by fire." Let us also not forget to note how the writing of polemical literature is an important element in the "preaching" of Dominic and his followers. The importance of this early Dominican evidence cannot be overstated. We have chronicled before us here essentially all the methods and tactics to be later employed by Friar Raymond of Peñafort and his associates in their mission to the Jews and Muslims of Spain.

96. Jordan, *On the Origins*, Chaps 23–25 in Brooke, 166–67.

6

Disputation & Reason: Peñafort to Llull

Inflamed with fires of charity, he [St Raymond] inspired a special devotion and reverence for himself among infidels also, to wit, Jews and Saracens, who admired the excellence of his honesty and were delighted by his sweet and reasonable speech.

—Peter Marsilio, OP

But since you [O Lord] have now brought me such happiness, I beg you . . . through grace and the illumination of this sovereign light you may help me to give light and direction to so many men who are in a state or in times of darkness, ignorant of the path of salvation.

—Blessed Ramon Llull, *Book of the Gentile and Three Wise Men*

FOR MANY, the celebrated Barcelona Disputation is seen as the symbolic "beginning of the end" of Jewish prosperity in Spain, or even Europe taken as a whole. Yet there is little about the event itself, or Raymond's alleged "orchestration" of it, which portended inevitable doom. Indeed, one might just as well find in it the medieval seeds of a modern sense of tolerance. As Maccoby describes it:

Nevertheless, the tone of the Christian attack is here much more conciliatory than in Paris. There are no threats of confiscation or burning of the Talmud depending on the result. The object is not to convict, but to win over. There are many reasons for this, from the religio-political situation in Spain to the character of Dominican missionary activity in the school of Raymund de Peñaforte, the aged scholar and missionary (later canonized) who set the tone of the debate though he did not himself participate in it as a disputant, preferring to give this role to the convert from Judaism, Pablo Christiani.[1]

1. Maccoby, *Judaism on Trial*, 39.

Friar Paul's worthy opponent was Rabbi Moses Nachmanides (*c.*1195–*c.*1270), considered not only a prestigious figure in the Jewish community of Catalonia, but one of the most outstanding in all of Jewish history writ large: "Commentary on the Torah, commentary on the Talmud, halakhic treatises, important formulations of spiritual doctrine, mystical speculation, communal leadership during a number of periods of crisis—all this constitutes the remarkable creativity of Rabbi Moses ben Nahman."[2]

We are largely indebted to the rabbi for the details of this encounter, which are reported at length in his Hebrew account, the *Vikuach,* for the Christian Latin account is very meager by contrast. Though there has been more than a century of ink spilt in rancor over the veracity of these accounts—usually according to denominational lines—as also to who won the engagement: friar or rabbi, it is not our purpose at present to retrace these labyrinthine paths (in a forthcoming work devoted more exclusively to the Barcelona Disputation this author hopes to revisit these issues); what we are seeking is a more detached and objective path through the great disputation, enough to give us an accurate sense of the new Dominican approach to Jewish mission and its impact on Dominicans and Jews. It seems safe to say that, although Nachmanides wrote his account to bolster the Jewish community in the face of a new and potentially dangerous "challenge" from the Christian "Other," much of what he writes is not only believable, but essentially corroborated in the briefer Latin account.[3] As for the latter, while it too contains apparent distortions, by and by it reflects the gist of the encounter from a Christian spectator.

Friar Paul and Rabbi Moses debated over the course of four days, between Friday July 20 and Friday July 27, 1263, before the king and his court and a crowd of Christian, as well as Jewish, subjects. It should be noted straight off that to suggest that the two disputants met on a level playing field is, of course, historically inaccurate. In the first place, the Ramban[4] and his Jewish audience had clearly been coerced into participating in the forum by the king at Dominican prompting.[5] Secondly, we ought to observe that Nachmanides' role was cast in a decidedly defensive posture. As Chazan remarks:

2. Chazan, *Barcelona and Beyond, The Disputation of 1263 and its Aftermath* (Berkeley: University of California Press, 1992), 36.

3. Cf. ibid.

4. *R*abbi *M*oses *b*en *N*achman; a common abbreviation.

5. Chazan, *Daggers of Faith,* 73; "This discrepancy in roles is revealed first in the convoking of the meeting in Barcelona. Both the Latin and Hebrew accounts emphasize that the discussion was not negotiated by the two parties; it was engineered by the Christian

The truth of Christianity was not to be put in question; rather, the Jews were to be refuted and shaken in their faith. The agenda . . . was indeed ordered in such a way as to make this possible. . . . This attack, through which the Christian side stood to lose nothing while the Jews were profoundly threatened, can only indicate Christian control. In addition, the four specific points chosen for the discussion likewise reflect a Christian point of view. They involve issues through which the truth of Christianity might be proved. No Jewish spokesman, given freedom of choice, would have selected such items for debate. Again, we emerge with a clear sense that the agenda was designed by the Christian side and forced on the Jews.[6]

On the other hand, Martin Cohen argues just the opposite. It wasn't a forum to disprove the errors of Judaism, so much as one to establish the truths of Catholicism, so *it* was the more vulnerable:

Only the cardinal principles of Christianity were placed on the agenda, and the burden of proof appeared to fall squarely on Paul's shoulders. Even the progression of the questions seemed to favor Nahmanides, for should he succeed in refuting one, the rest would be stripped of their meaning and victory would be his. And if Paul tried to buttress his case with statements from the rabbis, Nahmanides' unquestioned superiority in this area could be expected to foil his every thrust. Nahmanides' position could not have been stronger. With the weight of his knowledge and the apparent advantage of the agenda, nothing less than a lightning victory should have ensued.[7]

But Nachmanides was handcuffed by never really being allowed to lead. The king and the Dominicans made sure that, most of the time, his was a defensive posture. While scholars seem chiefly to assume that this was for done for cold, pragmatic reasons—to ensure a public Christian victory in this high-stakes contest—almost certainly the main reason was out of respect to Almighty God and His Only Son Jesus Christ, whose Mission and Testament were at stake. Fear of potential blasphemy must have been paramount in their precautions.

---

side and foisted on the Jews. More specifically, it resulted from powerful pressures exerted by the Dominicans on King James I of Aragon. Had the king refused to order Jewish participation, the clash would never have taken place. This is indicated succinctly by the Latin text: "Moses the Jew, called 'rabbi,' was summoned from Gerona by the lord king at the urging of the Dominicans and was present there along with many other Jews, who seemed reputed among other Jews most learned."

7. Martin A. Cohen, "Reflections on the Text and Context of the Disputation of Barcelona (1263)," *Hebrew Union College Annual* 35 (1964): 157–92; 164.

Even so, Rabbi Moses, it seems, did what he could to make his role a more active one, considering the concrete circumstances. He writes, for example:

> I replied, "I will do as my lord the King commands, if you will give me permission to speak as I wish." I was seeking thereby the permission of the King and of Fray Raymon of Pennaforte and his associates who were there.
>
> Fray Raymon of Pennaforte replied: "Provided only that you do not speak disrespectfully."
>
> I said to them, "I do not wish to have to submit to your judgment on that, but to speak as I wish on the matter of disputation, just as you say all that you wish; and I have enough understanding to speak with moderation on the matters of dispute just as you do, but let it be according to my own discretion." So they all gave me permission to speak freely."[8]

Nachmanides' statement is noteworthy on several accounts. It is, in fact, almost the only time he makes reference to Raymond of Peñafort in the context of the entire debate and Raymond's reply contains perhaps his only recorded words in regard to the whole matter of his Dominican missionary enterprise toward Jews. (Later on, either at the end of the debate or in synagogue a week later, Raymond gave a sermon on the Holy Trinity.) The fact that Nachmanides asked permission of the king and Peñafort by name has led scholars to the conclusion that the "infamous" friar was the true architect behind the debate. But it could just as well mean that Friar Raymond was the only Dominican for whom Nachmanides had even a modicum of respect, that the elderly saint was more amiable and agreeable than the upstart apostate, Paul Christiani. Friar Paul, in fact, seems the likely brainchild of the disputation, not Raymond—indeed, the rabbi says as much: "Are you the clever Jew who made this new discovery and became an apostate because of it? Are you the one who bade the King to assemble before you the sages of the Jews to hold a disputation over your discoveries? Do you think we have never heard this argument before?"[9]

Wishing to have more of a free hand in his own defense, Rabbi Moses specifically asks permission of Raymond of Peñafort. The former master-general grants him this permission as long as he does not blaspheme Christ or his Church. This incident is significant for at least two reasons. On the second day of the debate, Nachmanides again attempted to address James I and this time was cut off by the monarch himself: "I said

8. Maccoby, *Judaism on Trial*, 102.
9. Ibid., 135.

to our lord the king 'My lord, hear me.' But the King said to me: 'Let him [Paul] speak first, for he is the challenger.'"[10] Finally, on the last day of the debate, Nachmanides, weary of repeated interrogation, once more sought a more even-handed format from the king: "It is fair that for one day I should be the questioner and Fray Paul the answerer since so far, he has questioned me and I have answered him for three days running." The king replied: "Nevertheless, you answer him."[11] Besides showing the contrived nature of the theological contest, these exchanges show that King James was repeatedly unwilling to grant the Ramban any leeway. Raymond, on the other hand, by Nachmanides' account, was willing to let the rabbi have some liberty in his own defense. This may suggest a more accommodating attitude on the part of Peñafort than on that of the king. Later on, after Raymond's exposition on the Trinity and Nachmanides' rebuttal, we see a certain graciousness toward his opponent demonstrated once again:

> Then Fray Paul stood up and said that he believed in a perfect Unity, and together with it there is a Trinity, and that this is a matter so deep that even the angels and princes on high do not understand it.
>
> I stood up and said, "It is obvious that a person cannot believe what he does not know; Which means that the angels cannot believe in the Trinity." And Fray Paul's *companions made him keep silent.*[12] (emphasis mine)

As Maccoby suggests, it appears it was Peñafort who made Paul pipe down. He poses a sharp contrast between Donin, for example, and Peñafort:

> At Paris ... the virulent anti-Talmudic attitude of the main Christian disputant, Nicholas Donin ... [he thought] the Talmud was [a] wholly pernicious work, which ought to be expunged from the memory of man. Raymund de Peñaforte, however, had a much more civilized approach, towards both Jews and Muslims. He understood that in order to produce genuine conversions, he must enter into the culture and minds of his prospective converts. Accordingly, he set up academies where Dominican monks were set to work to study the Jewish and Muslim classics. This provided the first impulse for the study of Hebrew and Arabic at the universities.[13]

10. Ibid., 114.
11. Ibid., 134.
12. Ibid., 146.
13. Ibid., 41.

Furthermore, Maccoby's view is the only one actually supported by contemporary sources. As Peter Marsilio describes Raymond: "Inflamed with fires of charity, he inspired a special devotion and reverence for himself among infidels also, to wit, Jews and Saracens, who admired the excellence of his honesty and were delighted by his sweet and reasonable speech."[14] It would seem that Raymond's approach to Jews (and other non-Christians) was that of "sweet and reasonable" discourse stemming from a purported supernatural love, or *caritas*, for the salvation of their souls. This was certainly the Dominican ideal, as propounded by the life and work of the founder of the Order.

One could further point to another episode on the third day of the debate when Nachmanides countered Paul's Talmudic argumentation by quoting Maimonides: "King messiah is destined to arise for Israel, and he will build the Temple and gather the banished of Israel." At this, Friar Arnold of Segarra stood up and condemned Maimonides for speaking "lies."[15] He was then silenced by the king, who allowed Nachmanides to continue explaining the passage. Peñafort did not speak out, but remained silent. Had he considered that utterance blasphemous, he surely would have risen to Christ's defense. As previously mentioned, the one thing that Nachmanides quotes Raymond as saying to him is that he ought to speak "respectfully."

Although Raymond had no scruples about forced debates or, as we shall see, sermons coerced at Sabbath observances, nevertheless he held some store by respectful speech with regard to one's ideological opponent. Nachmanides certainly has nothing derogatory to say about Raymond's deportment during the proceedings. Furthermore, Raymond's remark that the rabbi may speak his mind so long as he does not speak disrespectfully (of Christ and the Christian faith) goes a long way toward explaining his involvement in the subsequent campaign to purge all Jewish books in Aragon of blasphemy, including the related prosecution of Nachmanides. In his Hebrew narrative, the rabbi claims to have spoken the following words:

> No, the real point of difference between Jews and Christians lies in what you say about the fundamental matter of the deity; a doctrine which is distasteful indeed. You, our lord King, are a Christian and the son of a Christian, and you have listened all your life to priests who have filled your brain and the marrow of your bones with this doctrine, and it has settled with you, because of that accustomed habit.

---

14. *Raymundiana*, I, 12.
15. Vose, *Dominicans, Muslims and Jews*, 171.

But the doctrine in which you believe, and which is the foundation of your faith, cannot be accepted by the reason, and nature affords no ground for it, nor have the prophets ever expressed it. Nor can even the miraculous stretch as far as this as I shall explain with full proofs in the right time and place, that the Creator of Heaven and earth resorted to the womb of a certain Jewess and grew there for nine months and was born as an infant, and afterwards grew up and was betrayed into the hands of his enemies who sentenced him to death and executed him, and that afterwards, as you say, he came to life and returned to his original place. The mind of a Jew, or any other person, cannot tolerate this; and you speak your words entirely in vain, for this is the root of our controversy.[16]

Not one, but many of the statements cited above could easily have given serious offense to the other side.[17] If the Ramban actually said them without receiving any censure, it attests to a formidable forbearance on the part of his medieval Christian contemporaries, something no modern Dominican detractor has acknowledged. Chazan has written that it is highly dubious that Nachmanides would have been given such free license.[18] The fact that he chose to include these remarks— presumably to bolster Jewish confidence in an hour of alleged Christian aggrandizement—largely explains subsequent Dominican, even papal, cries for his punishment.

The debate had been deliberately structured in such a way as not to impugn the faith. As the Latin text has it:

Deliberations were undertaken with the lord king and with certain Dominicans and Franciscans who were present, not that the faith of the Lord Jesus Christ—which because of its certitude cannot be placed in dispute—be put in the center of attention with the Jews as uncertain, but that the truth of that faith be made manifest in order to destroy the Jews' errors and to shake the confidence of many Jews. . . .

---

16. *Vikuach*, Maccoby trans., 119–20; based on the *Vikuach* of Nachmanides edited by Steinschneider, 1860; the apologetic "value" of Anselm's *Cur Deus homo*, and the likelihood that it was written for "real" Jews, not "hermenutical" ones or Christian heretics, seems appreciably strengthened in the wake of Nachmanides' words; cf. *Cur Deus homo*, 5.

17. Nachmanides himself writes that he, following Friar Raymond's discourse on the Holy Trinity, averred that "the angels cannot believe in the Trinity" (again because of Its alleged unintelligibility) and that "Fray Paul's companions made him keep silent," as the friar wished to retaliate to a perceived blasphemy. What would have been the ruckus had the rabbi really denied that *man*—the subject of Jesus's Revelation and Redemption—is equally incapable of accepting the alleged absurdity?

18. Chazan, *Barcelona and Beyond*, 48–49.

Friar Paul proposed to the said rabbi that, with the aid of God, he would prove from writings shared and accepted by the Jews the following contentions, in order: that the Messiah, who is called Christ, whom the Jews anticipate, has surely come already, also that the Messiah, as prophesied, would be divine and human; also that he suffered and was killed for the salvation of mankind; also that the laws and ceremonials ceased and should have ceased after the advent of the said Messiah.[19]

But Friar Paul's *fourth* proposition was not the critical one; surely it was his first proposition, that Jesus is the Christ! A devout Dominican

19. Yitzhak Baer, "The Disputations of R. Yehiel of Paris and of Nahmanides," (Hebrew). *Tarbiz* 2 (1930–1931): 185; Chazan's English translation, *Daggers of Faith*, 74; cf. Maccoby, *Judaism on Trial*, 147–150. Jeremy Cohen seizes upon the friar's last point as proof that the Dominicans considered Jews heretics:

> Having considered the attacks of Pablo Christiani and Raymond Martini on the Jews, we can now view the "school" of Raymond de Peñaforte not only as a specific group of friars but also as a school of thought, the proponent of a particular anti-Jewish polemical ideology: rabbinic Judaism had no place in Christendom, and every effort thus had to be made to convert its Jewish adherents. It was no accident that Raymond Martini followed in the *Pugio fidei* the agenda for Pablo Christian's debate with Nahmanides, and that the same crucial point, the fourth proposition on Pablo's agenda, underlay both friars' positions: contemporary Jewish observance of the Mosaic commandments was inherently improper and heretical even for the Jews. . . .
>
> Martini distinguishes three different genera of expressions of Jewish belief. First, he speaks of the law and prophecies of the Old Testament, which along with their correct interpretations would, albeit pre-figuratively, establish the truth of Christianity. These interpretations or traditiones were preserved by the Jews of the Bible as part of their oral tradition, which eventually came to be recorded by the rabbis of the Talmud. Such correct interpretations of Scripture must be extracted from rabbinic literature "like pearls out of a great dungheap." Second, in contradistinction to these select few traditiones, the vast majority of Talmudic teachings are described as the aforementioned dungheap, the head of a dragon or toad, or the venomous sting of the bee. This body of literature, replete with "absurdities," propagates the false beliefs "regarding the messiah and so many other matters which the Jews have believed from the time of Christ." Third, Martini identifies his present enemy, "the perfidy of the modern Jews," which expresses itself as both "impudence" and "evil." It is against this brand of Judaism that he intends to direct the Christological traditiones of the first. (As cited in Chazan, 174)

This is an attempt to gratuitously establish three categories out of Martini's text, corresponding to three historical stages of Judaism in his eyes, the first consisting of the Jews of the Old Testament, the second, the Jews of the Talmud who lived during and after the time of Christ, and the third "the *ludei moderni* of Martini's own day, (who) maintained the perverse beliefs of the rabbis who preceded them, inheriting and persisting in all the vices of talmudic Judaism." But as Chazan argues, the third group is really just a reiteration of the second: "Once again, the tripartite scheme means nothing. There are really only two groups for Friar Raymond (and all mainstream Christian theologians): pre-Christian Jews and post-Christian Jews." (Chazan, 174)

need not view rabbinic Judaism as "heresy" in order to simultaneously hold the view that "every effort thus had to be made to convert its Jewish adherents." The Christian priority was to see Jews come to know and love Jesus, not demonstrate their departure from biblical Judaism.[20] The only thing novel, therefore, in the approach of Raymond and his disciples was their use of the Talmud in their polemics to persuade Jews. Thus, as Chazan concludes, "There is ... no evidence in the Barcelona confrontation of a new ideological view of Judaism and the Jews."[21]

Raymond's methods—and motives—seem clear enough from those who knew him best:

> Also in the Hebrew language, with his counsel and favor, some friars have been instructed such that they are able to vanquish the ill will and errors of Jews, which before they were not able to do. Jews had been accustomed for a long time to deny audaciously the true text and the commentary of their own ancient sages as well as that of our saints, in places which pertain to the Catholic faith and are in accord with it. Furthermore, falsehoods and corruptions which Jews had inserted in the Bible, in many places which concern mysteries still hidden at the time of writing, about the Passion and other sacraments of the faith, are revealed by the Jews' authentic Scriptures to be forgeries of truth, which is to their maximum confusion and to the confirmation of the Christian faith. For that reason indeed, those who were being converted from the erroneous sect of the Saracens or of the Jews to the faith of the Lord Jesus Christ, had recourse very confidently to the venerable father, Friar Raymond, as to a singular refuge. As he had begotten them all in the Lord, he sought for them sustenance of life from kings and prelates of the Church, and while rejoicing with them he instructed them in the Catholic faith, strengthening and edifying them with salutary teachings and exempla.[22]

According to his biographer, then, Raymond directed that certain friars be trained in Hebrew and commence study, not only of the Old Testament, but also of the Talmud, in order that the "mysteries of the Passion and other sacraments of the faith, might be revealed through their authentic scriptural texts." The "mysteries of the Passion" are none

20. Chazan, *Daggers of Faith*, 170–73; "Thus, on close inspection, Cohen's case based on the Barcelona confrontation dissolves. The fourth item on the agenda was in no sense the crucial item; it is fully plausible that this issue was never raised at Barcelona. Friar Paul's intention was not to prove that present-day Judaism was a deviation from classical Judaism; his last goal was to prove the age-old Christian contention that Jewish law had been abrogated by the coming of the Messiah but to do so on the basis of rabbinic texts."

21. Ibid., 173.

22. *Raymundiana*, I, 32–33.

other than Paul Christiani's first three propositions from the Barcelona confrontation: (1) that Jesus, "the Christ" had already come, (2) that he was both true God and true man, and (3) that by his sufferings and death he has gained the grace of salvation for all sinners. This is the same core apologetic message to infidels as first propounded over a century-and-a-half earlier by Anselm in the *Cur Deus homo*.[23]

The "errors" of the Jews in the eyes of Peñafort and the Dominicans are the traditional ones ascribed to them, rejection of Christ's self-revelation and the sacraments of his Church, not the use of the Talmud per se. They are considered objectively guilty of "infidelity," or "blasphemy," not "heresy." There is a distinction between the two sins, and no one in Christendom was more familiar with the distinctions between sins than Raymond of Peñafort! In fact, he is quite explicit on the point in his *Summa confessorum*—in his own hand: "*Dictum est supra de Iudaeis, & pagani, qui per infidelitatem Deum inhonorant: nunc agendum de Haereticis, qui a fide deviantes in Deum multipliciter peccant.*"[24]

Far from "see[ing] no place for the Jews in Christendom ... [and] trying to extirpate manifestations of contemporary Judaism from Christian Europe," Raymond is quite clear in the same summa as to their continued right to exist (as also Muslims) and to do so unmolested:

> Moreover, as he says, Jews as well as Saracens ought to be moved more strongly to receive the Christian faith as their new religion by citations of authority, by reasoning, and by pleasant incentives, rather than by harshness. Furthermore, they are not to be compelled, for compelled acts of service do not please God, Who wants sincere ones (as 45 distinguishes). The Council of Toledo says the same, as it distinguishes in the same way concerning the Jews.[25]

The fact that Dominican leaders found numerous passages from the Talmud to be irreverent was enough to call for its censure. Blasphemy, as we have said, is as much a sin as heresy. Raymond of Peñafort made "every effort" to convert the Jews because they were considered infidels, not heretics; thus, he also made every effort to convert Muslims.

---

23. Notice also that, as Chazan contends, Friar Paul's fourth proposition, that the laws and ceremonials of Judaism have ceased to be necessary, is a superfluous corollary of the first three items on Paul's agenda, not the crucial point upon which Cohen rests his thesis—and is not included in the above account by Raymond's biographer, as are the other three.

24. *Summa de poenitentiae*, I, 5, 1.

25. Ibid., 1, 4, 1.

All this theory having been explored, however, there is still the question of how to reconcile the medieval Catholic ideal of tolerance as conceived by the Dominicans with the tumults and anxieties the Order clearly engendered in practice between the Christian populace and Jewish *aljamas* (communities) after the Barcelona Disputation. Let us briefly examine what occurred.

Urged on by the friars, on August 26, 1263, James I reissued his edict of 1242 allowing the Dominicans unfettered access to preach to Jews (or Muslims). The king reminded his officials: "You must oblige and if necessary force the Jews and Muslims, young and old, male and female to gather before the friars wherever and whenever and however they desire it; and they should listen to the words of the friars carefully and in silence."[26] Three days later, on August 29th, he sent a message to all the *aljamas* of the realm, announcing that Friar Paul Christiani would be visiting their synagogues, homes, or other suitable places "to preach the word of God or dispute or discuss holy Scripture with you ... [you are] to come to him and listen calmly and favorably and to humbly and reverently, without any calumny or subterfuge, respond to his questions about faith, and the holy Scriptures according to your knowledge; and to show him your books, which he requires to show you the truth."[27]

Letting an apostate Jew into their homes to lecture them on how their own books demonstrated the coming of the Messiah and therefore, the shortcomings of the continued practice of the Jewish faith—all without being able to enunciate (or gesticulate) the slightest sign of displeasure—was surely not a prospect any Jew would welcome with enthusiasm. Certainly there were protests and appeals to the king. Some members of the episcopacy and their parishioners could conceivably have added insult to injury by a stream of anti-Judaistic words and actions in those sultry summer days between the end-of-July Disputation and the end-of-August edicts. Indeed, we know that on one occasion James and his royal entourage were actually forced to brandish naked steel to quell an angry clerical mob.[28] Perhaps it was even this particular incident that moved the king to make an astonishing policy

26. Vose, *Dominicans, Muslims and Jews*, 153; cf. Baer, "The Disputations," 155; Heinrich Denifle, "Quellen zur Disputation Pablos Christiani mit Mose Nachmani zu Barcelona 1263," *Historisches Jahrbuch des Görresgesellschaft*, 8 (1887), 225–44 (234–35).

27. Ibid; Denifle, "Quellen zur Disputation Pablo," 235–36.

28. Baer, "The Disputations," 167; "The incident must have happened shortly after the Disputation at Barcelona ... the excesses were symptomatic of deep and widespread unrest."

reversal just one day after the release of his letter to the Jews.[29] He ordered his officials that:

> You may not compel or permit compelling Jews, their wives or children in any city or town of our realm to leave their neighborhood for the purpose of hearing sermons by Preaching Friars, still if some friar of the Preachers wishes to enter the *call* [Jewish quarter] or a synagogue in order to preach to them, they may listen if they wish; but we grant the Jews that they are not obligated to go outside their neighborhood to hear sermons or to hear sermons anywhere by force.[30]

The Jewish community had received, as it were, an eleventh-hour reprieve. Even further restrictions were imposed upon the Barcelona friars in an edict issued five years later: "Because of preaching done to you outside the *calls*, you often suffer insults and injuries from Christians. So if the friars or others wish to preach to you in your synagogues they may not come into the synagogues or *calls* to preach with a multitude of Christian people, but only with ten upright Christian men and no more."[31] Mark Johnston argues that these decrees "clearly recognize that Jews were suffering abuse from Christian mobs outside their neighborhoods."[32] He believes the "ten good men" (an obvious legal formula) were likely comprised of wealthy burghers who had a stake in ensuring peace in their town.

In addition to being subjected to mendicant preaching, however, Jews were aggrieved by a return to the censorship of their literature. The same day James announced that Friar Paul would be visiting Jewish precincts to preach, he issued another decree ordering Jews to expunge all passages from the Talmud which Friar Paul found blasphemous. Failure to comply would result in a stiff fine or even the consignment of whole texts to the flames. The king's edict specifically mentions Peñafort along with Raymond Martini and Friar Arnold of Segarre, the retired head of the Spanish Province, as composing the panel empowered to censor any instances

---

29. One could once again make the case that it was Raymond of Peñafort, James's confessor, who alone could have convinced the king to change his mind so quickly and completely, though this is perhaps even more speculative than the argument that it was Peñafort who dissuaded Pope Innocent IV from ordering mass burnings of the Talmud. The point is that given what little evidence we have to go on, one can just as easily "make" him a hero as a villain.

30. Mark D. Johnston, "Ramon Llull and the Compulsory Evangelization of Jews and Muslims," in *Iberia and the Mediterranean World of the Middle Ages, Studies in Honor of Robert I. Burns SJ*, vol. I, ed. Larry J. Simon (Leiden: E. J. Brill, 1995), 11; Denifle, "Quellen zur Disputation Pablo," 235–36.

31. Ibid., 12.

32. Ibid., 13.

of perceived insult.[33] But after seven months of confusion and protest, an edict of leniency was issued in March 1264. Jews were now given a month's grace to appear before a new appeals committee with the opportunity to defend suspect passages as innocent of offense against Jesus or the Holy Virgin. If they argued successfully they could keep their books.[34]

There is no real reason to question the sincerity of Raymond or the Dominican Order in this whole episode. As both Maccoby and Vose point out, the Barcelona censorship of 1263/4 was very different from that of Paris in 1242. The Spanish campaign to censor the Talmud was neither an attempt to exterminate Judaism, nor a mere "fishing expedition." There are, in fact, several passages from the Talmud which devout Christians could hardly view as anything but blasphemous:

> Jesus the Nazarene practiced magic and led astray and deceived Israel. (*Sanhedrin* 107b)
>
> It was taught: On the eve of Passover Yeshu [Jesus] the Nazarene was hung . . . a herald went forth and cried, "He is going forth to be stoned because he has practiced sorcery and enticed Israel to apostasy. Any one who can say anything in his favour, let him come forward and plead on his behalf." But since nothing was brought forward in his favour he has hanged on the eve of Passover! (Sanhedrin 43a)[35]

There is even a further passage (Gitt, 56b) where "Jesus is described as suffering in hell by being immersed in boiling excrement"![36]

James I's inquiry into the Talmud had represented a return to Innocent IV's "compromise" policy of twenty years earlier (which may itself have been mitigated by Peñafort). Jews would be allowed to keep their books, but they would be expunged of any derogatory references to Christ or the Virgin or any other perceived attacks on the faith. That Raymond of Peñafort heartily supported such measures, however, does not mean that he equated contemporary Jewish practice with heresy. Nor does it mean he was a "fanatic" and a persecutor. The case against Nachmanides that followed is, admittedly, indicative of mendicant belligerence, but (the now ninety-year old) Peñafort played the least offensive role.

At some point the censorship committee accused "Bonastrug de

---

33. Vose, *Dominicans, Muslims and Jews*, 171; Baer, "The Disputations," 156; Denifle, 236 (#5); Fernando Valls y Taberner, ed. "Diplomatari de San Ramón de Penyafort," *Analecta sacra tarraconensia* 5 (1929), 286–87.

34. Vose, *Dominicans, Muslims and Jews*, 173; Baer, "The Disputations," 156; Denifle, 238 (#7).

35. Sanhedrin, vol. I, *Babylonian Talmud*, 136–37.

36. Maccoby, 26.

Porta," a teacher of Girona, with having disparaged Christ and the Catholic faith. This is simply Nachmanides according to his Latin name.[37] The charge may have been based chiefly on the rabbi's assertion of the absurdity of God becoming man, or his quotation of Maimonides as also mentioned above, since it was the same Arnold of Segarre who took umbrage at his statement at the Disputation, who now sat on the tribunal that indicted him. Then, of course, there was the apostate Paul, who must have resented Nachmanides for remarks he made toward him in the debate and for the rabbi's portrayal of his "defeat" in the subsequent Hebrew account, which he wrote and quickly disseminated. Indeed, this publication is likely what triggered his prosecution. The case was not judged by the Dominicans, but by James and his royal advisors. Nachmanides' defense was that the king and Friar Raymond had granted him leave to argue his points; he should not now be punished for making use of that concession. Still, as the rabbi himself records, permission had been granted him by Raymond, "so long as you do not speak disrespectfully." By April 1265, the king had issued a comparatively light sentence. Nachmanides would serve two years' exile and his book would be burned.[38] When the Dominicans objected, the king responded by dispensing with punishment altogether; this on the heels of a separate decision freeing the Jews from subjection to any lingering Dominican censorship. The nonagenarian Peñafort, well acquainted with the king's temperamental character, would surely have seen the futility of arguing with him on these points.[39] Paul, however, was another story, and it is time we delved into his character more deeply.

Clearly, Friar Paul had a score to settle with Nachmanides, first as an ex-Jew, and second, as "the loser" in the *Vikuach*. James's reversal as regards the rabbi, in fact, apparently so infuriated Paul that he left the kingdom to complain to the new pope, Clement IV, who was actually an old ally of his from Provence when the pope was Guy Foulques, Archbishop of Narbonne and sponsor of Christian disputes with Jews.[40] If

37. Williams, *Adversus Judaeos*, 245; nt. 1; Vose, *Dominicans, Muslims and Jews*, 174; nt. 27; "Many medieval Jews had 'Romance' names as related alternatives to their Hebrew ones"; Chazan, *Barcelona*, 199–203; Burns, *Diplomatarium of the Crusader Kingdom of Valencia*, vol. I (Cambridge: Cambridge University Press, 1984), 101–2.

38. Vose, *Dominicans, Muslims and Jews*, 174; Baer, "The Disputations,"157; Denifle, 239.

39. The sovereign even once had his own confessor mutilated.

40. Chazan, "Archbishop Guy Fucoldi and his Jews," *Revue des études juives* 132 (1971), 587–94; "Confrontation in the Synagogue of Narbonne: A Christian Sermon and a Jewish Reply," *Harvard Theological Review* 67 (1974): 587–94; 445, 451–53, 457; Vose, *Dominicans, Muslims and Jews*, 143.

Paul is correctly identified, he is said not only to have disputed with his former co-religionists in southern France, but to have repeatedly denounced them for money-lending. More than this, he was infamous for digging up and expelling the bodies of Christian apostates who reverted to Judaism from Jewish cemeteries![41] Clement IV subsequently wrote a letter to James I, urging him to take a much harder line with the Jews (and Muslims) of his realm in general and to punish Nachmanides in particular for his "lies and blasphemies."[42] When as much as two years passed without the king taking any punitive action, Clement fired-off *Damnabili perfidia Judaeorum*, a bull (as its title suggests) dripping with anti-Judaism.[43] It concludes by admonishing the king to use his nobles and officials to force the Jews to "surrender the entire Talmud along with its commentaries and additions. All their books must be exhibited for inspection."[44] While texts found to conform to the Bible (Old Testament *and New*?) and judged free of error were to be returned to their owners, it seems unlikely that most texts would have fit this criterion. Those judged false, or even debatable, would be kept by the papacy until a final decision was made. This was practically Paris all over again ... this *was* Nicholas Donin all over again—only this time he wore a Dominican habit: "As one of those who will carry out the investigation of the books seized, the pope strongly recommends Paul Christiani, the bearer of this letter, who as a former Jew and zealous convert, has all the essential qualifications of expert knowledge of languages and of the heresies and errors found in these books and of Christian theology as well."[45]

For his part, King James the Conqueror was unmoved. His enactments a year later in October 1268 almost make him appear to be deliberately thumbing his nose at Rome. James, as we have seen, re-affirmed the right of Jews not to be subjected to preaching (and mob intimidation) outside their *call*, and also ordered that no more than ten "good men" might accompany preachers into their synagogues, as noted above. These privileges extended not only to the Jews of Barcelona, but Girona, Perpignan, and Montpellier, along with

---

41. Vose, *Dominicans, Muslims and Jews*, 143; J. Kobak, *Jeschurun* 6 (1868): 1–31; Joseph Shatzmiller, "Paulus Christianus: un aspect de son activité anti-juive," in *Hommages à Georges Vajda*, eds. G. Nahon and C. Touati (Louvain, 1980), 203–17; Chazan, "The Letter of R. Jacob ben Elijah to Friar Paul," *Jewish History* 6 (1992): 51–63.
42. Grayzel, *Church and the Jews*, 92–97.
43. Ibid., 97–99.
44. Ibid., 98.
45. Ibid.

clauses that blatantly defied Clement's and Paul's agenda. These included exemptions from most investigations concerning Hebrew books, dispensations from onerous sumptuary laws, permission to collect interest on loans at the rate of four *deniers* per pound per month.... Perhaps in response, Paul once more took his leave of the Crown of Aragon and moved on to Paris. There he resumed his anti-Jewish preaching and disputational activities with the support of a more compliant French monarchy.[46]

Paul might have been doubly motivated by the death of his papal patron a month later. One wonders if the Jews of Aragon viewed the pontiff's untimely demise (not to mention Paul's definitive departure) as a judgment of God—one could hardly blame them if they did.

One might also wonder whether the summation of all these troubling incidents is not itself the ultimate indictment of any alleged claim to Dominican "tolerance." Did not Clement have recourse to the word "heresy" when referring to Talmudic literature? Did he not employ Christiani and the Dominicans to the task of censorship and seizure? On the other hand, on what reasonable grounds should Raymond of Peñafort and his preaching program be held responsible for the obsessive actions of Christiani and Clement? Before the bar of history, doesn't Peñafort deserve to be tried as a separate defendant? Most of the *excesses* associated with the Barcelona Disputation and Dominican proselytism/censorship campaigns lie squarely with Christiani and Clement, one a self-loathing Jew, the other a rabid Jew-hater. No doubt Saul had internalized the stereotypical prejudices of surrounding Catholic Jew-haters, incorporating them part and parcel into "Paul," his new Christian alter ego. Only a self-contemptuous man, who had disturbed the graves of his own kin, could place himself at the service of a pope who routinely characterized his race as "reprehensible, ungrateful and injurious."[47] But to demonize the larger Dominican mission program by focusing on individuals such as these is to lose sight of the tradition of the penitential literature and tolerant dialogue of the Christian humanists of the twelfth-century renaissance.

The fact is, the Church did not need Nicholas Donin to tell it how "pernicious" the Talmud was before Christian apologists began studying Hebrew and rabbinic literature: witness Odo and Master Alan of twelfth-century Paris. Churchmen did not wait for Paul Christiani to upbraid his Jewish upbringing before mounting a campaign to proselytize Jews—it was because of the preaching of devoted men like St Ray-

46. Vose, *Dominicans, Muslims and Jews*, 178.
47. Grayzel, *Church and the Jews*, 97.

mond and St Dominic that Paul was converted in the first place, succumbing to the call of mendicancy itself.[48] What each of these "innovative" Christian apologists did share, however, was a deep and abiding interest in sin, repentance, and the eternal welfare of others. It was a sacra*mentality* which led them to compose manuals on vice—it was what prompted them to begin preaching to the unconverted. Efforts aimed at converting Jews only became a reality because a handful of heroically charitable men viewed them more than ever as brothers—even if brothers in need of correction. And this leads us back to the abstract.

The Catholic ideal of both proselytism and tolerance was based on the notion of the brotherhood of poor sinners in need of transformation in Christ. It was considered the highest compliment to the dignity of the "Other" to invite him to share in that greatest good, which the Christian already possessed. True, this meant disabusing him of alleged untruths, but always by force of reason, not compulsion. To call this "tolerance" is not to diminish in any way the obvious hardships that the Jewish *aljamas* experienced as a direct result of its implementation. The Catholic construct, however, actually came with built-in curbs against its own excesses. If the Dominicans in the Crown of Aragon are guilty of anything, it was not adhering to the self-imposed limits of the medieval Catholic conception of tolerance, as elaborated by their own Thomas Aquinas: "Now fraternal correction is directed to a brother's amendment: so that it is a matter of precept, in so far as it is necessary for that end, but not so as we have to correct our erring brother *at all places and times.*" (emphasis mine) The Angelic Doctor explains in his *Summa theologiae* that whereas the Catholic faith obliges men never to commit blasphemy, murder, adultery, or other violations of the Decalogue under any pretext, the converse, never missing any opportunity to practice the virtues (like fraternal correction), is not an obligation:

> Negative precepts bind always and for all times. On the other hand, acts of virtue must not be done anyhow, but by observing the due circumstances, which are requisite in order that an act be virtuous; namely, that it be done where, when, and how it ought to be done. And since the disposition of whatever is directed to the end depends on the formal aspect of the end, the chief of these circumstances of a virtuous act is this aspect of the end, which in this case is the good of virtue. If therefore such a circumstance be omitted from a virtuous act, as entirely takes away the good of virtue, such an act is contrary to a precept. If, however, the circumstance omitted from a virtuous act be such

48. Cohen, "Reflections on the Text," 108.

as not to destroy the virtue altogether, though it does not perfectly attain the good of virtue, it is not against a precept.[49]

When preaching leads to people pelting Jews with stones and when censoring blasphemies leads to vendettas against prominent Jewish leaders, it is time to forego fraternal admonition. Quoting Augustine, Aquinas argues this can even be a meritorious duty of charity: "If a man refrains from chiding and reproving wrongdoers, because he awaits a suitable time for so doing, or because he fears lest, if he does so, they may become worse, or hinder, oppress, or turn away from the faith, others who are weak and need to be instructed in a life of goodness and virtue, this does not seem to result from covetousness, but to be counseled by charity."[50]

Here again we see that authentic admonishing (or not admonishing) is fired not by the desire to eliminate an enemy, but to assist a *brother*: "'Since we ignore who is predestined and who is not, charity should so guide our feelings, that we wish all to be saved.' Consequently we ought to do our brethren the kindness of correcting them, with the hope of God's help."[51]

This being said, it nevertheless appears that men like Martini, Christiani, and at least some of their confreres had lost sight of the unspoken assumption of the-Jew-as-equivalent-to-Christian penitent. This is especially to be noted in the years following Peñafort's death. During the summer of 1279, for instance, anti-Jewish riots broke out in Huesca and Calatayud in connection with Dominican preaching campaigns. As Baer describes them: "In Huesca, a mob carried a simulated Torah scroll through the streets, to the accompaniment of derisive chants and mimicry, in a grotesque parody of Jewish rites. In Calatayud and several other places the populace actually stormed the walls of the judería and tore down the gates, while a sermon was being delivered inside."[52]

King Pedro III, successor to James the Conqueror, reissued his father's strictures against Christian rabble accompanying the friars into Jewish quarters, while at the same time instructing the Jews to once again listen patiently to the friars' sermons without complaint. It is hard not to conclude, however, that the Dominicans ultimately failed to practice the discretion of the confessor when admonishing non-Christian sinners. It is very likely that during this same simmering summer

---

49. *Summa theologiae*, II. II. 33. 2.
50. Ibid.
51. Ibid.
52. Baer, "The Disputations," 168.

Raymond Martini began circulating his newly completed *Pugio Fidei* among the friars and in his own disputations with Rabbi Ibn Adret.[53] Martini was perhaps the most famous pupil of Peñafort's *studia*, and the one who would later go on to teach at the school in Barcelona. We actually encountered him earlier in the list of friars to be sent to North Africa in 1250. Speaking of the friars who completed their language studies, Burns says of Martini, "The ideal graduate was a man like Ramon Marti, described shortly after his death as '*philosophus in arabico*.'"[54] It was in 1257, while Martini was working in Tunis, that he composed his *Explanatio simboli apostolorum*, "a tract addressed to all infidels which endeavored to prove the twelve articles of the Apostles Creed primarily with quotations from Scripture."[55] In 1260 Martini completed a *Summa* against the Qu'ran, which is now lost, along with an Arabic dictionary, the *Vocabulista in arabico*. But his chief contribution was his polemics directed toward Jews, the *Capistrum Iudeorum* in 1267 and the *Pugio Fidei adversus Mauroset Iudeos* in 1278.[56]

---

53. Vose, *Dominicans, Muslims and Jews*, 157–58; "The full significance of Martini's (and perhaps his fellows') having somehow at some point around 1279, preached to or debated with rabbis like Solomon Ibn Adret remains open to question. It may have been intended in part as a conversionary exercise, and arguments in the *Pugio* were apparently taken seriously enough to generate a Jewish response. Jews may in fact have been forced to attend mendicant sermons at Barcelona as mandated by the king; in any case there was undoubtedly at least a sense of danger in the air as pogrom rumors circulated about the region. Like Nachmanides before him, rabbi Solomon thus wrote to bolster the confidence of his coreligionists in a time of perceived need"; nt. 98: cf. Perles, R. *Salamo*, 54–6; Graetz, *History of the Jews*, vol. III, 622–23; Longpré, "Le B. Raymond Lulle," 198; Cohen, "Christian Adversary"; Hames, *Art*, 252–53, esp. nt. 21.

54. Burns, *Las Siete Partidas*, 95.

55. Cohen, *The Friars and the Jews*, 131; cf. Joseph M. March, "En Ramón Marty y la seva '*Explanatio simboli apostolorum*,' *Institut d'estudis catalans-Anuari*" (1908): 443–96.

56. Ibid., 164; "It was in his anti-Jewish writings, though, that Martini demonstrated the greatest advances in polemical methodology. In 1267 he wrote the *Capistrum Iudeorum*, a work that not only proffered prophetic evidence to establish the advent of the messiah but also refuted Jewish objections to such argumentation taken from rabbinic literature. The *Capistrum* revealed signs of a growing recourse to propaedeutic rational argumentation on Martini's part, an approach entirely lacking in the earlier *Explanatio*. Similarities between the *Capistrum* and the *Summa contra gentiles* have led some scholars to the conclusion that Aquinas consulted Martini's work while writing his own, finding the method of using sources currently regarded by the infidel as authoritative a very helpful technique. Martini, however, himself found the *Capistrum* ineffective for converting the Jews, apparently because they had refused to accept as evidence biblical or rabbinic sources adduced in their Latin translations. The friar consequently compiled the *Pugio fidei adversus Mauros et Iudeos*, a work completed in 1278, which marked the climax of his polemical career."

Fifteen volatile years after the Barcelona Disputation, his *Pugio* bears all the marks of a now poisoned estimation of the "Other":

> Behold, reader, how God, in view of their crimes, placed the Jews in a terrible state of perception, so that they do what ought not be done and is not becoming. And with what great guilt is that most abominable mouth, which quite often has blasphemed the Lord Jesus Christ, infected and punished! For as often as they circumcise an infant or an adult, they suck the penis orally for as long as blood emerges from it, desiring to obey the ... rabbis. They excuse this by saying that if this would not be done, all their infants would die, which is false. For the Saracens circumcise their infants and never do this abominable act.[57]

If accurate, such intimate knowledge of contemporary Jewish practice could only have come from someone like Paul Christiani. Indeed, in not a few places, one may discern Martini's debt to him.[58]

Besides attacking Jewish custom Martini also routinely derides rabbinical exegesis: "Know that countless evil and most impudent lies ... are in the Talmud and their other books with which I no longer wish to soil my parchment."[59] He adds, "Besides the spirit of fornication which is in their midst. ... The devil undoubtedly ... misled them and deprived them of a sense of understanding the truth, so that they are less intelligent than asses as regards divine scriptures."[60] Cohen calls this vindictive work "the magnum opus of the school of Raymond de Peñaforte." He would do better to affix the name Paul Christiani.[61] Let me be clear on this point. Paul's penchant is no knock on the Jewish community, as if it alone possessed the inherent capacity for producing megalo-virtuosos. The Catholic community has produced its share of obsessive intellectuals who, having once "gone over to the other side," would stop at nothing less than the complete conversion—and subver-

---

57. *Pugio Fidei*, 3.3.11.18, 786; Cohen, *Friars and the Jews*, 150.

58. Martin Cohen, *Friars and the Jews*, 176–77; Chazan, "From Friar Paul to Friar Raymond: The Development of Innovative Missionizing Argumentation," *Harvard Theological Review* 76:3 (1983): 289–306; *Daggers of Faith*, 115–36; although neither Cohen, nor Chazan argue Christiani's strong direct influence, each scholar nevertheless gives ample examples of Martini's indebtedness to Christiani's original argumentation against Nachmanides.

59. Ibid., 3.2.5.16, 573; 3.3.22.15–18, 932–33; Cohen, *Friars and the Jews*, 149.

60. Ibid., 3.3.21.23, 918; Cohen, *Friars and the Jews*, 147.

61. Even Raymond's sharpest detractors are seemingly gravitating toward this conclusion; in *Christ Killers* (2007), Cohen has dropped all reference to Raymond of Peñafort, limiting himself instead to an historical sketch of Christiani and Martini.

sion—of their former co-religionists; Julian the Apostate and Martin Luther spring to mind.[62]

Peñafort's detractors will be quick to point out that he was the friar who likely ordered Martini's composition in the first place, to which one could reply that he is *explicitly* named as commissioning Aquinas's *Summa contra gentiles*, and it is entirely *bereft* of Martini's anti-Judaistic animus. Cohen writes, "If one lends credence to the . . . tradition that Raymond of Penyafort solicited the composition of the *Contra gentiles* to buttress his missionary campaigns among Muslims and Jews, the work perhaps embodies Thomas' concurrence with his confrere's conviction that the presence of the Jew and the Saracen in Christendom served no positive purpose."[63] But John Hood writes in *Aquinas and the Jews*, "Thomas harbored no special malice toward Jews; he was not a Pablo Christiani or John of Capistrano, obsessed with converting Jews or whipping up popular enthusiasm against them. Even his demands that usury be suppressed were based on a moral conviction that usury was wrong [i.e., sinful] rather than on any hatred of Jews as such."[64]

What is more, the pejorative tone of the *Pugio* is completely inconsistent with what we do know of even possible Jewish estimation of Peñafort as cited above: "Inflamed with fires of charity, he inspired a special devotion and reverence for himself among infidels also, to wit, Jews and Saracens, who admired the excellence of his honesty and were delighted by his sweet and reasonable speech."[65] Paul, on the other hand, is the one charged by his own people that "he came . . . to destroy the remnant of Israel," one who "wanted to uproot everything."[66]

Indeed, the one possible reference to Peñafort in the *Pugio* is one of the few times in which we may still discern darkly the traditional Dominican approach to sinners: "I have been enjoined to put together, from those books of the Old Testament which the Jews receive, or even

---

62. Luther even employs the same terms as Martini: "The Catholic theologians are asses who do not know what they maintain, when they say that Christ has only destroyed the ceremonial law of the Old Testament, and not also the Ten Commandments," Martin Luther, *Commentary on Galatians*; cf. Patrick O'Hare, *The Facts About Luther* (Rockford, IL: TAN Books, 1987, reprint; Frederick Pustet Co., 1916), 114.

63. Cohen, *Living Letters*, 372.

64. Hood, 111.

65. *Raymundiana*, I, 12.

66. Cohen, *Friars and the Jews*, 128; cf. Chazan, "Confrontation," 452–53, 455–56; Adolph Neubauer, "Another Convert," *Jewish Quarterly Review* (1893), 714; and Solomon ibn Verga, *Shevet Yehudah*, 148.

from the Talmud and other authentic writings of theirs, *something that like a knife may be ready for preachers and priests of the Christian faith, to cut the bread of the Divine Word* whenever Jews are present at sermons and also indeed to cut the throat of their impiety and perfidy."[67] (emphasis mine) The latter sentiment is exceedingly grating on our ears, but in context ought to be less severe than it sounds. Vose, for example, writes: "Note the use of martial imagery, which was a hallmark of the Order in its foundational documents."[68] It would be closer to the mark, however, to hear in these lines the discordant and now-distant strains of the preacher-as-doctor of the penitential tradition. Compare Martini's use of the "knife" to that previous wielding by Alan of Lille:

> *The preacher should act like the material physician or medical doctor. For, just as the medical doctor, because of the diversity of diseases, varies the kinds of remedies, so the preacher ought to apply the remedies of admonitions.* For example, if he is preaching to the lustful, he may bring in authorities against lust, and discuss reasons against it; he may show it to be abominable to God and to mankind—indeed, how it stinks before God. *Now by warning he may cut, as with a knife, and now he may foster through consolation.* In a similar way let him dispute against other vices, accordingly as he may have seen his hearers ensnared by various vices. If he preaches to the poor, let him discuss poverty, commending poverty.[69] (emphasis mine)

Martini's *Pugio* is not the dagger of the assailant; it is the work-blade of the surgeon, of the doctor of souls—or at least it used to be.[70] We see here that the physician of the confessional, who preaches to the laity, ought to be the same as the doctor who now preaches to Jews and Muslims. In other words, non-Christians were deserving of the *same* treatment as the faithful—though, admittedly, in Martini's hands they were now liable to malpractice.

As Augustine and Aquinas had argued, it was wrong to correct the sinner if the correction was likely to make him "worse." In this context, riots against Jews and mob mockery of their religion surely destroyed all reasonable hope of genuine conversions. Traumatized Jewish appeals to

---

67. Raymund Martin, *Pugio Fidei adversus Mauros et Judaeos* (Paris: Apud Mathurinum Henault, 1651), 1.

68. Vose, *Dominicans, Muslims and Jews*, 127, nt. 146.

69. Alan of Lille, *Ars Praedicandi*, xxxxix, PL 107d (184).

70. The Dominicans certainly styled themselves as such, as we have already seen and cf. Ames, *Doctors of Souls*, Unpublished PhD dissertation, University of Notre Dame, 2002.

the Crown of Aragon and reciprocal restrictions thus imposed upon Dominican conduct can only mean that the Friars Preachers of the last third of the thirteenth-century were found wanting in the charity and prudence of their founders. It was rather a case of too much the dagger, not enough the poultice.

Did this disturb Raymond of Peñafort? If Peñafort really was the pioneer of charitable outreach to Jews and Muslims, why is there no record of his opposition to the tactics, if not the tone, of his Dominican confreres, especially of Christiani and Martini? Does not silence equal approbation? What is to be said for the saint in his separate, but related defense?

In his *Vitae fratrum*, completed six years *before* the Barcelona Disputation and Dominican censorship campaign, Friar Gerard of Frachet had this to say of the former master-general: "Afterwards [his resignation of 1240] he chose to live in the convent at Barcelona. Although sick and very weak, he is still living."[71] Frachet goes on to praise his master's sanctity, including promoting the spread of the faith among Muslims (Frachet makes curious omission of Jews) and his influence with civil authorities. It is to be highly doubted that the sick-and-very-weak-ninety-something took any active participation in the excesses of Dominican activities in the Crown of Aragon—much of which occurred after his death. His presence at the Disputation and his position on the censorship tribunal were likely ceremonial in nature due to his tremendous prestige. For all we know, the saint's synagogue sermon on the Holy Trinity was his "swan song." Indeed, his direct participation in those affairs which ultimately held some negative consequences for Jews was no worse than that of his sovereign King James, who is otherwise viewed as a tolerant and even-handed monarch.[72]

And if the saint was sorry to see the abuse of his methods of mission, we may yet have record of his opposition, albeit posthumously, and by the pen of a protégée: no less a personage than Ramon Llull.

---

71. *Vitae Fratrum*, 7; www.op.org/nigeriaop/kenny/VF7.htm.

72. In the words of Yom Assis, "Jaime I, himself a devout Christian, was prepared to encourage individual Jews to accept Christianity but was strongly opposed to all measures of coercion and pressure that were designed to destroy Jewish life. Jaime I acted as a Christian king as long as there was no danger to Jewish life and property," *The Golden Age of Aragonese Jewry* (London: Littman Library of Jewish Civilization, 1997), 51; cf. Chazan, *Barcelona and Beyond*, 32.

⊕

Whereas the present scholarly paradigm posits conversionist Christians driven to eliminate religious difference by baptizing all non-believers, subsuming them into one homogenous hegemon, "Christendom," the case of Ramon Llull (1234–1316) demonstrates quite the opposite. While the great apostle to Islam was born into one of the Catalan families who assisted James I in the conquest of Muslim Majorca in 1229, that king and caste evinced no interest in converting a now servile population:

> Neither Church nor King made any serious or sustained attempts to convert their Muslim captives to Christianity. . . . Baptism . . . [had] the potential to improve the terms of their emancipation . . . the drive to win the Majorcan slave population over to Christianity was neither endorsed nor set in motion by its Catalan masters, but rather sustained in defiance of them.
>
> The conversion of the captive Muslim population was of no interest either to the monarch or to those Christians who wielded any power and, therefore, received no official encouragement. Consequently, there is no reason to doubt that, when Llull subsequently called for the conversion of the Muslims, he was in fact, acting against the interests of the Christian community on Majorca as well as against the powerful military orders of the Temple and the Hospital.[73]

Thus, Llull's targeting of Jews and Muslims for conversion does not fit Moore's "decision[s] of princes and prelates" persecutory construct. The true motivations of this troubadour-"seneschal" to James the Conqueror are a well-known tale:

> One night he was sitting beside his bed, about to compose . . . a song to a lady whom he loved with a foolish love; and as he began to write this song, he looked to his right and saw our Lord Jesus Christ on the cross. . . . On the fourth occasion . . . when this vision appeared to him, he was absolutely terrified . . . his conscience reminded him of the guilt of his former life and his unworthiness to serve Christ. . . . At last, as a gift of the Father of lights, he thought about the gentleness, patience, and mercy which Christ showed and shows toward all sorts of sinners. . . . God wanted him, Ramon, to leave the world and dedicate

73. Fernando Domínguez and Jordi Gayá, "Life," in *Raimundus Lullus, An Introduction to His Life, Works, and Thought*, eds. Alexander Fidora and Josep E. Rubio (Turnhout: Brepolis, 2008), 29; cf. Lorenzo Perez, "Documentos conservados en los registros vaticanos relatives al primer Pontificado de Mallorca, 1230–1266," *Boletín de la Sociedad Arcqueológica Lluliana* 32 (1961–62), 48–66, here 52; 59; and ff; Álvaro Santamaria, *Ramon Llull y la Corona de Mallorca: sobre la elaboración de la 'Vita Raimundi Lulli'* (Palma de Mallorca, 1989).

himself totally to the service of Christ . . . to give up his life and soul for the sake of His love and honor; and to accomplish this by carrying out the task of converting to His worship and service the Saracens.[74]

It was personal sin, meditation on the Lord's Passion, and on his mercy toward "all sorts of sinners" that inspired Llull's extraordinary outreach to infidels. And whereas he had been moved by an adulterous love to write a song in praise of his presumed paramour, he would now spend the rest of his life consumed with writing "the best book in the world, against the errors of unbelievers"; in other words, he would become God's troubadour of mercy to the unconverted. Llull soon sold all his possessions and, after making provision for his family, set off for Paris, where he might gain the education he sorely lacked for his intended project. It is hard to miss the parallel between Llull and Waldo, between Llull and St Francis. More than mere hagiographical hyperbole, what we have chronicled here is the quintessential pious layman[75] to whom Alan of Lille, and later the mendicant Orders, had first ministered. Even the manner with which Llull sets out on his mission to Muslims, Jews, and other non-Christians is clearly inaugurated in penitential terms: "He set out for the shrines of Saint Mary of Rocamadour, Saint James, and other holy places."[76] Undergoing this penance, he might offer prayers in these places for possible martyrdom and the success of his program, which is described as follows:

> . . . [to] go to the pope, to kings, and to Christian princes to incite them and get them to institute . . . monasteries in which selected monks and others fit for the task would be brought together to learn the languages of the Saracens and other unbelievers, so that . . . one could always find the right people ready to send out to preach and demonstrate to the Saracens and other unbelievers the holy truth of the Catholic faith, which is that of Christ . . . accept dying for Christ in converting the unbelievers to His service; [and] to write the above-mentioned book.[77]

Either Llull had a genuine communication from God, or he was already familiar with the work of his namesake Peñafort and his Dom-

---

74. Raymond Llull, *A Contemporary Life* [*Vita coetanea*], 2–5, ed. and trans. Anthony Bonner (Barcelona, Woodbridge, UK: Barcino-Tamesis, 2010), 30–37; cf. also Bonner, *Selected Works of Ramon Llull*, vol. 1 (Princeton, NJ: Princeton University Press, 1985), 13–15.

75. Cf. Mark D. Johnston, *The Evangelical Rhetoric of Ramon Llull: Lay Learning and Piety in the Christian West Around 1300* (New York, NY: Oxford University Press, 1996).

76. Llull, *A Contemporary Life*, 9; Bonner, *Selected Works*, 37.

77. Bonner, *Selected Works*, 35–37.

inican language schools—or both. The resemblance between the two mission-programs is too striking to admit of other explanations. Furthermore, Llull informs us that he obtained a personal audience with Peñafort that had profound consequences for the course of both his life and ministry: "He was dissuaded from making this trip ['Paris, for the sake of learning grammar and acquiring other knowledge required for his tasks'] by the arguments and advice of his relatives and friends and most of all of Brother Ramon of the Dominicans . . . and those counsels made him return to his own city, that is, to Majorca."[78] How are we to view the relationship between these two towering figures in Christian mission to the unconverted? And what in particular are we to make of Peñafort's counsel to "forget Paris"?

E. Allison Peers, Llull's most prominent English biographer of the first half of the twentieth century, writes, "The life of the Dominican saint [Raymond of Peñafort] . . . will give some idea of the influence which his opinion would have upon Llull, who might well have derived most of his own ideals from the saint's achievements. Possibly the latter may have looked upon this young disciple as his successor."[79] Is there evidence for this speculation? Perhaps.

Llull relates the following story in his work, *Fèlix*:

> In a certain land a Christian monk once had such a long dispute with a Saracen king that he was able to persuade him that the Saracen religion was false; and the king understood, by the necessary reasons the monk had presented, that he was in a state of damnation. The king then asked the monk to prove to him by necessary reasons that the Christian faith was true, in which case he would convert to Christianity and be baptized, and he would place his country beneath the dominion of the Holy Church. The monk replied that he could not demonstrate it to be true by necessary reasons. The Saracen was most displeased with the monk's reply, saying that he had done a bad thing in taking him away from the Saracen faith in which he had always believed, if he could not give him necessary reasons concerning the Roman faith. He added that giving up one's faith for another was a matter of grave concern; but to leave a bad faith for a true one, involving necessity of reason, that is to say, to leave believing for understanding was quite acceptable. The king told the monk that if he could not give him understanding of the Christian faith, he would make him die a cruel

---

78. Llull, 10; Bonner, *Selected Works*, 36–39.

79. E. Allison Peers, *Ramon Lull, A Biography* (New York, NY: Ben Franklin, 1969; reprint of Society for Promoting Christian Knowledge, 1929), 36.

death. The monk fled, and the king died in error, from which came great harm to him and to all his land.[80]

The "monk" in question is almost certainly Raymond Martini.[81] Though the friar had written his notorious *Pugio* "principally against the Jews," his original training was in Arabic and for the proselytization of Muslims, and so he adds that his *Pugio* is also written "against the Saracens and other enemies of the true faith." Martini's alleged conduct toward Sultan Al-Mustansir so vexed Llull that he recounted this incident no less than seven times throughout his many works. Though there are deeper epistemological conundrums at stake, what should draw our attention here is the deafening reticence of the mendicant friar in the face of the Muslim ruler's obvious angst. In another version of the same story, the friar demolishes the Sultan's faith and then simply "hands him a list of Christian doctrines in Arabic telling him that he should read and believe them."[82] This is just one more example of that mechanical and apparently fruitless Dominican dialogue we witnessed against Jews in the mid-1260s and beyond. In this context, therefore, perhaps Ramon Llull's criticisms are also Raymond Peñafort's? How else are we to explain his discouragement of a Dominican vocation for the enthusiastic Llull? Wasn't Lull the perfect candidate for the aging saint's ongoing crusade for the souls of Jews and Saracens? Perhaps the now nonagenarian and pained Peñafort, knowing full well he was about to make account for his life and mission to his Maker, and having seen how "knowledge puffs up the wise" (1 Cor 8:1) in the case of his pupils Christiani and Martini as evidenced by their lack of charity, forestalled the same fate for Llull? Again, one might ask why else he should have actively discouraged such a promising Dominican candidate, unless he himself had nagging reservations about the methods and excesses of his own initiative? For all we know, he might have been the very one to counsel charity to Llull in all his efforts at dialogue.

We might uncover something about Peñafort and even more about the penitential origins of mission to infidels by examining another tale of Llull's *Fèlix* regarding the well-educated pastor of a large parish:

---

80. Llull, *Fèlix*, Book One, Bonner, *Selected Works*, II, 694.

81. Ephrem Longpré, "Le B. Raymond Lulle et Raymond Marti, O.P.," *Bolletti de la Societat Arqeologica Luliana* 44 (1933), 269–71, reprinted in *Estudios Lulianos* 13, (1969), 197–200; cf. also J. M. Abu-Nasr, *A History of the Maghrib* (Cambridge: Cambridge University Press, 1975), 140–43.

82. Harvey Hames, "Ramon Llull and his Jewish Contemporaries," address at International Conference on Inter-religious Dialogue in Ramon Llull, 9/15/01, Instituto de Estudos Avançados, Universidad de São Paulo, Brazil, www.ramonllull.net.

He had studied law so as to be able to advise those who confessed to him; but he had learned nothing of philosophy or theology, which was why he was unable to advise people as to how they could vivify virtues and mortify vices in their soul, but was able to advise them regarding worldly goods and how to make amends with them.... [A] man confessed to the sin of lust, and he asked the clergyman how he could, in accordance with nature, strengthen chastity and mortify lust in his soul; he then asked to be enlightened in matters of faith, for he often had doubts. The clergyman, however, was unable to give him any necessary reasons concerning these things. This man wondered why the task of confession was entrusted to such a man.[83]

Once again, as in the story of the mendicant and the sultan, a lack of knowledge of "necessary reasons" is to blame for not bolstering the Christian faith in a soul beset with doubt. This passage is notable on account of several facets. In the first instance, the connection between the theology of sin and sacrament and preaching to non-Christians could hardly be any clearer than in these two tales from Llull's *Felix*. Secondly, there is again an epistemological discrepancy between Dominican approaches based on "authorities" and Llull's overwhelming reliance on ontological reasoning, which shall constitute the heart of his Art, of which we shall shortly speak. Lastly, however, there is in these stories an implied criticism of the Dominican handling of mission. As Anthony Bonner, perhaps the chief Llullian-authority in English of the second half of the twentieth century, writes, "In the 1280s Llull criticized the Dominicans, this time rather directly, in his two novels *Blaquerna* and *Fèlix*. He accuses them, for instance, of being too legalistic (or decretalistic) in their training at Bologna, and as a result being too worldly in their outlook, as well as unable to counsel people in a properly human way in the confessional." He adds, "The reference to the Decretals [in *Blaquerna*] harbors, it seems to me, an implied criticism of Ramon de Penyafort, or at least his followers."[84] While I agree with the latter, I think it unlikely to be an attack on the celebrated friar-confessor,

83. Llull, *Fèlix*, 103; Bonner, *Selected Works*, 1034.

84. Bonner, "Ramon Llull and the Dominicans," *Catalan Review*, 4:4 (1990): 377–92; 385 and nt. 12; cf. *Blaquerna*, chap. 86, and *Fèlix*, chap. 103, cited in Juan Tusquets, "Relación de Ramón Llull con San Ramón de Penyafort y con la orden de Santo Domingo," in *Escritos del Vedat* 7 (1977): 177–95; Miquel Batllori, "Ramon de Penyafort I Ramon Llull," in *A través de la història I la cultura* (Montserrat, 1979), 58; cf. also Bonner, "L'aprenentatge intellectual de Ramon Llull," in *Studia in honorem prof. M. de Riquer* II (Barcelona: Quaderns Crema, 1987).

especially since Llull provides practically a portrait of Peñafort in another tale from the very same chapter.[85]

Llull's most famous apologetic treatise (among so many dozens), however, is his *Book of the Gentile and the Three Wise Men*, a work written more for the layman than the specialist. In this tale, a perplexed pagan philosopher searching for the meaning of life happens upon a Jew, a Christian, and a Muslim traveling through the forest. Prior to this fortuitous encounter, the three monotheists had just been instructed by mysterious Lady Intelligence in the rational grounds for interreligious dialogue, which are none other than Llull's own ontological principles or "necessary reasons." After having brought the Philosopher to rational belief in one God, each faith representative in turn provides him with cogent arguments for adopting his own religion. In this and in many other ways, Llull, unlike his Dominican contemporaries Martini and Christiani, is able to display the greatest sensitivity to his non-Christian protagonists. In the opening of the *Liber*, the Jew, the Christian, and the Muslim greet each other warmly and through their conversation evince genuine concern for each other's well-being. As Nederman writes, "Llull thereby establishes at once the tone of mutual respect and decorum for which the *Liber* has become known: Although members of competing faiths, the wise men conduct themselves in a dignified and convivial manner."[86] Or as Bonner observes of

> Llull's literary skill and his continual emphasis on the humanity of the four disputants. We have the Gentile's tears of sadness at the beginning and of joy at the end; the Jew's sorrow at the successive captivities of his race; and the Saracen's assertion of the temporal efficacy of his religion (resulting in the Muslim possession of the Holy Land). Then, too, there is the aspect of this work on which so many have commented, the exquisite courtesy of the participants towards one another. Perhaps, as has been suggested, Llull simply wished to offer a model of how such discussions should be conducted [*vis-à-vis* Martini and Christiani].

85. Bonner, "L'aprenentatge intellectual," 1035–1036; "There was once a saintly monk, very knowledgeable in theology and philosophy, who was confessor to a noble king. One day it came to pass that the king confessed a sin he had committed against a count from whom he had very wrongly taken a castle. The king confessed this sin and others, and the saintly monk gave a great deal of thought to the sins the king committed. After thinking about it for a long time, he, because of his great wisdom understood the origin of the sin, in which power of the soul it had originated, and how it had come to be committed. As a result, the holy priest knew how to confess the king, giving him convincing natural reasons as to the origin of his sin and how he should make atonement for it."

86. Nederman, *Worlds of Difference*, 30; "Varieties of Dialogue," in *Western Political Thought in Dialogue with Asia* (Lexington Books, 2009), 49.

Perhaps he also hoped in this way to make his Christian convictions more acceptable to his Muslim and Jewish adversaries. His tact even leads him to introduce an ending most surprising in a piece of medieval polemical literature.[87]

Llull has given us an example of medieval Catholic tolerance at its best. The three monotheists do not linger to hear the final decision of the Gentile as to which religion he has ultimately embraced. They act thus, so that "each . . . be free to choose his own religion," without prejudice from the Philosopher's choosing. Llull has, in fact, created a remarkable "space," free from threats of compulsion and even the pressure to conform to the group:

> An interreligious dialogue must take place in a neutral arena, that freedom of speech must be granted, even if everybody is well advised to avoid hurting remarks, that procedural rules are indispensable and that one has not the right to expect from the other that he give up or correct his religion if one is not willing to do the same . . . such dialogue is possible only if the interlocutors know much and are willing to learn more about the other religions.[88]

There is much of Abelard's approach in Llull's *Liber*: empathy, a desire to learn from the "Other," and reason as the ultimate criterion for religious validation:

> Abelard has taken a considerable step toward transforming the interreligious dialogue from a polemical to an edificatory tool. This fact has profound significance in turn for tolerance. Without denying that ultimate truth may be attained, Abelard in effect renders concordance problematic inasmuch as he postpones judgment because of the uncertainties and obscurities of doctrine (as well as the infirmities of human mental faculties). We must take seriously Abelard's claim that the value of dialogue is "learning." We discover the range of human beliefs, and their basis in reason, and thereby sharpen our ability to discriminate falsehoods and insupportable superstitions. We do not, however, establish truth, except perhaps provisionally, on condition that our understanding may be further deepened and transformed by additional debate and inquiry. The deferral of final judgment consequently implies the necessity of continuing toleration of questioning and dissent.[89]

87. Bonner, *Selected Works*, 97–98.

88. Vittorio Hösle, "Interreligious Dialogues during the Middle Ages and Early Modernity," in *Educating for Democracy, Paideia in an Age of Uncertainty*, eds. Alan M. Olson, David M. Steiner, and Irina S. Tuuli (Oxford: Rowman and Littlefield, 2004), 76.

89. Nederman, *Worlds of Difference*, 34.

Llull's dialogue, like that of Abelard before him, is not generated so much out of any fear that Jews and Muslims pose direct threats to Catholic society as out of a quest for the universal truth about God, man, and right conduct. As noted, before they engage in their exchange, Christian, Jew, and Muslim all agree upon a common philosophical groundwork as the basis for their search, and "that basis is none other than the Art itself."[90] Llull describes the Art in this way:

> The final intention of the Art is the discovery of truth. This intention is divided into four parts: the first is to love good; the second, to hate evil; the third, to know how to carry out the descent from the universal ... to the quest for and discovery of the particular about which we wish to know the truth; and the fourth, to offer a necessary demonstration of that which in the remaining sciences is only believable or probable in accordance with the truth. This art proceeds by means of these four intentions, since they are all directed towards the same goal, namely acquiring the science of discovering truth.[91]

Llull will use reason to come to common accord between the faiths. As Josep Rubio explains:

> Recourse to authorities is thus replaced in the Llullian Art by the ground common to the three religions of the Book, whereupon a logical mechanism enabling one to find the answers to the problems posed. In this sense, the Art has been viewed as a point of departure for inter-confessional dialogue, which Ramon Llull himself sets in dramatic form in *II. Llibre del gentil e dels tres savis* ... in order to make correct use of the Art, it is necessary to start out by having a predisposition to accept the truth, even if this means renouncing one's own faith should this be revealed to be false ... one's approach to the Art must be unencumbered by any form of prejudice and one must be fully prepared to accept the truth as the only valid conclusion, whatever this might be.[92]

This is almost the same estimation as of Abelard's work:

> Abelard was primarily concerned not with proving Jews wrong, but with understanding the supreme good and how that supreme good should be reached.... By drawing attention to the common ground that was the goal of the philosopher, the Jew, and the Christian,

---

90. Josep Enrico Rubio, "Thought: The Art," in *Raimundus Lullus, An Introduction*, 250.

91. Ibid., from *Ars universalis, Raymundi Lulli Opera Omnia*, ed. Ivo Salzinger et al., 8 vols. Mainz 1721–1742; (reprinted Frankfurt am Main, 1965).

92. Ibid., 246.

Abelard avoided the customary arguments generated by the uniqueness of the Christian claim. Such inquiry provided a better starting point for discussion of ethical precepts. Abelard's theological investigation similarly centered around the supreme good and its three-fold attributes of power, wisdom, and benignity as glimpsed by gentile philosophers, rather than the doctrine of the [I]ncarnation in particular .... Abelard was able to take ... ethical reflections much further in the form of debates of a philosopher with a Jew and with a Christian. He wanted to show that dialectical technique could become open-ended, in order to evaluate the common ground of different religious traditions and challenge Christians to move away from rigidly confrontational attitudes. [93]

Llull's Art begins, in fact, with sixteen universals or "Figures," among them Abelard's "power, wisdom, and benignity."[94] These attributes of God, synonymous with his Divine essence, were accepted by Christians, Jews, and Muslims alike. As Abelard deliberately omitted Christian doctrines such as the Trinity and the Incarnation from his discussion, so too Llull's Art and dialogue begin with first principles shriven of these teachings (one finds no universal for Three-ness or Son-ship in his quaternary Figures).[95] In Llull's case, however, he believed that such uniquely Christian beliefs were eventually demonstrable from these commonly accepted *dignitates*, or essential attributes of God. Fidora explains the underpinnings of Llull's Art:

> The fundamental qualities of God ... Llull called also *rationes* or *virtutes* ... a rendering of the Greek *axiôma* in the Latin translation of Aristotle's Metaphysics. In accordance with this tradition, Llull interprets the *dignitates* as *notiones per se notae*, as if intuitively comprehensible. As exemplary causes for Creation they are at the same time *principia essendi* and *principia intelligendi*. The essential attributes are, therefore, not just another object of philosophical reflection. Rather they are the overall enabling causes of Being and Cognizing.[96]

God's Goodness, Greatness, Eternity, Power, Wisdom, Will, Virtue, Truth, and Glory are first principles, therefore, and, as such, impossible to prove. But as Fidora points out, this did not detract from Llull's system, since the neo-Platonic idea that God's attributes are "embedded" in creation, "reflecting his glory, was a commonplace of medieval

---

93. Mews, "Abelard and Heloise," 39.

94. Rubio, "Thought: The Art," 254–55.

95. Trans. Marenbon, *Collationes*, xxxix; Rubio, "Thought: The Art," 245; 255.

96. Fidora, "Ramon Llull: Universal Saving Will and Universal Reason," in *Juden, Christen, und Muslime: Religionsdialoge im Mittelalter*, 127–28.

thought—the one that united the Jews, the Christians, and the Muslims in spite of all other differences."[97] Prominent within his science of reality were the virtues, likewise, commonly accepted by monotheists and ethical philosophers: Justice, Prudence, Fortitude, Temperance, Faith, Hope, Afterlife, Patience, and Charity.

The further details of Llull's Art need not detain us here. What is important for us to observe, however, is that just as in Anselm, Abelard, and others, consideration of God's perfections has brought Llull to consider the perfection and salvation of non-Christians (indeed, for Llull this is a metaphysical necessity). Lengthy musings on moral philosophy, virtue, and vice are at the heart of his outreach to sinful humanity. In the epilogue to his *Liber*, Llull's Philosopher offers an extended prayer of praise to God for the virtues he inculcates in men. The list begins with the traditional three: faith, hope, and especially charity, without which nothing human has value; though this is followed by the classical four—justice, prudence, fortitude, and temperance—it is sweet charity that moves a man to share this all-consuming-yet-unconsumed possession with his neighbor:

> And of what use to a man's heart are riches and blessings without charity? Sweet God, You who have enlightened and warmed me by the fire of charity, enlighten and warm with charity all those poor people lacking in charity who live in the land I come from, by which poverty they will be brought, through paths of darkness, to infinite, everlasting fire. . . . Do not let us forget justice in our prayer, for divine justice knows all my faults and can rightly punish me for my failings. . . . Let Him do with me what he will, for charity makes me love, fear, and worship God in his justice. . . . Prudence, you are the light of salvation . . . my understanding has long been in darkness because you were not a part of it. But since you have now brought me such happiness, I beg you . . . through grace and the illumination of this sovereign light you may help me to give light and direction to so many men who are in a state or in times of darkness, ignorant of the path of salvation.[98]

Penitential theology, which had its first stirrings in the works of twelfth-century clerics, has reached both a theoretical and practical apex in the formidable layman Ramon Llull.[99] The origin of outreach to non-Christians in the development of lay sanctity is perhaps, therefore, nowhere better evident than in Llull's case:

97. Ibid.

98. *Liber*, Epilogue; Bonner, *Selected Works*, 296–97.

99. As Nederman writes, "In sum, the tolerant tone of rational dialogue evident in Llull's twelfth-century predecessors is maintained and advanced in the *Liber*" (*Worlds*, 32).

His lifetime spent laboring for reform and evangelism represents superlatively the opportunities for intellectual and spiritual initiative open to Christian lay people in Western Europe around 1300. His appropriation of academic knowledge and emulation of clerical roles demonstrate emphatically a new sophistication in lay learning and piety. His contributions to such practices as vernacular education and organized popular devotion deserve far more investigation than they have received to date. As appreciation of his significance for these endeavors grows, the limited relevance of his activities to official programs for compulsory evangelization becomes more evident.[100]

Living as he did, as a Catalan in the Crown of Aragon, Llull, the reformed-sinner-turned-saint, could not help but reach out "with charity [to] all those poor people lacking in charity who live in the land I come from," Christian and non-Christian. Majorca, a former Muslim bastion, still boasted a significant Saracen presence, as, indeed, did Iberia as a whole. Llull's Art was the result of an ingenious attempt to fashion a yardstick independent of his own faith-tradition, which would nevertheless demonstrate the superiority of its truth claims when measured against its competitors.

For Llull, then, philosophical first principles were the indispensable keys for proselytizing non-Christian wise men. His *Ars Lulliana* postulated that the minds of Jews, Christians, and Muslims alike had access to God and the ontological realities of his creation. Indeed, as Llull definitively affirms: "Infidels are men like us and they share our [human] nature."[101]

---

100. Mark D. Johnston, "Ramon Lull and the Compulsory Evangelization of Jews and Muslims," 35.

101. Raimundus Lullus, *Lectura super Artem inventivam et Tabulam generalem*, Prologue, in: *Raymundi Lulli Opera omnia* [MOG] V, ed. I. Salzinger (Mainz: Häffner, 1729), 359–716; 360: "Ipsi infideles sunt homines, sicut et nos, et sunt de nostra natura," as cited in Annmarie C. Mayer, "Raymund Lull—A Key Figure of Interreligious Dialogue in Medieval Europe," *Bulletin ET* (*European Society for Catholic Theology*), 18 (2007/1–2): 204–14; 207.

Conclusion:
Tolerance & Transcendence

And if you refute me, I shan't be upset with you as you were with me; instead you'll go on record as my greatest benefactor.
                    —Socrates to Callicles, *Gorgias* (Zeyl translation)

To the Jews I became as a Jew, in order to win the Jews.... To those outside the law I became as one outside the law ... that I might win those outside the law.... I have become all things to all men, that I might by all means save some. I do it all for the sake of the gospel that I may share in its blessings.
                    (1 Cor 9:20–21, 23)—St Paul

[In] a single [political] state [exist] communities of human beings [who have] many [different] religious rules, [who] believe in opposite traditions and [who] degrade, deny, and mock each other's traditions. [But] the generally acknowledged rules bring them together.
                    —Ibn Daūd, *The Exalted Faith*

THE DEVELOPMENT of a scholastic theology of sin and mercy lies at the heart of the origins of Dominican mission to Jews and other non-Christians, and thus, at the heart of a uniquely Catholic kind of tolerance. St Anselm meditated on the mystery of the Incarnation and Redemption of the human race by Christ the God-man. He was the first Scholastic to attempt to use reason in the delineation of sin and the means for its atonement. Significant for us, his thought was not only to provide a more harmonious explanation for his fellow Christians, but also for those infidels who rejected the notion of God becoming man as philosophically and theologically absurd. The underlying assumption of the *Cur Deus homo* is that the intellects of Jews and Muslims are capable of processing rational arguments for the Christian faith. In this, his dialogue shares a definite ontological similarity to his famous proof for the existence of God. As to Anselm's motivation, he says quite explicitly that

255

it is his desire to see the mercy of God—"that than which a greater cannot be thought"—be properly reverenced by non-Christians united "with us . . . praising God's wise loving kindness." Anselm had no social agenda against Jews or Muslims. His concerns were clearly vertical, not horizontal. Interestingly, he would gladly answer their objections, but not those of Christian heretics. Though they are both in error, the two are separate to his mind. Alas, however, Anselm saw little chance of salvation for either group, nor did he hold out much hope for lay Christians living in the secular world. It was the early twelfth century. The devil's soldiers besieged every territory and few were safe except consecrated religious behind cloister walls. Those who aspired to sinlessness and salvation must find a monastery; the monks would not come to them.[1] The desire to seek holiness for (not the elimination of) "the Other" was a prerequisite for mission; thus there was no eleventh or twelfth-century campaign for the evangelization of Jews (or Muslims).

Peter Abelard was also a staunch believer in the power of human reason to probe the depths of the mystery of human iniquity and divine forgiveness. Building on Anselm's theological foundation, Abelard was the chief architect of a revolution in the psychology of ethics. He, more than any other, most clearly enunciated the principle that "sin" is not the will (inclination) to sin, but consent to that will; neither does sin reside in the sin committed, but in the intention of the sinner *to sin*. It was Abelard's inquiry into the mechanics of sin and virtue and the sacrament of penance which led him to an investigation of the beliefs of Jews and classical philosophers. Again, like Anselm, Abelard believed that Jews and pagans might be brought to Christianity through rational dialogue. He tried to persuade them, as he tried to persuade his colleagues, that human intention, not the literal application of the law, makes a man sinful or righteous. Abelard found condemnation from his peers for expounding his radical doctrines on sin, and especially for maintaining the position that the Jews who killed Christ did not even sin venially in doing so. Certain of his writings even speak of an eternal reward awaiting a segment of the unbaptized, and explicitly mention the sending of preachers. As we have seen, Abelard was clearly a man caught between two worlds: the traditional cloister and the emerging classroom.

It was in the schools of Paris that Abelard and others trained a new generation of budding scholars in his intention-based theories of sin and repentance. Odo the obscure and Bartholomew the bishop of Exeter both benefitted from their Abelardienne milieu. Like the master,

---

1. Though they undoubtedly prayed without ceasing for them.

Odo wrote a treatise on the virtues and vices. He too treated the three requirements necessary for the reconciliation of the sinner: *compunctio, confessio,* and *satisfactio.* Odo's study of sin and repentance led him to make explicit what was implicit in the dialogues of Abelard and Anselm: "If it is proper for us to exhort those who are fashioned in the faith to live better, surely we should recall the Jews from their erroneous disbelieving sect."[2] Obviously, while not a flattering portrayal, his statement posits a moral equivalency between believers of both religions: both are sinners in need of sanctity. As Abelard had characterized sin-as-wound and penance as the curative remedy of the confessor, so too, Odo justifies approaching Jews with preaching in the words of Christ: "They that be whole need not a physician, but they that are sick" (Matt 9:12). Odo made explicit the link between the pastoral work of the confessor and that of the preacher, as well as the need for both to minister not only to the Christian flock, but to the "lost sheep of the house of Israel" (Matt 15:24). The pursuit of holiness, not homogeneity, had brought him to this realization. Like his predecessors, Odo made use of rational arguments to answer Jewish objections to Christian premises, but what is more, he introduced the practical use of Hebrew to achieve his end. He stressed to his fellow churchmen that they must now take up the labor of learning the languages of their religious adversaries if their witnessing was to bear fruit. To substantiate his claim, Odo quotes the greatest Christian missionary—and Jewish convert: "I became as a Jew, that I might gain the Jews" (1 Cor 9:20). Odo's contemporary, Bartholomew, also drank deep from the wellspring of Parisian ethical erudition and sought to implement the learning of the schools in pastoral approaches to the faithful. He composed a groundbreaking *Penitential,* in which he sought to move beyond the mere lists of sins and penances of previous generations to a deeper appreciation between penitent and confessor. He urged understanding and wisdom on the part of the priest. The confessor must engage in a dialogue with the sinner, in order to judge the offense and its satisfaction. This deeper pastoral concern for the Christian flock also led Bartholomew to grudgingly advocate dialogue with sinners outside the fold. In his *Dialogus contra Judeos,* he makes it clear that his considerations for engaging Jews are not of this world: "We hold discussions with them for their own salvation."[3]

Like Bartholomew, Alan of Lille is associated with Paris and its pastoral concern for the moral problems of the laity. He, too, produced an innovative penitential guide for confessors, the *Liber poenitentialis,* as

2. Landgraf, "Le second livre," 126.
3. Hunt, "The Disputation," 147–48.

well as the *Ars praedicandi*, a handbook for preachers. Both works were among the first of their kind, and the sacramental theology of sin and repentance was the underlying connection between them. Abelard had posed an intensely personal relationship between the sinner and God, one in which the intention of the individual was key, both for the commission of the sin and for the absolving power of his contrition. Alan's contribution was to put Abelard's revolutionary thoughts into a form in which they might more easily spread to every priest in Christendom. As he writes in the *Ars*: "Remorse is ... the first medicine in the cure of sin.... Remorse is a spiritual washing of inner rebirth.... [Thus] according to the extent of filthiness, measure the amount of the washing; according to the severity of the sickness, measure out the quantity of medicine."[4] But if the sorrow of the penitent is the first medicine to be applied to the sickness of sin, the disease requires the further ministrations of a specialist, as Alan writes in the *Liber*: "The wise doctor, therefore, ought to follow the better course, and investigate all causes of the malady, without which he cannot determine the correct diagnosis."[5] Alan also views the role of the preacher in the same light as he does the confessor—as physician of souls: "The preacher should act like the material physician or medical doctor. For, just as the medical doctor, because of the diversity of diseases, varies the kinds of remedies, so the preacher ought to apply the remedies of admonitions."[6]

Interestingly, Alan's investigation of the theology of sin had led him to the conviction that sanctity was no longer the exclusive sanctuary of the cloistered; it was just as possible for secular souls. Thus, in his *Ars*, he urged a universal call to penance: to the poor, to the rich, to soldiers, lawyers, prelates, princes, monks, married persons, and many others.[7] This same vocation of sinlessness for the laity is recommended with equal vigor in the *Liber*. In Alan's eyes, holiness was no longer just for the holy. The minister of the sacrament of confession, acting with a doctor's discretion, should lead the penitents of all persuasions to perfection in Christ: from boys to bishops, from homosexuals to heretics. It was this conviction which motivated him to compose yet another treatise, the *De Fide Catholica*, or *Contra haereticos*. Unlike Anselm, who refused even to debate with the heterodox, Alan preached the Gospel to them in both word and work, likely personally visiting those regions of

---

4. G. R. Evans, trans. *The Art of Preaching*, 120–22.
5. Ibid., 15.
6. *Ars Praedicandi*, xxxxix, PL 107d (184).
7. Ibid.

southern France that were then enmeshed in false teaching. There was no longer any choice. It was the late twelfth and early thirteenth centuries and whole communities of Waldensians and Cathars were now thriving. Their very existence, in fact, gave ironic substantiation to Alan's notions of sustainable lay piety. But if lay persons, both Catholic and Cathar, were as capable as holy brothers of monastic virtue, then, in theory at least, so too were non-Christians. Alan therefore deemed it necessary not only to preach to Waldensians and Cathars but also included persuasive arguments toward Jews and Muslims in his *De Fide Catholica*. As we have seen, Alan's argumentation has led certain scholars to conclude that apologists like Alan saw infidels as definite threats to the unity and integrity of Christian society, just as much as heretics and lepers.[8] But it was the leprosy of sin that troubled Alan most, and, like a good doctor, he wished to minister to its victims in order to ensure unity of a different sort: "the unity of eternal beatitude."[9]

This is not to say, however, that Alan did not promote anti-Judaism with one hand while counteracting it with the other. His *Distinctiones dictionum theologicarum*, though not directly targeted at Jews (nor mainly material of his own making), nevertheless contains disparaging depictions of Jews on practically every page. "The fact that the *Summa 'Quot Modis'* gathers together numerous hostile references and organizes them in an alphabetical, easily searchable format is a significant development in the evolution of medieval anti-Jewish literature."[10] Yet, as Pearson points out, "However much it would shape the Christian conception of the Jew in centuries to come, it was also a reflection of the long tradition of anti-Jewish polemic which preceded it . . . in his dictionary, despite its many hostile references to Jews, Alan of Lille is only registering usages then current; he is not necessarily offering his personal view."[11] Alan and other Scholastics found themselves working within an anti-Jewish tradition that they themselves did not create. Under the circumstances, the marvel is not that in his *DDT* Alan reinforced traditional Jewish stereotypes, but that nowhere else in his entire lengthy corpus of works are such injurious insinuations found—not even in a *Contra Iudeos*! Indeed, as Pearson remarks, modern editors of the *De Fide Catholica* have made the few direct words he addresses to Jews harsher than they certainly were: "For example, in Migne the opening

8. Cohen, *Living Letters*, 157–58; 312.
9. *De Fide Catholica* IV, PL 210, 430a.
10. Pearson, "The Anti-Jewish Polemic," 105.
11. Ibid.

lines of the *Contra Iudeos* speak of the 'perverse beggarliness' (*perversam mendicitatem*) of the Jews (*DFC*, 400D). But the reading there should certainly be *perversam medietatem....* It refers to the obstinate 'half-wayness' (*medietas*) of Jews who believe in one God but not in the God who is both one and three—hence the Jews are 'halfway' to salvation, on the Christian view."[12]

The point is that Alan sees the world against such a vertical axis. He views Jews and Muslims through his sacra*mentality*: "If anyone shall have killed a Jew or a pagan . . . the victim was created in the image of God, and the killer has taken away the hope of future conversion."[13] Because they are created images of the Creator, *because they are sacrament*, anyone who kills them is liable to both temporal and spiritual consequences. Such crimes are also inexcusable, insofar as the Christian perpetrators have deprived these non-Christians of the opportunity of what is highest in this life—full membership in Christ's body the Church—and (presumably) eternal bliss in the world to come. Thus, on a purely pragmatic level, medieval missionary overtures to Jews, far from inciting violence against them, acted as a substantial curb against it. Lastly, it should be observed that the theology of sin and redemption, and its practical expression in the penitential manual of the confessor and handbook of the preacher, served as the true source for later Dominican efforts to convert Jews and Muslims in the next century.

Alan of Lille and his Parisian contemporaries all recognized the importance of moral theology and the simultaneous existence of a pastoral vacuum. As they saw it, because prelates were not preaching timeless truths to the faithful, heretics were eagerly filling their place with pernicious substitutes. Pope Innocent III addressed the issue both in his repeated urgings to the bishops and in his unprecedented and sustained use of Cistercian missionaries against the Cathars. But his greatest stroke was in approving the preaching enterprise of Bishop Diego of Osma and his coadjutor priest Dominic. Significant for our investigation, their life of apostolic poverty and preaching also gave pride of place to public debate. From the very beginning of the Order, the followers of St Dominic believed that frequent public disputation with their religious adversaries would achieve their adversaries' conversion. Both the heretics and the friars were allowed the opportunity to defend their respective positions. Furthermore, the practice of composing polemical literature was considered a key aspect of this preaching, and

12. Ibid., 98.
13. Longère, 77; *Liber Poenitentialis*, II, 58.

the deciding factor in establishing the authenticity of religious belief ought to be its "reasonableness." These are the same methods that were zealously employed by St Dominic's successor, St Raymond of Peñafort, in decades of mission to the Jews of Spain.

The testimony of the early Friars Preachers makes it clear that Dominic was motivated by a spirit of Christ-like self-sacrifice on behalf of others and that his passion permeated the embryonic Order. Far from engaging heretics and non-Christians from any desire for cultural homogeneity, Blessed Jordan of Saxony and other of Dominic's closest associates assure us that his motives were quite heavenly: " . . . with all his strength and most fervent zeal to win for Christ the souls he could; and their came within his heart a wonderful, almost unbelievable, longing for the salvation of all."[14] The witnesses to his sanctity are unanimous in their opinion that Dominic was "zealous for souls, not only those of Christians, but also of Saracens and other unbelievers. As evidence of this, he proposed to go to the pagans and die there for the faith, once he had organized his brethren."[15] The sincerity of the saint and his earliest followers would even seem to have been attested by non-Christians themselves, if Brother John of Spain is to be believed: "St Dominic was loved by everybody, rich and poor, *Jew* and pagan (there were many of these in Spain), in fact by everybody except for the heretics and enemies of the Church whom he pursued and refuted in debate and in preaching."[16] (emphasis mine) The ideology of the founder of the Dominican Order was not to "rid Europe" of those who "threatened the fabric of its existence," but to rid Christians, as well as non-Christians, of all attachment to sin. Even his celebrated debates with heretics have less to do with "ethnic cleansing" than with the "happy bath of repentance":[17]

> While he [a Cathar] was taking them [Dominic, a bishop, and others] through a wood somewhere, he led them astray so viciously, through thorns and thistles, that their feet and legs became quite covered in blood. The man of God endured all this with the utmost patience; breaking out into a hymn of praise to God, he encouraged the others to praise God too and to be patient. "My friends," he said, "hope in the Lord. Victory will be ours, because even now our sins are being washed away in blood." The heretic saw their extraordinary and blissful patience, and he was pricked with compunction at the good words

14. Jordan, *On the Origins*, Chap. 34; Brooke, 164.
15. *Acta Canonizationis s. Dominici* 12, in *Early Dominicans*, 84.
16. *Acta Canonizationis*, 74–75.
17. Alan of Lille, *The Art of Preaching*, 12–22.

spoken by the man of God, so he admitted the poisonous way he had deceived them, and renounced his heresy. When they reached the place of the debate, everything came to a satisfactory conclusion.[18]

What we see here is that sin and satisfaction for it, is at the heart of the conversion of others—even of successful debating! This is the Dominican sacra*mentality*, which was part and parcel of the friars' outreach. Dominican meditation on penitential theology found practical expression in many ways, but particularly in preaching and in the sacrament of confession. Dominic's vision of pastoral service to the masses accorded well with the designs of the papacy, as manifested in Canon Ten of the Fourth Lateran Council. Through a series of pronouncements between the years 1216 and 1221, Pope Honorius III crafted legal sanction for the Dominicans to act in the role of coadjutors and assistants to the bishops, as Lateran IV said, "Not only in the office of preaching, but in hearing confessions and imposing penances." In particular, his encyclical letter of February 1221, *Cum qui recipit prophetam*, ensured that Dominican priests should be accepted everywhere as confessors of the sacrament. The release of the letter coincided with the creation of the new Order's first manual for confessors, authorized by Dominic and composed by Friar Paul, the canon lawyer of Bologna. Paul's *Summa de poenitentia* borrowed from the work of previous penitential writers as well as from the wisdom of his master-general Dominic. He continued the now familiar metaphor of the confessor-as-doctor, who in his compassion used sweetness and soothing words to comfort and heal sick souls.[19]

The same concern for the salvation of souls that moved Dominic and Paul to create the *Summa de poenitentia*, also spurred the master-general to send his trusted friar to the pagan Cumans of Eastern Europe. It is because of his missionary exploits that the saintly Dominican was forever after fondly recalled as Paul of Hungary. We learn from Dominican chronicles that those friars who suffered and died in the attempt to convert these infidels did so not out of any calculated need to preserve Christendom's societal fabric, but to save sinners from hell; Anselm's monastic-fortress metaphor had certainly been turned on its head. Non-Christians were sinners, yes, but also brothers to whom a Christian ought to will the good as much as to himself, and the highest good was salvation in Jesus.

Like Paul before him, Friar Raymond of Peñafort had studied and

18. Gerald de Frachet, *Lives of the Brethren*, in Tugwell, 87–88.
19. Paul of Hungary, *Rationes poenitentiae*, *Florilegium Casinensis*, 193.

taught law at Bologna, entered the Dominican Order, and composed a *Summa de poenitentia* for confessors. Raymond's *summa* quickly became the most authoritative moral treatise in both the Order and Christendom at large. His reputation as a wise confessor was so strong, in fact, that, as we have seen, Pope Gregory IX appointed him his personal confessor, as well as papal penitentiary in charge of dispensing the pope's own absolution to penitents. Kings, counts, and country folk all received pardon from Peñafort's hands. It should come as no surprise, then, that the confessor of all confessors should be the one man most responsible for an unprecedented campaign to convert Jews and Muslims. No doubt he was the force behind *Cum hora undecima*, the pope's clarion call to universal evangelization in 1235, of which his own campaign to the Jews must be seen as part and parcel.

As master-general of the Dominican Order from 1238 to 1240, Raymond gave definitive codification to the ancient constitutions of the Friars Preachers and ensured that the vertical horizons of its saintly founder would long endure: "Our Order is ... instituted from the beginning for the preaching and the salvation of souls, and our study should be principally and ardently directed to this end with the greatest industry, so that we can be useful to the souls of our neighbors."[20] Following both the letter and the spirit of the law, Raymond, after resigning his generalship, and with the help of his successors, went about establishing Dominican schools of non-Christian languages in Spain and North Africa so that the friars might be more successful in preaching to the unconverted. (Thousands of Saracens are said to have been converted from Murcia and Tunis alone.)[21] Raymond's calls were echoed by John Wildehausen and Humbert of Romans, his saintly successors. Humbert made an impassioned plea for volunteers willing to forsake family and familiarity to learn foreign languages and spread the Gospel to infidel populations. The world is ailing for lack of Christ, therefore, "The company of preachers is the health of the world." The master-general is also significant for his remarks concerning Jews, that they do not constitute a threat to Christendom: "We allow the Jews to live with us, because they neither know how to cause us harm, nor are they capable of it; rather, they are ever prepared to serve."[22]

The Dominican approach to Jews and Muslims must be seen as an extension of the admonishment of the sinner, the penitential subject of

---

20. Mulchahey, *First the Bow is Bent,* 3.

21. *Raymundiana,* I, 12; 32.

22. Humbert, in J.D. Mansi, *Sacrorum Conciliorum Collectio,* 59 vols. (Venice, 1779–1782), 24, 115, as cited in Stow, "Hatred of the Jews or Love of the Church?" 82.

the preacher and confessor. As Aquinas writes, "The correction of a wrongdoer is twofold, one which applies a remedy to the sin considered as an evil of the sinner himself. This is fraternal correction properly so called, which is directed to the amendment of the sinner. Now to do away with anyone's evil is the same as to procure his good: and to procure a person's good is an act of charity, whereby we wish and do our friend well. Consequently fraternal correction also is an act of charity, because thereby we drive out our brother's evil, viz. sin."[23]

But if admonishing our friend the sinner was only likely to make him more stubborn in his sin, then admonishment was to be *foregone*. Indeed, God requires that one practice prudence and mercy toward one's neighbor, not the malevolent vigilance that awaits every opportunity to catch him in his sin: "As Augustine says (*De Doctr. Christ.* i, 28) ... that 'Our Lord warns us not to be listless in regard of one another's sins: not indeed by being on the lookout for something to denounce, but by correcting what we see': else we should become spies on the lives of others, which is against the saying of Proverbs 24:19: 'Lie not in wait, nor seek after wickedness in the house of the just, nor spoil his rest.'"[24] Thus, the medieval practice of preaching to sinners and proselytizing unbelievers came with its own built-in curbs against excesses that degrade the dignity of the "Other." This is medieval Catholic tolerance, which, as we have said, is not the passive restraint of hatred, but the active practice of love.

We would be negligent in our historical appraisal, however, if we did not observe that the Friars Preachers failed to practice the discretion of the confessor when admonishing non-Christian sinners, especially so among the Jews of Catalonia. According to their own Angelic Doctor, it was wrong to correct the sinner if the correction was likely to make him "worse." Manhandling Jews and mob jeering of Judaism were not only affronts to human dignity, they could not possibly lead to uncoerced conversions to Christianity. As we have noted already, Jewish appeals to the King and his repeated impositions upon mendicant preaching must mean that the Friars Preachers of the last third of the thirteenth-century were sorely lacking in the fraternal love of their saintly founders: they prized too much the dagger, not enough the poultice. They lost sight of the Jew as the prospective penitent, the proper subject of the preacher and confessor. But should the Dominicans be charged with setting in

23. *Summa theologiae*, II. II. 33. 1.
24. Ibid., 33. 2.

motion the calamitous chain of events that led to the wholesale defamation—in some instances the demise—of whole communities of Iberian Jews in the fourteenth and fifteenth centuries? The answer seems to lie with whether mendicant mission to the Jews should be judged by the benefit of hindsight or by the foregoing sacramental principles of charity that first spawned their effort. Perhaps the key is to consider them both in our deliberations.

A satisfactory verdict on Raymond of Peñafort seems equally as elusive as desirable. In the end, he was a medieval man: he had no scruples about forced debates or, as we have seen, sermons coerced at Sabbath observances. He was directly involved (from a Christian perspective perhaps justifiably so) in the prosecution which ultimately led to Nachmanides' exile. Nevertheless, we have it from the Ramban's own hand that Raymond allowed him some measure of free speech in his own defense, and that he—unlike his confreres—never interrupted him. Like Odo before him, Raymond saw the value of learning Hebrew (and Arabic). Like Alan of Lille, Raymond also encouraged the use of rabbinical literature in persuasive arguments against Jews. Dominican friars Paul Christiani and Raymond Martini relied heavily upon this innovative technique in their polemical exploits. Peñafort almost certainly asked both Martini and Aquinas to compose treatises their brethren might employ in preparation for persuading Jews and Muslims into the faith. And as his founder Dominic had given him an example in southern France, so too Raymond made a practice of debating-as-preaching, participating in, if not outright orchestrating, the celebrated Barcelona Confrontation between Friar Paul and Rabbi Moses Nachmanides. In both contexts, Catholic appeals were made to reason, to truth; that sphere to which (according to learned Christians and Jews) all men have inherent access.

Raymond did not mount his missionary effort to the Jews because he was a "Jew hater" who saw "no place for them in Christendom," but because the sacramental theology of sin and sanctity now *held* a place for them; for unlike previous penitentials, Raymond's *Summa* may, in fact, be the first manual for confessors to specifically include Jews and Muslims along with Christian sinners. This is a theology of inclusion, not exclusion: a medieval form of toleration based on human sinfulness and divine redemption. When Raymond repeats Gregory the Great's dictum that Jews ought to be approached by means of "sweet words,"[25]

25. "Both Jews and Saracens should be induced by authoritative texts, by reason, and by blandishments rather than by harshness, to accept anew the Christian faith. They should not, however, be compelled to do so, for forced servitude does not please God." *Decretals*, Chazan, *Church, State, and Jew*, 38.

(*blandimentis*) he is employing the same language as Alan of Lille (and other confessors) when approaching penitent sinners:

> Thus the priest is like a spiritual doctor, when the sinner, spiritually sick, approaches him. First, he ought to attract the sinner with words and soothe him with blandishments, that the sick person may more easily disclose the disease, that is . . . the sin. Thus, after detection of the sin, the priest, having first set forth words of blandishment, may conclude with blows of satisfaction, warning that the guilty one, led on by shame, must neither disavow his sins nor fear to admit his crimes before a man, for in confessing he speaks not to a man but to God.[26]

By including Pope Gregory's penitential approach to Jews in the Church's universal Code of Canon Law, and especially his *Sicut Iudeis*, Raymond assured himself a place in the history of toleration, even if he had never done anything else. Yet, we know he also had a hand in the Spanish *Siete Partidas* and that he took there the same tolerant approach as Gregory: "By barking is understood preaching, which arouses fear through speech; and by the staff the punishment which is given by the good works which they themselves do and exhort others to perform. However, the punishment by deed, should be imposed with moderation and great prudence, and with love and not ill will; in order that men may understand that it is done more through the love of God."[27]

As for Raymond's participation in, or planning of, the great Barcelona Debate, we agree with Maccoby's conclusion: "It becomes clear after some investigation, that the Barcelona disputation was the only one in which the conditions of the debate were relatively fair, and the Jewish side was allowed to develop its argument in relative freedom."[28] Still, the rabbi's participation was coerced and he himself was prosecuted for his portrayal of the event, perhaps even forced into exile—though this has more to do with possible embellishments in his dram-

---

26. *Liber poenitentialis*, 26; "The priest should further say that one who has confessed before the heavenly judge is not held to have been condemned but rather to have been absolved, showing also by multiple authority that guilt is blotted out by the confession of the sin. For authority says: Confess your sins to one another [Jam 5:16]. And elsewhere: I have said I will confess against myself, and Thou hast remitted the impiety of my sin [Ps 31:5, or in versions other than Douay, Ps 32:5], and so on. Even Christ Jesus commanded the cleansed lepers to show themselves to the priest [Lk 17:41]. Through which is signified that he who labors with spiritual leprosy ought to show himself to the priest through confession of his fault. Beyond this, the priest should teach that the sin uncovered in the present time will be covered on the Day of Judgment, but that the sin veiled at present will be revealed in the future."

27. *Las Siete Partidas, Book One*, XLII.

28. Maccoby, 11.

atic narrative than with his participation in the debate itself. The "persecution" of the rabbi was largely the work of Friar Paul and Clement IV. It was they who stubbornly tried to force the Crown to punish him. That James refused, and even curbed mendicant excesses, shows that one could support preaching to Jews and still consider oneself tolerant.

Despite repeated sins of commission and omission on the part of medieval Catholics toward their Jewish brethren, it is not historically accurate to affirm an outright malevolence in the mendicant theological tradition. Indeed, as we have seen, both Master Peñafort and King James sometimes exhibited a public prudence and restraint that other Christian leaders lacked. Both men clearly acknowledged the continued right of Jews, not only to exist, but to *defend* their faith. Llull, for his part, found fault with the exaggerated Dominican approach, but pursued the conversion of Jews and Muslims with equal intensity through his own unique methods of dialogue. Medieval ideals of tolerance were more versatile than is regularly imagined. As one scholar writes:

> Dominicans like Christiani and Martini failed to live up to their own principles . . . this very failure highlights an important aspect of culture often missed by historians inspired by "persecuting-society"-type paradigms; namely the fundamental openness of tradition/culture to contingency, which means that those immersed in a tradition have the potential for development (like Aquinas's thought on friendship and Peñafort's thoughts on tolerance), self-critique (like James of Aragon reversing his support of the disputation or Ramon Llull developing a modified path to mission in light of Dominican excesses), as well as failure and hypocrisy (Christiani, Martini).[29]

What we hope has become abundantly evident is that Dominican proselytism of Jews, Muslims, and pagans should be viewed more as an organic outgrowth of the twelfth-century renaissance in "penitential-lay sanctity," than that of the "persecuting society." As especially Aquinas and Llull demonstrate, the essence of Christian approaches to non-Christians lay not in intolerance, but in friendship; a desire to share one's highest good with the "Other." As Llull put it: "The final intention of the Art is the discovery of truth. This intention is divided . . . the first is to love good; the second, to hate evil; the third, to know how to carry out the descent from the universal."[30] As Pope Emeritus Benedict XVI put it in an international address:

---

29. "Review" by anonymous reader of one of the draft manuscripts of this book, 2.
30. Rubio, "Thought: The Art," in *Raimundus Lullus, An Introduction*, 250.

Christians of the nascent Church did not regard their missionary proc-
lamation as propaganda designed to enlarge their particular group, but
as an inner necessity, consequent upon the nature of their faith. . . .
The universality of God, and of reason open towards Him, is what gave
them the motivation—indeed, the obligation—to proclaim the message. They saw their faith as belonging, not to cultural custom that dif-
fers from one people to another, but to the domain of truth, which
concerns all people equally.[31]

Rational dialogues from Anselm to Ramon Llull reflect some of the
highest compliments ever paid to non-Christian intellects. Indeed, it
may be said that rational approaches to truth within the Jewish tradition itself, as evidenced by Maimonides and Ibn Daūd, invited such
Christian interest in non-Christian worlds. Medieval mendicant doctrine on proselytization and the dignity of the "Other," taken on its own
terms, would appear to have every right to the word "tolerant." Medieval *tolerantia* meant that non-Christians should not be forced to Christianity against their will; they had to be wooed:

> True dialogue implies being held accountable, as much to oneself as to
> others. If I truly desire dialogue, it is first necessary for me to come to
> terms with myself . . . then it is necessary for me to come to recognize
> that my interlocutor is not another me, but someone fundamentally
> different from me . . . even if the sharing of certain ideas leads us to a
> kind of unanimity. . . . I can love you or hate you, but if I want to
> engage in dialogue with you, I must recognize your otherness, your
> fundamental difference from me. . . . But I must not remain mute
> because you are Other: I must speak to you, provoke you, understand
> you—speak my love to you (you who are so close to me, you who are so
> far away from me) and at the same time let myself be won over by you.
> In this dangerous game, and it is much more than a game, you can lose
> your soul, I can lose my soul . . . I believe that certain authors of the
> twelfth and thirteenth century reached this fine point of tenuous grace,
> achieving a dialogue which can serve as a model for us today. . . .[32]

Especially in Aquinas and in Llull one finds a sensitivity to every-
man's sinfulness, brokenness, inability to follow the Truth. Even Raymond of Peñafort's other potential protégés, Christiani and Martini, are
compelled to "love their enemy" for his own spiritual welfare, as Bartholomew of Exeter once put it. Medieval Catholic belief in the power of
Truth to redeem ought not to be identified with an elitist will-to-power,

---

31. "Address to the Collège des Bernardins, Paris," September 12, 2008.
32. Dahan, *The Christian Polemic*, 118.

but with the mercy dispensed by a trained medical professional. Jews as much as any people were created in the image and likeness of God.

However, as we have seen, the sacramentality of the Middle Ages was a two-edged sword. While medievals upheld truth, they simultaneously belittled it, both in theory and practice. The Friars Preachers not only failed in fraternal love, they repeated opprobrious appellations of Jews with real-world consequences; they did not distinguish between the Jew-as-symbol and the individual Jew. As Guardini observes more generally of the shortcomings of the medieval approach to the world:

> The bold and pious structure of medieval existence had been able to arise and endure only because the eye for the reality of things was often blinded, the heart was protected from the possibilities of the world and the decisions were transferred to the realm of ethical and religious life. Medieval man adored God and obeyed the authority which the Lord of the world had placed within it. In this way he satisfied the ultimate truth, but often overlooked the penultimate: yet this is also truth and must not be crushed by the weight of the other. Consequently, his answers to the questions concerning the nature of the world were often prejudiced and uncritical and reduced it.... And since the world could not present itself to his view as that which it is, even his faith did not attain its proper confirmation.[33]

But as Gertrude von le Fort writes:

> Just as the meaning of the symbol does not necessarily coincide with the empiric character or condition of the individual who for the time being is its bearer, so also the essential quality that it designates is not restricted to the individual in question. We maintain, for instance, that from the point of view of her symbol, woman has a special affiliation with the religious sphere. To conclude from this that woman herself is particularly religious, or that she holds supremacy over man in this respect, would imply a complete misunderstanding of this book. The matter concerns itself with the figurative aspect of the religious quality, its visual representation; and this, as belonging to the symbol, has been in a special measure entrusted to woman.[34]

Might this sacramental understanding of reality not hold the key to reconciling the seemingly irreconcilable: traditional sentiments such as St Augustine's remark that "the Church admits and avows the Jewish people to be cursed, because after killing Christ they continue to till the

---

33. Guardini, *The World*, 16.

34. Von le Fort, *The Eternal Woman: the Timeless Meaning of the Feminine*, trans. Marie Cecilia Buehrle (San Francisco, CA: Ignatius Press, 2010; reprint of Bruce, 1954), 4.

ground of an earthly circumcision, an earthly Sabbath, an earthly Passover,"[35] and that of the Second Vatican Council, "[N]either all Jews indiscriminately at that time, nor Jews today, can be charged with crimes committed during his Passion. . . . [T]he Jews should not be spoken of as rejected or accursed as if this followed from Holy Scripture"?[36] Individual, empirical Jews are not "guilty," and must not be defamed, but as JEWS they bear the typological "symbol," PRODIGAL-IN-NEED-OF-REDEMPTION, nonetheless? In other words, JEW as EVERYMAN-since-the-Fall, symbolically standing for each one of us "poor banished children of Eve," of whom Cain, Hagar, and Esau are types? In this case, just as individual women are no more "religious" than individual men, could it be that to the mind of the Church, Jews have a symbol of "rejection" associated with them, even though individual Jews are *no* worse sinners than individual Christians? Or would such a suggestion be itself a perversion of the sacramental approach, of the kind that spawned centuries of anti-Jewish epithets and episodes? If this were a legitimate Catholic "sacramental" distinction, it would have at least this benefit: it would seemingly defuse, almost overnight, all existing tension between Paul's unflattering "typological" references to Jews,[37] and the sensitive and conciliatory remarks made toward actual Jewish people of the past fifty years.

Lastly, as this study began with the historiography of intolerance, it seems fitting it should end with it. Can we avoid the conclusion that if the medieval Dominicans failed to consistently embody their own ideals, their modern detractors have largely failed to acknowledge the existence of those ideals at all? We have seen that entire book-length studies, even those by otherwise sensitive scholars such as Chazan, are silent on the subject—that those who dominate the field today no longer subscribe to the objective notions of truth and love which medieval people did. Is this perhaps the principal reason such "tolerant" principles have been largely left unchronicled, let alone unheralded?

---

35. St Augustine, *Against Faustus*, 12:9–11; cf. above, Chapter 1, nt. 30.

36. *Nostrae Aetate* 4.

37. If this were so, one could still make distinctions between "legitimate" Pauline sacramental depictions of "Jews" by various churchmen down the ages and bastardized versions of this hermeneutic that are just plain anti-Judaistic/anti-Semitic—sometimes by the same authors.

The dogma of relativism has, however, yet another effect: Christian universalism, which is carried out concretely in mission, is no longer the obligatory handing on of a good meant for everyone, that is, of truth and love; with this presupposition, mission becomes the mere presumptuous attitude of a culture that imagines itself to be superior, that tramples upon a whole magnitude of religious cultures in the most shameful fashion, thus it is held, depriving those people of what is best: their own heritage.[38]

But modern moral relativists, as we have seen, find it exceedingly difficult to reconcile the Catholic claim to exclusive truth (fullness of truth is a better qualifier) and alleged tolerance for the "Other." They argue in the Enlightenment vein that it is precisely the absolute that must be sacrificed on the altars of tolerance for civilization to be perpetuated:

Hans Kelsen was expressing the spirit of our age when he represented the question of Pilate, "What is truth?" as being the sole appropriate attitude for determining the structure of society within the state, in the face of the great religious and moral difficulties of mankind. Truth is replaced by the decision of the majority, he says, precisely because there can be no truth in the sense of a binding and general accessible entity for man. Thus the multiplicity of cultures serves to demonstrate the relativism of all cultures. Culture is set against truth. This relativism, which is nowadays to be found, as a basic attitude of enlightened people, penetrating far into the realm of theology, is the most profound difficulty of our age.[39]

Or as the late Gustav Mensching put it:

Religious man . . . should consequently accept tolerance for the sake of "truth" in religion, without giving up his own religious standpoint. He should not only realize the life in religions other than his own but also be convinced about the "truth" of the statements made by other creeds concerning God and salvation. *This he should do if he conceives of truth not as something rationally comprehensible,* but as the abundance of symbolic-mythical aspects of the holy, and eternal, that appears differently to different men in their different stages of maturity.

Religious views should adapt themselves to what scientific study has disclosed. . . . On the basis of our present deepened insight into the formative laws of religious history, tolerance as acknowledgement of the different genuine possibilities of living encounter and relationship with the divine is an indispensable postulate. Today, intolerant claims of

---

38. Ratzinger, *Truth and Tolerance,* 73.
39. Ibid., 72.

absoluteness and fanatic persecutions of other beliefs and believers ... are always a lack of insight.[40] (emphasis mine)

The medieval Catholic origins of tolerance are something altogether different and therefore underappreciated:

> Nor ought it to be objected that the open-ended quality of their dialogues conveys a covert message: namely to teach the impossibility of achieving any rational agreement whatsoever. Both Abelard and Llull explicitly upheld the possibility of reaching agreement about the truths of faith through reason alone. Rather, the doubts they expressed were about the ease of such consensus, because of the complexities of the subject matter as well as the frailties of human mental faculties. It is this humility in the presence of other diverse and well thought-out faiths that forms the cornerstone of truly tolerant dialogue during the Latin Middle Ages.[41]

Recognition of man's changeableness—i.e., sinfulness—not truth's relativity, made medieval tolerance possible.

Ultimately, what is needed in Medieval Studies today is something analogous to Peter Brown's call for a radical revision of the Gibbon paradigm in Roman Studies: "A dogged *guerilla* against the dominant, melodramatic" construct; one which "amounts to nothing less than the hesitant search for a new language of historical change, indeed, for a new historical sensibility, attuned to different phenomena or prepared to view the same phenomena in a different, less sinister light."[42]

We may conclude, therefore, that not only the medieval Academy but the modern world has much to gain from a reappraisal of the Christian metaphysics of the Middle Ages and its practical application to modern moral dilemmas and dialogue. Again, to quote Pope Emeritus Benedict,

---

40. Gustav Mensching, *Tolerance and Truth in Religion* (University of Alabama Press, 1971; reprint of 1955 Quelle and Meyer), 167–68; or as Klaus Schreiner put it: "Only when the early modern state proceeded to make natural religion instead of a closed system of belief the consensus-shaping *vinculum societas*, it set free spaces of action in which individuals and groups could realize their rights of freedom of belief and conscience.... [O]nly the dissolution of the historically grown bonds between religion and justice, which restituted freedom to religion and prudence to justice, enabled the free expression of religion in a spirit of mutual patience," "Toleranz," in *Geschichtliche Grundbegriffe*, ed. Otto Bruner, Werner Conze, and Reinhart Koselleck (7 vols.; Stuttgart, 1972–92), VI, 445–605, as cited in Bejczy, "*Tolerantia*," 366–67.

41. Nederman, *Worlds of Difference*, 37.

42. Peter Brown, "The World of Late Antiquity Revisited," *Symbolae Osloenses* 72 (1997): 5–30; and his "Reply to comments," 10; Brown, of course, was referring to the Gibbonian "Decline and Fall" model of the last centuries of Greco-Roman civilization that so dominated classical studies prior to Brown's inauguration of "Late Antiquity."

"The West has long been endangered by this aversion to the questions which underlie its rationality, and can only suffer great harm thereby. The courage to engage the whole breadth of reason, and not the denial of its grandeur—this is the program with which a theology grounded in Biblical faith enters into the debates of our time."[43] Bejczy explains the danger inherent in the West's Enlightenment view of rationality: "Admitting the relativity of our truths, we should be reluctant to condemn the acts of our fellow human beings that differ from our own— that is the basic idea of our so-called tolerance. An idea that makes us morally defenseless if outright evil shows up." Ironically, by condemning medieval commitment to universally recognizable moral truths, today's intelligentsia could be throwing away the only true remedy to the escalating sectarian violence they so fear. Bejczy sums it up well:

> Medieval authors never doubted that they possessed the absolute truth, but they developed the concept of *tolerantia* as a way of getting along with the untrue. Medieval authors were never morally defenseless against outright evil and condemned it wherever they believed to find it, but still they advocated not to interfere with it if this seemed to be opportune. Obviously we do not have the same enemies as medieval people. Still, with regard to the question of how to handle the enemies we do have without going to the extremes of tyranny and inertia, the medieval doctrine of tolerance contains a lesson for our age as well.[44]

What a different world it would be if the U.S. and its allies had adopted a "medieval" stance of tolerance toward the "evil axis" regime of Iraq, and if Muslim zealots had long ago adopted the same posture toward the U.S. and Israel?

When one considers modern notions of tolerance based on moral equivalency, one is reminded of C. S. Lewis' remark concerning Britain's battle against Hitler's Germany: "What was the sense in saying the enemy were in the wrong unless Right is a real thing which the Nazis at bottom knew as well as we did and ought to have practiced?"[45] Without objectivist notions of truth—those medieval "generally acknowledged rules" of Aquinas and Ibn Daūd—by what grounds do we condemn anti-Semitic acts in any age, medieval or modern? At bottom, is our modern morality based on subjective sentiment and solidarity any more

---

43. His Holiness Pope Benedict XVI, "Address to the University of Regensburg," September 12, 2006.

44. Bejczy, "*Tolerantia*," 384.

45. C.S. Lewis, *Mere Christianity*, book 1 (New York, NY: Harper Collins, 2001, originally pub. 1952), 5.

"true" than the nihilism of the Nazi and Communist regimes, which liquidated millions of Jews and Christians? One Jew, who escaped the horrors of their grasp thanks to Christian charity, has left us a keen insight not only into modern moral relativism but into "medieval" Christian-Jewish tolerance and dialogue founded upon a sacramentality:

> Not a material but a spiritual principle is at stake in this, the only genuine world war. Today the fronts are still confused and the further developments are not to be foreseen. On the one side strands radical nihilism which no longer regards the human being as the *image of God* but as an amoral machine in a completely meaningless world. On the other side, on our side, stands the metaphysical, the religious concept of life, the conviction that this Cosmos was created by the spirit and that a spiritual meaning lives and breathes in every atom. It is indeed a war between the principles of life and death.[46] (emphasis mine)

The Austrian playwright Franz Werfel was so grateful to the Catholic inhabitants of the French town of Lourdes for sheltering him from the Gestapo that he made a vow to tell the story of its greatest heroine, St Bernadette Soubirous. In 1858, the illiterate peasant girl was said to have been privileged by repeated visits of the holy Virgin Mary, under her title, "The Immaculate Conception." Miracles of healing and conversion followed swiftly despite the atheist politicians' attempts to stop the faithful from worshipping at the grotto of the apparition. Mary, a Jewish mother without any stain of sin, reportedly asked the Christian faithful to offer prayers and penances for all poor sinners. As Werfel writes:

> "The Song of Bernadette" is a jubilant hymn to the spiritual meaning of the universe. Through the medium of this simple and charming personality, we see how even in our age of skepticism, divine powers are at work and how they raise an ignorant creature, favored by grace, beyond her own natural limits. Although the story takes place in a Catholic milieu it is not only bound to the Catholic form of life but concerns equally all men—Protestants and Jews—and all men whose hearts intuitively recognize the divine powers which in rare moments gloriously transfigure our daily reality.[47]

It is only within this mentality that Dominican outreach to Jews and other non-Christians can be understood as tolerance: a sacra*mentality*. As one of those sons of St Raymond of Peñafort put it: "Brothers who work for the salvation of men have heavier but more fruitful work to do

---

46. Franz Werfel, "Writing *Bernadette*," 126, as cited in Hans Wagener, *Understanding Franz Werfel* (Columbia, SC: University of South Carolina Press, 1993), 156–57.
47. Ibid.

than other religious who work for their own salvation. This work is full of unspeakable joy and in it they have the Blessed Virgin as their special helper."[48] It was a vision of the Holy Virgin which prompted Raymond to found the Order of Mercy, and another apparition which moved him to found his language schools for mission to Jews and Muslims (as was the case with Ramon Llull).[49]

It is an irony of history that the sins of Dominican preachers have come to overshadow their distinctly medieval Catholic brand of tolerance based on human sinfulness, that they are better known for stigmatizing the "Other" than for their own tenet of touting the Other as "the other self."[50] Modern historians have it within their power to further fathom the sacramentality of the Middle Ages, or they may leave it lost, a relic in the sands of time. If the latter, then Shakespeare was undoubtedly correct: "The evil that men do lives after them; the good is oft interred with their bones."

---

48. *Vitae Fratrum*, 1.6.

49. *Raymundiana*, I, 32; from anonymous life of Raymond manuscript from the Library of the University of Barcelona (Ar. 1-3-4); cf. Chapter 5, nt. 40.

50. *Summa theologiae*, II. II. 28. 1; cf. Chapter 5, nt. 17.

Index of Names

About the Author

EDMUND J. MAZZA is Professor of History at Azusa Pacific University in Los Angeles, where he teaches Ancient, Medieval, and Renaissance and Reformation History. Dr. Mazza has contributed chapters on these subjects for Cognella Press's forthcoming *A History of the Premodern World*. Mazza's research centers on the Medieval Mediterranean, especially the juxtaposition of sectarian communities: the controversies of Catholics, Cathars, and Waldensians; coexistence and conversion among Christians, Jews, and Muslims in Barcelona under James I; the inauguration of novel Dominican language schools in Hebrew and Arabic in Spain and North Africa under St. Raymond of Peñafort, OP, as well as the idiosyncratic and prolific apologetics of Blessed Ramon Llull. Dr. Mazza has produced teaching videos shot on location in Athens, Ephesus, Istanbul, Palermo, Naples, Venice, and Rome. Mazza was an invited scholar at Liberty Fund's 2015 San Diego seminar "*Convivencia and Reconquista*: Freedom and Responsibility in Medieval Spain." That same year he organized at New York University the conference "Conversing Conversion," celebrating the 750th anniversary of the birth of Dante. Dr. Mazza was also the organizer of "Christ Among the Medieval Mendicants," a 2013 conference commemorating the 750th anniversary of the Barcelona Debate and the institution of the Feast of Corpus Christi, co-sponsored by The Graduate Center of the City University of New York and the Morgan Library and Museum.